A Theology of Public Life

What has Washington to do with Jerusalem? In the raging
debates about the relationship between religion and
politics, no one has explored the religious benefits and
challenges of public engagement for Christian believers –
until now. This ground-breaking book defends and details
Christian believers' engagement in contemporary pluralistic public life, not from the perspective of some neutral
"public," but from the particular perspective of Christian
faith, arguing that such engagement enriches both public
life and Christian citizens' faith itself. As such it offers not
a "public theology," but a "theology of public life,"
analyzing the promise and perils of Christian public
engagement, and discussing the nature of civic commitment and prophetic critique, and the relation of a loving
faith to a liberal politics of justice. Theologically rich,
philosophically rigorous, politically, historically and
sociologically informed, this book advances contemporary
discussion of "religion and public life" in fundamental
ways.

CHARLES MATHEWES is Associate Professor of Religious
Studies, University of Virginia. His other publications
include *Evil and the Augustinian Tradition* (2001).

D1739381

Cambridge Studies in Christian Doctrine

Edited by

Professor DANIEL W. HARDY, *University of Cambridge*

Cambridge Studies in Christian Doctrine is an important series which aims to engage critically with the traditional doctrines of Christianity, and at the same time to locate and make sense of them within a secular context. Without losing sight of the authority of scripture and the traditions of the church, the books in this series subject pertinent dogmas and credal statements to careful scrutiny, analysing them in light of the insights of both church and society, and thereby practise theology in the fullest sense of the word.

Titles published in the series

A Theology of Public Life

CHARLES MATHEWES
University of Virginia

CAMBRIDGE UNIVERSITY PRESS
Cambridge, New York, Melbourne, Madrid, Cape Town, Singapore, São Paulo, Delhi

Cambridge University Press
The Edinburgh Building, Cambridge CB2 8RU, UK

Published in the United States of America by Cambridge University Press, New York

www.cambridge.org
Information on this title: www.cambridge.org/9780521832267

© Charles Mathewes 2007

This publication is in copyright. Subject to statutory exception
and to the provisions of relevant collective licensing agreements,
no reproduction of any part may take place without the written
permission of Cambridge University Press.

First published 2007
This digitally printed version 2008

A catalogue record for this publication is available from the British Library

ISBN 978-0-521-83226-7 hardback
ISBN 978-0-521-53990-6 paperback

Cambridge University Press has no responsibility for the persistence or
accuracy of URLs for external or third-party Internet websites referred to in
this publication, and does not guarantee that any content on such websites is,
or will remain, accurate or appropriate.

This book is for my mother
Martha Thomas Mathewes
IX.30.1935 – I.1.2006

She loves me like a rock
– Paul Simon

Saeculum autem hoc eremus est
Augustine, *sermo.* 4.9.9

Contents

Acknowledgments

The tale grew in the telling. It began with reflection on a sermon, given by Revd. Sam Portaro at Brent House at the University of Chicago, on the oddities of the agenda of "putting Christ back into Christmas" – the upshot of which was that Christ would not get into Christmas by some sort of willed politico-cultural imposition, but rather by being found already there, in the vulgar and kitschy desires that we various theological snobs sniff at. I have written this always thinking of his last line: "That, after all, is how Christ got into Christmas in the first place." That sermon, hundreds more, and the liturgies of which they were a part, shaped this book decisively; and so I thank Revd. Portaro, Revd. Bruce Epperly, Revd. Jeffrey Fishwick, Revd. Paula Kettlewell, and Revd. Jonathan Voorhees, and the communities of Brent House at the University of Chicago, St. Paul's Charlottesville, and Christ Church Charlottesville, for teaching me the way of Christ, albeit as awkwardly and abashedly as Episcopalians do that sort of thing.

Numerous colleagues have read parts of this book and offered useful advice; I especially thank Tal Brewer, John Bowlin, Luke Bretherton, Patrick Deneen, Eric Gregory, Paul Griffiths, Eric Jacobsen, Slavica Jakelić, Derek Jeffreys, Kristen Deede Johnson, Robin Lovin, Aristotle Papanikolaou, Chad Pecknold, Jon Schofer, Kathleen Skerritt, Darlene Weaver, Jim Wetzel, William Werpehowski, Paul Wright, Diane M. Yeager, and Phil Ziegler. When I met Oliver Davies, I recognized a sympathetic mind, with a kindred theological attitude. Continued discussions with William Schweiker, particularly throughout his Lilly-funded project on "Property,

Possession, and the Christian Faith," gave me whatever instruction I have on matters relating to religion and culture.

Several journals, and one publisher, were good enough to allow me to reprint material that first appeared in their pages. I have drawn on the following in this book: "On Using the World," in *Having: Property, Possession, and Religious Discourse*, ed. Charles Mathewes and William Schweiker (Grand Rapids: William B. Eerdmans, 2004); "Reconsidering the Role of Mainline Churches in Public Life," in *Theology Today*, 58.4 (January, 2002); "Faith, Hope, and Agony: Christian Political Participation Beyond Liberalism," in *The Annual of the Society of Christian Ethics*, 21 (2001); "Augustinian Anthropology: Interior intimo meo," in *Journal of Religious Ethics*, 27.2 (June, 1999); "Pluralism, Otherness, and the Augustinian Tradition," in *Modern Theology*, 14.1 (January, 1998).

I have worked in the Department of Religious Studies at the University of Virginia for the past nine years, and I have now lived here in Charlottesville longer than I have lived anywhere else in my life. Many graduate students helped me, especially Sarah Azaransky, Brantley Craig, Willis Jenkins, Emily Gravett, Karen Guth, Paul Macdonald, Jon Malesic, Angel Mendez, Mark Ryan, Keith Starkenburg, Jeff Vogel, and Chad Wayner. My colleagues in the department, particularly Jennifer Geddes, Asher Biemann, Larry Bouchard, Jim Childress, Jamie Ferriera, Charles Marsh, Margaret Mohrmann, Peter Ochs, and, during their time here, John Milbank, Gene Rogers and Corey Walker deserve great thanks. My department Chair, Harry Gamble, has been a welcome sage and supporter throughout. In Spring 2003 an undergraduate research seminar was dedicated to reading a draft of this book, and the students in that seminar – Patricia Amberly, Peter Andres, Sarah Jobe, Sarah McKim, Cate Oliver, and William Winters – contributed materially to it. I also thank Carl Trindle, Principle of Brown College at UVA, for sponsoring the seminar – and for much more.

A sabbatical at the Center for the Study of Religion at Princeton University also shaped the book. Robert Wuthnow, R. Marie Griffith, Anita Kline, Elliot Ratzman, Leora Batnitzky, Penny Edgell, Leigh Schmidt, Jeff Stout, and Lisa Sideris all gave generously of their time and attention. A seminar taught by Peter Brown and Neil McLynn while I was at Princeton – "Emperors and Bishops" – greatly aided my amateur understanding of late antiquity.

Sometime in my first month at Virginia I met James Davison Hunter, who soon after introduced me to his brainchild, the Institute for Advanced Studies in Culture. Ever since, I have been an underlaborer in the work of the Institute and its offspring, the Center on Religion and Democracy. It is no exaggeration to say that this book would not exist without the continual stimulation, provocation, and inspiration that this remarkable intellectual community has provided. I thank Joseph Davis, Justin Holcombe, Slavica Jakelic, Steven Jones, John Owen, Edward Song, and the many others who have argued and discussed with me the matters of this book. In the summer of 2002, CORD sponsored a manuscript workshop wherein my book and others were subjected to a week of meticulous attention from my fellow participants Pamela Cochran, Eric Gregory, Paul Lichterman, Ann Mongoven, and Brett Wilmot. Shelley Reese Sawyer's meticulous attention secured the workshop's success, and I am grateful to her as well. But I especially thank James Hunter for dedicating so much of his time and energy to ensure that others could think and write and talk and simply spend time living the life of the mind – not in an undisciplined, but in a supra-disciplined manner.

For their incessant patience, and gentle encouragement, never rising to the (well-warranted) level of threats, the next-to-last thanks must go to the good people at Cambridge University Press. I have been fortunate to have editors who care about my work, and I thank Kevin Taylor and Kate Brett for their long-suffering forbearance, acumen, and prudence. I am also immensely grateful to Dan Hardy, editor of the "Cambridge Studies in Christian Doctrine" series, for his faith, hope, and charity as regards this work, and particularly in his herculean labors in reading and re-reading its versions.

I thank all the above; but several people merit individual recognition.

My friend Josh Yates has been a boon companion throughout my time at Virginia. We arrived in Charlottesville the same semester, and since then we have been unindicted intellectual co-conspirators, occasional running partners, and significant financial underwriters of several local coffee shops. I am deeply grateful for the patience and charity that he has always shown me, as well as for his intelligence, generosity, and example.

My wife and colleague Jennifer Geddes remains my primary conversation partner, my most insightful critic, and my love. Her belief in this project, and in its author, carried them both through when things looked bleakest – and you, dear reader, owe her thanks for saving you from a seventh chapter.

Our daughter Isabelle was born during the composition of this book. Before she arrived, we never imagined working so hard, or being so happy. She is an ever-present reminder both of this book's immediate urgency and of its ultimate unimportance; I am not sure for which I am more grateful.

My mother, Martha Thomas Mathewes, has been with this book since before it began and with its author for some time before that as well. She is the person who first oriented me to the world, and she has always been my guiding star. If this book expresses an attitude, a way of living in the world, it is as much hers as anyone's. I hope she will approve.

Charlottesville, Virginia
January 6, 2006

Abbreviations for works by St. Augustine

ad Gal.	*expositio epistolae ad Galatas*
conf.	*confessiones*
contra acad.	*contra academicos*
DCD	*de civitate Dei*
DDC	*de doctrina Christiana*
de mor.	*de moribus ecclesiae catholicae*
de pat.	*de patientiae*
de Trin.	*de Trinitate*
DUC	*de utilitate credendi*
DVR	*de vera religione*
ennar.	*ennarationes in Psalmos*
ep.	*epistulae*
Gen. ad litt.	*de Genesi ad litteram*
in Io. ep.	*in Iohannis epistulam tractatus*
sermo.	*sermones*

Introduction: Life in the epilogue, during the world

A mirror for Christian citizens

What has Washington to do with Jerusalem? This book aims to ✓
answer this question. It provides Christian believers with one way to
understand why and how they should participate in public life. It
does so by offering a broadly Augustinian "theology of public life," a
picture of Christian life as it should be lived in public engagement.

The title foreshadows the argument. The book studies "public life,"
not simply "politics." "Public life" includes everything concerned with
the "public good" – everything from patently political actions such as
voting, campaigning for a candidate, or running for office, to less
directly political activities such as serving on a school board or plan-
ning commission, volunteering in a soup kitchen, and speaking in a
civic forum, and to arguably non-political behaviors, such as simply
talking to one's family, friends, co-workers, or strangers about public
matters of common concern.[1] Furthermore, this study is undertaken as
a "theology of public life," not a "public theology." Typically, "public
theologies" are self-destructively accommodationist: they let the "larger" secular world's self-understanding set the terms, and then ask
how religious faith contributes to the purposes of public life, so
understood. In contrast, a theology of public life defines "the public"
theologically, exploring its place in the created and fallen order and in
the economy of salvation.[2] Hence, whereas public theologies take as

---

1. See Shapiro 1990: 276, and Stiltner 1999.
2. For an analogous contrast between a theology of nature and a natural theology,
   see Schreiner 1995: 122.

their primary interlocutors non-believers skeptical of the civic propriety of religious engagement in public life, this theology of public life takes as its primary audience Christian believers unsure of the religious fruitfulness of civic engagement; and it argues to them that they can become better Christians, and their churches better Christian communities, through understanding and participating in public life as an ascetical process of spiritual formation.

Yet while Christians are its primary audience, all persons of good will who are interested in public life can read it with profit. Non-Christians will find explications of (what should be) the rationale for many of their Christian fellow citizens' public engagement, so they may use this book as a Baedeker, a dictionary to a language that many of their interlocutors employ; and they may also find that the book's theological analysis illuminates the structures and patterns that form (and deform) public life in advanced industrial societies. Furthermore, readers in other traditions may find help of a different sort; because the book offers an unapologetically particularistic approach that speaks to public matters without assuming that all its interlocutors share its local categories, they may find useful pro-vocation, viable support, and a suggestive model for analogous projects undertaken from within their own perspectives.

"Unapologetically particularistic" is key: using the first-order vernacular of Christian faith, it argues that Christians can and should be involved in public life both richly as citizens – working for the common good while remaining open, conversationally and otherwise, to those who do not share their views – and thoroughly *as Christians* – in ways ascetically appropriate to, and invigorating of, their spiritual formation, not least by opening their own convictions to genuine transformation by that engagement.

Such a project involves two distinct undertakings. First, it entails a theology of faithful Christian citizenship, which will unpack how the basic dynamics of faithful Christian existence promote Christians' engagement in public life during the world and inform their under-standing of the shape and purpose of such life. Second, it offers an ascetics of such citizenship, an analysis of how that citizenship should be lived by Christians as a means of training them in their funda-mental vocation as citizens of the kingdom of heaven, particularly considering those forces – material, structural, institutional, cultural, and intellectual – that mis-shape our engagement in public life today.

For many centuries there was a genre of political writing called the "mirror for Christian princes," wherein potentates could see what they should be striving to emulate as "godly rulers." This book is a mirror for Christian citizens. In public engagement, Christian believers do not seek simply to do the right thing; they also undertake a properly "ascetical" engagement with the world. Interpreting and endorsing that ascetical engagement is my ultimate aim here – a task captured in the phrase "during the world." Explaining this will take some time.

Why (and which) believers need a dogmatics of public life

The book builds upon previous debates on religion's role in public life, but does not contribute to it. It assumes that those debates have by and large ended, and that what we may call the accommodationists won, and the "public reason" advocates lost.

This was not supposed to happen. Once upon a time, the consensus (or near-consensus, anyway) was that religion was declining, increasingly marginalized, and in any event simply a mask for ideological debates more properly about material interests. Hence, most thinkers believed, religious convictions should be translated into a more properly "public" vernacular before entering the public sphere. A small minority – a faithful remnant, if you will – insisted that public life should accommodate particularistic religious voices; but they too were seen as relics, merely of antiquarian interest.

What a difference the last few decades have made. Each premise of the "public reason" argument has proven false. Quite clearly, religion is not, *pace* expectations, going away. Against predictions of inevitable secularization – and the concomitant marginalization of religious believers, languages, and arguments – sociologists, political scientists, and historians have shown that in modernity religion can and does remain vital in both private and public life, even as it changes its character.[3] Furthermore, religion *qua* religion seems often quite "functional" in modern societies. Given the substantial

---

3. See Asad 2003, Berger 1999, Casanova 1994, C. Smith 2003b. For a rival account see Norris and Inglehart 2004. For a good discussion of the mesmeric power that the "secularization frame" still has over the knowledge classes, from government bureaucrats to academics to journalists, see Cox 2003.

changes – some would say precipitous decline – in both the quantity and the quality of associational life, religious associations are increasingly important on purely secular "civic" grounds; church basements may just save us from bowling alone.[4] Finally, religious engagement is inescapable; much of our public life consists of debates concerned with the proper boundaries of religion, the "political legibility" of religious believers' concerns (Bivins 2003: 10).[5] The sociology behind the heretofore dominant "public reason" argument about religion in public life has simply been wrong. Furthermore, alongside the sociological evidence, philosophers have argued convincingly that there are no good normative reasons generically to constrain religious voices' participation, *qua* religious, in public life. They argue that such voices best contribute to public life when left to determine for themselves – on grounds determined by their own particular, local conditions – how precisely to frame their arguments.[6] Such philosophers see us entering an age of "post-secular" public discourse, in which the unapologetically robust use of patently particularistic languages will provide a genuine basis for a real dialogical openness (Coles 1997: 8).

But so far these thinkers have made this case only partially, from the perspective of the public sphere. Such civic arguments are important, of course. But faithful citizens must be convinced to act and speak in explicitly faithful ways. A theological case must be made to encourage civic action by such believers; and no one has yet tried to make it.

There are many believers who could be swayed by such arguments. They seem invisible in recent discussions about religion and public life, discussions that make much of divisions among and within religious communities; but that is because of a methodological mistake. The many recent taxonomies, in the United States and outside it, of believers' attitudes towards politics are too finely grained: they underplay the fact that most believers are

---

4. See Elshtain 1995, Sandel 1996, Putnam 2000, Verba *et al.* 1995, Bivins 2003, Casanova 1994, Hart 2001, Mahmood 2005, Mathewes 2002b, Macedo 2004 and Gibson 2003. I thank Erik Owens for discussions on these matters.
5. See Hunter 1990, Layman 2001, and Uslander 2002.
6. See Placher 1989, Jackson 1997, Wolterstorff 1997, Eberle 2002, Thiemann 1996, Connolly 1999, Perry 2003, Weithman 2002, Ochs and Levene 2002, and J. Stout 2004. For more social-scientific arguments to this effect, see Post 2003 and C. Smith 2003a.

more committed to their faith than to any political program flowing from their faith, that they recognize that asymmetry of commitment, and are comfortable with it. These believers populate crude categories like "religious right" and "religious left," "crunchy cons" and "progressive orthodox," in considerable numbers; in fact they make up the large majority of Christians – Orthodox, Roman Catholic, Mainline Protestant or Evangelical Protestant – in the developed world (and beyond it) today.

But by sorting them into those groups, we miss what they all ✳ fundamentally share – namely, a common sense of the obscure distance, and yet obscure connection, between their religious beliefs with their civic lives. Such believers are unseduced by the sharper (and false) clarity of right-wing religious ideologues, because they seem too immediately tied to a concrete political program; nor would they accept similarly rigid left-wing theologies, were any on offer.[7] Religious beliefs, they realize, do not typically translate immediately and easily into political behavior, and anyone who says otherwise, they suspect, is doing more salesmanship than theology.

To some this suspicion looks like hesitancy, and the hesitancy looks like it is anchored in tepid believing. And many of these believers' faith is all too frail. (More on that in a moment.) But the frailty of their belief does not cause their political hesitancy. If anything, the causality may go in the opposite direction: their hesitancy may be partly to blame for the tepidity of their faith. For they realize that there is *some* connection between their faith and their civic lives. Many of them are deeply interested in finding ways to render intelligible to themselves and to their neighbors the meaning and implications of their putative religious commitments. But the only models for faithful engagement they see are much too

---

7. This is most pointedly so for Mainline Protestants; see Wuthnow 2002 and Wuthnow 1997: 395: "the percentage of evangelicals who want mainline Protestants to have more influence is higher than the percentage of mainliners who want mainline Protestants to have more influence." But it is also true for Roman Catholics and Evangelicals; see Hollenbach 1997, C. Smith 1998 and 2000, Bramadat 2000, Noll 2002, G. Hughes 2003, and Steinfels 2004 (especially the essays by Murnion, and Leege and Mueller). It may seem odd to group Protestants and Catholics together, as well as mainliners and evangelicals, but it is practically accurate; significant ecclesial, political, and even theological differences no longer map onto denominational differences, but instead transect the denominations. For more on this see Wuthnow 1988.

tightly tied to immanent political agendas, and so they hesitate to engage their faith in civic life. Hence they judge that faithful engagement means a quite tight connection between belief and action, between faith and works; and from the works they can see, they judge that the faith that funds them is not worthwhile.

Can these bones live? Less likely resurrections have occurred. For such an event to occur, they need a better model of faith as a way of life, and a better model of how that faith may guide public engagement. That is what this book offers.

Still, their resurrection will not be an easy one. No resurrections are. To be precise, any attempt to encourage these believers towards richer engagement faces two large problems.

First, such believers are among the last adherents to the "public reason" view. They assume that public religious action is inevitably expressed in absolutist and intolerant fashion by the self-appointed spokesmen of the religious right and (again, however rarely seen) religious left. Because they find such action both civically imprudent and theologically impious, they think that religion should stay out of public life.

It may be that some readers of this book share this worry. So the following is directed as much at you as at such believers: no necessary connection exists between the public use of thick religious discourse and intolerant intellectual, cultural, or theological positions, or between "thin" modes of speech and open-minded and conversational ones. After all, the most visible case of religious believers accepting a Rawlsian etiquette of restraint in public life is precisely in the superficially secular "family values" strategy of quite conservative religious organizations; the 1960s United States civil rights movement was saturated with overt religious rhetoric; and anyway, the Roman Catholic Church's statements – some apparently "liberal," some "conservative," and all expressed in a largely undefensive, dialogical tone – are often welcoming and stern at the same time.[8] Furthermore, and speaking of the USA in particular, evidence suggests that such believers' hesitancy about explicitly religious engagement, out of concern for rising theologically inflected intolerance, has actually amounted to a self-fulfilling prophecy. Their shunning of religious rhetoric in public has

8. See Hertzke 1988.

permitted, and perhaps encouraged, the rising prominence of more ✳
strident and intolerant voices in public speech. It is not that there
was no religious discourse in public until the "religious right"
introduced it; to the contrary, the "religious right" was quietist
from the 1920s until the 1970s, and its current activism was
provoked by concerns about the "loss of our culture" after the
successes of progressive movements, themselves typically saturated
with often strident and intolerant religious discourse, up to that
point. What has actually happened in the last few decades is that
those religious voices attuned to the complexity of religion in public
life have effectively ceded the rhetorical high ground of thick discourse to extremist and often reactionary (whether right-wing or
left-wing) voices. Culture, like nature, abhors a vacuum, and bad
theology drives out good.[9]

These voices' self-imposed silence is much to be regretted, for
without them public life seems doomed to an ever sharper and
more damaging polarization. The changing religious demographics
of North America and Europe over the past several decades suggest
this. Some scholars have argued that immigration will transform
American religion into more pluralistic, eclectic, and tolerant forms
than any society before. Others, less sanguine, see immigration as
important, but not because it will make American religion more
diverse and eclectic; after all, the large majority of immigrants to
the USA are and will continue to be conservative Christians, from
Africa and Latin America – hardly obvious candidates to revolution-
ize religion in the USA, at least in the way that the starry-eyed
prophets anticipate. Meanwhile, Europe faces the emergence of
ghettoized immigrant populations who have been excluded from
the national cultures into the public sphere, and the rise of reactionary ethno-nationalisms (often with a religious patina) in
response.[10]

In short, believers' alienation from civic-religious engagement
will end only when they stop reinforcing the extremists' monopoly
on religious discourse by shunning such discourse, and instead take
it up again. Speaking civically, today we need to cultivate the public

9. See Hofrenning 1995, Apostolidis 2000, Harding 2000, Hart 2001, McCarraher
   2000, R. L. Wood 2002, and Marsh 2005.
10. See Eck 2001 and Wolfe 1998 for the optimistic view; see Gardella 2003, Jenkins
   2002, Nicholls 1989, and (implicitly) Noll 2002 for the more pessimistic one.

discourse of religious citizens, not further constrain it. Thoughtful secularists and sincere believers can agree that we need, not *less* religion in public, but *more*, of a richer kind – for such believers would be a welcome addition to civic discourse.

Any attempt to encourage such believers towards a richer religious engagement with civic life faces a second problem: these believers are often, to be frank, lousy believers. Their grip on Christian faith and life – or rather, Christian faith and life's grip on them – is often quite anemic, sadly confined to a mere spirituality. Many churches have become deeply co-opted by the therapeutic ethos of the culture, leading to declining membership and looser commitment even among those who remain. These churches, and their believers, are perceived, not without reason, as collaborating with these social trends, rather than offering any real resistance to them. They are in deep need of reformation, of a new Great Awakening – indeed, of any awakening at all.[11] Provoking these believers would have a powerful effect, not only on our common public life, but also on their own religious belief; but in this case, the cause of the improvement is indistinguishable with the improvement itself.

Yet all is not lost. Despite the many correct criticisms that thinkers from H. Richard Niebuhr to Stanley Hauerwas have leveled against those believers' ways of believing, we need not despise the noise of their solemn assemblies. For latent in their religious convictions is a sense that their beliefs should shape the way they live in this world. Even now they profess a deep commitment to justice, genuine community, and respect for others, albeit emerging most of the time in vague moral pieties – what Nancy Ammerman calls "Golden Rule Christianity." Furthermore, they have developed a particularly rich "style" of civic participation, one built on a strategy of stewardship and "bridging," creating spaces in which the events that constitute civil society – the town meetings, small groups, soup kitchens, and campaign rallies – can happen. Latent in their convictions are powerful motives for a style of public engagement that is both theologically profound and civically

11. See Fowler *et al.* 1999, McGreevy 2003, C. Smith 2005, Wuthnow 1997 and 1998a, Witten 1993, Hout *et al.* 2001. In Europe, see Gill 1999.

constructive.[12] Nor could this be easily changed, for it is wired into their churches' very being, and not just a bit of software in their minds. It is part of their *habitus*, too deep-rooted and organic to be painlessly or easily exchanged for another style of engagement. Theologies of the latter sort – often on offer by the received churches' harshest critics today – are hydroponic, unrooted in the lived realities of these churches' traditions. As such, such criticisms are symptomatic of our consumer societies' identity politics, which offer little more than the bad faith of a too-easy particularism. Real particularism is an achievement, the realization of a distinct character that can take a lifetime to develop; it cannot be simply purchased and put on instantaneously, like a pair of pre-faded stonewashed jeans, or a mass-produced "antique-looking" vase from Pottery Barn. At least these churches' style, in having a real past, offers the possibility for a real, concrete, future particularism – even if it too often fails to deliver on its promise.

Furthermore, while such critics attack the style, the style itself is not the problem; the problem is the absence of a theological rationale for it. These believers continue to volunteer and engage in civic activities at rates higher than other citizens (and particularly more than overt secularists and more rigid theocrats), but they lack a theological rationale for their civic engagements – an explanation for why they, as Christians, and members of these churches, should do this. They suffer from what Charles Taylor has called "the ethics of inarticulacy": a way of life guided by moral convictions whose articulation is blocked by its adherents' incapacity to express their metaphysical and theological background. And such activity must be complemented by some rationale, if it would be an intentional and organic part of a church's life, and handed on to new generations of the faithful.[13]

Such a theological rationale should explain why such Christians should care about public life, how they should be engaged in public life, as Christians, and what they should expect to have happen to them, as Christians, in that engagement. It would urge them toward a thicker appropriation of their faiths, an appropriation that would

---

12. See Ammerman 1997, R. S. Warner 1994, and Theusen 2002. See also Wuthnow on the importance of membership in more politically active congregations for training in skills for civic engagement (1998b and 1999b).
13. See Taylor 1989 and C. Smith 2005.

energize and inform their public engagement. Instead of arguing for the legitimacy of religion in public life, it would argue for the legitimacy of public life in religion. It would not ask, "What does God have to do with politics?" (see DiIulio and Dionne 2000), but instead, "What does politics have to do with God?" It would be a dogmatics of public life, which is what this book seeks to offer.

During the world: the dogmatics sketched

What will this dogmatics look like? First of all, it will not propound a system but sketch a communal way of life. Christian life is a life of inquiry into God, and the practices in which Christians engage do not simply assist that inquiry, they embody it. A "theology of public life" therefore includes a more concrete ascetical spirituality and ecclesiology of public life, which are manifest in and reinforced by a set of concrete practices, "spiritual" and otherwise.[14] Such a theology is well described as a normative ethnography of religious practices.

To do this we must confront the concrete challenges facing our attempts at ascetical formation, especially the fluidity and increasing marketization of our occupations, our relationships, and even our identities. In confronting these challenges we find that the best way to use them is to *endure* them – to see them as inescapable facts about our lives, realities which we experience most fundamentally by suffering them. Endurance is the crux of this proposal; it embodies the overall practice, the ascesis, that anchors this "theology of public life."

Enduring: an ascetical strategy

In talking about an asceticism based on an understanding of life as endurance, I have used two terms that need some unpacking before going further. Today "asceticism" suggests very thin, very bearded, near-naked men doing strange things to their bodies. All of those things can be part of an ascetic regimen. But none of them

---

14. See Greer 1986, Hadot 1995 and 2002, Charry 1997, Wuthnow 1998a and 2003, Sedgwick 1999, and Volf and Bass 2002. For challenges to such a spirituality, see Roof 1999, and M. F . Brown 1997.

gets to the heart of the matter. For all our interest in altering our bodies today – through physical exercise, surgery, even drugs – we are ignorant of the deep history of reflection on and practices of asceticism, so that, as Gavin Flood puts it, "the residues of ascetic practice in our culture have become mere technique" (Flood 2004: 1). Proper asceticism is a matter of vulnerability more than toughness; it is not so much about learning to grit one's teeth and bear it, but rather of learning to suffer in the right way, in order for the whole person, body and spirit, properly to be able to bear the weight of its ultimate destiny – which in Christianity means able to bear the weight of glory that is humanity's eschatological destiny.[15]

"Endurance" also needs some explanation. An ascetics of public life, built on a program of "enduring," uses engagement in public life to discipline one's dispositions. It does so by seeing that engagement most fundamentally as a form of suffering, of reception. Our lives in this world are more a matter of being acted upon than of acting. Such endurance is not fundamentally inert; passivity and activity are complexly intertwined therein, in a habituated receptivity, an alert waiting. The very etymology of waiting gets at this complexity; as Michael Raposa points out, the word *wait* "derives from the verb *to watch* and is associated with *wake*" (1999: 195 n. 1). This watchful waiting endurance is a positive mode of engagement with the world and with God in and through the world – an active, anticipatory, and welcoming responsiveness – organized through the theological virtues of faith, hope, and charity.

Yet the virtues so understood are not so much positive moral achievements as habits of resisting "making" anything out of ourselves; this is why we can talk about moral agency without falling into Pelagian presumptions of the necessity of moral heroism. Furthermore, they are not static states or conditions, they are dynamic and temporally organizing. They orient us most fundamentally to the temporal structure of our being, and of being itself. They give us our sense of timing, our "rhythm," and thereby order our desires and discipline our dispositions, teaching us to be properly vulnerable to God's grace, and especially the gift of Creation, given

15. See Asad 1993: 111–15, and Wimbush and Valantasis 1995, Charry 1997, Harpham 1987, and Roberts 1998. See P. Brown 1995 and 1992 and Lawless 2000 for Augustine's ascetical strategy, and DDC I.24.24-5 for Augustine's account of proper asceticism.

through the medium of time.[16] To endure virtuously means that we, as best we can, accept the gift that time most basically is. To imagine our life in the world as a matter of endurance is to see this life as a pilgrimage; it is to see oneself as a voyager, a *viator* in the world, in history. Pilgrimages are activities, but traditionally they are understood as a form of suffering, a way of traveling through the world that renders one vulnerable to presence – the presence of God, of the world, of others, even of oneself – in a new and self-altering way.[17]

To be so ascetic – to endure virtuously, to wait properly, to watch wakefully, to undertake what Augustine calls the "pilgrimage of our affections" (*DDC* 1.17.16) that this endurance entails – requires training, a training in how to inhabit time, how to take time, how to be patient. Anyone who has spent time around young children knows that to be patient requires serious discipline. We are like little children as regards this training, no matter how old we are. The most fundamental subject matter of our training, and in a way our most immediate tutor, is our desires: we must learn to desire aright. Yet the disciplining of our dispositions is at least as much a negative task as a positive one; at least as much about cultivating appropriate dissatisfactions as it is about realizing certain accomplished states of character; at least as much about the disruption of achievement by the recognition of our ongoing need for patience and waiting as it is about the apocalyptic presumptions of moral achievement. Our impatience is a general fact about the human condition, no matter what era or culture we inhabit; but it is made especially pointed for us by our contemporary consumer culture. "Consumer culture" is aptly named, for in it we are consumed with (and by) the idea of immediate gratification – whether of one's

16. For more on resisting the heroic and agonal temptations in the languages of virtue and practice more generally, see S. Jones 2002: 57–70 and Coakley 2002b.

17. See Augustine, *de pat.* My understanding of enduring parallels Coakley 2002a and 2002b and de Certeau 1992, and has some similarities with Hauerwas 2002, though as will become clear, I think that at times Hauerwas surrenders to the temptations that the language of "enduring" means to resist. On waiting see Vanstone 1983. On disciplinary practices, see Asad 1993: 134. On pilgrimage see Dyas 2001, especially the distinction between "life-pilgrimage" and "place-pilgrimage" (245–46), Constable 1976, for discussions of early Christian theologians' concerns regarding geographic pilgrimages, and Campo 2002; I thank Jason Danner for discussions on this.

physical appetites, one's intellectual habits, or one's existential identity.[18] Our typically manic-depressive lifestyle renders such pilgrimage almost unimaginable. In the face of an advertising culture that screams at us that we can, indeed must, "have it all," and have it all *now*, we have to learn to long, to long for the right – and in this life, impossible-to-"acquire" – "things." We must be "trained by our longings" to understand ourselves and others as beings whose longings, their persistent lacks, are crucial to our being (Harrison 2000: 97). Indeed "the whole life of a good Christian is a holy longing" (*in Io. ep.* 4.6), for we seek a goal unattainable in this world. We must learn to feel and dislike our condition of *distensio*, our experience of being overstretched, extended in confusing and disquieting ways. We must cultivate the right sorts of dissatisfactions – attending to the moments of dissatisfaction and, instead of dismissing them or downplaying their significance, we should acknowledge them as telling us something of the truth about our world, and our hopes for full and permanent happiness within it. We should feel an appropriate measure of "restlessness," a longing for something we know we will not fully find here, and a refusal to accept the false idols that we throw up for ourselves as distractions. We must learn to live during the world, not ultimately to expect to like it – in fact we must learn to allow ourselves, by and large, *not* to like it, where "liking" it means trying to find ourselves fully at home here.

This training is not easy, and has many pitfalls. We must not use it to confabulate a false wistfulness or a metaphysical nostalgia. The cultivation of dissatisfaction cannot be the cultivation of the snob, trained to sneer at all they come across; it is not a preemptive prophylactic against experience, but rather the implication of our increasingly profound inhabitation of our experience of desire – an experience that, on this account, we normally do not let ourselves fully feel. We should cultivate dissatisfactions with our dissatisfactions. (A saint can be all sorts of things – sad, angry, crabby, happy, dumb, cantankerous, beatific – but she or he cannot be complacent; coming to appreciate the difference between being at peace and being complacent is one of the most basic lessons saints can teach us.) We need a constant dispositional dislodgement; we must keep

18. I have been much educated on consumerism by V. Miller 2004 and Campbell 1987.

our disenchantment perpetually in motion. We should learn to live, as it were, in suspense, in resistance to closure. To borrow from Nietzsche, we should avoid being stuck, even to "avoiding being stuck" (which is precisely where most of Nietzsche's contemporary groupies fail to follow Nietzsche). With Augustine, again, we should learn to live as mendicants, begging constantly for forgiveness (*sermo.* 56.6.9), for in this life our justice lies in forgiveness of sins, not perfection of virtue (*DCD* 19.27). To do this, in other words, requires something more than skill; it requires grace.

This practice expresses, and reflexively relies upon, profound metaphysical and anthropological convictions. Metaphysically it means that "the world," insofar as it exists (or, better, claims to exist) autonomously, is a deeply compromised and compromising reality. And we also learn that the world is actually something other, namely, God's Creation.[19] When Creation fell and became "the world," it became less than what it once was, what it should be and what it will be yet again; it lives on "borrowed time" (Cavanaugh 1998: 228). And in inhabiting it so do we, who are the foremost exemplars of what was once great about it, and of what has gone so profoundly wrong with it. Anthropologically it affirms that the human is, as Rowan Williams puts it, "a creature animated by desire, whose characteristic marks are lack and hunger, who is made to be *this* kind of creature by a central and unforgettable absence, by lack and hunger" (1987: 69).[20] Because of this, we must be patient with our impatience; even as we recognize that this is not the home of our longings, we must not silence our hopes for real consummation, for a real realization of what we most deeply and truly desire. We are not seeking, as perhaps in Stoicism, to extinguish our hopes, but rather just the opposite – to learn to endure their persistence, and their irresolution. We must feel these hopes' full force and not seek to satiate them with the false consolations of consumer culture, to acknowledge that their satisfaction is deferred

19. See Davies 2004
20. See *sermo.* 38.1–2. See also Peter Brown on the psychology of politics in 2000: 322–25, and Markus on "eschatological restlessness" in 1970: 170. On *distensio*, see *conf.* 11.26 and the helpful discussion in O'Daly 1977, and Ricoeur 1984: 26–30. On pilgrimage in Augustine, see Claussen 1991 and Halliburton 1967. For the role of the community see van Bavel 1991 and Cavadini 2004. This insight extends behind Augustine, of course, even if he most fully develops it; see Betz 2000.

to a time beyond the ages of this prefab world, and to give that acknowledgment the weight it deserves.

Such a project – built on cultivating a sense of our own incompleteness, dissatisfactions, and even failures – may seem dissatisfying. But that dissatisfaction is part of what it aims to treat. We impatiently, apocalyptically expect solutions for our problems. But such "solutions" are generally snake oil. And as Franz Rosenzweig suggested, Christianity is best understood as providing a structure to our passion and suffering, not a solution to it (1985: 376).[21]

To endure our life in this way is to be attentive and wakeful, patient and long-suffering, to refuse to let the world have the last word on what it means, and yet to refuse also to presume to know what that last word will be. It is to live in the world, without accepting its immanent self-presentation. It is to live eschatologically within the world – to live *during the world*.

During the world

The phrase "during the world" may sound novel, but it is quite old. It appeared as long ago as 1435, in the will of one Richard Beauchamp, Earl of Warwick, who asked therein that a chapel be built with money from his estate, and "that there be said every day, during the Worlde ... three masses" in the chapel (G. Holmes 1962: 180). And the idea behind it is older still. The struggle to grasp the idea expressed by that phrase has been one of the primary tasks of Christian thought from its beginnings. A whole cosmology is packed into those three words, one suggesting a way of treating our earthly condition as crucially contingent, at least in the sense that our lives' significance is not absolutely determined by the immanent forces that both press upon us and (seem to) sustain us. The language of "world" suggests that we, as the namers of "the world," have an ability to step back and see it as a whole, to gain something like a perspicuous conceptual grasp on it. On this picture, we have some sort of ability, however partial, to transcend the world; the "horizon" of the world is not our absolute horizon, and does not ultimately define us. Indeed, by naming it, we define it (van Fraasen

21. See Batnitzsky 2000 and Santner 2001.

2002: 5–25). Our immurement in the world is in some way then not the whole story about us.

This capacity for transcendence is typically misunderstood. Many recognize it, only to get caught on the horns of a dilemma. If we are not absolutely in this world, how should we conceptualize our relation to it? Some suggest that we are made not for this world, but for some "other" one; for them we should struggle to understand how to relate to this world while we are in it, but seek ultimately that other world which is in some radical discontinuity with our existence now. Others insist that this world is the only one there is, and we should see our tendencies towards estrangement from it as temptations to be resisted. The options are stark: either this world or another. We are properly at home in this world, or we are "resident aliens." But both options are inadequate. It is simply bad faith to deny our world-transcendence, our recognition that the material conditions of our material lives are not all there is to say about us. Yet nor are we otherworldly, made for another place – a metaphysical Mars, perhaps – and for some obscure reason trapped in this one; the fantasy that we could be "altogether elsewhere," in a way that would be free of worldly engagements, makes our relation to the world altogether too accidental. Indeed, the temptation to think of ourselves as otherworldly in this way does not speak simply of our historical failures of imagination; that we experience it as a temptation reveals that our condition as "worldly," as existing in an environment in which we remain in complex dialogical relation, reaches to the depths of our self-understanding.

What such positions seem to forget is our conditioning by time as well as by space. We normally orient ourselves most primordially in space. We live after the triumph of *mathesis*, the mathematical spatialization of reality that was accomplished in early modernity.[22] But such a conceptualization is superficial. It implies that the world as we find it is a permanent and unalterable reality, in relation to which we are ultimately defined. This not only accepts our sinful belief that the way the world is, is "the way the world really always has been and will be"; it may also delude us into thinking that there is some place – namely, "the church" – in which we can stand that is fundamentally uncontaminated by "worldliness."

22. See Pickstock 1997: 135–66.

Christians should be oriented not by Newton's onto-theological grid but rather the biblical-historical narratives, and they should reconceive the world fundamentally temporally, as a duration. Christians are not otherworldly, but most fundamentally "other-temporalitied." "The world" is more primordially an era than a place.[23] More fundamental than the question of where we live is the question of when, and on this account we live in the "epilogue," the "after-Word," speaking Christologically (G. Steiner 1989: 93–4). We are, in the most profound way, *belated*; everything important to our fates – our sin and our salvation – has already occurred, or at least (in the latter case) has been inaugurated, if not fully accomplished. Our fate is secure, the victory is won; we are simply waiting for the final consummation. Given this condition as belated and yet waiting, we must, through grace, begin to learn to live in a new way in this passing age. We should understand the world as something we fundamentally must endure – not an absolute and unquestioned "given," but rather a contingent configuration of reality that will one day pass away.

This is what the phrase "during the world" is meant to bring to the fore. It suggests a period, episode, or era – a non-permanent condition, but one inescapable, for now – in which we find ourselves, and which we must live through. By so picturing the world temporally, many of our most cherished escapist metaphors are immediately rendered defunct. We cannot stand "outside" or "against" the world; we cannot fully participate in God's condescension *vis-à-vis* the world, because what the language – God's language – of "the world" condescends to is, in part, ourselves. Yet we know that this condition is impermanent: we must live in time, but we cannot rest content with(in) this dispensation as conclusive.[24]

So understood, "during the world" disabuses us of believing that the world is what we make it. Not at all: we are more fundamentally witnesses than *ex nihilo* agents. But we are not witnesses in the sense of innocent bystanders, whether to a crime or a car wreck; we are more like the audience in Greek tragedy, necessary for the play's realization, implicated in its truths, but not able to act to alter the

---

23. For a sociological deconstruction of "otherworldliness," see McRoberts 2003.
24. For discussions of the import of temporality, see Rudenfeld 2001, Coles 1997, D. Harvey 1990, G. Steiner 2001, and Baudrillard 1994. For a powerful alternative to this account, see Jenson 2004.

basic story. Yet it is not a tragic story, though the interim often does seem, at best, tragic. We live "in the middle," and it is from the middle that we have to begin. We must endure the present time and stand fast into an indeterminate future. The fact that the world will one day end, that it is not our ultimate frame of reference, does not entail the apocalypse's imminent arrival. Eschatology without imminent apocalypse: that is the tensive structure of commitment and longing that should shape human life here, during the world.[25]

An Augustinian worldliness

So we need a dogmatics of public life; and such a dogmatics will be fundamentally ascetical; and such an ascetical dogmatics will cultivate our ability to perceive our condition as one of living "during the world." But why would we seek to find inspiration for such a program in Augustine?

In an important way, the decision is simply pragmatic. Augustine's theological vision, vocabulary, and (to a lesser degree) attitude have shaped the traditions of Western Christianity more profoundly than any thinker other than St. Paul. To offer a theology of engagement able to speak to the audience this book wants to reach, splintered ecclesially and doctrinally in myriad ways, it is wise counsel to find a common root for all of them. Augustine is that root.

But there is a deeper, principled decision. Not only is Augustine's thought more readily apprehensible by the book's core audience; his thought is also especially fruitful for thinking about public life and "worldliness" more generally. This may be surprising, given Augustine's reputation as a metaphysical escapist and gloomy worldly pessimist. Thus part of this book's task is to explain why his reputation is wrong; and so the book insinuates, and occasionally explicitly urges, a particular revision of our understanding of the Augustinian tradition of Christian thought. I should briefly sketch this revision here.

---

25. For life "in the middle," see Bonhoeffer 1997: 28. Von Balthasar's contrast between "epic" and "dramatic" modes of theology is relevant here as well; see von Balthasar 1988a and Healey 2000. For more about the contrast between "eschatological" and "apocalyptic" modes of being, see the Introduction to Part I.

By using the phrase "the Augustinian *tradition*," I mean to draw guidance from Augustine's thought, without being trapped in the historical cul-de-sac of debates about what Augustine "really meant." The diverse interpretations are importantly due to different interpreters' judgments regarding Augustine's textual center of gravity, which typically begin from *de civitate Dei* or the *Confessions*.[26] In contrast, I argue that it is best to read Augustine as centered not around those texts but instead around his sermons, scriptural commentaries, and especially his one truly "gratuitous" work, *de Trinitate*. These texts depict the self as an active agent within a community in a continual process of conversion towards or away from the divine Trinity, of which it is itself an image and which is the soul's true origin and end. Such a picture of Augustine's thought is becoming increasingly common now, as these more centrally doctrinal writings have begun to receive the scholarly attention they deserve.[27]

So understood, Augustine's thought was developed by various descendants, from Cistercians such as Bernard of Clairvaux and Franciscans such as Bonaventure, and by the Reformed traditions, from Calvin to Edwards (and in a different way Schleiermacher), emphasizing the conversion of the affections as the fundamental site of the workings of grace in the world. In the twentieth century these themes were developed by the Niebuhrs and their intellectual descendants such as Paul Ramsey and, more recently, Oliver O'Donovan, Gilbert Meilaender, and Timothy Jackson.[28] This tradition offers a vital theological approach to the convictions and practices that shape Christian life.

This reading of the Augustinian tradition entails two things, one consonant with and one conflicting with current trends in theology

26. Methodologically see Mathewes 2001a, esp. Chapter 2; historically, see Dodaro 2004a.
27. This view is encouraged by recent historical work on Augustine by scholars such as Lewis Ayres, Michael Cameron, Robert Dodaro, Michael Fiedrowicz, and Thomas Martin; it will become increasingly common as the impact of the New City Press translations of the Augustine corpus into English make palpable for readers the enormous iceberg-like mass of sermons and commentaries heretofore kept from contemporary readers' easy appropriation. For a careful development of the importance of *de Trin.* for Augustine's "political" thought, see Dodaro 2004a: 147–81.
28. For a nice discussion of Niebuhr's legacy, see Werpehowski 2002. For a good analysis of Ramsey as not just Niebuhrian but Augustinian, see Davis 1991.

and ethics. First of all, it supports the popular emphasis on understanding moral life as a matter less of principles than of our
dynamic inhabitation of some set of moral virtues or dispositional
attunements. Augustine allows that one can be a Christian without
access to the Bible – such were the desert fathers and mothers – but
only if one's life is already governed by the theological virtues of
faith, hope, and love. These virtues are not a superficial optional
interpretation of the Christian life for Augustine; they provide
something like a fundamental structure for understanding the
shape of human existence for him. This is so because of his
understanding of the human as a temporal creature; as all the virtues are forms of *caritas*,[29] perhaps *caritas* is the fundamental mode
of inhabiting time, and thereby the fundamental mode of created
being itself. In this way this project emphasizes the dispositional
and conversionist character of religious commitment.[30]

Second, the "political" Augustine here presented proposes an
unusual assessment of the nature of the significance of "worldly"
political existence – and through this, a surprising picture of the
significance of "worldly" existence *tout court*. One typical problem of
political developments of Augustine is that they start with his
political prescriptions and do not see the theological sources of
those prescriptions; because of this, they often misunderstand even
his political prescriptions. But in fact at its core Augustine's thought
has no fundamentally political content at all, but is simply theological; and yet, precisely because Augustine's political insights
have no "natural" home in some properly political region of his
thought, coming to appreciate Augustine's "political" proposals,
such as they are, enables a deeper appreciation of the pro-creation
dynamism of his theology in general.[31]

Most concretely, many scholars attempt to impose a Procrustean
schema of "natural" and "supernatural" on his thought. For scholars

---

29. *De mor.* 15, 25, and Carney 1991: 33–34. For a specifically political development
of this point, see *ep.* 155 and 138, and Dodaro 2004b.
30. See *enchiridion* for more, and Studer 1990. For more on the value of thinking
about the moral life fundamentally in terms of virtues, see Porter 1990: 100–22.
31. As Robert Dodaro argues, Augustine was always at pains in his correspondence
with secular authorities to note the connections between even the most
mundane matters and the new life to which God calls us. See Dodaro 2004a:
7–10, 196–212. Also see Kevin Hughes's very insightful comments in 2005b:
145–46.

committed to this framework, Augustine seems to deny any genuine "natural" goods in politics, which they take to reveal his deep animus towards the conditions of our "worldly" life as a whole.[32] On such readings it can appear that, in Quentin Skinner's words, "Augustine's view of political society had merely been ancillary to an eschatology in which the life of the pilgrim on earth had been seen as little more than a preparation for the life to come" (1978: 50). If this were true, it would present a deep challenge to any attempt to argue for an Augustinian endorsement of public life. But in fact it is not true. Augustine's picture of the dynamics of divine sovereignty and intimacy, captured in his understanding of grace and love, happily stymies Procrustean categorizations such as "nature" and "supernature," and offers a more nuanced view of this-worldly life in general, and of public life in particular. Augustine certainly diverges from Aristotle insofar as the bishop insists, against the philosopher, that the human good does not climax in the parochial community of the human polis, and insofar as he affirms that a human life untouched by political sovereignty can still be a flourishing life. But Augustine is not so bleak as many have taken him to be about the possible benefits of worldly, communal, and perhaps even genuinely public, life. He was fully appreciative of the goods of worldly community and worldly things; his love for music, for example, is deep and abiding. The life of the saints in paradise, after all, is social and embodied, and the sociality and embodiment mark not only their relation with God, but their relations with one another as well. Some scholars have recently begun to realize this, but it remains an insight not yet fully digested.[33] Augustinians can affirm that public life can be a way for humans to come to participate in God. It can be understood ascetically, as a means of purifying the soul for God: the ascesis of citizenship can be understood as part of the ascesis of discipleship. This is a strongly postlapsarian vision of politics, yet it avoids any collapse into despair or anomie. Genuine goods can be pursued, and even partially achieved, through public life, but they are not properly secular political goods; no such goods exist.

32. See, e.g., Weithman 1992. For a broad survey of criticisms of Augustine's purported "otherworldliness," see Kirk 1966: 133–37.
33. For evidence that Augustine thought of politics as a good, see Burnell 1992 and von Heyking 2001.

More importantly still, Augustine's potentially positive assessment of public life is anchored in a deeper positive assessment of
worldliness than the received accounts allow. In fact, Augustine is in
many ways better positioned than Aquinas, conceptually speaking,
to make sense of Christian existence in the world; for unlike
Aquinas, Augustine was blessedly innocent of the conceptual
dichotomy of "nature" and "supernature" that burdened the
attempts of so many, including Aquinas, to interpret human existence. As God's love is the source of all being, we all always participate in God's love; even Satan is held in existence by God's love.
The split-level "nature" and "supernature" account, which neo-
Thomism found in Aquinas's thought (whether or not it is actually
in Aquinas himself) has no purchase in Augustine's. He could not
imagine that God's gratuitous creative activity for the world could
be quarantined from any space of "sheer nature" in the *saeculum*.
This is why so many thinkers inspired by Augustine in the past
century found the language of "nature" and "supernature" so foreign to his thought, and tried to overcome its deleterious effects by
running the terms together – so that Paul Ramsey argued for a "this-
worldly supernaturalism" and John Milbank demands that we
"supernaturalize the natural" rather than "naturalize the supernatural."[34]

Augustine's refusal to confabulate a nature–supernature distinction has many benefits for his theology. Most generally, it means
that the conceptual structure Augustine employs implicitly under-
scores the continuity between our present "worldly" condition and
the greater life yet to come. More specifically in political terms, it
reflects an ultimate overcoming of all boundaries, and a deep conceptual resistance to positing ultimate limits – based finally on
conceptual resistance to any concept of an ultimate "outside" or
exteriority to the divine providential plan. Even Satan in hell serves
God. This reveals that Augustine is a profound critic of what we
might call "the mythology of the exterior" – and suggests that that
mythology is, in some fundamental way, essentially a political
mythology. Augustine's is not a "politics of limits," at least not
ultimately; indeed, he is the greatest thinker of the idea that the

---

34. See Ramsey 1950: 132, and Milbank 1990b: 207. See also van Bavel 1987: 28,
    TeSelle 1970, De Lubac 1969, and Burrell 2004: 208–9.

problems that vex politics do not finally come from "outside" or "the other" or any sort of exteriority, but from inside – from us trying to escape, to get outside. Outside of what? Of God, ultimately. But for Augustine there is no outside; there are no ultimate enemies; all we must do is learn to love ourselves, one another, and God. In this way Augustine is the ultimate theorist and therapist of escapism.[35]

Conclusion

A project like this one runs just off the grooves carved by many previous texts in religion and politics. Hence it is likely to be misread in several different ways. Here I want to resist several misreadings of the book before readers settle comfortably into them.

First, this is not an apology for democracy. Tocqueville said, "Americans so completely confound Christianity with liberty that it is almost impossible to induce them to think of one without the other" (2004: 338). It is a wise warning. Democracy is not the "ideal" institutional state of Christian believers. Political life in the world has no "ideal" state. It is too *ad hoc* a condition for that. Democracy is not our divine destiny, and heaven is not a New England town meeting. Christians have survived many different political structures during the world. Good Christians live as subjects of the tyrannical autocracies of East and Central Asia, in the oligarchic kleptocracies of the Middle East, in the semi-democracies of Latin America, even in the completely "stateless" conditions across much of Africa. Public life can occur (imagine!) even where democracy is not. (Consider the "antipolitics" of Eastern Europe in the last decades of the Cold War or the "street liturgies" by Roman Catholic resisters in Chile under Pinochet.[36]) For most readers of this book, democratic structures exist and should be defended, sustained, and extended. But my goal is not to use faith to support our democratic culture, but the reverse, and more – to use our civic interactions with one another to deepen faith.

35. See Phillips 2001a.
36. See Konrád 1984 and Cavanaugh 1998.

Second, while this book is unapologetically theologically framed and ecclesially addressed, it is not finally an expression of in-house *ressentiment*. It is not an apocalyptic jeremiad against contemporary public life or "modernity" in general. Modernity has led to much confusion and vexation. But it has also offered immense goods. This book talks about both. There are good reasons to worry about the drift of public life in conditions of late modernity; but there are also reasons for hope. Apocalyptic jeremiads of ritualized renunciation do little to help anyone with anything, beyond offering the false comfort of a Pharisaic purgation, which will need to be re-performed tomorrow. They are a symptom of our problem, not a solution to it. So they have always been, for the assumed purity that jeremiads entail is always delusory. Christianity has always been a mongrel religion, combining in new ways language from a variety of Hebrew discourses with other, especially Hellenic and Roman, elements, so that even the most "original" Christian speech-acts were impure and hybrid – in ways that mirror the metaphysical miscegenation of Chalcedonian Christology. And in the opposite direction, no element of Christian discourse is immune from misuse and abuse because of its "distinctively Christian" pedigree; heresy debates are often about the right use of central terms of Christian discourse, not just about the language on the "margins" of the vocabulary. Proper use of the language stands or falls on its pragmatic validity, on what the language does for us and (more importantly) *to* us. We should resist such fantastic escapisms and face the fact that ours is a political world, and our fate is to live out our lives as crucially public creatures. (Even monastics are such, as was powerfully evidenced by the life of Thomas Merton.) I say this as much for ecclesial reasons as for civic ones: bad civic culture encourages an enervating servility and lassitude in its inhabitants that hinders the development of proper Christian persons. And good civic culture can become – and has become from time to time in the past – a particularly palpable site of the Spirit's presence in this world. Christians should be interested in thinking about public life, not just for their fates as citizens, but also for their fates as Christians.[37]

37. Latent here is an appreciative critique of Stanley Hauerwas; see Mathewes 2000. For more, see Gill 1999, esp. 19. On the civic engagement of the early churches, see Winter 1994.

This is not a matter of argument. <u>Christianity *just is* a public religion</u>. It is not a mystery cult, nor is it fundamentally esoteric; it lives in public. Vibrant Christian faith presses us outward towards one another, not centrally in terms of "charity work," doing nice things for those less fortunate than ourselves – though such good deeds are praiseworthy and needed – but as fellow citizens, and not just of a worldly state, but as citizens of the kingdom of heaven. This dynamism toward the other has historically been understood as evangelization, and that certainly has a role to play in its future. But it may perhaps be better manifest indirectly, in an unapologetic confessional openness about one's own motivations and rationale for operating in the public sphere. In any event, Christians will not know what "evangelism" might mean unless we think deeply about Christianity's missiological energies and how they should be best inhabited today. It is not anywhere near an effective strategy just to bury one's head in the sand and simply ignore this aspect of the faith. Vigorous Christian belief entails a serious commitment to expressing the faith. Conversely, a lack of expressing the faith leads to pallid believing. Christians cannot hide their lamp beneath a bushel; real Christians will not do so, and are not doing so.[38] But how, during the world, should that lamp be displayed? What shall Christians do now, in this weird after- and before-time? How can believers inhabit Christianity's "already" and "not yet"? Is humanity just marking time? Is it all, in John Courtney Murray's phrase, "just basket weaving" (Murray 1988)? How should we comport ourselves in this Epilogue, during the world?

Answering those questions is the point of this book. It does so in two steps. Part I explicates a theology of engagement – one which, while implicit in many theologies today, has not before been explicitly articulated. It explores how a certain picture of God and God's relation to the world plays out in understanding ourselves as appropriating the divine *energia*, "energy" or "activity," in our behavior in the world. Central to this new account is a revitalized and metaphysically vigorous picture of God's simultaneous immanence and transcendence: God's free sovereignty over creation and

---

38. See O'Donovan 1996: 212–14, Rausch 2004, and Abraham 1989. My understanding of evangelism and engagement is sympathetic with the deep logic of Abraham's understanding of evangelism as initiation. See also Stuckey 2003.

yet God's intimate ongoing involvement in sustaining all creation in being. Hence Part I attempts to offer a theological interpretation of the world as a form of participation, through Christ, in the church, in the divine *perichōrēsis*. This participation is distended by our fallen condition and our temporality, but it is participation nonetheless. And it is a participation necessarily mediated through the world, through our condition as existing in God's Creation. Creation is not the "background" to our redemption, it plays an essential role within it. The basic dynamics of this theological vision develop the dual dynamics of the inside going outside, and the outside coming within, to challenge our attempts to set up absolute boundaries in the world, between inside and outside. We sinfully use these boundaries (or try to use them) to separate ourselves – from those who are unclean, from our neighbors, and ultimately from God. But this separation is impossible, and in every way we are more eschatologically intimate with each and every other than we "naturally," in our fallen state, imagine. The question this part seeks to answer is simple: given this understanding of God and God's relation to Creation, how are we to understand our lives – before God, within creation, and with others – during the world?

Part II further develops Part I's answer to this question, by detailing how to understand and inhabit public life, civically and ascetically, during the world, in a theology of citizenship. The concept of "citizen" is the fundamental political category of modernity, the locus of political sovereignty, and thereby diverges from much premodern (and modern, and some postmodern) political theology by not fundamentally treating the political agent as a subject, and not taking the basic political question to be the question of proper obedience. The basic question is not one of the character of proper obedience to political authority, but the character of proper participation in public life. Given this, citizenship is usefully understood as a liturgy, not only as a communal activity (the root meaning of *leitourgia*), but also because, by engaging in apparently political activities, we are participating in properly theological activities as well. Yet this is not an argument that "politics," as we presently understand it, is a "proper sphere" of an intended order of creation; rather, the dynamics and longings captured in political activities are ultimately "ordered" to God. Again, this is an eschatologically inflected political theology: the liturgy we participate in now will find its proper meaning only before the Lord at the judgment day.

Yet our present participation in this liturgy can fit us for our parts in that greater liturgy to come. Existence in this culture, or any culture for that matter, will cultivate the soul; the only question is, how should it do so? How should we position ourselves "downstream" from cultural and political forces so that they may best shape our character? These chapters ask this question also, and thereby offer an ascetics of public life. Against both apocalypticism and consumerism, both of which tempt us towards false conclusions, false "ends," the virtues can find themselves purified through engagement in public life. The souls of Christians may be shaped by their public engagements in ways that train their longings here, while also offering a foretaste of their participation in the eschatological kingdom to come.

With all that said, let's get to it.

PART I

A theology of engagement

Wherever you turn your eyes the world can shine like transfiguration. You don't have to bring a thing to it except a little willingness to see. Only, who could have the courage to see it?

Marilynne Robinson, *Gilead*

Introduction to Part I

Part I of the book explicates the general theology of engagement that undergirds the explicitly political theology unpacked in
Part II. It explains how Christians should see the fundamental
theological dynamics of their faith as encouraging an ever deepening attachment to our created condition, and it suggests that those
dynamics are well articulated in an Augustinian vernacular.[1] Finding such a pro-creation agenda in Augustinian Christian thought
will likely surprise many readers. This Introduction explains why it
should not.

An Augustinian theology of engagement

Augustine's thought may seem an odd resource for a program
of worldly engagement. After all, Augustine often sounds as if he
thinks humans have fallen out of heaven into the world. But the
surface appearance of his rhetoric – couched in a late antique philosophical vernacular – is deceptive. The deep conceptual and
theological underpinnings of his account actually endorse a very
different view: a picture of humans as fallen out of creation – out of
our condition as creatures in a created world – and into a condition
in which we assume we must have absolute mastery over what we
see as a world fundamentally other than ourselves. Human sin is
"privation" in a way that is not merely etymologically related to
privacy: it is solitude, isolation, what Robert Markus calls "man's
liability to close in on himself … at bottom, sin [is] a retreat into

1. There are several strong affinities between this argument and Markham 2003.

privacy" (1990a: 51). Conversely, redemption is, in a way, publicity, presence to others, and most fundamentally to God – a turning back to God, the neighbor, and creation. For such an Augustinian account, our lives are properly seen as inextricably part of a larger created order, and we must come more fully to inhabit our created condition.

It is hard to isolate a starting point for Augustine's thinking. But certainly one of its sources lies in his acute theological analysis of our escapism – our condition as caught between our sinful pre-dilections towards interiorizing and privating *superbia* or "prideful-ness," and the kenotic ecstasy that is the grace of Christ anchored in the Father and kept inexpungeably, agonizingly, tantalizingly pre-sent in our hearts through the Holy Spirit. We find ourselves out of tune with the world, with our timing thrown off, and so we are tempted to endorse this estrangement, to name it as our natural condition. But this distempo is fundamentally accidental to the human condition; that is why we describe it as a "fall."[2]

In response to this condition of depraved and privated privacy, we should resist our persistent attempts to retreat further into our-selves (and resist the fantasy that such retreat is ever successfully possible). But this resistance cannot ever expect to make us happy in this life, because even as we undertake it, we and the world remain fallen, and so experience all our engagements as suffering. So we should come to be ever more fully open to the sufferings that mark our lives during the world, most fundamentally as a mode of being in time, indeed of receiving the gift of time itself from God.

But this openness to suffering, this practice of "confessional openness," itself holds a further potential pitfall. For one more of our canny strategies is to see such suffering as a technology we can employ to fix ourselves – a way we can keep in charge of ourselves, alone and autonomous – and thus just one more of privacy's guises. Yet not so; this suffering is not something you can use but some-thing that uses you, that trains you to be a new sort of person. Suffering is not something you do or achieve but something you accept, something you endure.

This theological picture is more apprehensible to us today than in much of the twentieth century because of the rehabilitation of the

---

2. On the accidental nature of sin, see H. R. Niebuhr 1989: 78.

theological insight, over the past several decades, that God's transcendence and immanence are more intimately interrelated than
most modern thinkers imagine. As Augustine put it, God is simultaneously "most high and most near, always absent and always
present" (conf. 6.3).[3] On this view, it is not possible for divine and
human causality to compete on the same "plane" of action, and so
there can be no profane saeculum where God is absent. We can couch
this basic insight in terms of Christology and salvation history.
God's activity in the world did not culminate in providing a sacred
example that entered into reality like a spaceman, hermetically
sealed from contamination by materiality: in Christ, God plunged
fully into materiality to redeem it, and our participation in that new
creation, through the sacramental mediation of the body of Christ,
is our salvation.[4]

Yet this theology does not finally rest in sheer accomplishment.
Christ's "coming" is the Son's unitary mission across all time, and
so Christ's saving work has both always and not yet been completed.
During the world, we should live adventally, celebrating the inau-
guration of our redemption, in and through our participation in
Christ's mission. The overall project of time is not yet concluded,
and so we must undergo the historical process of salvation knowing
that the consolations of redemption are not given to us immediately. Joy is not our imminent future; only the longing for joy is.

The ascetical engagement proposed here is a form of participating
in God's kenotic engagement with the world. By engaging in public
interactions with others and enduring the risks those engagements
entail, we come better to see and participate in God pro nobis.

Part 1 makes this case in three chapters. Building on the Augustinian insight that God is "more intimate to us than we are,"
Chapter 1 sketches this account's basic theological anthropology,
asking what sort of autonomy and agency are available to humans
given this powerful picture of God's role. Given our faith that God
will be all in all, what does "life before God" look like today?
Chapter 2 asks how we are supposed to inhabit "the world,"

3. See also Gen. ad litt. 8.26: "Without any distance or measure of space, by His
   immanent and transcendent power He is interior to all things because they are
   all in Him." For contemporary analogues, see Placher 1996 and Milbank et al.
   1999.
4. For the deep Pauline roots of this see Hubbard 2002.

understood as creation as a whole, given this picture of life before God: given our hope that we will eventually see God's sovereignty as governing all of history, how can we presently treat creation with respect for its relative integrity? Chapter 3 unpacks the implications of this picture for life with others: given the command to love one another, can we really make sense of the idea that in meeting strangers we must meet them as themselves, not just as God's mask? What does otherness amount to, in a world governed by a God as sovereign and all-suffusing as this?

In each case, we will see that the languages we use to understand these dimensions of our lives – the languages of selfhood, of the world, and of community – all turn out to have a theological core: God becomes the crucial grammatical anchor for understanding all three facets of existence. Indeed, each of the languages turns out to lead into the others. To speak about the self requires us to speak intelligently about the world that, in part, calls the self to communion; to speak about the world requires us to speak intelligently about the community of humans in which we find ourselves when we live in the world; and to ask about the destiny of the self, the world, and others is to ask about the destiny of all, which is to ask about God. Indeed, to "ask" at all is to begin a process of inquiry that can only "end" itself in inquiry into God. To be alive is to seek God; and all such seeking longs to become, and will eschatologically be consummated as, praiseful wonderment at God.[5]

But today we recognize that this process of seeking ever deeper communion is persistently vexed by our fallenness, and deferred by our existence in a history that has not yet run its course, so we best speak these languages by speaking in an eschatological – but not apocalyptic – "tense," that keeps us open in the present, and awaiting the world's completion in the eschaton.

As such a first-order theological project, Part I is an unusual beginning for a work on religion and public life. It will provoke two different responses in many readers. Some will find it problematically escapist. Others will find it all too this-worldly – indeed, apocalyptically so. Many of the people who will feel these temptations are those to whom this proposal is meant to appeal. The temptations are second nature to us. They identify real tensions for

5. See Mathewes 2002a.

any Augustinian proposal. But I think they should be resisted. Below I explain why.

Is the project otherworldly?

One set of challenges revolves around a deep suspicion, especially common among secularists, that a project like this one, with its emphasis on not finding the human's proper good in any immanent configuration of goods, inevitably promotes a certain kind of "otherworldliness" or "anti-worldliness." Such a suspicion can be expressed in two ways, metaphysically and existentially. Metaphysically, critics ask: How does the language of "the world," when granted any real weight, not tempt us to offer some total assessment of "the world" as a whole, which of necessity obscures the manifold complexities and contradictions within it? How can it be a language to engage the world, instead of being – as its grammar strongly implies it will be – a language to alienate ourselves from it, and thereby to excuse our indifference or outright hostility to it? Existentially, the critics suspect that the account suffers from a deep wistfulness and *ressentiment*, a despair at our existence that expresses itself in a longing to be altogether elsewhere. Those who hold such suspicions want us to feel the force of Hamm's exclamation in Beckett's *Endgame*, when he says, "Use your head, can't you, use your head, you're on earth, there's no cure for that!" There's no "cure," no technology of escape, they say; we are *in* this existence inescapably, and our being is determined totally by its shape.[6]

These suspicions merit substantial engagement, and this book returns to them repeatedly; I will only offer a summary of my response to them here. Speaking metaphysically, the value of this language lies in its immense critical leverage, its potential for a quite radical critique of the status quo. Admittedly the concept can be ruthlessly simplifying, but it allows us to "denaturalize" reality as we find it, to render radically contingent "the way the world is," and thus to open up an imaginative space of incredible opportunity. After all, the language of "the world" is irremediably a theological

---

6. Actually, Hamm says this twice; Beckett 1958: 53, 68. See Cavell 1976 and Adorno 2003b. These worries may be prominent among hardcore secularists, but they can be shared by others; see, e.g., M. O. Boyle 1997.

language: it enables us to imagine the world as a contingent expression of God's will. The capacity to imagine this is central to the Christian kerygma. God is always faithful, but God is also a living God, always able to do an utterly surprising new thing, swerving from our expectations, absolutely confounding our sinful presumptions to know the course of history. Not to name the world as "the world" would suggest otherwise: it would deny God's transcendence of creation. From a Christian perspective this would be both wrong and self-mutilating, for it would ignore the eschatological dynamics which Christianity (for good and ill, we should admit) contains.[7]

Speaking existentially, this suspicion's roots are found in its apparently supra-worldly "solution" to the tragedies of worldly existence – namely, the idea of *grace*, a force from outside the world that "rescues" us. But rescues us from what? Is not such a "supernatural" resolution to our problems simply an escapist pseudo-resolution of our problems at the cost of genuine confrontation with the serious challenges we face? To which we may reply that, admittedly, bad uses of "world" language can encourage an escapist mentality and work to dissipate or misdirect our energies. But the problem here is the misuse of the language, indeed a misuse still captive to a fundamentally immanentist imagination. Such bad positions allow themselves to be partially defined by a "worldly" horizon, and so indulge in otherworldly *ressentiment* precisely to the degree that they accept the credibility of that "worldly" stance.[8] Fear of such a "bad otherworldliness" cannot take center stage in any elaboration of Christian life during the world.

After all, in one sense this proposal is otherworldly; for only if we accept that our motives to love are not elicited or merited by what we call the world, and hence need not seek final validation therein, can we love the world as much as we want to. This is because our love is, as are our lives, gratuitous. Our love for the world is otherworldly in its origins, but it is equally a love for *the world*, as its

---

7. For examples of religion as a force for political reimagination, see Walzer 1970, Hill 1991, and Tanner 1992.
8. I am not opposed to conceiving the church as the ultimate human community. But the church cannot be understood via a derivative parallel to the world, presuming a prior polis on which it is reactively modeled. See Mathewes 2000.

object; only by accepting this love as otherworldly can we allow it to be as thoroughly worldly as we wish it to be. In this way "other-worldliness" enables its adherents to be more fully at home in the world than "immanentists" can be, because it allows us not to expect more from the world than it can provide, and thus not to be disappointed by it. We can care for the world as much as we do only if the source of our caring is not simply the world itself. In contrast, it is immanentism that is truly *un*worldly, for it tries to bend our transcendental longings back down into the world. Immanentism turns out to be a failure of imagination, a kind of repetition-compulsion: a refusal to see beyond (not see *the* beyond) the literal givens of the world's current configuration.[9]

Readers should not feel satisfied with these reassurances; the temptation towards otherworldliness is perennial and radical, and will not be neatly resolved during the world. But it is resistible. Exploring this temptation, and suggesting ways perpetually to resist it, form one of the themes of the rest of this book.

Is the project apocalyptic?

Another, deeper challenge to this account is that the language of "the world" inevitably takes on an apocalyptic cast, encouraging a presumptuous complacency wherein we identify our own expectations for the future with God's plan. Such critics worry that we inevitably invest the idea of "the world" with too clear and certain a profile in our thought, and do not allow the unmooring of the world from our expectations, and so it becomes little more than a projection device for our own wishes. Here the use of "world" language is problematic, not so much in itself as in its ability to be bent back into the service of our own self-interest. Not only is the language not self-correcting, it also fails to get at the deepest root of the problem, which is our attempt to control reality – if not space, then even more primordially, to control time. But we too are under God's judgment, and what we think and say we want must be relativized as well.

This is the core of the Jewish critique of Christian claims about Jesus' being the Messiah. This worry is that Christianity is

9. See Santner 2001.

fundamentally apocalyptic, an ongoing attempt to demand the Messiah – that it is, in short, a vast, sacrilegious self-indulgence. (It may also be one of the sources for post-modern critiques of Christianity as "onto-theology.") If Judaism is, as Michael Barnes has put it, the "primary otherness" with which Christianity is inescapably engaged, then this worry lies at the center of that engagement (Barnes 2002: 200).[10]

One must admit the bite of such critiques. Judaism is more purely adventral; but almost from its beginnings, Christianity has been finished. As we said, Christians live in the epilogue; we have, in an important way, finished our religious history. Even what is yet to come has quite literally been "scripted" for us in the book of Revelation. This is why apocalypticism is so fundamental a temptation for Christianity. In fact Christians have exhibited a wild and dangerous oscillation between emphasizing God's absolute immanence in history and God's absolute transcendence of history. Human history is charged with theophanic meanings, yet such a theophanic presence in the world is always troubled by the memorial repetition of our recognition of the absence of the yet to return Christ. Images both can and cannot reveal God; history is both sacred and profane; the world has and has not yet fully borne the weight of glory.

But Christians can frame these critiques internally to the language of their faith. Apocalypticism is not only a fundamental human temptation; it is one proper description of the root human fault itself, the attempt to usurp God's power as Lord of time, and as such should always be resisted. Nonetheless, our resistance to apocalyptic hyperbole cannot renounce the insight that that hyperbole attempts to express – that things today are not ultimately as they will be. The sheer dismissal of apocalyptic proclamations, and the repression of the emotions motivating those proclamations, would encourage an unthinking acceptance of the status quo. As Jürgen Moltmann has argued, "the loss of eschatology ... has always been the condition that makes possible the adaptation of Christianity to its environment and ... the self-surrender of faith" (1975: 41). We are better served if we recognize the value (and stubborn persistence) of the religious longings and the eschatological imagination, crystallized in "world" language, expressing

10. See Wyschogrod 1983, Rosenzweig 1985, and Novak 1989.

those longings, and if we acknowledge our inescapable struggle to resist the escapist temptations they present to us, rather than imagine we could ever truly clip our religious wings. We need a program of Christian formation that escapes the oscillation between the mindsets of "apocalypse now" and "same as it ever was" – a program that takes these worries with real seriousness, as a diagnosis of our sinfulness, yet still does not simply dismiss the energies that encourage bad apocalypticisms and settle back into a resigned acceptance of the status quo. We must identify and resist the many ways that the temptation towards ending manifests itself in our lives, while still keeping us vulnerable to the idea that the world we inhabit will, "in the end," end.

In seeking such a program of Christian formation we find much help in Augustine's work. He was the first major figure to use eschatology to resist a too literal apocalypticism, even as he remained convinced of the reality of the apocalypse.[11] He was deeply sensitive to the way humans could turn anything to sinful use, and he saw the dangers of a Christian complacency all too vividly in the church of his day. So his thought bears much promise for identifying and disarming these apocalyptic temptations, especially if we further develop the theological stance behind his own efforts to give determinate shape and programmatic structure to the recognition of the historical contingency of the created order.[12] We can do that by drawing a distinction between what we can call the apocalyptic and the eschatological imaginations.

Apocalypticism is fundamentally an epistemological attitude, a claim already to know. The Greek word *apokalyptō* means "to unveil" or "disclose"; it suggests a mindset that basically looks to the future as an already determined and knowable reality. On this definition, "apocalypticism" is a form of eschatological meteorology, of forecasting; in a weird way, to be apocalyptic is to be *post-*apocalyptic – to know already what is going to happen, and so to

11. See Pollmann 1999 and P. B. Harvey 1999.
12. The "apocalyptic" / "eschatological" contrast is not my own, though my use of it is somewhat idiosyncratic. (There is a vast historical literature on apocalypticism that I will not address.) A helpful and apparently similar contrast is elaborated in Alison 1996; another is P. Miller 2000, esp. 156. See also Keller 1996, S. O'Leary 1995, Boyer 1992, Harding 2000, and Bull 1995. For a powerful and interesting critique of the "already"/"not yet" structure of much eschatological thinking, see Jüngel 1989.

treat it as the past. This is a deep human temptation, and illuminates how we seek to understand history. Our desire to understand history is actually a desire to be able to say what it meant "in the end," a desire to have it finished, over – so that this desire entails a desire actually to escape history.[13]

In contrast, the eschatological imagination opposes all apocalypticisms, all temptations to anticipate the end of time. The eschatological imagination is most fundamentally ontological, for the Greek work *eschaton* means "a limit," "an edge," or "an end." It is a way to refuse a false knowingness about the future, and hence to enable real knowledge by keeping us open to the future and to the "new thing" that God is always almost about to accomplish. This imagination identifies the apocalyptic temptation as a temptation towards endings, and in response to this temptation most fundamentally enacts a resistance to our own sinful desire to end things. Theologically speaking, this desire for endings is an attempt to avoid God – a way of escaping our actual responsibility to understand and act in response to God's action upon us. The world will end, for the eschatological imagination; but we will not be the ones to end it. God's will is not captive to our expectations. The lesson of providence is not that history can be finally solved, like a cryptogram, but that it must be endured, inhabited as a mystery which we cannot fully understand from the inside, but which we cannot escape of our own powers. To paraphrase Reinhold Niebuhr, history offers no progressive triumph of good over evil; if anything, its tensions accentuate over time. We must not become too comfortable in any worldly dispensation, because we remain aware of its difference from our proper dispensation.

This distinction between the apocalyptic and eschatological imaginations is palpable in many Christian beliefs and practices. First of all, the church's life is not simply a matter of marking time. We *remember* Christ's death and we *proclaim* his resurrection, even as we await his coming in glory. That is, we have obligations to the past and the present as well as to the future. But, as William Cavanaugh puts it, "we live on borrowed time" (1998: 228): both past and present are genuine sites of blessedness, insofar as they participate in the eschatological redemption of all, a redemption inaugurated in

13. For examples see Eusebius 1976 and 1999.

Jesus Christ. It is not simply that we don't know yet what the significance of the present, of history, is; from within history, its significance is not yet fully determined. All of creation is a sentence that God has begun to speak, but which is not yet completed, and so we await its full meaning.

Of course, we should beware the temptation towards anti-nomianism here as well. We should not jettison the apocalyptic texts or thinkers from the tradition, or the eschatological energies they express; to do so would be just another form of apocalyptic closure – the closure of closure itself.[14] The dangers of oversensitivity to the apocalyptic temptation may be as great as indifference to it: speaking of H. Richard Niebuhr, who powerfully voiced "Protestant" suspicions of any determinate expectation in eschatology, Harry Stout suggests that "the lopsided praise of movement to the virtual exclusion of order can yield the mistaken image of (to paraphrase him) a church without creeds bringing people without codes into a kingdom without structure through the ministrations of crises without end" (1989: 98). Our waiting is a waiting *for*; our longing has a positive content.

Still, the worry about apocalypticism's temptations toward closure must remain; we must not ever let ourselves believe that we have "finally" answered it conclusively. Christianity must perpetually resist its own temptation towards concluding. We cannot ever expect, in this dispensation, a conclusion of our concludings, a final resolution of our desire for resolution. But the desire itself is significant; can we treat it not as an opponent to be defeated, but as a lesson God is trying to teach us?

Augustinians certainly think so. Ever since Eden, sinful human-ity's basic mental framework for interpreting history has been apocalyptic. Indeed, the Fall itself was the attempt by humans to seize for themselves God's sovereignty over all things, and one fundamental form of God's sovereignty is God's sovereignty over history. Sinful humanity imagines that such sovereignty can be expressed only in mastery, and the only kind of mastery we imagine is mastery over life; but we cannot give life, we can only take it away, and so mastery for humanity is the power of destruction, of

14. On resisting both "closure of the world" and "closure of the text," see Keller 1996: 19–20.

✶ death: humans, in seeking to be "like God," are like God only in mimicking God's power to kill. Ever since Eden we have not just been trying to claim the end of history; we have been trying to end history – not just to witness that end, but to be the agents of its accomplishment.

Such has been history's perpetual face. But lately things have, if anything, gotten worse. Our technology has caught up with that desire, and now we can fulfill the very apocalyptic longings we are supposed to have outgrown. Michel Foucault put it well: "For millennia man remained what he was for Aristotle: A living animal with the additional capacity for a political existence. Modern man is an animal whose politics places his existence as a living being in question" (1981: 143). At no point in the past did we need to confront our temptations towards apocalypticism as much as we do today, when these temptations saturate our political landscapes. This is so not only in regard to various millennial fringe groups, violent or otherwise; nor is it simply so as regards much of the contemporary populace, at least in the United States and in much of the developing world (remember that the most popular novels of the recent past have been the "Left Behind" series); most importantly, it is so as regards almost all kinds of radical and revolutionary politics, whether manifest on their face or buried in the deep structures of their thought.[15] To avoid confronting these temptations to apocalypticism is to be at their mercy. We need to think about apocalypticism precisely because it has become real today in a way it has never been before.

But the proof of the pudding is in the eating. And now that we have identified and articulated some worries about this proposal, and sketched how those worries do not immediately defeat the project, we must (at last!) begin the project itself. We turn to that now.

15. See Boyer 1992 and 2005, M. A. Bernstein 1994, and Cook 2004. A challenging counter-reading is Frykholm 2004, which I discuss in the Conclusion.

1

Life before God

<u>What does it mean to have faith?</u> What are the theological preconditions of a life lived out of faith? Most fundamentally, to have faith means to be determined, in two senses. First, it means to ✶ be determined as regards one's convictions – to be confident and persevering in them. Second, it means to be determined as regards one's identity – in the sense of moving from an indeterminate and amorphous sense of self to a more definite, determinate sense. So understood, <u>our "faith" defines us, gives us a determinate identity,</u> <u>which is manifest in the confidence with which we hold and express</u> <u>our convictions.</u>

But such "determination" has its dangers. It can ossify into the apocalyptic determination of presumptuousness – a conviction that we know already who we will fully be, and who we will ultimately become. We feel this temptation, and we feel it *as* a temptation, because we know we are incomplete, and we feel that that is bad, imperfect; absent such faith, the self may seem not a whole but as a *hole*, a vacuum that needs filling; much of our manic activity is driven by our panicked recognition that we need to do something to be a self (see Berger 1992: 111). Bad faith is a form of false closure, a pseudo-resolution of our inescapable human openness, during the world.

Some suggest that because of this all faith should be avoided, that we should live in determined resistance to such closure, in some form or another of skeptical suspension. But such determined resistance to determination is just one more form of bad faith. Our easy opposition between skepticism and "fidelity" masks the fact that real belief is difficult to achieve, even among – perhaps especially among – skepticism's most ardent enemies. This is the upshot of the last few decades of epistemological inquiry about the "groundlessness" of belief, and the inescapability of this condition: we are always already in a series of fiduciary relationships, always already "faith-full" beings.[1] We always need somewhere to stand, when evaluating our convictions; there is always something taken for granted.

What then should we do? We must acknowledge that determination, and faith, constitute our inescapable condition. Our saving grace is that true faith, genuinely inhabited, is relational – faith in something outside ourselves. True relational faith directs, orients, and opens us, in a way that will be resolved only eschatologically. In the meantime we must learn to face the terror of an open, yet to be determined, identity. As children, we go where we will; but when we have a mature faith, we will be girded and taken where we do not want to go.

✳   Faith, then, is a way of talking about the relationship between a living self and its sources of value, its identity, and its ultimate being. Faith is trust, the trust that God is in charge of our lives, and that it is God who makes our lives intelligible and narratable. To talk about faith is to use a language of the self and its "god." For Christians, to be a self is to be a self before God, in intimate and constituting relation with God. In talking about the Christian language of faith, that is, we are trying to find a language through which we can understand how we exist before God as selves.

This chapter explores Augustine's grammar of this language through detailing his theological anthropology – his picture of the human and its place in creation and before God, during the world. Augustine's importance to philosophical and theological anthropology, and its importance to his thought, cannot be denied.[2] Yet while Augustine's position is often praised in general terms, its details are typically kept comfortably at arm's length, because it seems too paradoxical to do what it seems to want to do. To be precise, two apparent paradoxes obstruct the full appreciation and appropriation of Augustine's thought by contemporary thinkers.

---

1. See M. Williams 1977, Cavell 1979, Plantinga 1993, and Foley 1993.
2. For the ambitious nature of Augustine's anthropology see van Bavel 1987: 27, and Burnell 2005.

The first concerns the nature of mind or human knowledge, and is ✳
captured in the claim that all knowledge is mediated by self-
knowledge, and that self-knowledge is itself mediated by knowledge
of God; to realize objective truth one must turn inward to the subject, and thereby outward to God. The second paradox concerns the
nature of human agency, and is captured in the claim that the self is
perfectly free when it is perfectly determined by God; true freedom
is found not only *through* but even *in* the divine imposition of pre-
venient grace. Many people find both claims difficult to understand.
How can subjectivity lead to objectivity? And how can freedom be
realized in and through servitude?

In fact the difficulties vexing our understanding of Augustine's
position reflect problems vexing our own purportedly superior
anthropologies, for it is precisely our modern philosophical categories that obstruct our understanding and appreciation of
Augustine. Indeed, both of the puzzles described above are caused
by a common flawed conception of autonomy. We commonly
understand autonomy to mean the subject's independence from
outside influence or formation; we thus take human knowing to be
a matter of matching subjective mental constructs with the "outside" world, and human freedom to be a matter of spontaneous
subjective decisions sparking our bodies to act in that world. I call
this a "subjectivist" conception of human being, because it invests
the human subject with priority in its existence; it assumes that our
knowing and believing, desiring and willing originate sponta-
neously in us, not as responses to what realities outside the subject
do to and through us. It offers us a language for understanding our
lives whose primary verb tense is active: the human knows, does, is.
This account is most fundamentally characterized by the priority it
gives human activity. Furthermore, it tends towards solipsism, for
on subjectivist grounds, as Emerson said, "use what language we
will, we can never say anything but what we are" (Emerson 1957:
271); and while transcendentalists may find comfort in that solipsistic narcissism, others might find it too cramping.[3]

While this modern model has permeated our language and our
consciousness, complaints about it are common. It is criticized as
conceptually incoherent, morally and politically problematic, and

3. See e.g. Connolly 1999.

theologically suspect. And it is all those things. But complaints alone will never dislodge it from our mindset. For that we need a better picture of human being, one that depicts us as we really are – one sensitive to the intricate interrelationship between our activities as thinking, willing, and acting beings, and the enframing reality which elicits our activities. As Gary Watson puts it, we must find "room in the world for ourselves" (Watson 1982: 14).

Augustine is often identified as the crucial ancestor of modern subjectivist anthropologies. His work is said to underwrite both Cartesian philosophy of mind and voluntarist theories of agency; he is accused of inventing the inner and inventing the will. And one cannot deny that Augustine's writings did indeed play a role in these developments. But these positions are actually *mis*readings of Augustine's views. In fact his actual account not only resists Cartesian and voluntarist pictures – pictures which his thought diagnoses as building out of convictions about the human that are themselves derivative of our sinful *superbia* – but also offers a radical alternative to them. Proper Augustinian anthropology understands human agency as always already related both to God and to the world, thereby chastening modern predilections for absolute autonomy while still affirming the individual's importance.[4]

Hence the air of paradox surrounding Augustine's anthropological claims arises from errors not in his views but in our own. For his two (to us) troublesome statements affirm important truths about the human, truths we must acknowledge today. And his account depicts the human condition (which is also the human dilemma) more comprehensively and accurately than any of the modern alternatives we presently possess. Most fundamentally, this account offers us a language for understanding human being whose fundamental verb tense is passive: the human is created, is known, is, to paraphrase Luther, more fundamentally acted upon than acting. To appreciate this, we must exorcise the received, putatively "neutral" philosophical categories in which Augustine's account is often presented, and replace them with a more theologically rich and supple vocabulary. The upshot of this exorcism will be a new understanding of what faithful existence before God looks like on

---

4. For a richly historical discussion of the nature of selfhood and relationality in Augustine's era, see Conybeare 2000: 131–60.

Augustinian terms – how it understands the human activities of knowing and acting as kenotic responses to God's eschatologically oriented primordial knowing and acting. Faith is not so much a state as it is an ascetical virtue: a form of interpretive orientation that resolves interpretive difficulties only by reorienting one's attention towards far more profoundly irresolvable mysteries. To have faith is to be a self; but to be a self for Augustine is not a self-enclosed cognition, but rather to be related to God in a certain way, as remembered by (and remembering) God, known by (and knowing) God, and willed by (and willing) God (de Trin. 14.12). To have faith is to "know" oneself as determined by another, radically transcendent but also absolutely immanent, reality: and that is what all call God.

Or so this chapter argues, first in terms of Augustine's epistemology, then in terms of his theory of agency. It concludes by showing how this thoroughly theological and eschatological account of human life during the world helps us develop a political theology based on a dynamic engagement with the world, to be spelled out in the following chapters. While many think Augustine's work overemphasizes human interiority, they miss the basic dynamic relationship of "interiority" and "exteriority" that actually governs his overall view. The crucial insight that his account brings to this project is the confounding of interiority and exteriority in God's creative and consummative action; and we will see it reappear again and again throughout this work.

Augustinian epistemology: against Platonic idealism

Augustine's epistemology, and his philosophy of mind more generally, are simultaneously deeply interesting and deeply perplexing. His basic epistemological move is inward; he emphasizes the interiority of the subject in a way that seems to undermine the importance of the external world. Yet he also sharply criticizes solipsism and skepticism, affirming our power to know objective truth. So Augustine can seem to be everywhere at once: equally the discoverer of the individual's interiority and the great apologist for the necessary role of dogmatic communal authority in intellectual activity.[5] Accordingly his texts seem, to modern readers, riddled

---

5. See Taylor 1989, MacIntyre 1988, and Crouse 1976.

with contradictions that cannot be explained by conscious changes of mind or patterns of development. But when properly understood, his account helps transform both the terms and the framework of our epistemology.

First of all we must understand Augustine's account as an extended critical engagement with a view with which it is often, ironically enough, identified – namely, Platonism. "Platonism" in contemporary philosophy most commonly functions as a straw, a difficulty in taking seriously the reality and significance of the material world – a difficulty that signifies some sort of other-worldliness or even anti-worldliness in the thinker who stands so accused. The issues of historical influence and appropriation, let alone what should count as "Platonism" and what should not (and how it is related to what Plato wrote or taught), are enormously complicated, and I make no pretense of resolving them here. Still, many thinkers have noted the deeply Platonic-sounding formulations pervading Augustine's writing, and some argue that he in some way "Christianized" Platonism, either baptizing it or, even worse, merely slapping a Christian veneer on what was essentially a (presumably non-Christian) Platonic philosophy. However, we should note what is rarely noted: Augustine was at least as critical as he was laudatory of Platonism, and if we attend to his criticisms we may develop a more nuanced appreciation of his engagement with Platonic thought more generally.[6]

In fact his accusations against "Platonism" arguably echo contemporary philosophical critique of Platonist philosophical stances. But Augustine goes deeper than contemporary philosophers do, offering an ontological critique of Platonism: in his account, Platonists depict our relation to the world as fundamentally contingent and properly accidental. They come to epistemological grief because of this depiction, for by assuming it they cannot grant full legitimacy to knowledge of worldly realities, but instead see all such "earthly" knowledge as essentially pseudo-knowledge, at best opaquely conveying the luminous truths that stand behind, but fundamentally unconnected to, it. And Augustine builds his own epistemology explicitly in opposition to this view. For him, humans are created as

---

6. For the best recent account making much (much too much, in my opinion) of Augustine's debts to Platonism in his philosophy of mind, see Cary 2000.

fully part of a larger creation, and thus our knowledge of it is genuine and authentic – albeit muddled, shadowy and broken by our corruption in sin, as all our knowledge is and shall be until the eschaton. But our sinful epistemological condition gives us no grounds for a radical resentment of materiality, as it does (on Augustine's understanding) for Platonists; rather, our condition should make us more fully aware of our sinfulness and long for the day we truly know all things, including the grains of sand and the sparrows of our world. Hence the problem with Platonists is not that they recognize some tension and occasional ill fit between ourselves and "existence" – any minimally plausible account of humans must do that – but rather that they conclude, on the basis of this ill fit, that we properly belong to another world, a world elsewhere. In contrast, Augustine thinks, we must trust the sincerity of God's creative act, and be committed to the world; for we are part of it, and in some sense unimaginable as detached therefrom. Far from being a "Platonist," Augustine's project is fundamentally oriented towards subverting the Platonic temptations towards imagining another world as our home.

To grasp this critique, however, we must begin where we are, with the epistemological categories we have today; as they are the ones we use to try, unsuccessfully, to understand Augustine, we must come to see why they must be transcended.

Mind's relationship to world

Our perplexities with Augustine's philosophy of mind arise because we read him as if he alternately advocated one or the other of two Procrustean positions that contemporary epistemology treats as mutually exclusive – epistemological internalism and externalism. The modern debate between advocates of these positions revolves around the question of epistemic justification or warrant for our beliefs, although the issues involved are ultimately not simply epistemological but also metaphysical, concerned with the relation of mind and world, subjectivity and objectivity.[7] Internalists argue that individuals are responsible for their epistemic apprehension of the world; the mind, that is, must somehow

7. See Foley 1993.

establish its relations to the world, typically by constructing some inner "picture" of that world. In contrast, externalists argue that an individual's epistemic standing is generally determined by external factors such that, rather than creating the world, the mind is somehow created *by* it. Each has legitimate concerns about the other. Internalists accuse externalists of reductionism, of annihilating subjectivity in favor of a scientistic reduction of agency to nomological causality. Externalists accuse internalists of idealism, of so bloating subjectivity that it cannot accommodate any real concept of a world outside the self at all. Both express an acute anxiety about the proper place of the mind "in" the world, about finding room in the world for our minds.

Aspects of this debate would sound familiar to Augustine. But the debate itself would bewilder him. Understanding that bewilderment can provoke a fruitful and transformative discomfort with the contemporary options. With the externalists, Augustine argues that our beliefs are largely beyond our control, because our minds are deeply responsive to extra-mental realities. But with the internalists he argues that our mental existence cannot be reduced to material-nomological causality, and that we remain importantly responsible for shaping our beliefs. According to him, epistemic justification does take place within the roughly autonomous space of subjectivity, but such justification proceeds only by affirming that an irreducible otherness stands at the heart of that subjectivity – the otherness of God. Augustine anchors his external realism, that is, in the inwardness of the mind's discernment of God. Objectivity is realized through subjectivity, but only because subjectivity has at its heart an objective reality.

A sketch of his epistemological development helps explain these claims. Augustine first formulates his position in arguments with Manichean rationalists and Academic skeptics. He tries to steer a middle course. Against the Academics' epistemic despair, exhibited in proposals for the total suspension of belief, he affirms that epistemic commitment is necessary and legitimate and that real knowledge is possible. Against the Manichees' rationalist complacencies, however, he argues that real knowledge is difficult to achieve and requires commitment to complex, communally authorized disciplines of belief formation and evaluation. In Augustine's view, we begin with innumerable beliefs, including some that we cannot

doubt, some we can doubt, and some we ought to doubt; but our ✳
epistemic abilities are perverted by sin, and so working towards a
more truthful knowledge requires real effort (and indeed communal
effort). We are responsible for reforming our epistemic faculties in
order to be positioned properly to secure true knowledge.[8]

Augustine's picture of the human inquirer reveals more general
facets of his anthropology, for he understands epistemology to be
part of the larger soteriological aim of human existence. Knowing
cannot be understood in isolation from the larger human project;
we acquire salvific knowledge by participating in a community
seeking salvation, and this participation reveals to us what we have
"really" wanted all along. Thus what begins as a critique of epistemological skepticism turns out to be, ultimately, a rich picture of
the self as broadly "determined" as to its loves and, through its
loves, its beliefs.[9]

Augustine most closely approaches epistemological externalism
in de Trinitate's critique of the Platonic doctrine of anamnesis, or
recollection, which he takes to claim "that the souls of men had
lived here even before they wore these bodies, and therefore
learning things is more a remembering of things already known
than a getting to know new things." On this picture, the self's
relation to everything, including itself, relies upon some ontological
form of "prior consent," so to speak – some sense that our approval
is primordial. This is a sort of ontological contract theory; in its
"original position," so to speak, reality is presented to us as something which we can take or leave.[10]

Augustine argues that this does not make proper sense of the
human capacities to know things, as it seems to imply that everyone
must have been a complete genius in a past life, in order to ensure
that all we know, we "know already" in a sense; yet "it is unlikely
that everybody was a geometer in a previous life, seeing that they

8. See Augustine's contra acad. and DUC for these arguments, and Collinge 1988;
   for contemporary elaborations and developments, see Wolterstorff 1984 and
   Aquino 2004. For a more technical analysis of such distortions, see Elster 1983.
9. See Gen. ad litt. books 7–9. See also Mathewes 2002a. In arguing that we are most
   fundamentally beings who love, Augustine's position resonates with some
   major work in recent philosophical anthropology on "the importance of what
   we care about." See Frankfurt 1988, Taylor 1989, Lear 1990, and McDowell 1994.
10. I do not think this was Plato's own doctrine; see Republic III, 412e–413b, on
    voluntariness and involuntariness in belief formation. For a general account of
    what Augustine is trying to do here see Ayres 1992 and 1995.

are such a rarity in the human race that it is a job even to find one"
(*de Trin.* 12.24). Knowledge due to precognition by the soul in some
preexistence does not resolve the epistemological problem, it
merely pushes the puzzle one step further back, where the question
arises again: How do we come to know in the first place? Augustine's response is telling:

> The conclusion we should rather draw is that the nature of the
> mind has been so established by the disposition of its creator that it
> is subjoined [*subiunctum* – "joined under"] to intelligible things in
> the order of nature, and so it sees such truths in a kind of non-bodily
> light that is *sui generis*, just as our eyes of flesh see all things that lie
> around us in this bodily light, a light they were created to be
> receptive of and to match. It is not because the eyes already knew
> the difference between black and white before they were created in
> this flesh, that they can tell the difference now without being
> taught it. (*De Trin.* 12.24)

Our most basic epistemic relation to reality is not achieved through
heroic agential activity, not even via "recollection"; rather, our
minds are "created to be receptive of" reality, and God has "sub-
joined" the knower to the known.

The root problem for Platonists, Augustine thinks, is that they
assume that knowing creation is a derivative exercise of the intellect, not what the mind was made for. For Augustine, in contrast – at
least by the time he wrote *de Trinitate* – the activity of knowing
creation is much more fundamental to the mind's existence. Indeed,
we might say that we are created to know both creation (ourselves
included) and God, and the proper question of epistemology is how
those two are related.

Augustine's critique is not simply a narrow technical criticism of a
bad philosophical argument; it reveals a fundamentally different
understanding of humanity's relationship to the world. This becomes
clear when we note the otherworldly trajectories that a Platonist
epistemology may tacitly encourage. It suggests that knowing is an
activity primarily directed at extra-worldly objects, only derivatively
diverted to this-worldly, "mundane" objects, and thereby implies
that the activity of knowing is not primarily an activity at home in
this world. By refusing this epistemology, Augustine closes off a very
powerful temptation towards otherworldliness.

One may think this is taking things a bit too far. Is not Augustine at least Platonic in deploying a psychology – a picture of the soul – in which memory plays a considerable part? But here again, surface similarities between Platonists' discussions of memory and Augustine's *memoria* mask fundamental differences. Augustine rejects more than the Platonist picture of how the mind relates to the external material world; he makes parallel arguments in discussing the self's interiority and in particular its self-knowledge. He argues that the mind is created by God in a way that entails its direct (if partial) acquaintance not only with its world, but with itself and its God – direct in the sense of unmediated by any faculty or power of *memoria*. This claim makes its appearance as early as *de magistro*'s discussion of Christ as the "Inner Teacher," and by the time he wrote the mature *de Trinitate* he explicitly rejects the belief that there was a time when *memoria* was wholly "potential," simply a space in which to store future memories. If *memoria* were initially mere potential, then it could not be the self's ineradicable basis; but it is just this inescapable self-presence that, for Augustine, phenomenological attention to ourselves evidences (and which, incidentally, demonstrates the falsity of the skeptic's claims to the possibility of total suspension of commitment).[11] He holds that, on the contrary, *memoria* is not a capacity but an actuality, a presence, the necessary presence of the self to itself: "The mind, after all, is not adventitious to itself," Augustine argues,

> as though the mind-which-was-not-yet came from somewhere else to the same mind-which-already-was;[12] or as though it did not come from somewhere else, but in the mind-which-already-was should be born the same mind-which-was-not-yet, just as in the mind-which-already-was arises a faith-which-was-not-before; or as though after getting to know itself it should by recollection see itself fixed in its own memory, as if it had not been there before it got to know itself.

"The truth," Augustine concludes, "is that from the moment it began to be it never stopped remembering itself, never stopped understanding itself, never stopped loving itself" (*de Trin.* 14.13). The mind's self-awareness is not accidental; it is the necessary self-presence that enables the self to act and to reflect.

---

11. See Burnyeat 1987.
12. I have reversed the two terms of this contrast for clarity's sake.

While the reality of this ineradicable self-presence seems to establish a special *sui generis* space for the mind, in fact it entails the opposite: the mind is *not* its own self-enclosed reality. According to Augustine, we must trust in interior realities as much as in exterior ones, because God is at the core of both. Because Augustine's epistemology is Christoform, even in our knowing we are subject to a divine other. *De magistro*'s theological claim that Christ is "the inner teacher" bears deep epistemological and ontological implications: the ineliminable presence of the Logos in the world is the condition for the world's intelligibility. Christ's presence within the soul is more a transcendental presupposition of our constitution than a positivistic observation; wherever truth is, there is Christ.[13] The mind is not in the Cartesian cogito's nowhere, with epistemic relations to the "outside world" that are fundamentally contingent; rather, the self knows itself as already, and indeed always already, a self in the world and before God. Even before exerting any effort, it cannot help but know God – for, as Augustine says, "God is closer to me than myself" (*interior intimo meo*) (*conf.* 3.6; see also 10.16–27).

Our recognition of God's primordial presence in the self should undo our pretensions to solipsism, and help us see how our relations to the world – particularly our dependence on various authorities to inform our minds and our desires – are also "internal" to the self, not accidental to its constitution. So while Augustine's analysis of *memoria* may appear similar to Platonism, and may appear to warrant a straightforwardly internalist picture of the mind, in fact it entails that the self is externally determined even in self-knowledge – that the self, in knowing itself, no more epistemically bootstraps its way to cognition than it does in knowing the outer world. The self's epistemic reality is fundamentally given to it, and the self is "warranted" in believing in those realities because it cannot find a way to disbelieve them. Talk of the self's "interiority" misleads if one imagines it (as is usual) as a sort of inner private chamber; interiority is rather a way of conceiving the fact that the self is, at its base, always facing the reality of God. Augustine's putative internalism is turned inside out, and it turns out to look quite a lot like epistemological externalism; but this

---

13. See *DVR* 30.56–31.58, and 43.81–44.82, Burnyeat 1987, and Cloeren 1985.

semi-externalism is warranted by seemingly internalist ontological arguments about the nature of the mind's interiority.

Such modern categories simply cannot be workably applied to Augustine's thought. The distinction between externalism and internalism, so popular in modern thought, distorts the complexities of human existence that Augustine so meticulously untangles and details. We should conclude, that is, that the terms themselves need to be at least transformed, if not transcended.

A contemporary Augustinian epistemology

An Augustinian epistemology can incorporate what is good and true in both internalism and externalism while responding to the concerns about each. Internalists are often accused of subjectivist relativism, but Augustine's account understands subjectivity as always already involved with an objective reality that it cannot ignore, but at best (and at worst) can only deny. (Hence the primordial epistemological problem is not simple error, but self-deception.) On the other hand, externalists are often accused of being fideists, whose theories of purely external "warrant" win only a Pyrrhic victory because they apparently eliminate any legitimization beyond the simple fact of belief, hence reducing our cognitive responsibilities in ways that make us epistemically indistinguishable from thermometers, merely gauging changes in our environment; but Augustine's account acknowledges the agent's responsibility for her or his own epistemological proper functioning – not through direct voluntary control over belief, but through the agent's indirect voluntary influence over the conditions that produce her or his beliefs. And because Augustine acknowledges this, he commends certain activities – both solitary introspective and communal confessional ones – that help reconstruct certain religiously and morally significant epistemic modules.[14] While we cannot choose our beliefs, we can, to some degree, choose the communities that will shape our beliefs.

Nonetheless, while these activities have as an indirect benefit the creation of epistemic warrant – by shaping our epistemic modules to modify what we are warranted in believing – that is not their

14. See Alston 1991, Audi 1986: 165, and McDowell 1995: 882.

main end, nor is it of salvific importance. Augustine argues that epistemology is not an *a priori* necessary prelude to positive inquiry; we need it to get to God only because our minds have been deformed by sin. Furthermore, Augustine's acknowledgment of individual responsibility for, and participation in, the reconstruction of one's epistemic framework does not undermine the broader picture of the self as determined in its beliefs by things beyond its control. Our lives' meaning is found, not in the production of true beliefs (were it so, we might happily pass our days adding numbers together), but in a loving relationship with God and our neighbor; and insofar as that relationship eventuates in knowledge, it is not the representational activity of a mental projector on the windowless inside wall of our skull, but a knowledge that we suffer by acknowledging that God and the neighbor present themselves to us, unmediated by any subjective scrim. Knowledge is not most fundamentally an achievement but a suffering of presence, one we confess more fundamentally than we achieve.[15]

One might say that we work out our epistemic responsibilities in fear and trembling. For Augustine, the fact of our responsibility does not deny the relevance of external determinants. While we need (and are responsible for) some voluntary introspective practices to reform our ways of believing, we should avoid "naturalizing" such practices into a general "epistemic voluntarism" because we need such practices only because of our sin. Sin introduces us to epistemology's discipline – or better, sin introduces that discipline into us: the Fall affects our minds by disordering our wills, and we must engage in voluntary, *ad hoc*, and more or less ramshackle practices to recover (or better, to re-receive) our epistemological openness to God and the world.[16] With St. Paul, Augustine thinks that our present vision is only partial and that our voluntary believing will be transformed into indubitable (hence involuntary) knowledge.

This epistemological lesson, about the self's epistemic apprehensions as externally warranted, is part of a larger lesson we should

15. On knowledge as suffering, see Ochs 2000: 64; see also Lash 1988: 217: "It only seems easy to speak about our experience and knowledge of God and his ways in the measure that we insulate our religious speech and theological imagination from the endlessly complex and disturbing world in which that speech finds reference." I thank Paul Macdonald for conversations regarding these matters.
16. For ways to develop this project, see Foley 1993 and Zagzebski 1996.

learn: the ineradicable tension between the person and God. For Augustine, epistemological relations are in some sense finally reducible to theological ones. Our intellectual nature is just as created as our material nature, and it is not the human's action "out into" the world, but God's action on the soul, that is the fundamental fact from which epistemology must begin. This relationship is seen not only in the givenness of epistemic self-presence – the self-presence that vexes the Academic skeptics – but also, and perhaps more fully, in the ontological and axiological givenness of the self's loves, in the always already present claim on the self of some value-creating and value-sustaining commitments to the world. *Memoria* and *mens* are thus only part of the story; we must also acknowledge the self's *amor*, love or "attunement," and through *amor* the orientation of the self's *voluntas*, or will. Augustine's epistemology turns into ontology, and this ontology finally turns out to be theology.

Augustinian agency

Augustine thus commends our cultivation of epistemological practices for ultimately soteriological – that is, practical – purposes. Yet this shift from a concern with knowledge to a concern with action can seem simply to flip us from the frying pan into the fire, for, like his epistemology, Augustine's account of human action seems both deeply interesting and deeply perplexing, and for the same reasons.[17] His fundamental claim is that human freedom is achieved in the imposition of divine sovereignty, that true liberty is realized in servitude. How can this be? Most scholars think that Augustine's account fails; they think his absolutist account of grace is simply incompatible with true human freedom. Others, most prominently James Wetzel, argue that his work is actually a subtle and complex form of Stoic compatibilism refashioned in Christian terms.[18] Both sides agree that his position is indefensible – that he cannot correctly affirm genuine human freedom and genuine divine sovereignty.

17. As will become clear in this chapter, there is an indirect relationship between these debates about action and current epistemological debates. See Mele 1995: 173, where he argues for a "negative historical constraint" on autonomy. For extended reflection on this see McDowell 1992.
18. For the former, see Burnaby 1938; for the latter, see Wetzel 1992 and Djuth 1990.

This debate has precedents reaching back even to Augustine's contemporaries, and this very dichotomy was urged on him by his Pelagian opponents. But he himself resisted both options as Procrustean temptations, and we can follow him in affirming both human and divine freedom. Augustine's account does not, despite received theological lore, utterly reject human freedom in favor of grace; on the contrary, grace *is* freedom. But to understand this requires reconceiving freedom and, through it, grace.

The problem of agency

As in the case of the apparently conflicting elements in Augustine's epistemology, our confusion about Augustine's account of agency is interestingly related to contemporary debates about the nature of action and free will, particularly the debate between "compatibilist" and "incompatibilist" accounts of free will. "Incompatibilists" claim that human agents are effectively autonomous, in some sense spontaneous springs of action, while "compatibilists" claim that humans are simply parts of a larger causal framework that begins and ends outside of them.[19] This debate is ultimately about the place of human agency in human nature, the role of freedom in our personhood. But this debate seems destined to end in stalemate, for, on our received understanding of agency, it seems impossible to reconcile freedom with our existence as worldly, as having a world. In part, this problem is due to misconstruals of what it is to exist in a world, as philosophers of both the continental and analytic persuasion have argued.[20] But it is also in part due to misconstruals of what freedom really is.

A satisfactory account of agency will combine broadly voluntarist intuitions about "the importance of what we care about" in making our willing genuinely ours, with broadly cognitivist intuitions about the necessary coherence of our motivational affections and our evaluational judgments. One of the best such accounts is offered by Susan Wolf. She acknowledges that the world plays an important

---

19. See Watson 1982. For good presentations of libertarianism, see van Inwagen 1983 and Clarke 2003.
20. See Dreyfus 1991 and Lear 1990.

part in free agency, but she does not explain precisely how that fact should change our understanding of agency.[21] She acknowledges that the world has a normative structure of right and wrong, and that that normative structure determines the character of some human action – action that is reasonable and intelligible, *because* it is good. Thus for Wolf freedom is asymmetrical: explanations of bad actions can appeal only to the fact of human choice, while explanations of good actions can appeal also to the way the world is. (The good action can be explained by some version of the claim that "the agent saw the right thing to do, and did that," where "the right thing to do" is visibly, perhaps we would say obviously, the right thing not only to the agent, but also to us, assumed to be impartial judges from the point of view of the universe, so to speak.) Bad action is finally inexplicable and indeterminate, while good action can have a legitimate explanation and hence can be seen as determined.

But while Wolf properly points out the asymmetry in freedom, she does not develop the obvious implications of her insight, namely, that human agency is bound up in important ways with an external "natural" structure.[22] Augustine does just this. His treatment of agency is not only more coherent than his modern critics suggest; it can also show us a way out of the swamp in which some of the best contemporary treatments of freedom are mired. Crucial here will be how his theological anthropology accommodates the best of what modern concepts of autonomy offer without obliging us to accept their ideologically modern baggage. We will see how next.

Sin, freedom, and grace

Augustine conceives of freedom and autonomy in terms of integrity – the full integration of a person's decisions and desires,

---

21. The following summary uses Wolf 1986 and 1990. My criticisms of Wolf here parallel those of Wetzel 1992.

22. Wolf's sense of "determinism" equivocates between *hard* determinism, in which the good's sway on us is best described as a form of control, and *soft* determinism, whereby we "determine" ourselves to be governed by the good in a way that leaves undisturbed the questions of so-called "metaphysical" freedom. But surely on the latter account, the will may now be psychologically determined to do the good – and morally incapable of doing otherwise – only on the assumption that at some prior point the will freely chose to act in such a way that it would become so determined. On this see B. Williams 1995, and van Inwagen 1989. For a similar proposal to Wolf's, see R. Stout 1996.

her willing and her wanting – in a way that indirectly implicates the external world in the achievement of freedom. In Augustine's view, freedom is a matter of having an integrated and hence intelligible will – a will that is yours because you can make sense of its commands.[23] This condition of intelligibility relates freedom to extra-subjective reality through the object-directed nature of desire. On Augustine's model, one has true freedom if one's will is the integral expression of one's desires, desires that are construed as properly basic – that is, not ultimately under one's voluntary control (as if a perpetual regress ending only in a voluntaristic fiat of "decisiveness" were a form of control [*pace* Frankfurt 1988: 168–70]), but are expressions of the agent's nature. Without such integration, the will's irrationality forbids us from seeing it as in any important way our own.

Augustine's account depicts us as free, and hence autonomous, not simply when our wills take a certain shape, but when we love (and thus will) a certain end. And his faith that God created the world good allows him to make two basic claims about our present state of disintegration, one about its cause and one about its cure.

First, the introduction of evil into a wholly good creation is fundamentally a negative act – ontologically privational and hence intellectually incomprehensible. That such an act is strictly speaking inexplicable (and even inconceivable) does not, alas, render it impossible; rather, it tells us something of the nature of wicked acts themselves. They are at heart purely negative, a nay-saying to the world, and hence most fundamentally done not out of bad reasons but rather out of no reason at all. Having asked, "How can a nature which is good, however changeable, before it has an evil will, be the cause of any evil – the cause, that is, of that evil will itself?" Augustine could only answer that the human capacity for arational revolt is simply part of what it means to have free will (DCD 12.6). Sin is the perverse manifestation of our godlike faculty of freedom,

---

23. For good discussions of this see de Trin. 15.38, ennar. 121.1, and conf. 13.10. John Burnaby puts it well: love for Augustine is the *motus animi*, the movement of the soul, and hence it is not simply an emotion but rather "the directive energy of the will in its most general aspect" (1938: 94).

the *ex nihilo* that stays *nihilum*. There is no efficient cause, only a *de*ficient one:

> One should not try to find an efficient cause for a wrong choice. It is not a matter of efficiency, but of deficiency; the evil will is not effective but defective. For to begin to have an evil will, is to defect from Him who is the Supreme Existence, to something of less reality. To try to discover the causes of such defections – deficient, not efficient causes – is like trying to see darkness, or hear silence.

Augustine concludes that there is "no efficient natural or (if we may so call it) 'essential' cause of evil choice, since the evil of mutable spirits arises from the evil choice itself, [which] diminishes and corrupts the goodness of nature." This *causa deficiens*, this deficient causality, has its own proper description wholly in what it is not, in its failure to be a good act: "And this evil choice consists solely in falling away from God and deserting him, a defection whose cause is deficient, in the sense of being wanting – for there is no cause" (*DCD* 12.7). As T. D. J. Chappell argues, an act of original wickedness, which divides a previously good will and leads to the habituation of sin, is built on *folly*, on no good reason at all.[24] To seek a "cause" for sin is to try to render it intelligible, and hence to render it explicable, but that would bring it back into the explanatory fabric of the cosmos, the violation of which is what sin quite literally is.

Second, sin is a one-way street. Though we may call it folly, it alienates us from ourselves and destroys the integrity of will and desire with which we were created. The will guides the agent according to what the will loves; good action is the action of an integrated self while wicked action is not. But an agent, once gone wrong, cannot reintegrate herself; for the only instrument she would have for such reintegration is itself sullied by the disintegration. The self's decision to love the wrong end can never succeed, for the self is hard-wired to seek right relationship with God; yet if it attempts to return to loving the right ends, it finds that its continued attraction (or addiction) to wrong loves prevents such a conversion. In this state of disintegration, the self still possesses freedom of choice, but its loves are internally divided and so the will, enslaved by its own free choice, cannot will anything fully. Augustine vividly depicts this in *Confessions*: once fallen, the

---

24. See T. D. J. Chappell 1995. For more, see Mathewes 2001a, ch.2.

will's loves conflict, and the self is perpetually torn apart by its divergent loves.

> The soul (*animus*) commands the body, and is obeyed at once; the soul commands itself and meets resistance. The soul commands the hand to move and there is such readiness that you can hardly distinguish the command from its execution. Yet the soul is soul, whereas the hand is body. The soul commands the soul to will; the soul is itself, but it does not do it. ... The trouble is that it does not totally will, nor therefore totally commands. Insofar as it wills, it commands; and insofar as it does not will, to that degree it commands not. Will is commanding itself to be will ... but it does not fully give the command, so that what it commands is not done. For if the will were full, it would not command itself to be full will, for it would be so already. It is therefore ... a sickness of the soul to be so weighed down by habit (*consuetudine*) that it cannot wholly rise even with the support of truth. Thus there are two wills in us, because neither of them is total; and what is lacking in the one is present in the other. (*Conf.* 8.9)

In this situation, we cannot realize our longed-for integrity because to do so we would have fully to will that integrity already – and if that were possible, we would already be integrated. No bootstrapping techniques will help you here; the dissenting will is not an alien force, but as much part of the self as is the properly desiring will. You cannot fully identify with part of yourself against another part of yourself; you are helpless before the dis-integrity of your loves. What needs correction is not something you control; what needs correction is you yourself. The dissenting will cannot be eliminated or evaded; it must be converted. What has been so put asunder, only God can put together.

We should resist, however, one temptation present in language about the "divided will." The struggle that takes place in the self is not simply a struggle "in" the arena of "the will." As James Wetzel points out, Augustine does not posit any autonomous faculty of the will at all; indeed, to do so would be Pelagian.[25] To imagine that the conceptual distinction between reason and will points to fundamentally discrete faculties in the self is to confuse vocabulary with ontology. No part of the self is a neutral spectator in this contest.

25. See Wetzel 1992: 7–8.

The scope of the problem cannot be less than the whole human being, as the human is an organic, dynamic whole. Agency implies rationality, which in turn has ontological implications: humans have the capacity to act, but our action is unintelligible without recourse to our evaluations, and our evaluations are (or, following Wolf, should be) significantly determined by the world. The problem of the divided will implicates the whole agent's total dynamic relation with God and the world. Hence the debates about free will are best framed as fundamentally metaphysical debates, arguments about the nature of the world and the person's place within it, rather than simply anthropological debates about the internal hydraulics of agents.

For Augustine, the way up is the same as the way down. Agents recover their freedom through the reintegration of their affective structure, through their loves' conversion back to congruity with their natural desires. But the self is not able to accomplish this reintegration by its own power; it is always an event of divine grace. It is not simply a "worldly" or "moral" achievement. After the Fall, it certainly involves effort and labor on our part; but such effort is caused more by our entropic attachment to sin working against God's grace shed in our hearts. The unified soul is not an immanent, realized fact, but an eschatological achievement of Christ in the Father working through the Holy Spirit.

In light of this we can see how Augustine's account of freedom, though in some ways seeming libertarian, nonetheless implicates extra-agential realities in the recovery of free will. Through the human's desires, the objective world is always already within the subject; the agent has certain desires for reality that the agent cannot completely deny. "Objectivity," taken to mean all that is not the subject, determines the shape of the subjective, orients it toward certain ends, by being already within the subject; thus, the conversion of the subject's affective structure is simply the recognition and affirmation of the self's existence in this world. Basic human desires are good and to be trusted; our failure lies in our inability firmly to trust them. Accordingly, the recovery of our freedom requires our deep reappropriation of those desires. (Contrary to common opinion, Augustine's concern with the body derives not from an obsessive hatred of it, but rather from his sense that the dissonances felt in (not only by) our bodies reveals the central theological problematic, namely, agency's dis-integrity with nature.[26]) The human fault lies in attempting to deny our nature; to be fully and properly natural beings would be to return to a state of grace. Like the knowing subject, then, the acting agent finds her place in the world and before God because she finds the world and God at its heart.

The reception of grace here described has eschatological, ecclesiological, and sacramental dimensions. Eschatologically, Augustine does not take this recognition of objective, or at least extra-subjective, forces at work in the self's reintegration to support any sense of solidity in or accomplishment by ourselves. Nothing is yet "accomplished"; all we feel now are the first fruits of an integrity and wholeness that we will properly possess only in the eschaton, and which at present we only proleptically "borrow" from that coming kingdom. Any confidence on our part that we (at last!) know who we are called to be, in a final determinate sense, is dangerously apocalyptic; rather, whatever reintegration we experience should make us feel our past instability and present weakness all the more palpably. (Hence "progress" in deification in this life typically takes the form of increasing recognition of our frailty and sinfulness.) This inescapably involves one's community: to be reintegrated is to relearn how to love aright, and we learn this through discipline, a discipline both interior and exterior, communal and individual. It may sound easy to love, but Augustine is no romantic; relearning to love, while partially intuitive, is also importantly counterintuitive, and we need others' tutoring, particularly the others of the "school of charity," the church. As John Milbank says, "love is a highly complex, learned practice" (Milbank 1990b: 236; see also O'Donovan 1980: 130–5). And this reintegration, effected in and by the community, occurs therein most centrally in and through the liturgical and sacramental practices of the community.

So understood, the self, existing in time, is fundamentally unstable. Many find in Augustine's anthropology a longing for some sort of metaphysical stability and security; but in fact his account of the human in time begins from the premise that our existence in the present moment is too evanescent, too slippery, to anchor a stable, pure, and secure self. Here again, Augustine seeks a language

---

26. See Mathewes 2001b and Fredriksen 1990.

or vocabulary for a self who suffers, one more passive than active, a self whose most basic experience is one of witnessing her life, whose being is "given" to her as a gift. And yet this self participates actively in her life, most fundamentally through ecstatically responsive *confession* of this givenness – the retrospective, proleptic, articulate witnessing of, and affirmative participation in, God's governance of the course of one's life. God gives us even our self-knowledge: we understand ourselves as gifts of God, creatures whose proper and eschatological mode of being is an ecstatic and responsive confession of our own giftedness which is simultaneously articulate gratitude to God for our giftedness, but creatures whose current postlapsarian mode of being is a waiting for our "completion" in infinite being and love in the consummation on what Catherine Pickstock has aptly called "the eschatological morning" (1997: 273). To learn to speak our being in this way is a difficult lesson; in this life we are never more than children at doing it.[27]

Augustine's account of agency offers an account of asymmetrical freedom similar to Wolf's, but he develops it within a richer metaphysic and reverses her asymmetry. According to Wolf, we are responsible for good action even if we are determined to it, while, were we psychologically determined to bad acts, that determination would exculpate us. According to Augustine, we are never responsible for good action precisely because it has a reason, and hence a cause, beyond us in God; but we are ultimately responsible for bad action, for we are the final, if irrational, cause of it:

> Now if we conclude that a good will also has no efficient cause, we
> must beware of giving the idea that the good will of the good angels
> is uncaused in the sense of being co-eternal with God. In fact, since
> the angels were themselves created, it follows that their will must
> also be created ... [and thus] as soon as they were created they
> adhered to their Creator with that love with which they were
> created. And the rebellious angels were separated from fellowship
> with the good [angels] by [their] act of will (which was evil in the
> very fact that they fell away from the good will), and they would not
> have fallen away, had they not willed to do so. (*DCD* 12.9)[28]

---

27. For more, see Mathewes 2002a and 2003, Mennell 1994, and J. S. O'Leary 1985.
28. For a congruent later elaboration of these themes, see Anselm 1998.

Some thoughtful, more philosophically minded exponents of Augustine, such as James Wetzel, find this a weakness in Augustine's philosophical account. They argue that Augustine's account of original sin poses intractable problems to his overall account because the originary sin, on this account, must be radically spontaneous, and the thrust of Augustine's overall anthropology is directed at showing that our pretensions at possessing such agency are pridefully delusionary (1992: 201–17).

But while Augustine did in fact conclude that while voluntary sin, in the case of the Fall, is not intelligible *qua* voluntary sin, it is still real, because it can be seen as the perverse affirmation of some lesser good over a greater, if it is to be seen as intelligible, and hence as an action at all. Voluntary sin is thus possible, albeit under the guise of affirming some other, lesser good (as can be seen in the *confessiones*' story of the delight the young Augustine took in the community of thieves stealing the pears in the garden). It can exist, though never properly as "voluntary sin"; we can define it as an act that fails to be itself.

This may sound paradoxical. But for Augustine the paradox lies in the limits of our own comprehension, not in reality itself. We do not sufficiently attend to the cosmological and historical dimensions of Augustine's account of sin. He admitted that an act of pure voluntary sin was impossible for humans to undertake; it would require a power of agency so unconditioned as to be effectively suprahuman. But such suprahuman entities exist: the angels. We often forget that for Augustine it is not only goodness that is suprahuman; evil is as well. There is a cosmological dimension to the story of the Fall, for all the main actors in what we think of as "the human moral drama" are, crucially, not human (or, in Christ's case, not merely human): our corruption stems from our temptation by the angel Satan, who was already corrupted by a wholly self-willed act of radical evil, and our salvation stems from the redemptive act of God. And there is a historical dimension to the Fall as well: humans are not created wicked, but become so, in a technical sense, accidentally. We are, of course, responsible for this accident, as it occurred because of our free will. But to say that does not explain why our free will was actualized in this manner. What it shows us is that humans can so violate the order of things that their acts violate not only the moral law and the laws of nature, but even the order of intelligibility itself. Such actions cannot be understood, but only described. And we had this freedom before the Fall, but lost it in the Fall, and became chained to sin. Grace does not "restore" this capacity to us; rather, grace is the refusal henceforth to use this "capacity" to revolt.

The philosophical criticisms of Augustine's account, then, miss these cosmological and historical elements of the story of our freedom – how, in Augustine's account, our freedom has changed across time. In eliding this aspect of Augustine's analysis, such critics subtly alter the overall picture that Augustine proposes. It is simply not the case that grace – conceived as the absolute love of God and hence not finally distinct in form or content from the original love offered to (and at that time accepted by) Adam and Eve before the Fall – is totally determinate. If it were, human beings could not have fallen as they did, unless God willed their sin. But Augustine is not a Calvinist. Thus there is a significant "libertarian" leaven needed in what the philosophical critics take to be Augustine's compatibilist dough; and the leaven changes the whole in significant ways – not least in challenging the adequacy of terms such as "libertarian" and "compatibilist" for describing Augustine's thought.

Augustine's account refashions our understanding of the place of agency in the world and before God, and thereby refutes characterizations of his account of divine sovereignty as heteronomous – for there is no self, strictly speaking, apart from and primordially independent of God. God, recall, is "closer to me than myself." We are most fully free when we assent to being the sorts of beings we already are, and though we are permitted partially to dissent from God's plan, our dissent cannot be more than partial; God's loving sustenance of us forbids us to annihilate ourselves so totally as that. Furthermore, this picture affirms that God's goodness, as manifest in and by the world, should be (and gracefully is) met by an "active gratitude" that responds, in its microcosmic integrity, to the integrity of the world.[29] What Augustine teaches is that we must trust both the world and our true desires – that we must, in fact, trust the world through and in those desires.

29. For this formulation of the idea, I am indebted to Derek Jeffreys.

Augustinian anthropology and theology: reimagining autonomy

Far from being incoherent, Augustine's work offers an account of human agency far superior to dominant modern pictures. As moderns we typically conceive of ourselves as *ex nihilo* actors and knowers, subjects originally alone and outside of the world and intervening in it, bootstrapping ourselves into knowledge and pulling ourselves into existence by the hair.[30] Augustine does not share this faith, and with good reason. His theological anthropology illuminates how we exist as fundamentally part of a larger order – in the world and before God – in ways superior to contemporary alternatives. It has implications beyond our mere self-understanding. We turn to those now.

Reimagining autonomy after Augustine

The worries that Augustine's theological anthropology elicits from us reflect deep confusions about the character of our existence, confusions rooted in our understanding of autonomy. We typically picture autonomy as an ideal of total self-determination, but ultimately this picture is totally alienating: it not only implausibly immunizes humans against any worldly influences, but also undermines the very possibility of our own intelligibility. It is simultaneously existentialist and consumerist, Jean-Paul Sartre at the Wal-Mart(re), making our agency a futile passion.

On what grounds can the self be understood to determine itself? Perhaps we are willing to say that "Because I willed it" is the best we can do for an explanation for one's actions, and that such is the price of freedom. But this misses the point, because as a reflective agent I have no reason to identify with this "I" that stands at the fount of all my actions. Indeed, this "I" seems to be less *me* than an alien thing at the base of my agency. Thus this picture of autonomy, so often assumed today, does not secure me from any outside interference, but just the opposite: it transfers my agency to an unintelligible, hence effectively external, voluntary force. In securing the self's reality against determinism, this picture of

30. See Burrell 2004: 147 and *passim*.

autonomy goes too far, and leaves the self a gilded bird in an iron cage.[31]

This confused account of autonomy urges us to see Augustine's account as either a subjectivist, indeed solipsistic, egoism or an objectivist determinism. On the one hand, many miss the way in which Augustine anchors the self in the created world by placing the divine other at the heart of the created self. Such critics thus mistake Augustine's anthropology for a solipsistic egoism, both because it seems that his eudaimonism allows self-interest to elbow out all genuine concern for the other (though the word "genuine" shows already how very tenuous this worry is), and because it seems that his concern for the inner depths of the mind turns the world into merely intellectual stimulation of only secondary importance.[32] On the other hand, many miss the way in which Augustine grounds the limits of agency and virtue in the very character of agency and virtue. They thus mistake Augustine's anthropology for a heteronomous determinism, because it seems that his account of grace subverts the role of true human agency, reducing us to puppets whose strings are the vectors of "vertical" causality emanating from God. In brief, both interpretive routes end in the worry that on Augustine's account either the self obliterates all otherness, including God, or that otherness consumes the self.

These worries are misplaced, and gain the plausibility they have for us as a result of modern subjectivism of the sort exemplified by Descartes. If one begins with the Cartesian *cogito*, uprooted from the world, then not only is one stuck with Descartes's problem of getting from the mind to the world, but anything outside the mind will be alien to it and thus a threat to it, a contender against it. But we need not begin with the Cartesian *cogito*; the mind, as John McDowell puts it, simply "ain't in the head" (1992: 39). Mind is always already related to other realities, and is "given" to itself from outside of itself. For Augustine, the "giftedness" of mind is not simply an epistemological fact, or merely an ontological one, but properly a theological truth: <u>mind is from God.</u> The very features of

31. See Asad 1993: 13, on the relation between modern concepts of autonomy and consumerism. For connections between consumerism and nihilism, see B. Schwartz 2004, Friedman 1990, and Block 2002. I thank Markella Rutherford for conversations regarding these issues.
32. See O'Donovan 1980.

his anthropology that we, in our resolute subjectivism, find contradictory are the features that, rightly understood, could model a way to overcome the dichotomies that make it so difficult for us to understand how we can think, and will, and act responsibly.

Towards an Augustinian understanding of engagement

Once we revise our understanding of Augustine's thought, we see that preconceived ideas about Augustinian "politics" need changing as well. The most popular representations of Augustine depict the self as isolated from others, trapped in self-ignorance, and able to think of the good only negatively, in terms of a perennially absent God. This eventuates in politically minimalist interpretations of Augustinian politics. But such interpretations are more decisively stamped by our modern understanding of the self than by Augustine's. When we exorcise this understanding of the self, new possibilities appear.

First, as regards worries about "otherworldliness," what is assumed by such concerns is that the world as it stands is somehow a relatively coherent, relatively integral whole (say, a "body") within which religious commitments (which are often understood to be merely "spiritual") can at best "supervene" upon or complement material reality. Augustine's theology helps here by reminding us that the concept of a pure "nature" is a fable. Grace is not a *superradditum* to nature, but rather an integral part of the created order. In this dispensation, the political realm cannot be finally forbidden as a place of theophany, though neither can it be assumed as structurally inevitable. Chapter 2 will discuss these issues in more detail.

The question of moral rationality, and of the cognitive status of religious claims, seems to be at its heart a question of how our subjective experiences of valuing can be legitimated in a world of plural subjectivities and plural value claims. Often Augustine is invoked as a thinker who insisted on the necessary secularity of the public realm, for fear of an idolatrous caesaropapism. The contemporary worry expressed here, fundamentally about "intolerance," is captive to a dichotomy between what has been labeled "objectivism" and "relativism," between the desire to defuse subjectivity by scientistically reducing subjects to objects, and the affirmation of "pluralism" as a simple capitulation to difference. While most thinkers recognize this dichotomy as misleading, if not downright pernicious, we have had little success in overcoming it. (Witness the interminable debate between "communitarians" and "liberals" in political theory and theology.) Our failure here reflects the belief that within an ontology that pictures the world as an archipelago of alterities, each negotiating its way around the others, it is morally insensitive not to worry that one's imposition of one set of beliefs on another is really nothing but an imposition. (This is one good reason why some of the best accounts of political community today, such as Judith Shklar's *Ordinary Vices* and Jeffrey Stout's *Ethics After Babel*, are grounded on fear.)

Suppose, however, that we approach questions of moral and religious rationality, and thus the nature of pluralist communities, from the Augustinian assumption that otherness is already at the base of the self. Doing this would give us more patience. We would admit that the attempt to engage one another most fully as particular and historical persons, an engagement including "rational" debate (whatever that may turn out to be), may yet allow us to find an account of genuinely universal moral and religious reason; meanwhile, in the interim, we are in no way required to surrender our own local rationalities (as if it were some mark of neighborly respect to blindfold everyone out of despair of coming to a common point of view). Furthermore, Augustine's account offers us a new vision of what reason is. It is not an autonomous, critical-transcendental evaluative module, for that would have all the problems of modern conceptions of autonomy discussed above; rather, it is most fundamentally a form of *attention*, attending to the ends the agent desires, and deciding how best to pursue those ends. Reason really is, or truly ought to be, the slave of the passions; but the passions themselves are not merely subjective whimsies, but rather have a normative structure and metaphysical valence, as indicative of the manifold relations between ourselves and the rest of the world. Augustinians therefore see the question of "toleration" much more complexly as a matter of dialogue and conversation, dedicated not to avoiding confrontations with one another but to attempting to engage each other's "otherness" genuinely. Otherness is not a negative challenge, a Leibnizian "windowless monad," or a sheer mass of antimatter. It is a positive gift, eliciting in us the responsibility to transform our lives in and through the other's reception. Chapter 3 will discuss these issues more thoroughly.

The final question is the political one of the relations between individuals, their various associations and communities, and the political community that demands, legitimately or illegitimately, their final commitment in the *saeculum*. This too is a form of the question of how we should accommodate otherness – though this time within our own community, however "thick" it may be. In such debates, Augustine plays a crucial role as a straw man: radical communitarians accuse him of promoting "Constantinianism," while more liberal thinkers accuse him of authoritarianism and anti-individualism in politics. Both groups worry that Augustine's emphasis on communal authority can elide true otherness, whether that otherness be another community or an individual person. Historically, both have reasons for their concern. But should we respond to the fact that society is immoral by suggesting that smaller groups, or individuals, will somehow be more upright? Or should we surrender our most proximate political power to some extra-human institution or text, whether that is Scripture or the Constitution? Surely any such "surrender" is not what it claims to be, but rather a simple refusal of responsibility for our own interpretations of such texts. The political problematic is continuous with the theological problematic, and can be neither resolved by the liberal public/private distinction, nor avoided by the radical communitarian inside/outside dichotomy. Augustine's theological anthropology, depicting us all as always both inside and outside the community, because we are inside and outside ourselves – can lead to strong claims about the importance of public life. Part II of this book explores these points.

Conclusion

In their various ways, these disparate worries all expose a crucial disjunction between Augustine's thought and our own received intuitions, the relation between selfhood and otherness. We, as moderns and as fallen humans, understand ourselves as properly our ownmost possession – fundamentally separate from one another, from the world, and from God. But this self-understanding, on Augustine's picture, is delusory. It is why we can speak of the fundamental human fault as *superbia*, and why privacy, on a philosophical and theological level, is so ultimately dubious for this tradition. But it is as much an expression of nihilating despair as it is of presumptive pride; for this presumption of self-possession, which requires the self to posit an abyss between itself and the rest of creation, may well be secondary to the despair that imagines that God has abandoned us.

Augustine's theology shows how grace works against this pride and despair. On his account, we have abandoned God, but God's action in Christ, from the beginning of time, will be the way that God overcomes our estrangement and returns us to God – and through God, to our neighbors, to creation, and even to ourselves. The ground of his theological anthropology is his conviction that at the core of the self is an other, God; but this other is more intimate to me than I am to myself – *interior intimo meo*. As Denys Turner has argued, for Augustine "the language of interiority is self-subverting"; to go deeply into the mind is to go *beyond* it; to turn inward and descend into the self is simultaneously to reach outward and ascend to God (1995: 69). Augustine's basic moves, especially his arguments about human knowing and acting, and the place of the human knower and actor in the world and before God, begin from this insight. The world is not finally fractured into self and other; the divisions and separations marking every moment in our fallen world do not reach down to the basic character of reality itself.

Augustine's theology is, then, all about learning how to be committed to the world and to God in the right way. This is a picture none of us fully understands, let alone fully accepts; yet our understanding of it is thus irremediably associated with a hopefulness that its true intelligibility will be made eschatologically apprehensible. But how do we practically inhabit this eschatological hopefulness? That is the topic of Chapter 2.

2

Life in the world

We say amisse,
This or that is:
Thy word is all, if we could spell.   George Herbert, "The Flower"

What does it mean to live in hope? And what are the theological preconditions and implications of a life so lived? In hope, we see the world as revelatory of more than its immediate, and superficial, self-presentation. In hope we affirm our confidence in God's sovereignty, and our conviction that God will be all in all. In hope, we see the world as intelligible only as God's story – not properly a "world," with the spurious posture of autonomy that that word conveys, but rather as *Creation*, an event, irrepressibly expressing a self-transcending reference, the act of a loving Creator. We see the world as significant, the "semiosis" of God, and we live in the world, during the world, in hope, by participating in that semiosis – by treating the world as not exhaustively immanently and immediately significant, but as crucially transcendentally and eschatologically significant.

But today, during the world, it is not obvious that the world "means" more than itself, that it has a significance, and significa-tion, beyond the literal. Augustine recognized this difficulty: "The existence of the world is a matter of observation, the existence of God a matter of belief" (*DCD* 11.4). So hope must find a way to bring to expression this currently obscure but theologically foundational fact. We must find an ontology that can bear the weight of our hope – a language through which we can see the world as broken but still significant, albeit significant in ways that will be made fully clear only in the eschaton. That is what this chapter tries to sketch.

Chapter 1 argued, against many critics' suspicions, that an Augustinian theological anthropology offers a quite plausible and attractive picture of the human in the world and before God. This picture presents the self as fundamentally a *sufferer*, more passive than active, whose being is "given" to it as a gift, and who properly participates in her or his being through ecstatically responsive confession of this givenness, a confession first of all to God, but to creation as well. But such a defense of the Augustinian account does not silence critics' concerns so much as relocate them: once driven from their positions criticizing Augustine's direct theological anthropology, they reposition themselves and shift their fire on to the implications of that vision for our dealings with the world. For many thoughtful people are troubled by what they see as that vision's implications, namely, an inevitably estranged and instrumental view of the world. They fear that such an attitude is hazardous to our very existence; we are living so far beyond our means that our present behavior threatens to consume our future. Whether we agree with these fears or not, it is hard to deny that we are caught in ways of life that seem excessive and destructive. This is not a matter of individuals' wanton rapaciousness; there are material and structural forces shaping our behavior. But those structural forces did not pop up *ex nihilo*; they are at least partly caused by broadly cultural realities, by our behavior and beliefs. Many thinkers locate the root of the problem in our inherited religious traditions, whether living or merely a cultural residue. While the details of the problem are disputed, the structure of the critics' diagnoses and their proposed remedies are identical: they diagnose our root problem to be a residual "otherworldliness" surviving as a relic of our earlier religious worldviews, and they prescribe as a purgative a more diligent worldliness, a love for immanent material existence – a more emphatic affirmation of the intrinsic value and fragility of both non-human nature and human society.[1] And if we want to change them, at least part of our energy must be dedicated to changing those behaviors and beliefs. How can we do this?

1. See L. White 1967, Lovibond 1982, and Keller 1997. For a nice contrast, see Rupp 2001.

Typically this otherworldliness manifests itself, the critics believe, in a fundamentally instrumentalizing attitude towards the material world. One of the most popular targets for such charges is the traditional language of "using the world." And the most prominent spokesperson for this view is Augustine. He contrasts two basic attitudes that we can take towards things: "using" them and "enjoying" them. To enjoy something is to value it wholly in itself and for itself; to use something is to value it for its instrumental value for another end. The object of enjoyment is that which allows the enjoyer to flourish; thus the eye enjoys the light by which it sees (*DCD* 8.8). What makes us flourish? No material thing in itself; thus we should "use" the material things of this world and, properly speaking, "enjoy" only the wholly immaterial reality of God (*DDC* 1.3.3–4.4).[2] A radical instrumentalism seems latent here, one which undermines all attempts to invest other creatures with genuine value; Augustine's thought seems to instrumentalize all creation – even, at times, the divine – for the sake of the self. In brief, the challenge is one fundamentally against Augustine's eudaimonism, to the effect that any ethic finally oriented towards the self's exclusive happiness must deny the final independence of others. This charge has textual support in Augustine's writings, especially in his notorious claim that the two "cities" of humanity are distinguished by their loves, "the earthly city [governed] by a love of self carried even to contempt of God, the celestial city [governed] by a love of God carried even to contempt of self" (*DCD* 14.28). The critics understand Augustine as suggesting that love of God, and not just love but even *concern* for the world, finally are incompatible.

Unsurprisingly, this account has not received many hosannas in recent years. The general project designated by this language – which I shall call the use-paradigm – is taken to represent the nihilistic, world-hating, life-denying, ascetical and (nastily) "metaphysical" attitude of the anti-ecological "other." Normally it is contrasted with another view, apparently diametrically opposed;

2. There are interesting and complex questions about the status of other humans in this text; for a fascinating account of this, focusing on how hard Augustine found it to construct an adequate language within which to articulate the right relation to the neighbor in the world, see O'Donovan 1982. More generally see Baer 1996, van Bavel 1986, and O'Donovan 1980.

"loving the world."[3] Here we will not directly assess the contemporary alternatives to this position, but we should note that the slogan of "loving the world" gains determinate meaning by what Nietzsche would call "nay-saying," an activity of externalizing and denouncing what one does not want – without determining whether what one does not want is actually there, or only a fable concocted by one's imagination. And yet in the case of "loving the world," what is denounced is in fact a fable. We need a more complex analysis of what these purportedly contrasting slogans in fact obscure.

We can begin this analysis by looking at what, beyond slogans, these critics offer as an alternative. They typically propose a respectful recognition of and sensitivity to limits, a recognition that human aims must be restrained by some absolute boundaries, that human desires may simply not be justifiably realizable. Different thinkers understand these limits differently, but the formal analysis of the problem is the same: our Promethean tendency always to overstep, never to be satisfied, never to have enough. For them we must observe proper limits, without which we will inevitably destroy whatever happiness we have with our various rapacities.

Such claims echo ancient Stoic demands that we live in accord with *nomos*, and that such life primarily involves a practice of restraint on our part. But this is wrong. Of course we should recognize the propriety of limits, of basic commandments that must not be violated, basic covenants that cannot be broken. But God's desire for humans is not fundamentally proscriptive, concerned with setting limits.[4] And humans would be mutilated by attempts to make our longings perfectly finite and mundane. Instead, we should seek not fundamentally to limit our desires, but to have them reoriented towards their properly infinite end. We should care about the world not more, but in a different way than we currently do. Our loves must be not restrained but reoriented. By aiming to recover the practices Augustine once designated with the phrase "using the world," perhaps we can make ourselves less ravenous creatures, and hopefully place less strain on our world.

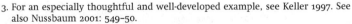

3. For an especially thoughtful and well-developed example, see Keller 1997. See also Nussbaum 2001: 549–50.
4. For a good discussion of this, see Barth 1957: 553.

To begin to support these claims moves us quickly towards a general ontology of creation *as* Creation, an ontology that can explain why no "enough" will work. Sketching such an ontology is this chapter's task. The reasons for our persistent psychological transgression go deep in us, and indeed in the fabric of the cosmos itself. The world is not defined by finitude, and so our desires are not so fixable and limitable; we are always called beyond ourselves by creation's excessiveness. The problem is not that we remain too otherworldly, but that we are not "otherworldly" enough; better, the proper language we should use to understand our condition is not the fundamentally secularist language of "otherworldliness," but rather the fundamentally religious language of idolatry. We have made an idol out of the world. This does not mean that the idol is intrinsically evil; on the contrary, typically the created things made into idols are themselves victims of the idolaters.

Modernity's quarrel with Augustine is thus fundamentally about ontology, about the nature of creation itself. To understand this ontology, we must begin by undertaking a careful analysis of the two apparently quite distinct tasks which the language of "use" plays in Augustinian thought. For "use" is not simply a straight-forward axiological and ethical term for Augustine; it bears an equally primordial exegetical and semiotic significance. For Augus-tinians, to talk about "using" things is to speak simultaneously in a moral and hermeneutical register.

Doing this involves offering a far more theological reading of the practical human project than is common today, and not only among non-religious people. Effectively most of us are secular moralists, imagining that morality is a fundamentally this-worldly reality, one built around apparently mundane virtues like pru-dence.[5] Yet even so this-worldly a virtue as prudence hides theolo-gical valences; for, as the philosopher Peter Geach has argued, "'prudence' and 'providence' are in origin two forms of the same Latin word; etymologies are often misleading, this one is not" (1977: 70). The human adventure in this world is never simply mundane. This is not one more argument for the moral necessity of God.[6]

---

5. See McCloskey 1994, D. M. Nelson 1992, Baier 1994, and Hariman 2003.
6. See Taylor 1989 and Gamwell 1995 for two powerful examples of such arguments.

Such arguments suggest that God's value lies in underwriting, orienting, and energizing our moral projects; they thereby instrumentalize what should be ultimate. But providence fundamentally transforms our "moral" projects, and God will change us radically in ways we, before the eschaton, cannot foresee. Our understanding of the relation between prudence and providence must be transfigured. True prudence is a deeply theologically informed approach to valuing and inhabiting our existence, one that is properly characterized by the phrase "using the world."

Understanding the anthropological, theological, and ontological implications of this phrase is the task of this chapter. The use-paradigm recognizes that our desires are not fully satisfied by any assemblage of worldly goods. Those who wish to contain prudence wholly within "worldly" interests cannot do so, because real prudence tells, against them, of the illimitable nature of our desires. Nonetheless, this use-paradigm is not hostile to or dismissive of the world, for it sees the world itself as an expression of God, the medium through which we encounter God. It is not so much self-centered as self-subverting: in approaching the world in this way, we find that we do not so much use the world as discover that God is using the world, and us in it, for purposes which we only glimpse short of the eschaton. This use-paradigm implies a surprisingly powerful and theologically insightful vision of life in the world, a vision that we can yet inhabit. A new version of the tradition of Augustinian religious asceticism reveals and in turn relies on a powerful, and attractive, ontology which we would do well to recover. The chapter first abstractly sketches the crucial ontological claims of this picture. It then describes the meaning of Augustine's language of "use" and "enjoyment." Finally, it explores how this use-paradigm reflects a general theological ethic, a general account of how to understand "life in the world" as life lived when "the world" is properly understood as Creation.

From scarcity to gratuity: an Augustinian ontology of creation

We begin from the idea that the basic ontological fact for Augustine is that creation is a work of love, and shows the marks of love – so much so that love is itself the fundamental ontological truth about creation.[7] Augustine's profoundly dynamic picture of love connects our "worldly" activities to our putatively "other worldly" concerns. His account of love is dynamic in two directions. To be worldly, we find we must raise issues that are properly theological, while our theological interests are always cashed out in worldly ways. And both of these dynamics, drawing "worldly" and "otherworldly" concerns together, are rooted in the Augustinian analysis and diagnosis, simultaneously psychological and ontological, of the variety of human loves that should be properly ordered according to *caritas*, the principal and root love of the soul for God.

It is precisely on this issue – the true nature and proper reorientation of the self's loves – that many critics think the Augustinian account is deeply flawed. Such critics accuse Augustinians of so fixating on the self's salvation that everything else is instrumentalized for the sake of the self. Typically they stop at the psychological picture Augustinians propose; but the basic objection is really to the account of creation from which this psychology springs. The critics charge that this Augustinian psychology and ontology of love attempts to serve two masters at once – namely, the local, particular, immanent attachments we have to worldly things, and the universal and transcendent attachment we supposedly have to God. They worry that these two objects of love inevitably come to oppose one another, and that the worldly loves inevitably lose.[8]

This worry is typically directed at the use-paradigm.[9] There are two aspects to this charge. The first, more easily dealt with, is the claim that the eudaimonist ethic implied in the use-paradigm ultimately instrumentalizes all of material reality including other people for the pursuit of an immaterial – and typically for the critics, at least *less* real – end, rendering genuine relationships impossible. The second, and more difficult, is the claim that Augustine's use of this distinction instrumentalizes even the divine for the self's own ends. But in fact the real issue is ontology – the nature of Creation itself – and so finally we must address that.

---

7. The sketch here offered has many affinities with Davies 2004.
8. See Nygren 1957; for a response, see Burnaby 1938 and 1970.
9. See O'Connor 1983.

Love as dynamic from psychology to ontology

The accusation that eudaimonism leads inexorably to global instrumentalism is simply the suspicion that the distinction between use and enjoyment, once put in play, swiftly transforms genuine concern for the other into rapacious self-interest. But Augustinians can challenge this accusation, on both anthropological and ontological grounds.

Speaking anthropologically, they can challenge the picture of the self the accusation assumes – a picture which grants the self a sort of absolute Cartesian self-subsistence in which it is not genuinely involved with anything outside of itself. To the contrary, as Chapter 1 argued, Augustinians insist that we exist necessarily *in* a world: we are "hard-wired," so to speak, with other-regard, and our abandonment of others harms us more immediately than it harms others.

Our condition as so hard-wired is best seen through appreciating the central place Augustine's psychology reserves for the concept of love. Love (*amor*) is the "root" of the soul, and when the soul is properly oriented in the love that is *caritas*, it is a unifying force, equally for our own self-integrity, our relationship with God, and our relationship with our neighbor.[10] In loving rightly, one becomes an instrument of God, a vehicle for God's love of the world. How this is manifest differs as regards objects and humans. As regards objects, one discovers that *caritas* entails that one treat them not as one's proper possession but as fundamentally part of God's natural order; hence one is called to respect their integrity and essential autonomy from one's own self-interest. (This does not mean never intervening in non-human nature, or treating all of creation as "wilderness," for some parts of the non-human world require our intimate involvement, in stewardship and shepherding.[11]) As regards people, one discovers that *caritas* is community-building: as this energy directs the self toward conversion back to God, it also urges the self to seek communion with others. Nor is such *caritas*-funded respect really a

---

10. See *in Io. ep* 1.12; 10.10. Theologically speaking, not only is God's love for us prior to our love for God, but when we love, there is a "mutual indwelling," we in God and God in us. See *in Io. ep.*, 7.6–7; 8.14.
11. Too often some sort of human/nature divide is implied in ecology; for stimulating challenges to this, see Cronon 1995 and Milbank 1997: 257–67. I thank Willis Jenkins for conversations on these matters.

form of violence, for it puts no pressure on us to be intolerant of others' difference from us; we love others in friendship and treat them as we would God (*in Io. ep.* 8.5). But this is not simply a new *technique* for political life; Augustine aims for an affective revolution which would transfigure politics. When Augustine says, "Love and do what *you* will," he does not mean "Do what you will, insofar as that 'you' designates the you that you were before love reoriented your affections" rather, love has so transformed you that you now behave in a new way (*in Io. ep.* 7.8).

The egocentric perspective may be where we start from in this fallen life, and we may be generally teleological in our behavior; but proper attention to our most basic desires reveals to us that many of those most basic desires implicate us in reciprocal relations with realities outside ourselves.[12] While we are entrusted with the care of ourselves in a special way, not only are genuine self-concern and genuine other-regard compatible, but the former even requires the latter. For Augustine, the self loves both the neighbor and God, though the two cannot be loved apart from each other. In fact neighbor-love is given existential precedence for us today, because it is more concrete, palpably demanding, and less readily susceptible to self-deception; hence "in loving the brother whom you see, you will be loving God at the same time."[13] The relative independence of humans as legitimate subjects of proximately final worthiness is ensured, for Augustine, by Christ's injunction that the greatest of the commandments is to love God, and the second greatest is to love one's neighbor as oneself.

Ontology and confession

The anthropological response to the skeptical accusations about eudaimonism is not the only one. There is an ontological response as well, one that rejects the idea that love is a zero-sum

12. This is how I read Augustine's discussion of the necessary theological and anthropological presuppositions of "Love" in *de Trin.* 8. The most famous form of this argument is that of Bishop Butler: "Love of our neighbor would teach us thus to appropriate to ourselves his good and welfare, to consider ourselves as having a real share in his happiness" (1983: 59). I thank Eric Gregory for conversations regarding this.

13. See also *de Trin.* 8.8.12 and *ad Gal.* 45. For a relentlessly developed account of this, see Canning 1993, esp. 420: "Turning to the neighbor forms such an integral part of human turning to God that the latter may be defined by it."

game – that our "reserves" of love are finite and must be carefully marshalled, like water in a drought.[14] But this is a misperception. The world is love because God is love; hence, by loving through God, we love ourselves and all creation most perfectly (*ep.* 140.21.53–8). This is not simply romantic praise of reality; it has implications for the nature of reality itself: the universe we inhabit is not finally finite in the way that classical thinkers held, and our inhabitation of it is not finally a matter of knowing one's place, of fitting into a slot in the finite bureaucracy of natural categories. The real problem with our loves – their perversion towards worldly things – is not at its heart a problem of love's quantity, but of love's quality, so to speak, love's ordering. Our fundamental problem is not scarcity but excess, the excess of emotion and passion, of violence and desire, of goods and evils. The problem is not that we have too little; it is that we have too much – too much desire to be satisfied, too many things to love. These excesses readily attach (and attach us) to wrong causes and false gods. In contrast to the classical ideal of the wisely (and wearily) prudential sage, his *exemplum* of the actor in public life is that of the judge, the "public servant" torn by the excesses he must confront – excesses of wants and needs, of violence and desires, of goods and evils. For Augustine the fundamental difficulty we face is not how to make the most of a diminished thing, but rather how to respond to the gratuities visited upon us in a world where axiological mercantilism no longer applies, if ever it did.

This plenitude is not simply a fact about creation but is rooted in the nature of God, for Augustine; particularly in the dialectical character of God's transcendence and immanence, the participatory yet monarchial ontology that this dialectic entails, and the way this dialectic underlies and illuminates his understanding of love, particularly love as fundamentally excessive, of necessity gratuitous. God is "the cause which causes and is not caused" – the most real, indeed perfect existence, in which all other realities, insofar as they exist, have their being (*DCD* 5.9).[15] God is both the absolutely

---

14. For a general suspicion of monotheism relying on such a vision of scarce goods, see R. Schwartz 1997: x–xi. I thank Leora Batnitzky for calling my attention to this work.

15. See further *Gen. ad litt.* 8.26: "Without any distance or measure of space, by His immanent and transcendent power He is interior to all things because they are all in Him."

transcendent source of all existence – because God is immune from the imperfections and mutations which mark all of our "this-worldly" existence – and yet (and yet therefore), the essentially immanent presence of all existence – because God is precisely the life and truth by which we participate in, and know, existence. But God is not captured within such realities, but always transcends them; that is in part (negatively) what it means for God to be infinite.

So all of reality is made by something, and lives from something, that is "more" than that reality itself. Humanity in particular, by being made in the *imago Dei* and made for communion with God, is more than itself; and the more that it is, is love. A certain form of love is what the self finally *is*. Today, in our current sinful state of grasping egoism, what this right love is – what we essentially are – is not easily visible to us. But a way has been made available to us, in Christ: we should love the world because God loves it, and in the way that God loves it – which is a depth of love so great that God enters into the world in the person of the Son. But we must love the world *in God*, by participating in God's love of it. By participating in God's love of the world (and in particular in God's love of the people of the world) we come to know God; but "knowing God" here is not just spectatorial observation and representation, but rather real participation: we "know" precisely insofar as we manifest God's love, insofar as we become sacraments of it. (This is because all love is God's love, and in a way all love simply *is* God.) So the world is love because God is love. Hence Augustine's account of love, while psychological, is also and at least equally ontological; it is a claim about the nature of love itself, and by extension of the nature(s) of what we love.

Because God is love, and loves creation with the sincerity of God's whole being, our "worldly" and "otherworldly" loves are not autonomous, not even relatively so; reflection on one pole ineluctably leads to the other. How does our love of the world lead to love of God? Why can't our worldly concerns stay merely mundane? The Augustinian reply is straightforward, though it does not admit of direct validation: they cannot stay mundane because *we* are not simply mundane. Our loves are not simply loves of created goods; we cannot "clip" our desires to restrict them to the purportedly "natural" world. The world simply does not satisfy all our desires.

They are as gratuitous as the rest of creation. This need not deni-grate worldly things; it only acknowledges that, genuine goods though they may be, they are not all we seek – after all, happiness and security, if one wishes to distinguish them, are not the sorts of things we can purchase (no matter what advertisements say). Indeed, this account offers a more humane vision of worldly goods, as it reminds us that we ought to avoid an attitude of overvaluing them, which will lead inevitably to our being disappointed by them. His command that we use the world is not fundamentally about how we should act towards other things, but rather about what effect we should expect other things to have on us – that we should not expect them to do more than they were designed to do for us. This is sound practical advice; material things are simply too frail to do duty as adequate theological stand-ins, and to expect such per-fection is a mark of moral immaturity. Accusations that Augustine is a "misamorist" (e.g. Baier 1994) fail to see that he is not worried merely that we could harm ourselves in loving others, but more basically that we will harm them, expect too much from them, in treating them as our "ultimate good" – such treatment abuses their finitude. Given this setting, we can try to change our desires, or allow that their horizon extends beyond the world. Augustinians opt for the latter course, and so aim proximately to use but not enjoy the worldly goods. Hence worldly concerns, far from needing to be made theological, always already *are* theological: care for the world already is a mode of comportment which has as one of its purposes the satisfaction of theological longings, however normally misconstrued these longings (and their "satisfactions") may be.

All this means that "instrumentalizing" some things for the sake of others is an inevitable fact of who we are as creatures – creatures who organize ourselves around, and orient ourselves by, axiological "navigation points." For Augustine our "use" of worldly things is inevitable; what can change is simply the use to which we put them. Everyone worships some "god," some central axiological value around which they organize their lives, and for which they instru-mentalize other things, aims, and, at times, even people. One cannot not love: as Augustine put it, "there is no one who does not love; but he asks what he should love. Therefore I do not exhort you not to love, but to choose what we should love" (*sermo* 34.2). We ought to try not to suppress our affections, but to reorient them. The contrast between "enjoy" and "use" does not distinguish what should be loved from what should not be loved; it is rather a contrast in how one should value things. As Rowan Williams put it, "The language of *uti* is designed to warn against an attitude towards any future person or object that terminates their meaning in their capacity to satisfy my desire, that treats them as the end of desire, conceiving my meaning in terms of them and theirs in terms of me" (1989b: 140). The use-proposal urges us, not to instrumentalize the neighbor, but to value all things for their real worth – as God values them, in love. Augustine is not Kant's sap; his use of "use" is not most fundamentally a prescription to treat all things as means, but a proscription, forbidding us to expect things to be God, and forbidding us from acting as if we deserved from them some sort of ultimate happiness.

Yet not only are even our worldly concerns inevitably theological; Augustine's theology – understood as a practice of *imitatio Dei* (as the mode of *participatio Dei*) – is equally worldly, concerned with the right order and valuation of the world. His God is not the deistically indifferent and static watchmaker, but is rather a triune God whose inner being is always already in dynamic relation, and whose relationship to the world is one of life-giving immanent empowerment (as well as transcendent sovereignty). If we come to know God through our deepening inhabitation of love of our neighbors, the converse is also true: we know our neighbors properly only insofar as we know them in and through God, in and through God's knowing them. We know God through engagement with the world, and we know the world through deepening engagement with God. Far from being an essentially extrinsic *superadditum* to some presumptively wholly "natural" end, this participation in God, as gratuitous and "unnatural" as it seems, is our natural destiny. God has decided to be "God-for-us," and so we ultimately participate in that gratuitous love; and in this world, we turn to God, we are converted to *amor Dei*, through loving our neighbors. (Recall here Augustine's insistence that neighbor-love can give determinate shape to love of God.) If our worldly involvements press us to confront the root source of our love, our *caritas*, that reflection in turn forces us to confront the givens of our attachments and affections. The world turns out on Augustinian grounds to be not just the inert arena of our salvation, but also a dynamic partner with us in working that salvation out. Augustine's two dynamics, that is, force the human to be worldly and otherworldly simultaneously, because we are naturally "supernatural."

How can love guide life in this world? How are we to enact love in a world where love has no place to rest its head? Augustine's answer lies in the idea of the activity of confession, a double confession, itself doubly doubled. This confession is double first of all in what it is about: initially one's sin, but also praise of God; secondly it is double in its audience: both to God and to one's fellow humans (*ennar.* 138.1; *in Io. ep.* 1.6). The primordial theological activity of confession, that is, is both profoundly private and public, psychological and political, "vertical" and "horizontal." "Confession" here does not mean what we typically take it to mean; it is not fundamentally an exhibitionism, that desperate (and violent) stand-in for openness which is manifest so pathetically on TV talk shows. It is not fundamentally about the communication of autobiographical data; it is more an orientation, an awareness of and openness to the others surrounding oneself – an openness to transforming, and being transformed by, them. In it we find ourselves decentered, we find that we are no longer the main object of our purposes, but participate in something not primarily our own. This confession, then, is itself a turning to the other, not in the interests of mutual narcissism – which makes the other only a consolation prize for having to be already ourselves – but as an openness to transforming, and being transformed by, the other.

There is no security in this. But none should be anticipated, or even hoped for, in this life. Our hopes must anticipate a transcendental satisfaction, and we should seek to be "trained by longing" for the end (*in Io. ep.* 4.6). But this training takes place here, and we cannot escape it, or the conditions of this journey, before our completion.[16]

Contrary to common suspicions, then, Augustine's project is not world-denying but world-affirming; it simply affirms more than the "material" world. So understood, his proposal helps us resist the

---

16. This is the root of Augustine's criticism of Donatism. For him, the heresy of the Donatists is that they assume a dualism between world and God and seek to abandon the world; against this Augustine replies, "Were there no saints in the world at large? Was it right for you to condemn them unheard?" *In Io. ep.* 1.12–13.

various reductionist materialisms so powerful today, for it acknowledges that our ends transcend any worldly satisfaction, but are revealed through our worldly loves to stretch towards a transcendent God who is present in, but not exhausted by, creation.

Right "use": towards an Augustinian materialism

Now that we have sketched the fundamental ontology and dynamics of Augustine's *caritas*, we must articulate how this account plays out practically in human existence. The language of "use" turns out to be the proper form for love's practical expression. How does this language do this without fundamentally instrumentalizing the world? Here I argue first that, in context, Augustine's use-paradigm is a way of affirming the value of the world, and second that this paradigm should eventuate in practices of using that are all forms of stewardship of creation.

Augustine's use of "use"

Augustine uses the rhetoric of "use" to detail and promote the fundamental mode of comportment that he favors for our worldly existence. The use-paradigm was his attempt to formulate, against the opposition both of the asceticism then popular in elite Christian circles and of the puritanical conservativism prevalent among cultured pagans, a distinctly Christian rationale for apprehending and rightly valuing the world. It attempts to show how we can affirm the goodness of the created order as created, without treating it as an ultimate good.

Part of our failure to understand Augustine is due to semantic changes: his word *utor*, which we translate as "to use," is as John Rist notes a standard "Latin locution – found also in earlier English, e.g. 'He used him well' – indicating how people are to be 'treated'; the notion of exploitation is not to be read into it" (1994: 163–4).[17] It no longer has that flexibility in most modern languages. Beyond language difficulties, however, we also fail to appreciate how his philosophical theology complicates his practical proposal somewhat. The dialectic of divine immanence and divine transcendence

17. See also *de Trin.* 10.17.

so basic to his theology and ontology gives the charges of dualism their superficial credibility, yet also forbids dualism any genuine place in the schema. It underlies and connects the various terms Augustinians use to describe sin, and gives that language its illuminative, analytic, and practical power. That dialectic serves as the metaphysical link between the basically theological language of "sin as idolatry" and the initially therapeutic language of "sin as disordered loves": disordered loves are essentially idolatrous, for they cause us to worship an idol of our own making as God, and idolatry is necessarily a matter of disordered loves, for it calls us to love and worship some partial end as the source of our true fulfillment. God's immanence thus serves to remind us of the enormous impiety of any ontological favoritism of some segment of creation over another. But if God is in all things, God is not simply the sum of all things, not identical with creation as a whole; God's transcendence means that to worship all things as God is to miss the point just as egregiously. It is dangerous to say that God is somewhere in particular, but it can be just as dangerous to say that God is everywhere, or nowhere. The dialectic of transcendence and immanence serves as a critical tool against all forms of idolatry, both those that implant God too immanently within the world, and those that remove God too transcendently from it.

Furthermore, Augustine's texts are always shaped by deeply felt practical and pastoral purposes; doctrine is made for humans, not humans for doctrine. The rhetoric of Augustine's call for us to love God even to the contempt of the world is, in this light, a rhetorical aid to help change our order of loves, grounded on his conviction that this conversion will occur only by transforming our desperate attempts to rest in and on things of this world.[18] The use-paradigm in general, and particularly his more extreme formulations of it (such as his language of *contemptus mundi* and *contemptus sui*), often tempt people to think that he locates the problem finally in the objects of our loves; but Augustine treats each of these errors as formally identical manifestations of idolatry. The real problem with each form of sin is not the disparate objects, but the sort of love they express towards these objects. The worry here is more dispositional

18. A strategy employed elsewhere as well; see Calvin's *Institutes*, II.viii.54, on the role of "love of neighbor" as using our self-love against ourselves.

than metaphysical: Augustine does not want us not to love the world, but rather to change how we love it, as a whole and in its component parts.[19]

Such an affirmation of the world was almost unheard of in Augustine's day. His era has been called, not without reason, an "age of anxiety"; while it is hard to establish any psychological pessimism intrinsic to the era, the rhetorical forms of the age tended to encourage expressions of a fundamentally negative assessment of worldly existence – and this rhetoric in all likelihood had an effect on, if not an origin in, the consciousness of individual thinkers. Yet despite these larger cultural (and even perhaps ecclesial) tendencies, Augustine became "ever more deeply convinced that human beings had been created to embrace the material world" (P. Brown 1988: 425; see also R.Williams 1994). His position grew like a pearl around his central, granular insight: we are part of the world, and we are in a way the vehicles of God's love for the world, vessels of the world's redemption, just as we were the engines of its corruption. No straightforward dualism – neither the Manichees' evasion of responsibility, nor the Pelagians' furiously juridical moralism – would do. The world is not ultimately the problem; we are. Indeed, for him, dualism is simply one more form of escapism; the use-paradigm helps us resist all escapisms and insists instead on the necessity of our engagement with the world. His proposal of the use-paradigm was meant rhetorically, not to restrict his contemporaries' participation in the physical world, but to urge them towards such participation, against their temptations at recoil from it – to flush them out of their safe caves (and, if not down from their ivory towers, off of their marble stēlai) back out into the world.[20] In terms of marriage and human sexuality, in terms of the Christian's responsibilities towards the civic order, in terms of the mixed nature of the church – in case after case after case, Augustine encouraged Christians to move towards deeper commitment to "worldly" affairs, and to distinguish themselves from those who would seek to escape this condition.

Thus the use-paradigm does not disallow love of the world; it simply attempts to advise us how best to inhabit that altogether appropriate love. But what does that advice come to? That is what we turn to next.

19. See R. Williams 1989a: 11.
20. See Markus 1990b.

Practices of using

So Augustine thought that our worldly attachments were of soteriological import. But we must not hear in this a semi-Pelagian proposal of a salvific technology, as if we can choose to do this. We do not do the changing; we are changed, by God, and made vessels of *caritas*, which we should have been all along. Augustine wants us to understand ourselves as suffering our ongoing transformation by God of all of our various loves into an integral framework anchored in *amor Dei*. To elucidate this idea, this section discusses two facets of this transformation: how we should understand "possession," and how we should understand disposession, or giving away. Both of these practices reflect Augustine's broader theological depiction of our problem in terms of gratuity rather than scarcity.

As regards possessive use of objects, the first thing to note is that "using" objects does not mean treating them as fundamentally disposable. To use something does not mean *not* to love it, for some things that are to be used are also to be loved, albeit not all things. Nor need use and enjoyment be sequential, so that humans would "use" now and defer enjoyment for later. God's transcendent presence is not temporally teleological (in any straightforward sense, at least). We do not use and then enjoy; we must enjoy God now, simultaneously with using God's creation. One may well "use" objects properly by treasuring them, by respecting their autonomy from one's own particular interests; we respect the mundane goodness of things as they are separate from us, as they are in God.

This is more apparent in aesthetics than in ethics.[21] In so treasuring objects – whether pieces of art, or beloved books, or what have you – one finds that their increased intrinsic value gives them more autonomy. They are, so to speak, less yours, less an extension of your ego, and more themselves, the more you love them. Value overflows your own subjective grasping of things, and inheres in the things themselves: you can love things so much, that is, that you feel others must come to value them as well, that you must share them with others. Art is not art unless it is displayed; the object is

---

21. As Iris Murdoch suggests, "virtue is *au fond* the same in the artist as in the good man in that it is a selfless attention to nature" (1970: 41; see also 86–91). Cf. Soskice 1992, which provides a useful and provocative challenge to this proposal.

made more valuable by being communicated to others. Hence even material goods can be gratuitously pleasurable: they need not always imply a zero-sum system, in which the possession of a thing by one forbids its possession by others.[22] And what goes for material goods goes too for immaterial ones; as Augustine says:

> A man's possession of goodness is in no way diminished by the arrival, or the continuance, of a sharer in it; indeed, goodness is a possession enjoyed more widely by the united affection of partners in that possession in proportion to the harmony that exists among them. In fact, anyone who refuses to enjoy this possession in partnership will not enjoy it at all; and he will find that he possesses it in ampler measure in proportion to his ability to love his partner in it. (DCD 15.5)

In "possessing" things in this way – a way which, again, entails acknowledging their rightful autonomy – one is already moving towards understanding how we might undertake various practices of giving.

This Christian attitude towards materiality as part of a larger worldview, captured in the language of *caritas*, differed dramatically from the alternatives available on its appearance, such as the pagan Roman practice of euergetism, of giving elaborate parties for the poor. Euergetism was a form of social capital for the Roman nobility, a way of showing their magnanimity, and thus was necessarily tied to naming or knowing the giver, for their greater glory; Christian charity, in contrast, was exemplified in (and idealized as) anonymous giving, a giving whose aim was realized not in the visible response of recipients or one's peers but rather in the giving (which was always a sharing) itself.[23] For Christians the point of *caritas* was the communal repetition and participation in God's gracious love of creation (through the Trinity).[24] Giving is not so much an act of the self as the self's new mode of being.

Practically, speaking about non-human creation, the general form of this behavior is stewardship: the cultivating and agapic care for

22. For more on Augustine on property, see MacQueen 1972 and T. Martin 2005. For antecedents for such an "Augustinian materialism," see Innes 1995.
23. Of course both euergetism and *caritas* are ideal types. See Veyne 1990: 19-34, P. Brown 2002, 1992: 89-91, 96, and 1997: 30-1. For a general historical overview, see Davis 1996. For Augustine in particular, see DCD 2.20; 5.15, and Canning 1993: 420.
24. These rival visions of "glory" will appear again in Chapter 5 below.

things other than oneself, not on the grounds that such care is ultimately what the self wants, but rather because it is what the things as designed by God elicit from us. This stewardship is a form of prudence – a prudence that knows that the value of worldly things lies not simply in their immanent literality but also in their significance, in what they are for; a prudence that chooses therefore not to hoard but to store up treasures in heaven. This prudence is a quiet virtue, of self-effacing modesty, distinguished by the quality of the attention it encourages to what is before you. It is a virtue that cannot be given a useful abstract, theoretical formulation, but can only be exhibited in practice.[25]

Yet a question still pesters us: Is such a "prudence" really possible? All of this may sound attractive, and even plausible, as a way of managing our attachments to the world. But the image of control folded into the idea of "managing" is precisely what many (including, of course, Augustinians) find problematic about this account. "Management" seems a way of cooling our passions until they are lukewarm at best. But this is impossible, critics argue: either the warmth of the attachments will decay ever further until they end in cold indifference, or (or perhaps alongside this) the attempt at management will fail to get at those passions which drive us most deeply, and so contribute to our unknowing of ourselves. Either way, managing our passions seems problematic as a strategy for existence. We seem to be back with the problem of the Puritans, seeking to domesticate what is essentially undomesticable. Any such attempt at managing our loves will undermine their profundity as loves – that is, as *pathē*, passions, things we suffer, things which we cannot command. This is a general worry about any "theological ethic" – the worry that, rhetorically at least, such proposals simply offer us new technologies: devices which ultimately retain the self's sovereignty, leaving it in final control – as the serpent says, like God. How could prudence and providence conceivably cohere?

To answer this question, we must recall that this Augustinian materialism is not the most basic level of the theology. It is premised on the right love of God and on the idea that our lives are found

---

25. For an example, see the discussion of Augustine's own "prudential" exercise of authority in Chapter 4 below.

ecstatically and exegetically in wondering inquiry into God. We turn to that next.

Prudence and providence: inhabiting the hermeneutics of *caritas*

This chapter first explored the ontological framework that legitimates the perceptual change necessary to move from a picture of reality as fundamentally finite, with the basic problem being one of scarcity, to a picture of reality as a superabundant plenitude, with the basic problem being one of gratuity. Following this, the chapter then detailed the practical contours of our response to this gratuity. But we have not yet addressed the deep theological question of how this response is not just one more way of managing reality rather than a genuine way of participating in God's work. We still may think of "our" prudence as a polite though ultimately autonomous response to God's providence, rather than seeing it as the way we participate in the rhythms of God's providence. We have not yet grasped the real inner connection between prudence and providence.

We grasp this by realizing that the logic of the use-paradigm shifts from an "ethical" register to a "hermeneutical" and exegetical one – or rather, that the inner logic of the ethical is revealed as having been fundamentally exegetical all along. And it is at this point that prudence and providence come together. For Augustine, the use-paradigm is not finally a freestanding ethical "technology of the self" which he recommends for our autonomous projects of self-formation; it is rather a description of the practical interpretive framework which all people, whether they acknowledge it or not, employ. Distinguishing between "use" and "enjoyment" is not most fundamentally an ethical strategy, but rather an inescapable anthropological-hermeneutical activity. The ethical enactment of the use-paradigm is, for Augustine, simply (though not merely) our manifestation of this interpretive framework in and through the materiality of our lives. It is the way we come to inhabit the hermeneutics of charity.

In arguing this, it will help briefly to explore Augustine's most elaborate discussion of the use-paradigm, found in *de doctrina Christiana*. Here the use-paradigm is not most fundamentally deployed ethically but exegetically, within the context of Augustine's account of *doctrina* – a term referring not only to the content of what is taught but also and more deeply to the process of learning itself – and specifically as the regulative framework for interpreting Scripture. More specifically it gets deployed as a tool in the exegesis which Augustine sees as the primary practice of faith. The project of "using" the world turns out to be our basic mode of comportment in this life only because that comportment is more fundamentally an act of interpretation, and to be more precise, an act of exegesis – initially of the Bible, but fundamentally of the whole world, revealing it to be what R. A. Markus calls a "cosmic text" (1996: 34; see also Greer 1986). In this final section I want to sketch something of the radical consequences of this fact through exploring briefly the story of the Christian life as sketched in *de doctrina*.[26]

The nature of "Christian teaching"

We begin by deconstructing the "received story" of *de doctrina Christiana*. Typically the work is presented as a constitution, the "charter of Christian culture," concerned essentially with the validation, systematization, and communication of a determinate and closed set of doctrines by authenticated preachers to a passive audience awaiting tutelage. On this account, the text is concerned with two things: how to discover the doctrines, and then how to preach what is discovered. We undertake the process of discovery centrally by interpreting Scripture, guided by Augustine's hermeneutical rules, discerning through its signs God's purposes for us. We then proceed to preach this, both by our lips and in our lives. Such is *de doctrina*'s received story.

But some of the book's elements reveal fractures in this story, and if we attend to them more fully, a quite different picture appears. First, Augustine's techniques of exegesis are not wholly distinguished from his ecclesiology, his vision of the church. The Bible is the central and primary text, but it is neither immediately nor ultimately a necessary text; there are monks in the wilderness who

---

26. For more see Griffiths 1999, Bright 1999, Van Fleteren and Schnaubelt 2002, Dawson 2002, Pollmann 1996, Turner 1995b, Young 1997. More generally, see also Jacobs 2001a and 2001b.

have no access to the Bible but who are living holy lives (*DDC* 1.39.43). What matters is that we participate in the body of Christ, and practice the rule of charity. This participation entails active scriptural interpretation as well: exegesis is not essentially a special spiritual performance of a cognitive elite, it is fundamentally a practice of the whole church, both together and in its component individuals. Indeed, the activity of exegesis is in a way just what the church most fundamentally *is*.

Furthermore, the internal structure and external boundaries of the church are profoundly unstable, and this complicates the top-down "flowchart" model of ecclesial-pedagogical management that some seem to take the text to support. The practice of exegesis involves all the possible readers in the church. Any interpretation that can advance the rule of charity is legitimate, and so all believers are properly full participants in the communal exploration of God's word: as Gerald Bruns puts it, "these mysteries, so far from being incomprehensible to the many, are accessible to every sort of understanding – capable of being taken now in one sense, now in another ... The Scriptures are a public rather than a secret text; the truth has been tempered to a plurality of understandings" (1984: 161). This is part of why Augustine affirms the church's reality as mixed; there are saints living outside the *ecclesia*, and there are citizens of the earthly city present in the visible church.[27] The body of Christ is wounded at its side and is not now seamless. We may say, then, that the community of interpreters is open both "horizontally" – to those outside it – and "vertically" – to all those within it, no matter what their literacy.

Second, the practices and products of textual analysis, as we usually understand it, are not the ultimate point of this hermeneutics of *caritas*, in two ways. First of all, scriptural exegesis is not understood as an algorithmic device for producing the right doctrinal formulae, or generating the "plain sense" of the text, understood as a conversation-stopper. Many have noted that Augustine's exegesis is promiscuous, open to multiple readings and endless allegory. But the purpose of this exegetical promiscuity is not to showboat, or develop useful exegetical muscles; it is more

---

27. This is visible most famously in *DCD* but is also present in *DDC* and in his general preaching against the Donatists, in *in Io. ep.*

fully to subvert the boundaries of text and world, to show how the world is read through the text. Exegesis precedes ontology; indeed, ontology is but a province of exegesis. As Rowan Williams says, "The sign-quality of the world is not to be trivialized into a mere system of ciphers, puzzles that yield solutions, fixed material symbols for a fixed immaterial object or set of objects" (1989b: 146). Secondly, the interpretive endlessness thus recommended reveals that the Bible is not read ultimately as a cryptogrammatical end in itself; it is read to understand God's plan for the world, and ultimately as a vehicle for understanding God. "Learning from Scripture is a *process* – not a triumphant moment of penetration and mastery, but an extended play of invitation and exploration" (R. Williams 1989b: 142). In reading the "signs" and "things" of the Bible, we discover that the history recorded therein is best understood allegorically, as a language God speaks to us. Not only do we read the signs to get at the things; we grasp the things when we grasp them as signs – we must understand them as things which finally refer beyond themselves to something else.[28] From this Augustine draws the larger conclusion that the world itself is God's sign, God's poem. We must come to see and understand the "sign-character" of the world, its reality as fundamentally semiotic.

Nonetheless, Augustine is not quite aligned with contemporary intertextual theological approaches. His hermeneutical playfulness is not finally frivolous or narcissistically confined to textuality; it is ontological in its ambitions, and eschatological in its orientation. Augustine is sensitive to how the metaphor of "world as text" can encourage a "resting in the book" without moving out from it into the world. Again, Rowan Williams has it right: "Only when, by the grace of Christ, we know that we live entirely in a world of signs are we set free for the restlessness that is our destiny as rational creatures" (1989b: 141). We should be suspicious of a too exclusive attention to the "literal sense" of the Bible, and affirm not just the validity but even the necessity of paraphrase. We should avoid what R. A. Markus calls a "servitude to the literal" (1996: 23). Paraphrase is

---

28. I am indebted to Michael Cameron for enormously helpful conversations about Augustine's understandings of signs and things, and for a reading of selections from his forthcoming book on Augustine's *ennar.* On the sacramental and textual character of the world in late antique thinking, see Conybeare 2000: 91–130.

not, in fact, a heresy; it is the life of the text. The "literal sense" is an eschatological sense, and during the world a regulative sense – one that does not resolve problems so much as encourage us to discover how our world and our time can be found intelligibly in the text.[29] Insofar as it aims at extracting from the text a rather systematic theological and doctrinal grammar, such a project is, ironically enough, at once too instrumentalizing of the Bible (in the sense of exploiting its texts for a thoroughly fixed *a priori* purpose) and not instrumentalizing enough (in the sense of refusing to develop the Bible beyond itself). We must resist "carnal" or literal readings which anxiously assume that we must be in charge, and that we must achieve the right representation of understanding "inside" our heads. Such an aesthetic focus is premised upon a Cartesian account of understanding as representation; but if, as Wittgenstein said, understanding is most primordially "knowing how to go on," the community as a whole undertakes "exegesis" of Scripture by enacting the Scriptures in the everyday life of the church. Scripture is not an aesthetic artifact to be admired; it is a workbook, and our engagement with it is our entry into a broader mode of comportment during the world. The ultimate aim is not to get the Bible "right" in some sort of representational manner, but to find ways to use it.[30]

This gets us to the third and last major modification we must make to the usual story of *de doctrina Christiana*. For if exegesis is not finally a textual practice aimed at a right representation of the Scriptures as an artifact, the nature of "preaching" in this setting is also significantly different from what we usually take it to be. It is not the top-down transferal of some propositionally determinate semantic content from the preacher's intellect to the audience's, like a memo; it is the attempt to exhibit, and to invite others more fully to enter into, the ongoing communal activity of exploring the

---

29. See R. Williams 1991: 132 and Tanner 1987.
30. See Markus 1996. Gerald Bruns argues that the medieval analysis of the "four senses of scripture" worked to contain and control exegesis, so that the scholastics were opposed to "licentious interpretation," and "medieval hermeneutics appears to be less a method of polysemy than a critique of it" (1992: 140). In contrast, Mary Carruthers argues that the "levels" of exegesis are best construed "as 'stages' of a continuous action." See Carruthers 1992: 165. For an interesting defense of allegorical reading in late antiquity, see Lamberton 1986.

world as framed and illuminated by the Scriptures.[31] As Augustine says, a preacher's life is her or his truest speech (*DDC* 4.29.61; see also T. Martin 1998).

In light of these modifications to the usual story, we can see that *de doctrina Christiana* is not about the project of "figuring out" how to find and authorize some determinate set of doctrinal beliefs in the Bible and then to impress them into the souls of a stupefied audience of *rudes* in the pews.[32] Understandings of Augustine that assume some such approach inevitably attribute to him some sort of "semiotic anxiety" (see Irvine 1994: 265–71). But what a modern academic habitually sees as anxiety is simply, for Augustinians, the life of the church. We must "think of interpretation on the model of a social practice rather than as a certain type of mental operation" (Bruns 1984: 164), a practice whose aim is twofold. First of all, and this admits (though only theoretically) of some real realization, the community aims to train itself to come to see through the Bible's eyes – to use the Scriptures as lenses, in Calvin's phrase. *De doctrina Christiana* is a theo-political ethnography of sorts, depicting a community of interpreters, working together in an ongoing and endless process of interpreting Scripture as the key for understanding their lives, and consequently bringing the wisdom gained existentially thereby to the task of interpreting Scripture. The goal of this communal enterprise is not the realization of some apocalyptically final and stable complete "decryption" of the text, for such is not to be had; we are too finite and too flawed, and the text is infinitely rich.[33] Rather, second, the church uses the Bible to discern God's word in the world – or better, to discern the world as God's word, as *sacramentum*, theophanic, charged with divine significance. And the emotion felt through this practice of discernment is not anxiety but rather the intoxicating anticipatory hopefulness of the joy to come in the eschaton. The fundamental liturgy of the church is this practice of communally using Scripture as a device for transforming vision, a tool to help us see and speak aright.

31. There is no need to understand this "understanding" as literally a "content." See Bruns 1984: 162.
32. See Harmless 1995.
33. See Markus 1996.

*Reality as semiotic and Christianity as a pilgrimage
of "reading"*

This has substantial implications. First of all, it deepens our
sense of the meaning of "use." We should "use" things of this
world, not enjoy them, so that invisible things are seen by the
visible (*DDC* 1.4.4). But this "using" should not inflate us with
arrogance. It is not we who are finally "using" the world; rather, it is
God who primarily "uses" the world, and us in it. We do not alleg-
orize: God does. The idea of "use" finds its primary home not in
axiology, as an account of instrumentalizing value, but in semiotics:
God uses created things to signify something beyond the literal
meaning of the things. This does not devalue objects at all; to the
contrary, God loves and affirms every atom of the world, but their
value is not in themselves but in their "significance" in the entire
divine economy. If anything, this invests objects with a depth of
significance that a thin immanentism cannot accommodate.

This tells us of the sacramentality of created reality as a whole.
Action is semiotic because being itself is semiotic; events are not
dumb but "eloquent" (*DCD* 11.18). We do not impose meaning on
them, but discern (always partially) their true significance; and in
doing so we enter ever more fully into the song of God's love, the
doxological joy which is our proper, endless, end. Hence, the church
uses the Bible to discern God's word in and throughout the world – or
better, to discern the world *as* God's word, as *sacramentum*, theophanic, charged with divine significance, as ecstatic signs more
fundamentally than dumb things. As R. A. Markus says, Augustine's
"theory of signs ... spills over" into a general "hermeneutic of
human experience": what begins as exegesis becomes ontology –
more accurately, ontology is shown to be a province of exegesis – and
the world is revealed to be, as Markus puts it, a "cosmic text" (1996:
34). We ultimately aim to "understand" God, where "understanding"
is realized and manifest as love; we seek to apprehend the thundering
poem of Creation, to hear its enormous roar, in order more fully to
join in the song, to know and participate in what we have been singing
all along.[34]

---

34. For useful worries about loose "sacramentality" talk, see R. Williams 2000:
217–8; for a useful clarification see Ward 2000: 156–61.

This reading of the text implicitly suggests that *doctrina Christiana*, "Christian teaching," is the church's basic mission, and indeed its very being, both formally and materially. Rather than exclusively signifying the content of faith, *doctrina* at least as importantly refers to the form of faith. It is a guidebook for how to live as a church, as the body of Christ on its way through the world. It is about the teaching and learning of Christian life, the process of becoming disciplined as Christians, which is to say becoming the children and the people of God. Exegesis is our mode of being-in-the-world: not a being-towards-death, but a being-towards-understanding, a being-towards-comprehension. We exist as auditors, caught in the middle of hearing a sentence addressed to us; we know it is addressed to us, but we do not know where or how it will end, even as we know what it will end with, in some sense. This is a way of proleptically participating in the eschaton, in the final opening of the book that will mark the closing of history. Again, as Rowan Williams says, "A language which indefinitely postpones fulfillment or enjoyment is appropriate to the Christian discipline of spiritual homelessness, to the character of the believing life as pilgrimage" (1989b: 142–3). We read the world through the text, but with full knowledge that this reading, this whole mode of life, cannot be settled while we remain pilgrims, before the eschaton. Indeed, the deeper we read, the more powerfully we feel our tensive incompleteness, our *distensio* during the world.

Still, this pilgrimage of reading is not without some notion of its destination; and *doctrina* gives the church its goal – exploration into God, the cultivation of wonder, and the practice of glorifying God that is its consequence. Crucially, this practice of wonder, of theological inquiry, is not primarily speculative and propositional, but affective and perceptual, a change in how we apprehend the world. As Nicholas Lash says, "problems of knowledge are problems of ethics and not of epistemology or 'engineering'" (1988: 275, see 207). Both exegesis and preaching blossom into ethics, but "ethics" is equally a form of theological hermeneutics and aesthetics, oriented towards rendering intelligible (and articulate) our loves as our fundamental mode of participation in, and hence understanding of, God. In being this, *de doctrina* alters our vision of the "ethical" project – the ethos – of Christian life. Ethics certainly has something to do with that life, but it is not finally about right action, but about

<u>right understanding</u>. What we distinguish as exegesis, ecclesiology, liturgy, and ethics are all facets of a larger project, which directs us toward a central theological "inquiry," which is primarily about God and secondarily about our loves (because God is our loves) – a project best described as a hermeneutics of charity.

The upshot of all this is to re-situate "ethics" not as a doing or a becoming but as part of an act of interpretive response. It does not eventuate in anything approaching a moral algorithm, a simple moral calculus for dealing with quandaries; but such algorithms are really last-ditch attempts at being good, and so should not be any-one's primary aim. (As Albert Camus noted, "when one has no character, one *must* rely on a method" [1956: 11].) Such explicit the-ories are of course helpful, and intercommunal ethics do benefit from well worked out principled programs. But such programs are not the core of Christian morality, and cannot be: for in dealing with a living God, one cannot finally rely on any principles, but on God alone, and on our faithfulness as guided by God, for guidance. Nor on this picture is ethics attempting primarily to master the future, to shape it to a predetermined intention, as the management model would have it; it is primarily retrospective, undertaking a process of discovery, of coming to see what one's past has meant, what the present may signify, and what the future promises. That is all one can do with providence: discover it. Instead of being algorithmic and prospective, it is retrospective, dialogical, conversational, and working on our dispositions and our vision, the manifold ways we apprehend reality. It begins out of an "act" of interpretation, out of some answer to the question "What is going on?" And its content is interpretation as well, insofar as its responsive action itself man-ifests some interpretation of one's action-prompting situation. Pru-dence is the discernment of what is going on – what God is doing now – and in so being, it itself leads to the *imitatio Dei*, and the participation in the ongoing work of providence. The truly prudent thing to do is to inquire into our lives and try to discern in them what we "already know" must be there – God's awesome providential work. The primary "user" of the use-paradigm is God, and our task is to "discover" how God is using us and all creation as signs, to come to understand the language that we always already are.

And here is the connection between "prudence" and "providence" to which the beginning of this chapter alluded. A true prudence – a

proper use – involves treating things gratuitously, as more fundamentally contingent gifts rather than necessities, and hence imi-
tating (and hence participating in) God's *ex nihilo* creation. It is a
liturgical way of being-in-the-world, an active and practical participation in God's creation. In that project we are stewards, first and
foremost, of ourselves – we are not properly our own possession.
But speaking environmentally, we are also lexicographers of being,
appointed "readers" who not only with our lips but in our lives
articulate the Word, and preserve or cultivate the semiotic character
of being. God-talk (theology) and God-work (theurgy) are two sides of
the same coin; one who is prudent in the right sense loves the
world, not just as God loves it, but in God.[35]

Just what, in less abstract, more human terms, would all this look
like? Briefly put, it broadens our understanding of liturgy, and deepens our idea of exegesis. On this account, worldly action should be
performed not just for its immanent value, but because it is exploration into God, a mode of inquiring into God, and it should be interpreted communally as such. On this account the churches are, first
and foremost, communities of interpretation, composing a polyphonic and historically extended conversation involving all members
in the central practice of coming to understand Scripture, and
by living out their understanding return to Scripture with an ever
deeper, ever renewed sense of wonder and insight into their riches. In
a way this can be seen as a form of Christian midrash, though the
activity is more overtly inclusive of modes of interpretation which are
not obviously "interpretation" at all, much less interpretation of a
particular text: I think here of such activities as working in soup
kitchens, setting up alliances with other churches and religious
groups, possibly demonstrating for political causes. All of this
becomes intelligible as a "liturgy" of the church, the work whereby a
collection of disparate individuals comes together in community to
begin the infinite task of understanding.[36] And this liturgy may

---

35. The idea that an action's reality is in part determined by the self-understanding
of the actor who undertakes it has a solid philosophical pedigree. As G. E. M.
Anscombe puts it, action always takes place "under a description" 1958: §§
23–6. I note that the Crucifixion should inform our *imitatio Dei*; but I will not
discuss that complex topic here.
36. See Cavanaugh 1998, Bruns 1992; 105, 117–18, and Leyerle 2004.

indeed involve participants who do not yet properly inhabit the church. We will see more about this in Part II of this book.

Conclusion

Thus, even in Augustine's initial formulations of this proposal, the proposal is as far from otherworldliness as possible. It postulates a dualism between what happens in "this" world and "the next"; instead it assumes that this world is already a shadow of the next, and that therefore it has no independent ontological existence apart from its eschatological consummation. There is no fundamental difference in character (though there is considerable difference in degree) between what people do in the churches today and what all will do on the eschatological morning. This world is God's intended object: it is simply not yet consummated, and if we "use" it properly, we can participate, albeit partially and proleptically, in its ultimate character *as* consummated even today.

Such "use" is ultimately an ecclesial project, the work of the churches, in teaching their faithful what it means to be stewards of a creation not yet come to fulfillment. On this view, one can only speak of the "world" as a regulative idea, one which gains its integrity from within the web of practices that constitute the church. Only by participating in the project of the church – and *not* just by being a "theist" – can one gain the sort of integral vision of experience to begin talking about the world. This is an eschatologically inflected hermeneutical claim: only from the perspective of the churches will the world become finally intelligible as what it is: as the promise, not yet – despite all our waywardness – broken, of God's gratuitous and transfiguring work to be accomplished on us and all creation.

All of this leaves us with an interesting problem, whose implications we have not yet fully worked out: What about other people? How should we understand how Christians are to treat them? The traditional description has been: Christians should behave lovingly towards them, as God does. But in what does this love consist? This is the topic of Chapter 3.

3

Life together

The conceit of the social worker: "We're all here on earth to help the others. What on earth the others are here for, I don't know."
W. H. Auden, *The Dyer's Hand*

What does it mean to live in love? If we think of love as something wider than sexually erotic attraction, we will see that experiences of "falling in love" – with friends, books, professions, preoccupations – are far more common in our lives than a narrow fixation on romance will lead us to believe. We never choose love, pick it from a menu of equally viable, equally distant options; we discover that we are already in love, already mixed up with the other, our fates intertwined.[1] Only then, after we discover we are in love, our voluntary agency plays a role; for then we must decide what to do about our newly recognized condition.

What does it mean to try to live in God's love and in love for others, within this dispensation? What does it mean to try genuinely to live *with* others, not just *nearby* them, during the world? Properly speaking, human love is participation in God's agapic and kenotic attention to and delighted "waiting on" creation, a love most centrally oriented for us towards the neighbor (Vanstone 1983: 115). But today, during the world, such love is hard to imagine in its fullness; even those little loves that we manage to inhabit often seem to exist only as long as they stand out against the cooler, more callous, and less profound relations. Any honest talk of love must acknowledge its vexed condition in our world today, just as any

1. See Vanstone 1978: 39–54, and 1983: 97–9.

genuine love must be, in part, a mournful, vexed love. Yet despite these many vexations, we still seek out one another. What is it about us that makes us do this? To answer this question implies a theology of human community that makes sense of the idea that our destiny, and the destiny of the world before God, is found not in separation from one another but in convergence, in the final communion of the eschaton. Sketching such a theology is the purpose of this chapter.

Chapter 1 argued that Augustinian theology offers an account of faithful living, by providing a language within which we can understand humanity's relation to God, and more specifically can understand ourselves as gifts of God, whose fundamental proper mode of being is an ecstatic and responsive confession of that gift, and whose whole being waits completion until the eschatological consummation. Chapter 2 argued that this tradition offers an account of hopeful living, by providing a language through which we can understand the relationship between creation and God, and more specifically can understand creation as a whole as a further gift of God, through which we can love God and whose full being will be given to it only in the eschatological consummation. But we still have another dimension of our existence that merits extended attention: our relationship with one another, with the neighbor and the stranger. Christianity has always described and proscribed that relationship as one lived in love. What does that mean?

This chapter offers a language whereby we can see human community as fully realized only eschatologically, but also see our life even now as a proleptic participation in the true kingdom of God. Understanding our lives in this way should lead us towards a practice of confessional openness before others – Christian and non-Christian alike – as (ultimately) other members of that eschatological community. Our attempts to realize community here and now, partial and halting as they are, are discrete traces of our proper prelapsarian orientation towards communion – traces we must acknowledge and allow, even as we remain wary of their inflection by our sinful self-interest and tendency to conflate our egos with those of others. And the successes of our attempts at such communion are properly proleptic realizations of that eschatological communion – momentary realizations that we should acknowledge, allow and even encourage, but which we cannot delude ourselves

into imagining as regularly and "normally" achievable in this dis- ✳
pensation. Our longing for genuine community cannot be denied,
and while we should not use that longing as the sole load-bearing
pillar of a political theology, it should shape all aspects of that
theology.

Such is the basic grammar of the account sketched here. In order
to flesh it out, we will frame this discussion by talking about the
hardest case, the case of those with whom we share few fundamental commitments – others who are not members of our religious community. How should Christians live with non-believers
and with "other-believers"? Augustine's program for engaging these
most "other" others turns out to bear significant lessons for our
relations with even our most intimate others; it offers a legitimation
for engaging with otherness, and an explanation of what happens in
such engagements, in which we engage with others knowing that
we may well transform them – and be transformed by them. ✳

A focus on Christian relations with non-Christians may seem a
surprising place to begin a theological discussion of human community, but in fact reflection on radical difference has had a place in
Christian thought for a long time. Christianity has had a complex
and often ambivalent assessment of "the other." Like most human
communities, the Christian tradition is wary of aliens, non-Christians, whom it sees as strange and possibly dangerous; and yet the
tradition is well aware of its founder's commands to openness
towards the lost and victimized, the stranger and the other. Christian theology is founded upon the reconciliation of otherness: it
proclaims the reconciliation of humanity to God, and affirms,
within the Trinity itself, the revelation that some others have
always been reconciled. But because we are sinners, we forget our
obligations to be open to strangers. The tradition recognizes this
fact and seeks to remind us constantly to return to such openness –
not, of course, to capitulate to the others, but rather in order to be
authentically vulnerable, able to change, in ways their presence
elicits in us. In this way, the dialogue between the self and the
other, the "same" and the "different," plays a deep role throughout
the history of Christian thought.

Today is no different. But recent discussions of this issue have
deemphasized the received concern with Christianity's relation to
the "secular other," and focused instead on Christianity's relation

to other religions – on the theological significance of religious pluralism, and the proper theological response to it. The challenge of pluralism is very profound, for it reveals that in religious pluralism theology confronts a primordial theological problem: the problem of otherness. What the contemporary world calls pluralism we should see, in theological terms, as the fundamental challenge of otherness, a challenge demanding a rich theological response. Modern thought in general, and modern theology in particular, is ill-equipped to help us here, as it is committed more to avoiding than to confronting the challenge.

This chapter finds resources to do better in the work of the Augustinian tradition.[2] Yet many doubt whether Augustine and his inheritors can offer any such assistance. Indeed, many who are occupied with the "problem of otherness" identify Augustine himself as a particularly problematic figure in the obliteration of otherness, the first "master of oppression" – to such a degree that one of the most thoughtful and thorough of such critics, William Connolly, once labeled the modern fixation on identity and its hostility towards difference "the Augustinian imperative."[3] The core accusation here is analogous to the one instigating Chapter 2: belief in God, at least the ruthlessly serious sort of belief promoted by Augustine, necessarily entails the instrumentalization of other people to serve the believer's romance with God (which is inevitably, for these critics, at least as much the believer's romance with a particular, and particularly narrow, vision of his or her own self). The centrality of God for believers, so the critics say, leads inevitably to treating others as mere occasions or opportunities for exhibiting your commitment to God. Genuine otherness is subjugated to the reign of the same.

But again, such accusations are too sweeping in their anathematization of Augustine. Certainly the worries are not baseless, but

---

2. For Augustine's own views on dialogue and toleration in general, see Bowlin 1997, M. J. White 1994, Rohr 1967, and Vanderspoel 1990. For Jewish accounts with intriguingly similar proposals, see Dorff 2000 and Novak 1989; for an Islamic one, see Sachedina 2001.

3. See Connolly 2002a. In his second edition he changes his approach to Augustine, describing it as "the Augustinian temptation," for a fuller investigation of Augustine on *caritas* suggests that "there may be a promising tension between the Augustinian affirmation of love and the doctrine through which it is adumbrated" (2002a: xxiii). I thank Kathleen Skerrett for conversations regarding this.

they are not the final word on Augustine's thought. Even the critics would agree that otherness cannot be *too* other, particularly in regard to God: that would stumble backwards into a dangerous sort of cosmological dualism. Hence there is no serious reason to endorse the sort of radical incommensurability so many thinkers give lip service to today. Yet at the same time this theology has an eschatological dimension, and so can accommodate a "not yet" character to its absolute claims: as we experience it today, some absolute otherness *is* real, not just as the "positive" otherness exemplified in the perichoretic existence of the Triune God (which will remain even in the eschaton) but also as the negative otherness through which we so often encounter others in this world, due to the Fall; and such experiences of otherness are an ineliminable part of our experience during the world. Far from inevitably under-writing oppression, Augustine's thought can help us see the full complexity and deep theological meaning of the challenge of plur-alism and otherness, as manifesting the otherness present most fundamentally in the otherness of the divine Trinity, and through it in the relationships between that Trinity and humans, and in the relationships among ourselves. Because of this, Augustinians treat "the problem of otherness" as from the beginning a problem demanding a thoroughly theological answer.

To explore and unpack this claim is the aim of this chapter. It does this in three steps. First, it suggests that the challenge of pluralism should be understood as one manifestation of the more fundamental theological challenge of otherness, and suggests how work done in interreligious dialogue can help with this project. Second, it sketches how an Augustinian approach can help us do this, by critically engaging the best broadly Augustinian proposal regarding pluralism and otherness, that of John Milbank. Third, it presents an account of how the Augustinian tradition can be wel-coming of otherness in a rich and complexly dialogical manner.

From pluralism to engagement

We are only now realizing the radical character of the chal-lenge of pluralism. The existence of apparently mutually incompat-ible ways of understanding and guiding human life confronts us as sheer sociopolitical fact, a reality that demands a rich and systematic response by every community today. Lee Yearley puts it well: today we "must develop those virtues that will enable us to understand, judge, and deal with ideals of human flourishing that confront us but appear to differ markedly from our own" (1992: 2). We must understand other positions in their particularity, as traditions whose complexity and depth rival our own; we must deal with these other positions as traditions making claims to truth that contest our own; and we must judge between these views, both as making claims on us and as positions held by others whom we respect and with whom we share a world. Currently, we do this very poorly; at the practical level and the theoretical level, we seem more committed to living in the vicinity of one another than to life genuinely with one another.[4] How can we do better? How can we realistically acknowledge this pluralism, opening ourselves to disagreement and critique, while yet remaining fully and authentically ourselves – not pretending to others (or deluding ourselves) that we are empty of convictions but non-defensively holding our beliefs as true? To answer this question, we must first see what kind of challenge it is, and then determine how we should respond to it.

The failure of secular toleration

In this section modern secular approaches to addressing otherness will be critiqued. But that modern secularism has failings, even decisive ones, simply marks it as human. Despite its many failings, secular modernity is not only our condition; it has also led to many valuable things, especially the deeper estimation of the value of simple worldly existence, and its associated promotion of ideas of individual human dignity in the *saeculum*, and concern for the *saeculum* itself (expressed most palpably in environmentalism). Ian Markham is right: "The Enlightenment and its child, secularism, have taught the church much that is true about God's relations to the world" (Markham 2003: 29). Most notably, the challenge of dealing with others, in a respectful manner, seems to be prominent now in a way it was not in earlier eras, and that seems at least in part due to the emergence of modern (even liberal) notions of respect for persons' autonomy. However problematically developed

4. For empirical evidence see Wuthnow 2005.

those intuitions have been in modernity, it is important to acknowledge the lessons we have learned as moderns.[5]

But modern "respect" is our attempt to address a genuine prob- ✳ lem inadequately. That is, we cannot fully recognize how deeply pluralism challenges us if we understand that challenge as it is usually understood today, as "the problem of pluralism" *simpliciter*. This description depicts it in purely formal terms, as the epistemological problem of toleration. But this pseudo-resolution is unsatisfactory for us, because it obscures the real theological significance of the challenge, and illegitimately and unsuccessfully attempts to evade it. If the fundamental problem of modern politics is pluralism, this is a fundamentally religious problem, and it must be confronted as such.[6]

The received and inadequate strategy is the strategy of "secularism" – the strategy that marginalizes every form of what it sees as contestable "faith commitments," and permits into "public" human discourse nothing more than what it sees as uncontestable "common sense," however that is described (and it has been described in quite various ways indeed in the history of the secularist strategy). (On this definition, "secularism" does not denote the material realities of contemporary, religiously pluralist societies; it is only one interpretation of how to inhabit and regulate such societies.) When political thinkers confronted the apparently ✳ intractable differences among extra-subjective authorities – differences which, they believed, led to bloody religious wars – they replaced such authorities with new, typically subjective epistemologies, in the hope that these new epistemologies would settle disputes through universally shared criteria.[7] In practice, however, thinkers constructed not a neutral decision procedure but rather a "lowest common denominator" approach to rational discourse,[8] which allowed most activities to go on, but expelled explicitly religious discourse – or indeed any discourse about "values" – from the public

---

5. See Taylor 1989.
6. See Gamwell 1995, Walzer 1997, and Heyd 1996. For interesting (and iconoclastic) historical accounts of the development of toleration, see Murphy 2001 and Nederman 2000.
7. See Hirschman 1977, Cavanaugh 1995, and Asad 2003.
8. See J. Stout 1981, esp. his depiction of how the French Huguenots developed such an account in 236–8.

sphere of "facts."[9] Over time this resolution, originally meant only as a pragmatic stop-gap, ossified into the rigid meta-narrative of "secularism." Because reasoned discourse could run only through strictly laid out patterns, rationality suffered a hardening of the arteries.

In that sclerosis, one sees the birth of secularism. To save its cities, Europe destroyed its churches; it staved off destruction only at the cost of rendering religious beliefs at best vestigial to, and at worst parasitic upon, the daily life of its communities. The secularist strategy assumed that even with religious values quarantined from public, people would share enough common ground to adjudicate their differences without recourse to their "deep" metaphysical and religious convictions; that is to say, it assumed that the sources for peoples' "publicly relevant" views, now hidden behind a discursively impenetrable curtain, would remain similar enough to one another to ensure that all debate could be settled without reference to the deeper metaphysical and theological frameworks that sponsored their "properly public" positions.

This did two things. First, it made those deeper frameworks seem vestigial or superfluous to the proper functioning of the "practical" commitments. If those frameworks were not the ineliminable context of those commitments, or if they were merely secondary (and, usually, essentially subjective) "interpretations" serving as metaphysical background scenery to the practical essence of the views, they were immaterial. One could be a good person without any (even tacit) metaphysical or theological basis for one's views. (Such is the view of many people today.) The problem with this is that it encourages an "ethics of inarticulacy" that is problematic in itself (because it encourages a metaethical aphasia in people) and disastrous in its consequences (because it renders unimportant the communication of such views to children, rendering each generation less and less able to explain why it acts and thinks the way it does – until a point of complete moral inarticulacy is reached, a condition that it seems safe to say is not conducive to a morally vigorous society).[10]

9. Beyond Max Weber, I am thinking, more philosophically, of Sabina Lovibond's analysis of "the metaphysics of commuter-land" (1982: 96), and, more politically, Elshtain 1981. See also Sperber's fascinating discussion of "cognitive apartheid" (1985: 62).
10. See C. Taylor 1989, and C. Smith 2005.

Second, this strategy made it impossible for its adherents to argue in good faith with those who did not share their fundamental views. Such arguments, when they occurred, could not be recognized for what they were: theologically and metaphysically rich arguments between fundamentally different positions. Instead, they had to be redescribed as really sharing a similar vocabulary – namely, the vocabulary of liberal individualism – or as not really argument at all, not genuine contributions to debate.[11] That is to say, secularism despaired of the possibility of genuine engagement, and fruitful argument, over fundamental differences. It chose instead to construct public (and presumably "neutral") canons of argument, rules that delimited the proper scope (and depth) of argument, in the hope that interlocutors' convictions would never be so diverse that those canons could not usefully govern whatever argument turned out to be necessary.

But that hope has turned out to be false. The steadily increasing pluralism of Western culture has slowly undermined the plausibility of this secularist strategy, and the collapse of the uncontestable "commonsensical" seems effectively accomplished. As William Connolly puts it, today we face "recurrent situations where interdependent constituencies honor different moral sources and are unlikely to be moved by argument or inspiration to embrace the same source" (2002a: xxiii). In our day, the unsteady truce in place since the Treaty of Westphalia in 1648 seems increasingly fragile; many doubt whether it remains either politically viable or philosophically tenable. Thus John Rawls's putatively universal theory of justice has devolved into a chastened defense of "justice as fairness" as "political not metaphysical"; the pressure bearing down on this and similar accounts has transformed them from confident universalisms to humbled provincialisms, and they will certainly suffer further decay.[12]

Nonetheless, the recent historical pressures the secularist strategy has suffered are not its root problem; secularism faces deep conceptual problems, especially its construal of human autonomy

---

11. This is what gives United States Supreme Court jurisprudence on religion matters its odd air of profound incoherence and maddening blindness to that incoherence. For more on this see S. D. Smith 1995 and Thiemann 1996.
12. See Eberle 2002 and Rawls 1993. Even as so provincial, Rawls's account may be incoherent; see Gamwell 1995 and Weenar 1995. See also Orlie 1997.

✳

in dogmatically subjectivist terms, that stymie its response to pluralism as well. An ontology that forbids creation any real participation or communion in God has a hard time avoiding the conclusion that the world is fundamentally a collection of solitudes. This has direct effects on expectations for genuine engagement. Even the Connolly passage cited above suggests a despair of actually changing minds, a despair alluded to in his elegantly understated claim that we "are unlikely to be moved by argument or inspiration to embrace the same source," a claim that reveals that he intends not to help us understand how properly to engage one another, but rather to help us live with our different views, by recognizing that we "honor different moral sources" and by urging us stoically to "*affirm* this condition as a persistent condition of existence ... [in order] to respond to it without deep resentment" (2002a: xxii).[13] Such views manifest a despair of communicating across the chasm separating one person from another – a structural inability to imagine us crossing the boundaries isolating each of us, an inability that is conceptually as fundamental to the system as any phenomenological sense of the futility of such an effort.

Defenders of the secularist strategy have sought various forms of response to the problem; but in the end the best defenses simply come down to denials that the problem is real. (Because any real recognition would spell the end of the secularist strategy – even though not, of course, the reality of "secular" societies – this response is not surprising.) Most interesting, because most revealing, is the response that Jonathan Rauch calls "apatheism" (Rauch 2003). "Apatheism," for Rauch, is the view that one simply does not care what another's religious beliefs are. In effect this is a reassertion of a proposal for toleration that actually comes down to a sort of laissez-faire indifference, a willed ignorance and self-blinding concerning the other with whom one is engaged. Such are the straits to which an intellectual movement of several centuries' duration has been reduced.[14]

---

13. See xxiii: "Cultivate those elements in your faith that allow it to forge relations of presumptive generosity with others and ... to come to terms affirmatively with how human it is for others to contest specific dimensions that feel like the bedrock to you." For his picture of cognition and of the human's intellectual relation to it, see xxi.

14. See Sachedina 2001: 35 for a good criticism of this.

More subtle thinkers realize that such evasion is simply symptomatic of the problem it is meant to solve. As Melissa Orlie has
argued, "self and other, internal and external, are always inside one
another, even as our most common sense of group and individual
identity tends to obscure that fact" (1999: 143). Romand Coles has ✳
gone so far as to argue that we live in a "post-secularist" age, and
the recognition of the crisis of secularism has become something
like common knowledge in contemporary public culture, even
though many academics have yet to realize it.[15]

But pluralism challenges more than simply secularist toleration;
it challenges contemporary theology on theological grounds as well.
For Christian theology all questions of otherness are related to that
most basic otherness, that of God, and so must be seen as in part
manifestations of the challenge of divine otherness.[16] But much
modern theology cannot handle this challenge; modern understandings of self and world cannot easily accommodate this apparent divine otherness, as expressed in traditional theistic
affirmations.[17] In pluralism, what initially seems a contingent
political question is revealed to be a deep and inescapable metaphysical issue. As Oliver Davies has aptly put it, "In the modern
world our encounter with otherness begins not at the borders of the
self, but rather *within the self*, at the very core of our identity, and in a
way that challenges the self-possession of the subject" (2001: xvi).
Pluralism merely reminds us of this basic challenge, a challenge
that begins at home, in the challenge of the achievement of human
identity and community to any degree; to achieve such community,
we must find a more adequate response to the challenge of pluralism than secularist solutions allow us.[18] The challenge of pluralism
is thus an allegory for the broader and more basic challenge of
otherness; and we must face that challenge not because of historically contingent socio-political reasons, but for properly theological
ones.

If pluralism's challenge to modern theology is caused by such
theology's difficulties in thinking about the relationship between

15. See Coles 1997.
16. See Tracy 1991: 73–6, 95, and Barnes 2002.
17. See Tanner 1988.
18. See Lyotard 1989.

the self and the other, it is aggravated by such theology's tendency to take as its main interlocutor the fundamentally non-religious challenge of modern secularism, either as a rival which must be rejected, or as a fact which must be accepted. But secularism today requires at least massive rethinking, if not outright rejection, precisely because it cannot truly handle the deep challenge of pluralism. Thus much modern theology offers us little help in our problem because it accedes, implicitly or explicitly, to secularism's false resolution of the problem of pluralism, and engages in a project of theological reconstruction intended to render belief immune from challenge by other positions. Some of these projects express a (properly Christian) desire for universality, but can be so universal only at the cost of sacrificing their distinctness in order to enter the "public" realm; others express (again, a properly Christian) concern with affirming the distinctness of the Christian message, but assume that such affirmations entail the systematic rejection of engagement with non-Christians and a turn inward into the church. On either account, otherness is not so much included as occluded, not acknowledged but subsumed – or cast into the outer darkness. Such theological positions give us little help in confronting pluralism, because they are committed to ignoring it. We must do better.

The prospects for genuine dialogue

Theology should reframe its understanding of dialogue with others, rejecting as the dominant frame the apologetic debate with secular modernity, and replacing it with an understanding informed by dialogue with other major religious traditions. Here the primary task is not somehow besting the representatives of secularism, but instead deepening our understanding of the real meaning of each side's views. As Augustine DiNoia puts it, "if in modern theology the basic question was, how can a modern person believe this doctrine? then in postmodern theology the basic question has become, how can the deep intelligibility of this doctrine be exhibited?" (1990: 516). If we seek a theology that will help us understand the consequences of genuine engagement with others, we should look not to the apologetic debates with modern

Western secularism, but to the encounter between Christianity and the other "world religions."[19]

This does not mean that Christians should shun modern atheists or agnostics. They should continue to engage them, as allies and as conversation partners. But such engagements should not set the basic frame within which Christians understand the project of engaging others more generally. Often the grounds on which secularists are best engaged are cramping and narrow for Christians. But they are cramping and narrow for others too. Most of the others whom Christians will engage are devout religious believers; secularists, of various stripes, are a minority. For the sake of their full range of interlocutors, Christians ought not allow themselves to grow too facile with the constricted discourse that secularists find most comfortable. In engaging other religious traditions, the interlocutors meet on essentially equal terms: each brings complex and quite contestable metaphysical, axiological, and anthropological convictions to the conversation; each can recognize that their views can be intelligibly challenged; and all are vividly aware that they may well learn something from the other. Here the encounter can be a genuine encounter, and not the fundamental indifference to one another (or the meticulous avoidance of one another) urged by secularists.[20]

But "dialogue" as it is usually understood is insufficient. Contemporary accounts of interreligious dialogue are still dominated by a tired trio of options – namely, "exclusivism," "inclusivism," and "pluralism" – which are themselves Procrustean categories transferred from modern theology's debate with Western secularists on to interreligious dialogue. Such projects do not engage in genuine dialogue with other positions so much as construct arguments that preemptively deny the need for such dialogue. "Exclusivism" explicitly refuses such dialogue, and asserts the irrelevance of other religions; however, "inclusivism" and "pluralism" equally attempt to be "open" to alternative positions, only to stiff-arm the genuine risk of dialogue in favor of remaining within their own conceptual schemes. Inclusivists claim that other religions should be understood

---

19. And, indeed, it can apply to the global ecumenical dialogue as well; see Irvin 1994: 173.
20. I have learned much here from conversations with Paul Griffiths, and from Novak 1989.

as saying in different (and less adequate) ways what Christians truly say and so are only superficially different; pluralists, on the other hand, assert that, just as Christian inclusivists claim that all are "anonymous Christians," so in fact all are anonymous pluralists.[21] What each does is deny that in the encounter with the other, the other may offer a word to the self that the self may need to hear. These positions do not really respond to the challenge of religious pluralism, but attempt to avoid and thereby sterilize it.

Yet each has some merit. Exclusivism acknowledges the distinctiveness of Christian claims, inclusivism recognizes the universality of Christian claims, and pluralism affirms that differences between religions relativize every religion's claims. In a sense, then, each position expresses a distinct theological virtue: exclusivism expresses faith in the truth of Christianity, inclusivism expresses hope in the ultimate truth of Christianity, and pluralism expresses a humble charity for those in other religions. What is lacking in each is any accommodation of the necessity of the other virtues.

Fortunately new approaches have begun to emerge. Following philosophers such as Alasdair MacIntyre and Charles Taylor, thinkers like Michael Barnes, J. A. DiNoia, Paul J. Griffiths, and Mark Heim exhibit how genuine interreligious dialogue can proceed, and thereby synthesize the insights of the accounts described above in a harmonious whole.[22] Their work rejects meta-theoretical debate in favor of the concrete give and take of particular conversations; they recognize, as David Tracy puts it, that "dialogue itself is first a practice ... before theories on dialogue or conclusions on the results of dialogue are forthcoming" (1991: 76). They recognize difference, acknowledge the reality of very different traditions making conflicting claims to truth, and affirm the necessity of engaging these conflicting claims in rich and systematic argument. They confirm that the challenge of pluralism cannot be dissolved by philosophical or theological fiat, but demands engagement. These accounts all encourage and develop genuine interreligious dialogue

21. And so pluralism signifies, as John Milbank has put it, the "total obliteration" of particularity and the victory of Western universal (read: corporate) McReason. See 1990a: 175. For a positive proposal in line with the critical perspective taken by Milbank here, see Tanner 1993.

22. See especially DiNoia 1993, Griffiths 1991, and Heim 1995. See also Rescher 1993.

with the (explicit or implicit) intention of advancing understanding, ✳
both of self and of other, for all parties involved.[23] They accommodate all three theological virtues within one system as a way of
addressing the challenges of interreligious dialogue. They accept
(with charity) the distinctness of various positions, they acknowledge (with hope) the truth claims of each, and yet they still affirm
(in faith) their own position as containing salvific truth. But these
positions are not simply better answers to the same questions;
rather, they transform our vision of the problem, depicting it not as
a resolvable puzzle, but as an ongoing debate. The positions serve
not as conclusions, but as first moves in a debate that is only
eschatologically terminable. They do not tell us how to defuse the
dangers of religious pluralism, but rather show us how to go about
finding out what religious pluralism means.

The most theologically well-developed such account is that of
Michael Barnes, who begins from the assumption that dialogue is
theologically important and goes on to explore the implications of
that claim for the theological project and Christian life more
broadly. Dialogue provides us with a new way of learning about
God: "The question for a theology of dialogue is not how the
otherness revealed at the heart of selfhood can be synchronised into
a more or less grand strategy, but how, more radically and yet more
humbly, a certain passivity in the face of the other is to be recog-
nised as *intrinsic* to the Christian vocation itself" (2002: 129). But this
passivity is not the helplessness of the victim but the hopefulness of
the recipient of gifts; passivity before others is rooted in passivity
before the Lord.

The lesson of such work extends beyond formal interreligious
dialogue, and speaks to the way any theological inquiry should go
forward today. Theological inquiry needs a *metanoia* from a stance
that is defensive, apologetic, and finally concerned with clear and
distinct boundaries, to a necessarily dialogical and impure mode of
theologizing. While appreciating differences as needful, we also
must find ways genuinely to have real engagement, real conversation; and such a project will always find commonalities beyond (but

23. This is not the only way to read these thinkers; for example, Francis X. Clooney
uses DiNoia to develop a *collectio*, a "reading together" of two traditions (for
Clooney, Hinduism and Christianity) which appropriates one (the Hindu) for
the purposes of the latter (the Christian) – see Clooney 1992: 21.

not necessarily before) the differences. We must remain well aware
of the temptation narcissistically to project oneself upon the other;
but we keep aware of that temptation in order better to pursue, as
part of our authentic project, the task of finding the other in oneself. Theology is always an "impure" practice, one that works over a
given set of materials, which one can modify but which cannot be
wholly replaced by another language altogether.[24]

Understanding dialogue in this way entails both reinterpreting
the theological status of such dialogue and reframing the character
of our engagement in it. On a practical level, it suggests that we
reconceive dialogue not so much as speaking but as more fundamentally a form of listening, of hearing, of receiving. "Dialogue"
looks quite different if it is organized around a primary act of listening rather than speaking. Speaking is important, of course, but
in our world what we most palpably lack is not more noise, but
silence. Perhaps dialogue should be understood most fundamentally
as not about "us" speaking to "them," or about all of us talking, but
about all participants listening, both to one another and to one's
own voice. It may be surprising who we, and others, turn out to be.[25]

More profoundly still, speaking in properly theological terms, this
loving passivity before the Lord is the passivity of one who has faith
and hope, virtues that should characterize all our dealings during
the world. Barnes puts it well: "If it is the case that the hope, which
the act of facing the other inspires, returns Christians to the anarchic – the 'beginninglessness' – roots of their own faith in Moses's
encounter with the God of the Covenant at Sinai, can we not speak
of Christ as present, if not in the face of the other, then in the *act*
of facing?" (2002: 238). We see in dialogue and in the exchange
that it enables the possibility of communion, albeit proleptically as

24. The longing for such purity is the premier temptation of so-called "Yale
school" theology; while it focuses on the systematic and expository tasks of
theology in a salutary way, at times it is tempted towards a narcissitic and
defensive solipsism of this sort, in which exposition is ultimately indifferent to
otherness because of an overriding defensiveness and anxious commitment to
purity. There are deep theological matters at issue here: yes, theology does put
new wine in new wineskins, but God's work does have a historical continuity
from creation to eschaton; to claim otherwise is to practice a Gnostic method if
not profess Gnostic principles. For models of undefensive theology see Tanner
1997 and R. Williams 1999. See also Jenson's criticism of George Lindbeck in
1997: 18–20.

25. See R. Williams 1999: 332 and Muers 2004.

a foretaste of the kingdom of God. Dialogue is, then, the core condition of the human being *coram Deo*; in the encounter with the
other, that is to say, is more than a whiff of the day of judgment; and
our conversion to welcoming the other is in part the change from
our own seeking of justice to our own seeking of fellow lovers. So
understood, the encounter with the other should not be governed
by cringing fear at imminent prosecutorial judgment, but by overwhelming gratitude and joy at being received and accepted on the
basis of a merit not our own.

Following Chapter 2, this approach can be expanded into a systematic theological proposal regarding engagement in general, the
challenge of living with others *simpliciter* – connected with a picture
of God, the world, and ourselves – in order to offer it the greatest
purchase on the practices that inform our lives. Most fundamentally
we should interpret the challenges of life together as the challenges
facing the achievement of any community, and most fundamentally
Creation's community with God. If we look more deeply, we see
therein the kernel of the vision of the Beloved Community, the
kingdom of God, of which all human community today is but a
shadow and towards which all human community today points.
That is, we see in dialogue, and in the encounter with the other that
dialogue assumes, a proleptic foretaste of the kingdom of God. The
remainder of this chapter explains this vision.[26]

From engagement to communion

The challenge of pluralism confronts theology as both a contingent socio-historical problem and a basic problematic essential to
the theological tradition. Recent accounts of how to respond to
religious pluralism greatly assist our attempts to construct a theological response to the challenge of pluralism in general; but in order
genuinely to understand and comprehensively to accommodate the
full dimensions of such a response, we need a systematic theological
account. The Augustinian tradition offers great resources for this
project because of its conviction of God's absolute immanence to and

26. Augustine is not the exclusively adequate source, or obviously superior over all
    possible alternatives; for a position not explicitly Augustinian that resonates
    with my own, see Healey 2000.

absolute transcendence of creation, and its conversionist theology, which understands that the love of God is at best only partially and provisionally appropriated in any human life during the world. Together these elements undergird a vision of community which sees our encounters with one another during the world as proleptic figurings of the coming eschatological communion. Until then, we live in eschatological suspense; because of both our perspective and the structure of the time-bound world, redemption and damnation remain open questions until the end times.

This eschatologically conversionist worldview decisively informs Augustine's understanding of the human subject in its relations to others. Chapter 1 argued that the human is literally eccentric, with its center of gravity "outside" itself – or rather, that that "outside" has been *inside* all along. So Augustine presses dialectic to its most radical point, suggesting that the self is itself perhaps a dialectic, a dialectic between itself and God. Hence, all fallen creatures are fallen not so much from God (as they could not exist were they so to fall), but rather from themselves. One basic (perhaps *the* most basic) description of sin is self-division, and conversion is not so much the reunion of two separate entities as it is the reconciliation of the self to itself, its acceptance of its relation to its source.

 This Augustinian account sees conversion as partly a matter of growing into a new knowledge of difference – a new knowledge of what separates humans from one another. In becoming something new, one understands one's previous beliefs differently, and may (and indeed *ought to*) thereby come to a deeper awareness of and sensitivity to the differences separating persons from one another. But this conversion is fully realized only when one grasps it within a larger theological frame, as developing the dispositions necessary to reorient our loves (and thus our lives) toward God; hence the changes effected by that new knowledge of this-worldly differences both reflect and partially embody the more fundamental theological conversion of the self towards right relation to God. This is a conversion from a zero-sum picture of justice as fundamentally securing our separation from one another to a picture of justice as infused with love.[27] The return to

27. While this "justice versus love" contrast could be taken in anti-Jewish ways, it should not be so read: the "justice" transcended is a fallen justice, what appears as justice to those whose fundamental desire is to *avoid* being judged.

right relation with God, and the elimination of untoward differences between God and humans (and among humans as well), are thus accomplished not by shunning other humans, but by engaging them; not by turning away, but by turning towards. Conversion does not draw humans out of the world; rather it puts them more fully, and more properly, *into* it.

There is a real irony here. Many people think of converts as zealots. And certainly there is something of the anxiety of the new member of the club that floats in the air around new believers, as the magician's smoke lingers after the trick is done. But such zealotry does not properly reflect the new belief; rather it is a dangerous mixture of two things. First, it reflects the kind of obsessive focus that the new lover feels for the object of his or her affections; one is intoxicated by one's new faith. Second, it reveals a sinful anxiety that one is not "really" a proper believer – an anxious fervor to reassure oneself of one's grasp on the truth given the recent seismic shifts in one's existential self-understanding. The former can be expected to fade over time; but the latter may be more persistent, and is fundamentally an escapist temptation, a desire totally to renounce who you were "before." But such renunciation is an incoherent temptation that must be resisted; maturity leads one to see one's life as an integrated whole of a sort (such is one story of *confessiones*).[28] True conversion should make you more open, more vulnerable to the world. But of course such maturity is rarely realized, and those rare cases, only partially; so this conversion is not in this life accomplished, but always just being begun.

Given all this, "engagement" of a certain sort is a theological imperative, and Augustine's work enables us to understand the theological significance of the fact of pluralism – understood as the mutually conflicting truth claims of the self and the other – as a facet of the broader and more basic problem of otherness itself. Augustine's own use of dialogue is well documented. He discerned in pagan civilization truths that prefigured the Gospel "seeds of reason" present due to the inescapable relation of all humans to God, and thus as always already Christian truths; and so he demanded, and

"Justice" here is reducible to desire to be *left alone*. And Augustine will identify, diagnose, and refuse this picture of justice without mercy.

28. See Mathewes 2003.

practiced, genuine and thoroughgoing investigation of the pagan world to see what it could teach him.[29] But his work allows us to go beyond these relatively common affirmations by connecting such appropriation with the broader question of otherness. This tradition can affirm that the Christian church can in fact engage in genuine conversation with others, in a way that leads to deeper under-standing for all parties involved. This tradition can teach us the full meaning of, and the proper response to, the challenge of pluralism. Indeed, it helps us not only construct an account of the challenge of pluralism; it also helps us identify, critique, and resist our tendencies to want to avoid it.

This can be seen in one of the most ambitious attempts to appropriate Augustine's thought in decades, namely, John Milbank's audacious and impressive project. But ironically, Milbank's work is less adequate as a constructive response to the challenge of pluralism, in part because, paradoxically enough, it still accepts the horizon of options proposed by the "secular" reason it disparages. By describing the limitations of Milbank's project, I mean both to affirm his critique and critique his affirmations, to take his work beyond its own horizon, and show what a more thoroughly Augustinian response to pluralism requires.

Milbank sounds like Connolly when he claims that it is "better to replace 'dialogue' with 'mutual suspicion'," and understand con-versation as nothing but ideology critique (1990a: 190). Milbank seems captive to Connolly's despair of the possibility of genuine engagement, of changing minds. Like Connolly, Milbank's project seems in part effectively to want to help us explain why we need not engage one another, rather than allow us to do just that. But the difficulty with this is the manifest historical reality that dialogue *has* taken place at times, and, while modern interpretations of dialogue may be irremediably tainted with rationalist and totalizing assumptions, that is no reason to jettison the possibility of dialogue *tout court*. Furthermore, his own practice tells against such a rejec-tion, for whatever else one says about his work, one cannot deny it is argumentative; and he is obliged to offer some sort of account of what goes on in our heads when we become convinced by his

---

29. On the "use" of pagan work for Christian purposes, see *DDC* 2.19.29–40.61.

arguments. Hence he does not so much reject dialogue as refuse to theorize it.

The problem here seems to be rooted in his implicit agreement with his secular postmodern interlocutors, that reality is in fact marked by radical incommensurability – that reality itself is a collection of alterities, fractured into regions without an ultimate enframing reality. (Chapter 5 discusses this more.) Of course Milbank's basic aim is to oppose this belief, and offer instead the Christian "meta-narrative" as the integrating queen of the sciences yet again, able to "place" all other discourses. But in fact, at least when he discusses the possibility of argument and dialogue, he seems to forget this insistence and instead to accept a picture of human thinking as inescapably parochially local.

His agreement with this picture seems deeply connected to a dimension of his proposal which may cripple attempts at dialogue. This is his rhetorical insistence that the basic problem of modernity is its *nihilism*, its worship of death. For him, modern thinkers, and modernity itself, are not properly understood to be affirming some genuine goods, albeit in ways that overvalue them; rather, modern thinkers are best understood as affirming nothingness, death, the abyss.[30] There is certainly historical precedent for making this claim in the tradition, stretching back at least to Paul. Furthermore, it is hard to deny that affirmation of death has an explicit role in some of the more grotesque modern political and philosophical movements. And there is something to be said for arguing that the basic structure of sin is itself nihilistic – affirming the nothing that is not God rather than assenting to the infinity that is God.[31] But Milbank emphasizes this and ignores the traditional connection between nihilism and idolatry. Idolatry helps here because it renders sinful desires intelligible to us as distorted desires for proper ends, thereby establishing tendrils of intelligibility between "we" who have accepted grace and thus God, and "they" who have not done so; this troubles our desire to identify with one side over the other. But Milbank's exclusive rhetoric of nihilism severs any such links, and so he cannot talk to his opponents, he can only talk about them.

30. His collaborator Catherine Pickstock expresses this, more starkly still, as necrophilia (see Pickstock 1997).
31. See Mathewes 2001a.

Milbank's account is not fundamentally wrong; it simply remains too tied to modern theology's conversation with secularism to help us directly with the challenge of pluralism and otherness. Reinhard Hütter's critique of him as "not Augustinian enough" is correct (Hütter 1992: 116). He focuses on the apologetic Augustine, as evidenced by *Theology and Social Theory*'s almost exclusive attention to *de civitate Dei*. But this is unfortunate, for that is the one text Augustine shaped with a non-Christian audience explicitly in mind. Milbank's work would have been better served with a more comprehensive vision of Augustine's entire project, and especially his account of the way of the human "into" God – topics taken up especially in *confessiones* and *de Trinitate* – which would entail a more complicated theological anthropology.

There seem to be two things holding him back at this point. One is insufficient attention to the self's messy complexity. The other is his implicit assent to the modernist "either/or" picture of rationality, its overly stark dichotomy of "objectivism" and "relativism" (R. J. Bernstein 1983). As to the first, Milbank seems reluctant to develop his theological anthropology in an Augustinian fashion, to warrant a limited but important role for argument. Augustinian anthropology insists that "suspicion" reinforces the need for genuine dialogue; it advocates an approach which subjects all particular claims to rationality, including our own, to critique, but still recognizes – against all postmodern nihilistic resignation about truth – the need and capability for argument. This account depicts the self with a rich and complex inner life, a life which is plural at its heart, with the sinful self in conflict with itself and its God over the battlefield of its sinful will to self-disintegration and self-annihilation, the self struggling towards an (only eschatologically realized) integrity. Furthermore, even that integrity is realized only by ecstatic participation, through Christ and in the church, in the perichoretic communion of the Trinity.

As for rationality, he claims that "no fundamental account [of society or history], in the sense of something *neutral*, *rational*, and *universal*, is really available" (380, emph. added). But why are these three necessarily associated? Why not claim a universal reason that is *not* neutral? (In fact, what would it mean for reason to *be* neutral in the first place?) The problem latent in the fact that different people claim different things as "obvious" can be accommodated (on Augustine's account) by acknowledging the importance of the noetic fall of the mind and the distorting effects of sin on our belief-forming activities; we must engage in certain practices in order to become rational. Hence we can claim absolute, universal, and rational truth for Christianity, *and* privilege that discourse, *and* yet claim that we can (and must, when possible) still engage others in dialogue, which may eventuate in real argument – even if not in some putatively "neutral" court of appeal, still in a genuinely dialogical way.

In sum, Milbank's work only partially escapes the constraining modernist categories it condemns. Because of this, as powerful as it is, it does not adequately comprehend the viability and value of argument, and the durability and flexibility of the concept of truth, and is led towards an unfortunate and anachronistic "aestheticism" about truth which simply reproduces the "inverted mirror image" (MacIntyre 1988: 353) of the modern understandings of truth and reason he aims to oppose.[32] His project, for all its power as critical diagnosis, does not offer much constructive help for a theology of engagement; it is too apocalyptically impatient to take the time necessary to develop such a theology.

To do better, we need a more complex picture of the self, one that depicts the self as always already involved in dialogue. We also need a finer-grained depiction of dialogue, one attentive to its theological relevance, than Milbank provides. There are resources for such a project. Most importantly, Oliver Davies, in his magisterial *A Theology of Compassion*, has developed a systematic picture of selfhood as dialogical. That work is premised on the insight driving this chapter, namely that we need a theology that enables genuine dialogue – one that, as Davies has aptly put it, "must in the first

32. Recently, he has claimed that "we should only be convinced by rhetoric where it persuades us of the truth, but on the other hand truth *is* what is persuasive, namely what attracts and does not compel" (1997: 250), but he does not develop this thought; and by the time of *Truth in Aquinas* (2001) Milbank and his co-author Catherine Pickstock describe our participation in truth in ontological, liturgical and eschatological categories, as opposed to immanentist and individualist epistemological ones. They depict faith and reason as "phases within a single extension," a single mode of human intellectual relation with the world and God (2001: 21). Yet the connection between this picture and that offered in *Theology and Social Theory* remains obscure; and he continues to focus on nihilism to the detriment of idolatry, thus continuing to leave unclear exactly how humans ought to be conceived as always participating, in some way, however perverted, in the truth.

place accommodate the specifically *dialectical* encounter with the other" (2001: xvii). Davies himself proposes a theological anthropology that can conceptually accommodate the possibility and reality of such encounters. He bases this anthropology on a phenomenological analysis of compassion, upon which he builds a general picture of the self as fundamentally disposed towards engagement with the other – an engagement which is not an aggressive grasping of the other, but rather a mode of kenotic openness and even vulnerability before them. One might be tempted to say that this mode of kenotic openness "completes" the self, but Davies cannily does not give in to this temptation, for he is wary of any teleological conclusion to selfhood. Instead he says that through this engagement, "the self undergoes a transformation ... a movement from 'existence' to 'being,' which is a heightened or intensified state of existence," really a "transfiguration" (45).[33]

Davies's proposal is primarily concerned with engaging recent philosophical trends in order to articulate a general "kenotic ontology": a way of speaking about being that understands the desire for communion – for encountering, engaging, and reconciling with othernesses – to be fundamental to the nature of reality itself. But we can develop it for our purposes, in order to discover what sorts of practices, and modes of engagement, such an understanding of kenotic selfhood enables for engaging others. For this task, Augustine's work may help because he grasps the central fact of human existence: that we are "possessed" by a divine other, that we are in an ineliminable relationship with God. Of course, in sin God remains "within" the self, but the self is, in a sense, "outside" of itself; and the corruption of will renders the self helpless to save itself. (Hence *conf.* 10 is, among other things, a critique of the epistemological optimism of his earlier soliloquies and dialogues.) Yet even as sinners, revolting against our reliance on God to be, to act, and to know, we are nonetheless absolutely dependent on God. Indeed we "possess" our being by participating in God, and will properly receive it only at the eschaton, when we participate fully in the body of Christ, and thereby in the *perichōrēsis* of which our engagements today are but shadows.

---

33. Davies suggests that this kenosis is infinite; see Davies 2001: 220–1.

What does it mean, both metaphysically and practically, to say that the self is not simply its own possession, but is possessed by, and participates in, another? That question drove Augustine's theological investigations throughout his career, and we discussed it in depth in Chapter 1. It is not visible in *de Trinitate*, which aims to help believers dialectically grow in understanding the divine through a deepening understanding of the self, and vice versa; a movement of deepening understanding which leads to the realization that the self's proper mode of worldly being is always one in relation to, and imitative of, the divine Trinity.[34] As Lewis Ayres has said, for Augustine, "the human person is in the image of God when she or he has a life centered around the attempt to discern how a Christian must live in order to fulfill God's command of love. Through making progress in such a life – a progress which includes lapses from which one recovers – one comes to understand the Trinitarian mystery more closely" (1995: 269). The whole of *de Trinitate* is meant to teach "the education of desire," to educate agents' desires towards right love of God, and to teach agents that their desires, however crooked, have always already had God as their proper final end all along. Engagement with others is not simply an optional extra on this account; reaching out to others is in a fundamental way just what it is to live a properly flourishing human life. Indeed, to reach out to others is inescapable; in some basic way we just *are* that reaching out.

Engagement as proleptic communion

All that said, it is not enough simply to endorse dialogue. The description of engagement as "dialogue" is insufficient; we should redefine it as a flawed, provisional, proleptic participation in the body of Christ, and through Christ in the divine *perichōrēsis* that is our ultimate destiny. This is our last task in this chapter, to show how this understanding of dialogue can be converted to a genuine Augustinian interpretation of, and response to, the challenge of pluralism.

The virtues of engagement

Augustine's theology offers an account of selfhood rich enough to encourage the kind of engagement we need, in no small

---

34. *De Trin.* is in this way a recapitulation of *conf.* 10. See O'Donnell 1994: 234.

part by arguing that such engagement is unavoidable for real human life. But we must still construct the details of an Augustinian account of engagement in our fallen world. Such engagement will be fundamentally both epistemological and moral, as right understanding and right action go hand in hand. What Ayres calls "the education of desire" requires participation in practices that develop traits and characteristics that advance the process of conversion. In such practices, engagement can play a critical role. Indeed, engagement is a requirement of the Christian life as such; openness to others, to "the stranger," identifies the Christian community as that place where the good news is brought to, and received by, an estranged world.[35] Through describing this project, theology plays a direct and essential role in forming and informing our moral life; more particularly, the doctrine of the Trinity plays an internal role in understanding moral life properly, especially as seen through its manifestation in the three theological virtues.[36]

Because anthropological and epistemological issues illumine these moral concerns, we first explored the former above. For Augustine, the Word is in the world and in ourselves, even if we do not fully recognize it; so we use engagement, in all its forms from the loving communion of marriage to the dialogical community of debate, in order more fully to grasp that Word and appropriate those capacities that make the "arguments" (conceived broadly) that mark all such communion during the world ultimately superfluous. On this account, reason is both an immanent reality (as something we have partial knowledge of) and a transcendental ideal (as something whose final coherence yet escapes us). One lives in a faith, not based in any belief in one's own superiority, but grounded in a certainty that that faith offers genuinely salvific truth. We employ this (true) reason in faith, in the hope that we will one day meet it, as love, face to face.

It is thus a theological truth that the self must be open to engagement with others; for, since the self constantly requires further conversion from sin in this life, absolute closure is itself

35. Here I build on Jones and Fowl 1991: 73-4.
36. Furthermore, it is not only the case that the doctrine of the Trinity illuminates the distinct pattern of Christian ethics; the converse is equally true; we understand theological doctrines to the degree that we weave them into our everyday lives. Thus the sort of "application" proposed here is internal to our "theoretical" understanding of the Trinity. For two helpful discussions of this, see Pinches 1987 and L. G. Jones 1990.

absolutely closed off for humans. All understanding is provisional, open to revision.[37] But the distinctly Christian character of this affirmation makes it something more than mere "toleration," strictly speaking: it is an imperative for humble dialogical engagement that would seem problematically invasive to most proponents of toleration.[38]

This theological imperative for engagement is grounded on the fact that the transcendent yet immanent presence of the *Logos* in the world is tightly tied to the immanent practices in which humans engage in living out their lives within the Christian narrative. Here the life lived ascetically in seeking to inhabit the virtues becomes vitally important. Because dialogical engagement finds its place within the work of the Christian community's ongoing conversion – specifically, the ecclesiological and soteriological pattern of developing the theological virtues in community with others – it finds its place in Christian life *simpliciter*. Thus our practices of engagement are understood by Augustinians as exercises of the theological virtues.

The Augustinian tradition assumes that Christianity is true, though we do not, short of the eschaton, fully understand its meaning(s); furthermore, dialogical engagement reveals to the theologian both something about her interlocutor's position, and something about Christian faith. It either demonstrates how that other position is incorrect, or it reveals how that position already agrees with Christianity or reveals something new whose insights may aid Christian faith; for Christians, by demonstrating their faith's ability to meet such critiques, this dialogue either reveals resources latent in the faith which allow it to meet critiques, or it enriches the theologian's (and, by extension, the community's) understanding of the faith's manifest resources by revealing something of the depth of its insights. In fact, in any particular dialogue, all four things can happen, and often do. Thus, Augustine claimed:

> No doubt many matters pertaining to the catholic faith are not only more diligently investigated when they are attacked by the feverish

---

37. Hence much of Augustine's writing – especially his commentaries, but also the later books of *conf.* and much of *de Trin.* – is in the *subjunctive*, the conditional mode. Especially given the rhetorical commonplaces of his time, this is remarkable. I am indebted to Paul J. Griffiths for this insight. See also Cavadini 2004.
38. See Fodor 1995, esp. 20.

> restlessness of the heretics, but are more clearly understood and more fervently expounded for the sake of defending them against these enemies. Thus the controversy stirred up by the adversary affords occasion for instruction. (*DCD* 16.2)[39]

Thus, dogmatic exposition, which begins by assuming the truth of Christianity, engages others both for their own sake, and in order to deepen one's own understanding of one's own faith.

The operative virtue for dogmatic exposition is the virtue of faith. For Augustine, faith is a foundational premise: it is the touchstone by which one can finally claim to be speaking the truth. Dogmatic engagement with other traditions is made possible, indeed valuable, by the appropriation of faith. Again, this is not arrogance but *arrogantia fidei*, a confidence not in oneself, but in the tradition to which one gives one's putative and partly incomprehending assent. Faith motivates us dogmatically to engage others, because it tells us that we have some explicit purchase on the truth, and should deepen that purchase and offer it to others. In dialogue, dogmatic statements function as starting–points for inquiry, not as conclusions susceptible only to acceptance or rejection. In such inquiry, one rediscovers the distinctness of one's tradition, its uniqueness as a message of truth in a world riddled with falsity. In the courage of faith, we know our place as the distinct place of the Christian truth.

But faith cannot be proven but only confessed, and thus the dogmatic form is always complemented and supported by the confessional motive. Confession recognizes that the self does not so much grasp the truth as it is grasped by it; if in the dogmatic form of inquiry we claim an apprehension of the truth, through confession we acknowledge our imperfect grasp on it – or, rather, its imperfect grasp on us. Here the activity is seen fundamentally as inquiry and not as defensive, preemptive dogmatic proclamation; confession is the activity of the soul humbled by the taste of truth it has had, and hungry for more (see also H. R. Niebuhr 1941: 21–5).

In confessional mode, engagement with others does not become arrogantly condescending or hostile, but rather seeks ways to make sense both of how people may disagree and of why one remains confident of the truth to which one witnesses. To demonstrate this

---

39. For a similar argument from a different source see Aquinas, *Summa Theologiae*, Ia.1.8.

"dogmatic humility" we can borrow, perhaps surprisingly, from John Milbank's discussion of ontological disagreements on the analogy of hearing different musics. When we confront people with radically divergent ontological assumptions from our own, Milbank argues, we must confess that there is no way, at present, to settle our disagreement. We cannot communally determine whether we live in chaos or in an only seemingly chaotic, but actually historically *endless* baroque harmony, with many near-resolutions and false endings, which will realize closure only in the eschaton. Our faith that we live in the latter is ultimately unfounded, in the sense that we begin from it and can offer no proof for it (though of course we have evidence for it, as do those who assume the alternative) (1990b: 279).[40] We can insist that our interlocutors are missing the point of the music, that their timing is off, though all we have done in this is reached the proper level of profundity in the debate; for it is not a matter simply of propositional coherence or referentiality, but of a more fundamental matter of attunement to the world.

How will our recognition of the profundity of this disagreement not lead us back towards the kind of Stoic resignation and despair of which we accused putative "postmoderns," like Connolly and Milbank himself, earlier in this chapter? What we find we need is latent precisely in our accusation against them, of despair: we need hope. And indeed the virtue most visible in the practice of confession is hope. For Augustine, hope is an eschatological anticipation of the fulfillment of the soul's desires and directs the soul's movement. Hope is thus comforting, in part because it is always correlated with humility: inquiry into the meaning of the truths that one always only partially apprehends is both propelled by humility, by the recognition of one's ignorance and misunderstanding, and drawn forward by hope, by the comforting confidence that further inquiry will lead to deeper understanding. In confession, one learns more fully the flawed and finite condition one shares with all humans. In the humility of hope, we know our place as the common human place of finite and fallible understanding.[41]

---

40. For an interesting critique of Milbank's musical metaphor, see Skerrett 2003: 801.
41. A good example is Milbank 1990a: 190: in encounters with other traditions, we should "expect to constantly receive Christ again" and so advance "the continual work of conversion." See also Schlabach 1994.

Yet hope also disturbs us. It forbids us from turning away from disagreements that seem interminable. It refuses us the false consolation of resignation and despair. And it does so for the same reasons it comforts us – for it tells us that more is coming, that the new is not yet fully delivered to us, that we cannot come to conclusions yet – even the conclusion that some arguments are absolutely inconclusive. In this way our recognition of the profundity of our disagreements with one another does not anesthetize us to the fact that disagreement remains a problem, something that will one day be overcome; these disagreements, and how we have struggled in them, and against them, are part of the whole for which God will come to judge us.

Hence faith and hope, dogmatism and confessionalism, are complementary virtues for engagement. Dogmatic faith is necessary for one's self-understanding, as one must believe something firmly; yet it is tempered by the confession of one's all too limited understanding, a confession made only in the hope that one can deepen that understanding. One should be both confident in the truth of one's claims, and humble regarding one's understanding of those same claims, even as one is making them. One engages others convinced that one's message is genuinely important for them, and yet recognizing that through the engagement with them one will learn from them, further deepening one's own understanding. Honesty about both oneself and the message one has grasped requires both faith and hope, dogmatism and confessionalism, confidence and humility.

Such engagement is our basic mode of existence, even within ourselves, between the believer and the unbeliever within all of us – or between the unbeliever that is still too much us, and Christ in our soul.[42] This conviction warrants us in engaging others in both dogmatic confidence (about our own beliefs, and about the relevance of those beliefs to others) and confessed humility (about the frailty of our own understanding, and the possible assistance of others). But this dialogue is finally judgment: if, as Michael Barnes puts it, "God is both host and guest" therein, we experience that dialogue as a judgment, eschatologically deferred (2002: 192). Augustine's most

---

42. Or perhaps not; the other way to see this is as the overcoming of all dialectical reason, as Milbank has argued (1990b: 389, 404–5), though I think the dispute here is a false one. Milbank may too tightly associate the idea of "dialectic" with Hegelianism.

basic conviction (and not his alone) is that this dialectic within the believer is fundamental to the human ontological situation as fallen children of God – both participants in, and dissenters from, the truth which testifies to itself in our inmost hearts, people who will one day stand before God naked, unadorned, awaiting judgment. Perhaps that judgment is what we hear now, in the silences after we have spoken. In this way Augustine's account manages not only to accommodate the broadly outgoing energies captured traditionally in evangelism, it also explains how those energies should be inhabited during the world, before the eschatological accomplishment of their purposes, and how those energies are themselves modes of our proleptic participation in the last judgment, the final naming of reality for what it is, was, and always will be.[43]

Furthermore, our recognition that that eschatological accomplishment awaits us in the future means that, in this life, our engagements are characterized by the same eschatological longing that colors all aspects of Christian life. Thus this tradition's instigating motivation, and its expectation for what can be realized in the present and its hope for what will be accomplished in the future – in brief, the whole temporally extended understanding which it brings to its engagements – is decisively enframed eschatologically. In this eschatological waiting, the Augustinian tradition brings together its confidence and its humility under the form of *caritas*, the love of God. Because all the virtues are forms of *caritas* for Augustine, and especially as the love of neighbor is itself rooted in *caritas* (because only therein can one recognize the dignity of the neighbor as flowing from God's love for all creation), one finds that one's motives are wholly explicable only by recourse to that distinctly Christian term. It is only by the light of the love of the Triune God that the soul can come to engage otherness, and such engagement is the cognitive and conative appropriation of that divine *caritas* as it is always already moving in the soul's life.

All this works to warrant, indeed necessitate, a humbly confessed particularism. We should confess the dogma we hold, and our material affirmations should reinforce our formal procedures. We work from within Christian convictions, and both our motives and our basic premises are distinctly Christian; but the very confidence

43. See R. Williams 1999: 330.

with which we hold our beliefs, and our understanding of the epistemological implications of those beliefs, should make us always eager to engage other positions in dialogue. We are confident of the tradition's basic story: humanity is in self-dividing revolt from God, and God has become incarnate in Christ, and continues to act in the world in the Holy Spirit, in order to restore us to our proper end. Furthermore, our faith in this story entails that we see ourselves as at best understanding its meaning only in a mirror darkly; and this vision gives us a fundamentally Christian motive for engagement – *caritas* – a practice that synthesizes confession and dogmatism into a unitary yet triune action charged with faith, hope, and love.

How dialogue would proceed, and where it would lead

How would such dialogue proceed? It can happen in a number of different ways. One way would be for the tradition to recognize and attempt to engage an alternative tradition which puts a different "spin" upon many of the same fundamental propositions it affirms. In such a situation, the tradition can learn something of the power of its own position; and it can teach some of the more obscure, but nonetheless entailed, implications of those propositions. Much modern apologetics is the attempt to do this, and it continues as part of the broader projects of thinkers such as Charles Taylor. Another way would be for the tradition to meet a fundamentally different position, one whose basic beliefs differ primordially from its own. In such situations, it would see a tradition so different from itself that it could learn something of the distinct meaning of its own position; and, from the strange face of its interlocutor, it might discover resources hitherto unknown within its own tradition, resources which it might do well explicitly to appropriate, if it could. These two positions seem to exhaust the possibilities, although there may be others.[44]

Such dialogical argument is not predictable *a priori*. For one to judge in which of these two categories a particular conversation

---

44. For a different but compatible approach, see Ian Markham's discussions of "assimilation, resistance, and overhearing" as three strategies for theological engagement (2003: 48–61).

belongs is a judgment properly, if always at best provisionally, made only by engaging in the conversation itself, and seeing where it leads. It may be that Buddhist–Christian dialogue, for example, will reveal a basic set of affirmations shared by both sides about the relation between self and ultimate reality, one which problematizes the reality of the self before ultimate reality (thus Hick 1990); or it may be that the dialogue reveals fundamental differences between the traditions about their basic affirmations about the constitution of persons (thus Griffiths 1991). Probably more than one of these lessons will be apparent; certainly Christian engagements with various exemplary modern secular Western thinkers reveals both deep continuities in affirmations about the worth of the individual (thus Taylor 1989), and fundamental differences in understandings of the human project (thus MacIntyre 1990; Plantinga 1992). Such complexity is no surprise, for in such conversations, both the ramified traditions of thought we inhabit and those we confront reveal themselves to be far more complex and rich sources for moral and metaphysical reflection than we can anticipate. Traditions contain multitudes. As Karl Barth famously wrote, "God may speak to us through Russian Communism, a flute concerto, a blossoming shrub, or a dead dog ... The boundary between the church and the secular world can still take at any time a different course from that which we think we discern" (Barth 1975: 55). In any event, it is only within and through such conversation that such discoveries can be made.

So understood, such engagements are internal to the theological project of deepening understanding. While some would label such discourse "merely apologetic," and insist on its basically "ancillary" or "subsidiary" function relative to the (proper) "internal" uses of such discourse, the Augustinian tradition denies that such a distinction between forms of discourse can be ultimately sustained. There is a properly theological reason for this: a large part of apologetics' internal use is precisely to help believers achieve a more adequate understanding of their faith. On this earth we are *all* too much unbelievers, seeing in a glass darkly, and there is no absolute chasm separating the kind of understanding available to believers and non-believers, because there is no absolute chasm – not yet – separating believers and non-believers. Hermeneutical accessibility has always been the ground of Christianity's putative

universality. Non-believers can come to a less superficial understanding of the Christian religion by removing misconceptions.
Apologetics is argumentative; but argument can be, and in dialogical charity it *is*, for both parties, a matter of deepening understanding.

This reveals some very interesting things about theology itself.
The theological project is not one of demonstration, of some final
quod erat demonstrandum; its purpose as *fides quaerens intellectum* precludes that as humanly attainable. Rather it is a process of growth
into the Christian faith, by necessity a dialogical process of discovering what it means to reproduce the pattern of Christ's life and
death (and, through God's grace, resurrection), and hence to come
to know God. We seek and find God only to discover that that discovery itself renews our desire to seek and find God in ever more
powerful ways. There is no need, however, to claim that only those
within the faith can grow in understanding; such a claim would
make conversion narratives impossible. Indeed, on the Augustinian
account, this is what all humans do in this life, and possibly in
the next.

Augustine's theology thus offers a response to the challenge of
pluralism that does not collapse into relativism or universalism.
Christians are distinguished from non-Christians, not simply by a
deeper understanding of the concepts of the Christian language,
but also because they actively engage in the church's life of more
fully appropriating the grace of Christ and making that grace
manifest to "the world." This is what it means to witness. Thus, for
such an apologetics, there is no formal difference between putatively religious communities and self-confessedly non-religious (or
irreligious) communities. The program remains the same: confront
interlocutors with as much common ground as you can, and use
that common ground to work towards a common understanding of
both worldviews. The greater the extent to which the worldviews
conflict – as long as the conflict leaves space for intelligible comparison – the better, the more clearly, you can delineate and
understand each.

To find such arenas of fruitful dialogue, we should look for
conceptual spaces (or moments) that provide Christians and their
neighbors – secular or otherwise – with sufficient common ground to
have a conversation, yet also provide an issue (or issues) sufficiently

in dispute to give their conversation a subject. Only in such arenas can apologetic discourse take place, and then only when both sides consider it sufficiently important and proper for such discourse to proceed. Such projects isolate topics of dispute, clarify the framework necessary for such disputes to have a genuine weight for both parties, and use the disputes to seek both to increase Christians' understanding of the commitments that should guide their lives and to inform both themselves and their interlocutors of why different, though perhaps apparently similar, commitments are antithetical to the Christian faith. Such engagements are fundamentally *ad hoc*, centrally meant to identify and compare the divergent anthropological and metaphysical assumptions supporting the two accounts, and then to see where that comparison takes us. Here the initial task is descriptive: it attempts to clarify the differences separating the two accounts. From such description normative claims may be derived, but for such claims to be redeemed the descriptive prolegomenon must first be engaged.[45]

Out of this, an authentic vernacular for genuine dialogue and cooperation can develop. But we should not delude ourselves into thinking that this vernacular perfectly translates our primary languages into an unobjectionable "neutral" third language. We need not a "moral Esperanto" but something like inter-traditional pidgins, semi-languages that enable us to interact on matters of common concern without deluding ourselves that the tongue we use in those moments could ever be our home. It would be like trying to live on a rickety rope-and-plank bridge, above an abyss of empty platitudes. (And we can also thus imagine a kind of "secularism" as a pidgin secularism.[46])

By calling it a "pidgin" we remind ourselves to avoid growing too comfortable with it. Our command of it should always remain awkward and halting, reminding us that we are speaking a broken language, a stop-gap, even though we speak it in order to reach some sort of community with others – so that we remember always that our attempts at such community, insofar as they seek to bring

---

45. See Griffiths's (1991) constraints on the NOIA principle, largely (though not exclusively) of a socio-political nature, Werpehowski 1986, and DiNoia 1993.
46. For a Jewish parallel, see David Novak's proposal that Jewish–Christian dialogue should seek not convergence but rather "significant overlappings" that respect the two traditions' autonomy (in 2000: 124).

us into communion without the explicit presence of God, stand under the judgment of Babel. Yet this is not an artificially fabricated difficulty; it is not as if we *could* easily speak in this language and are merely "pretending" to speak it poorly. If the language is properly understood, and properly used, if we are trying authentically to be the particular believers that we are, the difficulty is organically there.

Some will wonder why we are supposed to aim at failure – or at what, to them, looks disappointingly minimal. They will suggest that such a limited achievement is too constraining for us, and that somehow we should find some way of communicating smoothly between all such views. But why? Why should we assume that comfort is what we should reasonably expect, or what we should aim for? Maybe a level of awkwardness, of difficulty and confusion, of Babel-like vexation, is actually better for us, as it keeps in our minds the brokenness of our communion with each other without God. In engaging others, we should be reminded of our sin not only in our failings, but in our successes as well.

Furthermore, in so practically recognizing the difficulties in genuine communion, we acknowledge the distance yet to be traveled between the shadowy engagement we can have here and now and the real communion for which we see all such engagement longing. So even our challenges become spiritually productive for us, gesturing yet again at the difficulties between our dialogues here and our ultimate participation, through Christ and in the church, in the perichoretic communion that is our eschatological destiny.

Conclusion

Christian theology should understand the challenge of pluralism as a manifestation of the more theologically primordial challenge of otherness; seen in this context, recent works on religious pluralism are helpful but must be placed within a more systematic theological framework. Augustinian themes can help here, particularly regarding the centrality of conversion in inquiry and in the Christian life as a whole, and regarding the use of engaging with others as a means of conversion, for both one's interlocutors and oneself. Approaching the issue in this way transforms our vision of the problem we face. Just as the essential challenge is not properly pluralism but otherness, dialogue is best understood not simply epistemologically but theologically – within the framework of the Augustinian account of the theological virtues, and as one manifestation of our engagement with God. As the self is always already involved in dialogue, with itself and with God, dialogue with others is not a radical change, and can correct, enrich, and guide the self's development.

The above account of dialogue implies and in part elaborates an account of inquiry and rational discourse *simpliciter*, an account which says that such discourse is never in fact *simpliciter*, for two reasons. First, we are never purely believers, and hence we must always engage in dialogue, both within ourselves and with others, in order both to deepen our understanding and to be welcoming to others. Rational discourse is essentially an ongoing project that can never conclude, at least this side of the eschaton; the ascent to truth is never complete, and all claims to absolute certainty should be doubted. Against all Cartesian misprisions of Augustine, Augustinian epistemology is essentially ramshackle. Second, such discourse is not purely a formal matter, never strictly and abstractly theoretical, without ontological commitments; negatively, certain pictures of the world are ruled out for it, and positively, it must always take its place in a living history of (quite literally) passionate inquiry. Thus this is not a solipsistic sort of self-knowledge, for it is directly related to the degree of knowledge that one possesses about the, or some, "other." The degree to which one can understand the differences separating one from another is certainly an index of the depth of one's own self-knowledge, but it is also, and equally importantly, an index of the depth of one's faith, one's knowledge and love of God and, through God, of one's neighbor.

Knowing is inevitably contextual; to know at all, one must know one's place, the context within which one speaks. Knowing is also inevitably relational; each form of one's knowledge is related to every other, and all forms of knowledge relate the self to some other. For Christianity, this means that to know any other is finally to know the ultimate other – God. To deny, as many seem to desire to deny, that we must try to grasp the "radical otherness" of this most radical other, whenever and wherever we find it, in such a way as to render it not quite so radically other, is in effect a refusal to know, and, in the end, a failure of charity.

Yet if we accept this argument, how precisely should charity be manifest? With this chapter we have completed our sketch of a general theology of engagement. We now need to see how this program works itself out in more specific form in public engagement, how it may inform the development of a concrete strategy of participation in public life, a theology of citizenship. Part II of this book undertakes this project.

PART II

The liturgy of citizenship

Christians are not different from others in where they live, or how they talk, or in their lifestyle. They do not live in cities of their own, or speak a peculiar language, or follow an eccentric way of life. Their doctrine is not an invention of inquisitive and restless thinkers, nor do they put forward a merely human teaching, as some people do. They live where they happen to live, in Greek or barbarian cities; they follow local custom in clothing and food and daily life, yet they always give proof of their own citizenship. They live in their own homelands, but as resident aliens. They share everything as citizens, and endure everything as foreigners. Every foreign land is their fatherland, and yet for them every fatherland is a foreign land ... They busy themselves on earth, but their citizenship is in heaven. *Letter to Diognetus*

In this life our justice consists more in the forgiveness of sins than the perfection of virtues. Augustine, *de civitate Dei* 19.27

Introduction to Part II

Part I offered an Augustinian theology of engagement: a proposal that sees the human's basic desire to be one of ever deepening communion with God, a communion that is realized, in this world, not through a sinful detachment from the world, but rather through a proper engagement with it. Indeed, the fundamental human fault is nothing other than such escapism – detachment, retreat, contraction, *privatio* – the delusion that our embeddedness in creation is finally accidental to our "essential" nature. Not so: God is most fundamentally found not by escaping the self, the world, or other people, but by engaging them; such engagement shapes us in ways good for our souls and the souls of our interlocutors. Our basic mode of engagement should be a practice of "confessional openness" – to the world, to one another, and ultimately to God's continuing gift to us of God's own being and (thus) our being, in and through time. It is our continued willingness to endure the new, to endure the time God gives us – to endure life during the world – that gives this practice its fundamental shape. The basic disposition out of which this should be done is a confessing and humble *caritas* that ever seeks the face of God in all such encounters, as the ultimate otherness with which we inevitably and intimately engage.

Part II specifies this general account in an Augustinian theology of citizenship – a theological analysis of faithful civic engagement during the world as part of God's providential economy. This theology will show how such engagement can occur in contemporary public life, and urge Christian citizens to give appropriate attention to the civic and political order, alongside appropriate

✳ resistance to inevitable tendencies (in this life) towards political closure – attention and resistance that are achieved via faith, hope, and love. It will also explain how Christians should use an ascetical vocabulary, again building upon the theological virtues, to understand their civic obligations to help discipline of their souls. Christians' public engagement during the world is not only civically viable and even vital; it also shapes them gratefully to receive, and joyfully to communicate, God's redemptive and consummative gift, and thereby helps to fit Christians for bearing the weight of glory, for citizenship in the heavenly kingdom to come.

In doing this, the theology sketches one account of "the liturgy of citizenship." Citizenship is obviously liturgical in a civic sense, as *leitourgia* is simply "the work of the people" and civic order is nothing if not such a work. But it can be a liturgy in another, theologically more proper sense – an activity that the body of Christ undertakes in doxological praise of God as Creator, Sustainer, and Redeemer. To claim that civic life can be liturgical in this sense is to suggest that civic life can be performed in a way that is continuous with the liturgy of the blessed in heaven that is our eschatological destiny.[1] This part attempts to show that these two liturgies are performable as two sides of the same coin, that the former is embedded and comes to fruition in the latter.

The challenge of our contemporary civic condition

The idea that public life today offers any kind of training for redemption will sound surprising. Many worry that contemporary public and especially "political" life is deeply problematic today.[2] Different scholars approach this issue in different ways. Some see the problem as one of a polarizing culture war fuelled by the rise of a pernicious identity politics, while others see the problem as the rise of a massive anomic disaffection with, and defection from, civic life. In fact both diagnoses identify aspects of a larger problem – namely, the disappearance of any real practice of politics and the

---

1. On the political implications of liturgy see Pickstock 1997, Cavanaugh 1999: 195, and especially Black 1997: 648 n.6: while in the pagan world *leitourgia* was "service rendered by wealthy citizens," for Christians liturgy is what the whole people of God do together.
2. See Sandel 1996, Barber 1988, and Isaac 1997.

loss of a rich and authentically political vernacular. Long-term structural and material changes in contemporary societies corrode "social capital," and consumerist markets inevitably change their participants from "political" agents into fundamentally consumerist creatures.[3] Today people resist understanding themselves as citizens at all; they more easily understand themselves as customers of the state, or as purely private people with no particular civic identity or obligations.

The problem is partly measurable in quantitative terms, in the malaise, anomie, and deep suspicion that many citizens increasingly feel towards their governments. Robert Putnam famously claimed that America is increasingly "bowling alone," and that this change in behavior is emblematic of a broader decline in American associational life, and indeed of associational life across advanced industrial societies more generally. Citizens of these societies vote less, pay less and less attention to public affairs, are involved in fewer associations, and in general are increasingly atomized, anomic, privatized subjects of government rather than participants within it.[4] As Theda Skocpol puts it, "Variety and voice have surely been enhanced in the new American civic universe ... But the gains in voice and public leverage have mainly accrued to the top tiers of U.S. society" (2004: 14).[5] Something has changed, and dramatically, about the amount of engagement with centrally public affairs in the past few decades.

But quantitative descriptions only get us so far. The problem is not simply apathy, but also positive repugnance: as E. J. Dionne argues, Americans *hate* politics.[6] Yet citizens' (certainly justifiable) disgust at contemporary politics explains little. After all, expressions of public suspicion of and hostility towards politics is nothing new, and in fact public discourse was significantly nastier in earlier eras than in our own – involving duels, assaults, and mob riots. But that is precisely the point. Today, when canings, riots, and physical violence have disappeared – more or less – from the public sphere, citizens use the ugliness of public life to justify large-scale defection

---

3. See Isaac 2003: 117–18, Hunter 2000, Bell 1996, Taylor 1989, Bauman 1999: 158–61.
4. See Patterson 2002, and Putnam 2002.
5. In her article, Skocpol does not even mention churches as a possible source of cross-class association.
6. See Dionne 1991.

from public engagement. In earlier eras, people complained in order to rally others to engagement; today complaint is more typically an excuse to stay on the sidelines. Even those who do participate in voluntary associations act in ways that, to use Nina Eliasoph's incisive phrase, "avoid politics," avoid thinking of their associations as devices for, or moments of, involving themselves in genuinely political action (Eliasoph 1998). Hence the common lament about the decline of civic culture not only designates a problem in public life; in an important way, the lament is itself part of the problem. Politics has disappeared, in crucial part, because we have despaired of it.

Our weariness (and our wariness) derives, in important part, from a failure of political imagination, of our fundamental "social imaginary" of public life, the set of precognitive assumptions about citizenship and freedom that frame our understanding of public life (Taylor 2004). We lack a way to recognize the other as significantly other, someone who is genuinely other to us, yet whose very otherness is part of her or his relevance to our political deliberations, and thus who elicits some sort of "recognition" from us, not just a laissez-faire indifference.[7] And we avoid confronting this failure by falling into cynicism.[8] We have grown increasingly uncomfortable and suspicious of any pretense to be speaking out of concern for "the public good." Instead we redescribe the give and take of political bargaining as either the despairing and nihilistic *de gustibus non est disputandem* attitude of consumerist indifference, or in the terrified terms of moral crusade against the minions of some Great Satan *du jour*.[9] We cannot imagine politics as more than the agglomeration of power by individuals or groups for finally selfish ends. This is a self-fulfilling prophecy: because the public sphere seems increasingly destructive, corrosive, and ugly, citizens increasingly imagine that civic engagement is inevitably duplicitous and corrupting; and so they approach any civic engagement they actually do undertake with less and less of the goodwill needed to improve its condition. As Oliver Bennett has argued, "in the postmodern world cultural pessimism is . . . not only a judgment about

7. See Taylor 1992.
8. On cynicism, see Frank 1997, Goldfarb 1991, Bewes 1997, and Chaloupka 1999.
9. On the collapse of "politics," see Hirschman 1970 and Isaac 1997; for examples beyond the United States, see Schoppa 2001 and Colburn 2002.

our culture, but also a structure of feeling that is increasingly produced by our culture" (2001: 193). The degradation of human existence into a sort of half-life lived in the dim light of smoky quasi-lobbying renders suspicious, or worthy of suspicion, all our cares and commitments; it contaminates our personal lives with suspicions most appropriate to gunboat diplomacy.

Yet our despair, and the problems it expresses, has immediate material causes, most centrally in the institutional fact of the rise of the state in the modern era. Whether or not it is intentionally planned, the state's growth over the past two centuries has been considerable. The modern state has enormous powers not only of social organization but even of existential creation; through education, civic rituals, and governmental/military service, it plays a fundamental role in quite literally creating its citizens. Its growth and increasing centralization have occurred even against the best efforts of individual officeholders.[10] The state is the overwhelming fact about most modern societies, and especially about civic life in those societies.[11] Today people see government more as something we have than as something we do; most of us most of the time, and all of us some of the time, are content to wallow in consumerist spectatorship rather than participate in civic action.

The rise of the state has led to the managerial bureaucratization of politics: the camouflaging of political issues in the grey, faceless discourse of policy wonks and the legal arcana of the judiciary. There is much to be grateful for in this. Procedural fairness has been increased, and any particular citizen is more likely to be treated as equal to any other by the governmental structures. But there have been losses as well, most particularly in the declining opportunities for genuine engagement in the running of one's local, regional, or national civic affairs. The rise of an elite of policy experts with their own, typically econometric language, along with the increasing import of the mandarin legal class, have led to a situation where ordinary citizens are rendered increasingly illiterate and inarticulate regarding matters that concern them.[12] The "big questions" are increasingly unasked in politics; questions about the obligation of

---

10. See Morone 1998.
11. See E. Weber 1976 and Wuthnow 1988.
12. See Habermas 1984, Brint 1994, Sandel 1996, Eliasoph 1998, P. D. Hall 1984, Casanova 1994, Hart 2001, Wuthnow and Evans 2002, and Mathewes 2002b. For

the state to its citizens, to the founders in the past, and to future generations, about the whole "nature and destiny of mankind" – all this has the dubious glitter of falling confetti at a political rally. Furthermore, politics changes from a project of self- and community-creation to a project of providing services, from a vision of politics as participation to politics as consumption. Indeed, governments often explicitly speak this way, describing their citizens as "customers." At times the state implicitly becomes not just a service provider but a therapist, as when it prescribes and proscribes proper forms of self-understanding and emotional presentation.[13]

Alongside the state, other cultural forces are at work as well, combining in a "feedback loop" with the structural forces to aggravate each other's effects. The rise of our vast and polyphonous media is crucial here; it represents us to ourselves in distorting ways.[14] Equally importantly, recent decades have seen the rise of "postmaterialist" values among the populations of advanced industrial societies. "Postmaterialist" concerns emerge as central for citizens when the traditional meat-and-potatoes issues of politics (or better: guns and butter), issues of scarcity and security, have been reliably resolved at the "end of history," a resolution that permits citizens to focus on, well, less self-interested concerns about the environment, equality of opportunity, and other such "symbolic" concerns. Politics becomes less a matter of "material interest" and more a matter of expressive value commitments. (Such postmaterial concerns may sound like the boutique "radical chic" leftism of liberal elites, but in fact postmaterial political programs are as easily conservative: many of the culture-war controversies of recent decades – about flag-burning, federal funding for art, curricular questions, capital punishment, and abortion – exemplify the

one example of the alarming trend in liberal political theory towards reliance on experts, see Warren 1999.

13. On the rise of "citizens as consumers," see Crenson and Ginsberg 2002. For more on the "therapeutic state," see Nolan 1998 and Polsky 1991. On consumerism and political life, see Campbell 1987, Scitovsky 1992, Turow 1997, Halter 2000, Lane 2000, Binder 2002, Micheletti 2003, and L. Cohen 2003. On consumerism and religion see Wuthnow 1994, N. Boyle 1998, and C. Smith 2005. More generally see Bell 1988, Coleman 1996, Dalton et al. 1984, Everett 1997, Ferree et al. 2002, Gainsborough 2001, Hart 2001, Lakoff 2002, Morone 1998, Nagel 2001, Oliver 2001, Perry 1999, and Sandler and Schoenbrod 2003.

14. See Turow 1997, Baker 1994, Jackall and Hirota 2000, Wilhelm 2000, and Barney 2000.

postmaterial thesis on both sides of the argument.[15]) The emergence of postmaterial values in the general populace presents public life with a number of difficulties. Most importantly, political parties have a harder time mobilizing postmaterialists in sustained and systematic ways: because they understand their personal activity as unproblematically political, and because they are so reflexively individualistic, they are wary of long-term costly commitments to political parties. Thus the populace is paradoxically more politicized, but curiously less politically organized and mobilized.[16]

The consequences of these changes on the kind of citizens produced in and by the political order are profound. The ideal citizen of a democratic polity is dispositionally deeply committed to voluntary participation in government, vitally but skeptically engaged with the political structures and authorities, and earnestly interested in working and debating with others regarding the shape and actions of the polity. But contemporary civic life encourages not committed participation but passive lassitude, not skeptical attention but cynical ignorance, not respectful engagement but apathetic indifference. Contemporary citizens are taught by the media and the culture to be consumers, and to see public affairs as a realm of ugly self-interest covered with a thin frosting of dissemblingly altruistic (or alarmist) rhetoric. They are treated by their government as customers to be served, not co-owners of the state.[17]

In this setting it is no surprise that many choose not to "voice" their complaints but instead simply "exit" from civic life altogether, retreating into a warren of cynicism. But this is a profound mistake. Every political order shapes the souls of its constituents, whether they participate in it directly or not; if anything, democratic political structures do so more ferociously than any other. The "loss of politics" is not only politically disastrous; it also distorts the character of the persons the culture produces in important ways. The pressures that reduce such a polity's inhabitants from "political" agents into fundamentally consumerist subjects also work on our

15. For a provocative complaint about this change in political life, see Frank 2004.
16. See Inglehart 1990, Dalton 2000, and Brooks 2000. For a powerful counter-argument to the sort I am making, see Lichterman 1996.
17. For an interesting (if overwrought) discussion of the importance and effect of modern managerial techniques in making citizens, see C. R. Miller 2001. See also Eliasoph 1998.

overall moral self-understandings, misshaping our understanding of agency and responsibility.[18] Contemporary "individualism" is closer to the autistic solipsism of extreme consumerism than to genuine autonomy or real independence. Hegel's claim that reading the morning paper is the modern version of morning prayer is false only to the extent that newspapers have been replaced by even more vaporous modes of delivering pseudo-information, such as television and the internet, making our lives ever more amenable to the pure fungibility and commensurability that consumer capitalism requires.[19] The attempt to "exit" public life is not only not a solution; it is actually just one more symptom of the problem.

The poverty of contemporary liberal political theory

In thinking about these matters, we are ill served by current "liberal" political theory, which is captive to parochial debates that, while perhaps originally provoked by real-world concerns, have today at best only an oblique connection to actual human existence.[20] Indeed, "liberalism" itself has suffered a sort of "Babylonian captivity" among academic theorists who conflate liberal political theory and actual "liberal democratic" societies. The latter is not the best description of the constellation of political institutions, practices, and dispositions that characterize our societies (explicit attention to republican themes would be better); but it is at least a viable description. But there is a considerable gap between the polity we inhabit, under any description, and the currently fashionable liberal political theories that purport to describe and underlie it.[21] Self-professed "liberal" political theorists have sacrificed the breadth of pre-academic political thought for a narrow range of puzzles that are rigorously articulable in their own analytic framework. In so doing they set a too comfortable task for thinkers and play a problematically restrictive role in public deliberation.

---

18. See Hammond 1992, McClay 1994, Bell 1996, Bauman 1999, Fowler 1999, Hunter 2000, and Isaac 2003. See Seligman 2000 for a pessimistic assessment of this, and Wolfe 2001 for a celebration of this.
19. Compare Bauman: "'News' is mostly a tool of forgetting, a way of crowding out yesterday's headlines from the audience's consciousness" (1987: 167).
20. In all that follows I have been much educated by Isaac 1997 and 2003, Brinkley 1998, and Johnston 1994.
21. See J. Stout 2004, Berkowitz 1999, and Galston 1991.

"Liberal political theory" is a family of associated political assumptions and projects. It aims to establish a consensual adjudicative framework and set of political structures that fundamentally autonomous individuals will find legitimate, in order to avoid seriously contentious, hence socially straining, public dispute – all of which is in the service of resolving complex socio-political issues in pluralistic societies while securing a stable "non-political" space for individuals to pursue their "private" interests with the minimum of interference by one another.[22] Yet this project is crucially flawed. The focus on structural or institutional projects – establishing just structures of deliberation, decision-making, and complaint – entails a deeply technological model of "political" thinking; this model is impatient with problems that are not yet clearly defined, much less ones that have no clear route to a solution, and hence it severely limits its ability to see, let alone address, the deepest problems we face today.[23] Furthermore, the aim of articulating political structures that can be ideally affirmed by all – or if not affirmed, at least not legitimately contested – is both dubious and dangerous. The conceptual framework underpinning this fixation on consent is premised on a dubious philosophical anthropology that focuses attention on the secondary question of consent while ignoring the question of how to shape humans into real agents.[24] And the aim of maximal consent slides easily into the dangerous habit of delegitimizing dissent, preemptively ruling impossible principled dissent to the proposed picture of the political order. The received liberal fixation on the ideal of consent as the holy grail of political theory implies a "dangerous utopia of reconciliation" (Mouffe 2000: 14) and renders liberal theory blind to the ineliminable presence of conflict and disagreement, which in turn means that such political thought must finally long to eliminate, not foster, dissent – which leads to the complete annihilation of politics itself. Liberal political theory ⚹ claims to aim at consent, but instead regularly hits the target of silence. *Solitudinem faciunt, et pacem appellant*: they make a desolation, and call it peace.[25]

---

22. See Waldron 1987: 127, Bird 1999, and Fowler 1999: 123.
23. See Galston 1991: 161–2, Bertram 1997, and Mehta 1995.
24. See Sandel 1982, Wolterstorff 1996, and Kahn 2004.
25. The Tacitus passage is from his *Agricola*, § 30. See also Herzog 1989, Rescher 1993, Mehta 1995, and Shiffrin 1999.

The concern with legitimization reflects liberal theory's belief that the great danger of political life is the polarization of opponents, due to irreconcilable (usually religious) differences, and ultimately degenerating into warfare. All political imaginations have their nightmares, and the nightmare of the liberal imagination is the horrific religious wars of the sixteenth and seventeenth centuries.[26] They fear that, given our situation of real value-pluralism, we must primarily ensure that that pluralism does not fracture the political order; all other challenges flow down in a descending scale of seriousness therefrom.[27] But this is a woefully narrow aperture through which to view politics, highlighting those problems that best fit this model of difficulty, such as abortion, while ignoring other worries, such as declining civic engagement. Furthermore, this focus forces liberal political theory to propound an inaccurate picture of the present, assumes a bad history, and presents a false political ancestry. Let me say something about these three failings.

First, its picture of the present reality of religion is fundamentally ideological – captive to a deep and resilient ignorance about religion, and motivated more by necessities internal to the logic of the belief system than by the result of any attempt actually to look and see what religion is doing in (and for) the culture. It constructs religious believers as the unspoken "other" against which "we" define ourselves. On its picture, for example, America is split between decent, right-thinking liberal moderates who are content to let others do what they want, so long as they can sip their lattes, flip through *The New York Times*, and zip to the organic market in their SUVs; and psychologically corseted redneck rubes who mutter darkly about black helicopters and UN conspiracies and pause from stacking school boards, propagating patriarchy, and promoting creationism only to bomb abortion clinics and field-strip their M-16s.[28]

---

26. One example of the fear of religion may be found in Rawls 1999: 182, under the index heading "Christianity." The entire entry is as follows: "Christianity: and heresy, 21, 166n; persecuting zeal of, its curse, 21, 166n." See also Shklar 1984, and Juergensmeyer 1993 and 2000.
27. See Beiner 1992. For an example of the sorts of worries that such a liberalism has difficulties expressing, see Fukuyama 2002.
28. Examples are depressingly legion: for two, see Rosenblum 2000 and Macedo 2000. For good examples of alternative visions, see Casanova 1994 and Mahmood 2005. For studies of the root causes of this ignorance, see C. Smith 2003b and Carter 1994.

Second, its history is equally dubious. The central political dynamic of the early modern era was not the creation of political tolerance as a reaction to interreligious violence, but rather the rise of the centralized and absolutist state as the locus of all legitimate violence and political sovereignty, out of a world of far more various (complementary and conflictual) structures of political authority. The ruthless simplification of the political ecosystem during the era of the birth of the Westphalian state was the real story behind the violence of the religious wars, which were significantly (though not exclusively) exploited as convenient excuses for the further entrenchment of power on the part of various political actors; as Richard Dunn put it, the Holy Roman Emperor "Charles V's soldiers sacked Rome, not Wittenberg, in 1527" (1970: 6). This is true also about our own day – the "religious war" lens through which so many contemporary problems are seen turns out to be perniciously false. That is to say, the received wisdom about Yugoslavia is wrong: it was not the eruption of antique (or "primitive") religious and ethnic identities and hostilities so much as it was the fabrication and exploitation of such identities for primarily political (not to mention criminal) purposes.[29] After all, the famous doctrine of *cuius regio eius religio*, purportedly one of the building-blocks of toleration, is equally a doctrine of intolerance – of the legitimation of a ruler's right to compel his subjects to believe as he did, no matter what others outside the realm may wish. The belief that "the liberal state" is the response to the challenge of pluralism gets things the wrong way round; pluralism is a problem only when you have a monotheism of the state, when the state claims to be the only game in town as regards power and authority. Without such an essentially aggrandizing political structure, diversity in belief, and heterogeneity on the ground, is much less difficult. Pluralism is a central problem for modern states not because of pluralism, but because of modern states.[30]

---

29. Against, e.g., the *Weltanschauung* of the previously referenced books by Juergensmeyer, see Sells 1996, and D. Martin 1997: 7–9, 16–17.
30. See Tilly 1975, 1989, and 1993, Cavanaugh 1995, van Creveld 1999, Ertman 1997, Murphy 2001, and Philpott 2001. For discussions of the effect the rise of the state had on political theory, see Skinner 1978: 352–8, Viroli 1992: 3, and Bauman 1999: 169–70. For the role of liberal thought in imperialism, see Mehta 1995.

Third, this error is not simply due to bad history; it allows it to pretend to a deeper ancestry than it can properly affirm. For liberal political theory really begins not in the sixteenth and seventeenth centuries, but in post-World War II anxieties about totalitarianism, populist mass movements, and "the true believer" pervasive (at least in political writing) in that era.[31] The liberal paradigm arose as an anxious response to concerns that the modern liberal nation-state – a rare creature in 1945 – was under attack from the Left and the Right, in a mortal struggle for the future of what Arthur Schlesinger Jr. called "the vital center." Driven by this anxiety, liberal theorists marginalized all those who opposed liberalism as reactionaries or relics of the past, a crotchety old lunatic fringe of back-country wackos who should be ignored or, better, put on cognitive reservations until they die off.[32] While such marginalizations might have been cognitively comforting for liberal theorists, they had the disastrous consequence of leaving liberalism unequipped, when actual anti-liberals appeared as real and important players on the scene (as they occasionally do), with any response to them other than sneers and name-calling.[33]

In general we can summarize these challenges by saying that liberal political theory is, paradoxically, not a theory about politics at all, but a theory about avoiding politics.[34] Given its picture of rights-bearing individuals as primary, it focuses on how best to leave one another alone, and the most basic human commitments it presumes are non-political commitments (which often means "private" commitments) – while the most basic "political" commitment it presumes in its participants is the commitment to live in proximity

---

31. Isaac 1997: 26–8. See also Brinkley 1998: 296–7, Gary 1999, and Halberstam 1999.
32. See Barber 1988: 31.
33. See Isaac 1997: 26–8 and Brinkley 1998: 296–7; for an example of the dyspeptic rhetoric of a cornered self-proclaimed "liberal," see S. Holmes 1993. For an example of this elitism in present-day theorizing see Warren 1999: 358–9 – in a society as complex as our own, we must accept an "epistemic division of labor" vis-à-vis politics; not just regretfully as a *de facto* necessity, but even as a *de jure* appropriate structure. Reinstitute an intellectual-managerial elite. See also Zolo 1992 for remarks on the "Singapore Model." See also Hart 2001: 221 and Isaac 1997.
34. As Paul Khan says, "liberalism is a political theory without any understanding of politics" (Kahn 2004: 182). See Barber 1988, Newey 2001, Isaac *et al.* 1999, and Kahn 2004. This could explain what Ronald Beiner (1997: 17) calls the fundamental *boredom* of liberal political theory. For more on boredom see Svendsen 2005.

to each other, a commitment it expects to be "freestanding," autonomous relative to any other convictions those participants may possess. (Rawls's celebrated egalitarian interventionism, for example, is only provisionally interventionary, the ultimate justification for which is humans' fundamental separateness from each other. For Rawls we should be egalitarians, that is, because this is the way to be most generally least intrusive.) There is no sense, in contemporary liberal political theory, that politics and public life in general – in the sense of taking responsibility for running the polity – is any sort of intrinsic good. Even if it is available for individuals to "go into" politics, what they will find there, in the liberal utopia at least, is not politics but bureaucracy, the administration of a managerial program determined on other than political grounds. In a way, liberal political theory is actually a despair of politics, of the possibility of political life itself.

The recovery of politics

It is hard for those unacquainted with the field of political theory to understand how profoundly captive the imagination of liberal political theory has been to these *ideés fixes*. It is the danger of any ideology that manages to consolidate its hold over an intelligentsia; almost inevitably the blinkered scholastic protocols of the discipline eclipse a clear-eyed vision of reality as the most important criterion for assessing a proposal's significance.

Some have escaped this hegemonic imagination. Some inside the machine recognize its inadequacies, and offer "political liberalism" or "civic liberalism" or "liberal republicanism" – a liberalism that works to correct such tendencies – as workable modifications.[35] And others, from quite different perspectives, are dissatisfied with the received pieties and demonologies of the status quo, and often especially with its understanding of the role (or proper lack of a role) of religion in public life.[36] Such thinkers have begun to discuss real politics again. They realize that received "liberal" political thought leaves something unthought – namely, the idea that political

35. See Macedo 1993 and 2000, Dagger 1997, Pettit 1997, Raz 1988, and Sunstein 1996.
36. See, for example, Galston 1991, Orlie 1997, Connolly 1999, and Deneen 2005.

life can be more than a device for securing for oneself a set of political rights, that it is an immanent good, available only by participating in public life. These thinkers want to recover those practices of political engagement that comprise the practice of citizenship. Reflecting on the revolutionary experiences of 1989 in Eastern and Central Europe, they recognize the value of political engagement itself.[37] As Adam Michnik put it, "we must live as if there is political space," and thereby create the conditions for the reality of such political space to appear (Schell 1986: 47). We must resurrect public discourse, reaffirm the need for commitment to civic purposes and civic projects, and cultivate a multidimensional culture of deliberation about such concerns. By engaging others in the public square, such thinkers argue, we can achieve, in the words of Michael Sandel, "a good in common that we cannot know alone" (1982: 183). Such a program, these thinkers hope, will reinvigorate our public life and can help replenish the dangerously alkaloid soil of contemporary civic culture.

Yet for all their diagnostic power, these visions remain frustratingly vague about how to reinvigorate public life. In part we lack a political grammar, a capacity for political conversation among members of a society. Contemporary sociologists argue that without a vocabulary, there can be no vision; and as earlier social theorists taught us, without a vision, the people perish.[38] So these political thinkers have some sense of the goal, but cannot see the way to it.

Christians can do better, for they have a very rich "political grammar" latent in their faith. Many of them are implicitly still operating through these grammars, albeit partially and often unconsciously. An explicit appropriation of such a grammar can help them become what Antonio Gramsci called "organic intellectuals": not simply people who "act" through and in their thinking, but people whose thinking regularly has as part of its intentional concern the "public good" and how best to think about the public

---

37. See Isaac 1997, Kumar 2001, Glenn 2001, and Kenney 2002.
38. While the language of "political grammar" may seem merely metaphorical, in fact it may be more than that; there appears to be a "strong positive relationship" between verbal articulateness and political and civic engagement. (Interestingly enough, exceptional mathematical ability seems to be strongly negatively related to such engagement.) See Nie and Hillygus 2001: 39–42. For more on the connection between "civic grammars" and social life, see Eliasoph 1998, Hart 2001, Lichterman 2005, and Alexander 2003.

good. Christian churches can become hospitable sites for the sorts of open-ended (and open-sided) political movements akin to what sociologists call "new social movements": not just groups of people who care about and act for political aims, but intentional communities whose self-understanding and very mode of existence embody resistance to the ongoing "colonization" of the public sphere by narrowly technical forms of rationalization that threaten to devour it.[39] They can do this by articulating a theology of citizenship for today. This theology will urge Christians to participate in public life in a way that accepts appropriate responsibility for that participation. This is important: the best vocabulary for understanding our engagement in public life is one organized not around obedience, but rather around participation.[40] Against some profound political views, these chapters will argue that the basic problem of contemporary politics is not legitimate authority but energized engagement, because the deep fact of modern public life is that *all* members of a community are ultimately responsible for its sustenance, and so must come to take ownership of that community.

Furthermore, a Christian understanding of civic engagement can offer explicit resistance to the oscillation between fanaticism and anomie to which wholly secular political programs seem prone. Christians can both recognize the necessity of civic engagement and resist the inevitable trajectories of fallen political structures towards self-aggrandization and apocalyptic finality. East of Eden, the realm of the "political" is not a direct reflection of the divine, but rather a sphere in which we participate in the divine obliquely, in an indirect and often confused way. We properly participate in the political realm, not by recognizing the sovereignty of God as communicated through the political structures in which we find ourselves, but rather by recognizing the sovereignty of God indirectly and obliquely, through our resistance to those structures' implicitly imperialistic tendencies. It is an eschatological, not apocalyptic, mode of civic engagement: we properly participate in public life by

---

39. See Melucci 1989, Laraña *et al.* 1994, Jasper 1997, Lichterman 1996, and Pichardo 1997.
40. Naturally the language of participation does integrate a language of obedience within it – as love, not law, and through concepts of fidelity and covenant – but this should not be allowed to obscure the radically different originating concepts.

resisting the "closure" of what passes for politics today, that is, by resisting the inevitable gravitational tug of any political order towards claiming final sovereignty over every other possible locus of human attachment, including especially the church, the neighbor, and the stranger.

Such a program raises concerns, for both believers and secular thinkers. I address them next.

How faith is good for civic engagement, and how civic engagement is good for faith

Many secularist thinkers will meet this proposal with skepticism. They worry that Christian engagement in civic order will not respect the integrity and proprieties of that order – that Christians will dismiss its immanent logic and goals, and exploit civic life for fundamentally non-civic aims. And they have reason to be so concerned. Much of what Christians do in the public realm is oblique to received political categories, because many practices of Christian citizenship are what Jason Bivins calls "politically illegible" – practices whose "public" character is hard to see from within the regnant political vocabulary (2003: 10, 157–8). Fasting can be a public act, as can be praying, working in a soup kitchen, even reading various texts, or going on pilgrimage; similarly, civil disobedience at military bases, at prisons, at abortion clinics, in civil rights causes – all these actions seem politically urgent to some and simply incoherent, sometimes futile, and even occasionally destabilizing to others.[41] In such cases Christians do care about public life, but not for the reasons that the *saeculum* uses to induce and sustain such caring, but for what they see as better reasons, of their own.[42]

Secular thinkers may find such forms of civic engagement threatening, not least because they challenge the received political language and practices, both materially and formally. But as Tocqueville realized, this pressure is part of Christianity's pragmatic value for public life.[43] It is part of the genius of liberal democratic thought in the last several centuries to realize that healthy civic

---

41. Recall the impact that reading the Koran, and then going on *hajj*, had on Malcolm X.
42. I have learned much on these matters from the work of Oliver O'Donovan.
43. For arguments of this sort see Bivins 2003: 171–5 and Mahmood 2005.

order is a matter more of allowing public life to flourish, rather than of constructing it.

More fundamentally still, secular thinkers will be uncomfortable about Christians' understanding of the destiny of public life itself. Against the too easy refusals of much contemporary secular political thought, for Christians public life should be properly, ultimately, one more form of love, of seeking communion, of seeking the Beloved Community.[44] Hence Christans affirm that politics turns out to be theology, a way of seeking God. Here is the deepest tension, on this Augustinian proposal, between Christian engagement in public life and that public life's professed self-understanding.

This tension – this ill fit between our civic energies and the political channels through which they run – will not be overcome in this dispensation. Secularists recognize this as well; the most intelligent theorists of modernity in general, and liberal democracy in particular, repeatedly insist that ambivalence and skepticism, not unqualified enthusiastic affirmation, are the most appropriate attitudes for modern citizens in the face of the many costs and benefits of our world. Why should it seem a failure of a position if it eventuates in an intelligible and even articulate account of why we might feel, and endorse, such ambivalence and skepticism?

Indeed, we might say that this tension, highlighted by Christian civic commitment, speaks to a tension inherent in the practice of liberal democracy itself. On the Augustinian account, we all have in our hearts a memory of and longing for real communion, communion of the sort that contemporary liberal theory, by seeking to quarantine it within the domestic "private" sphere, too simply denies. Liberalism is problematic and should not be uncontested in public life, both because it is not uncontested in our hearts, and because "liberalism" itself is on both sides of the struggle, at once a *modus vivendi* and a longing for the Beloved Community.[45] And the theological virtues, when manifest by believers in a pluralistic public sphere, create a politically rich site for living in that tension – a tension that is, in this world, good to make palpable, both for Christians and for others.

But secular critics are not the most troubling ones. Some of the most alluring contemporary theologies recoil in horror at the idea

44. See Marsh 2005.   45. See Tomasi 2001.

of a theology of citizenship. For them, real Christian faith puts one absolutely at odds with all worldly civic identities, because worldly identities immediately demand an idolatrous degree of fidelity from their members. Furthermore, they worry that the language of "contribution" inches slowly into collaboration, so ensuring that any theology of citizenship eventually becomes a theology *for* citizenship.

These worries are partly right. But their partial validity does not warrant the total recoil they encourage. Of course political identities can become idolatrous; even secular liberal democrats recognize that. Hence most polities today explicitly permit (even if they can over time implicitly subvert) far more complex forms of associative affiliation than is acknowledged in a "nation versus church" dichotomy. And the theatricalized rhetoric of opposing the demonic nation-state in which such theologies indulge simply camouflages their unwillingness to think seriously about how their adherents' various political activities can be made properly intelligible. In fact, saying one is avoiding it by mouthing certain *bon mots* about the state is insufficient, and often gets one into deeper trouble. The most powerful such oppositional theologian, Stanley Hauerwas, unwittingly contributes to identity politics, by making "Christian" easily consumable as one more identity marker.[46] The real question is not even how the fidelities – to nation and to God – are to be ordered, for the liberal state typically grants sufficient religious liberty to believers; the real, the pressing question is how they are to be related.

The answer offered here is broadly Augustinian, but with a difference: it avoids the categories that fuel the interminable arguments about the proper heritage of Augustine's political theology occupying much recent work. These debates are roughly between what we can call "Lutheran" and "Thomist" proposals for an Augustinian politics. To "Lutherans," Augustine thinks that politics is only negatively and instrumentally useful in securing the stability of order ("peace" is too rich a term here); politics, then, is a consequence of the Fall. On the "Thomist" view, politics is a proper and natural good, that would have existed even had we not fallen, as a function of the need for some coordinating authority to govern the

46. See Mathewes 2000 and J. Stout 2004.

complexity of human society.[47] Debate between these two positions is interminable, because both views have exegetical evidence on their side. The "Lutheran" view rightly points out that Augustine understood the necessity of "rule" to be a consequence of the Fall – after all, the only "natural" hierarchy he allowed was the family; the "Thomist" view rightly sees that Augustine still insists that social life is fundamental to human flourishing.[48] But both sides mistakenly impose an anachronistic concept of "politics" on to Augustine's thought, and so neither can see what Augustine was actually trying to do. In fact, *pace* Arendt, who claimed that Augustine was the last ancient man to understand what "public life" was, "the political" was precisely the concept that he lacked. For all his familiarity with the Roman civic republican tradition of historiography and political thought, he talked not about politics but about ruling, or government, and he saw the "external" government of a social body as continuous with each individual's psychological governance of himself or herself. Just as the mind needs to govern the appetites and passions that direct and shape the will, so the ruler must govern the populace for the greater good of the body politic.[49] Augustine's thinking about governance is anchored in his insistence that Christians must support the *ordo* of society, both passively (by obeying its laws) and actively (by serving in its military and in positions of civic authority), in order to help it secure some approximation of order and peace. Christians may disobey it only if it actively forbids worship of the true God, and even then disobedience is to be exclusively concerned with continuing that worship (*DCD* 19.19). As members of the political community, of course, Christians should plead for more justice and petition the authorities to rectify injustices, and what we have of Augustine's correspondence suggests that he was quite active in such

47. See Markus 1970, Deane 1963, R. Niebuhr 1953, O'Donovan 1987, Weithman 1992, and von Heyking 2001 for examples of these views. For salutary worries about such accounts, see TeSelle 1998.
48. See *DCD* 19.15, and K. Hughes 2005b, Burnell 1992, Doughtery 1990: 206, and R. Williams 1987: 62–3.
49. See Cranz 1972: 345. Even once we restrict ourselves to government, Augustine's concept of "the state" is very different from our own – really the state is just *army* and *courts*; the state was most important at the margins of Roman society, not at its center (see McLynn 1999). For more on "body politic," see Kantorowicz 1957.

importuning.[50] But such activity was done by some (ecclesial) authorities to other (civic) authorities, not conceived as the duty of citizens. Our concept of politics is not a topic of focused attention for Augustine, and so we will find little direct help in his work.[51]

Our proposed Augustinian theology must be mediated by others, and so we begin from Paul Ramsey's statement: "The mere fact that a man is a citizen elsewhere keeps him from being only a citizen here" (1961: xxi). This emphasizes the difference Christianity will make, while insisting that believers remain more or less directly engaged political actors during the world. Christianity does not suggest that its adherents keep the faith by withdrawing from civic engagement, but by engaging more fully in it – more precisely, through a kind of civic engagement that is sensitive to how life in this polity allows and/or hinders Christians' fundamental activity, the worship of God with their lips and in their lives.

To think about the relationship of public engagement and Christian faith in this way may seem to offer a merely contingent addition to real Christian life. And many Christians today do believe that "public life" is optional for Christians. Historically it has been often so understood; indeed, Christian thought largely learned the broader value of public engagement for human beings from modern secular thinkers. (It is a pointless indulgence to argue that Christians could have learned it from their own tradition; the fact is they did not.) But as Part I argued, there is a sense in which Christian life is fundamentally public in character. And taken up into the theological ambit of Christian faith, such participation offers a potentially rich and vigorous form of participation in God's order that Christians should appropriate.

Christianity's "publicity" can be lived in many different ways – by anchorites and hermits and monastics as well as Christian political agitators – and none of these is necessarily more "public" than any other. For the primordial sense of "public" is not in the *saeculum* at all; Christian life is lived in the ultimate public, *coram Deo*, before

---

50. See esp. Dodaro 2004a: 196–212.
51. More precisely, the problem is that, when *we* look for Augustine's political insights, it is only those matters that register with us as recognizably "political" matters. In fact, as I discuss in Chapter 4, he reflected on broadly though recognizably political matters in his discussions of ecclesial authority and religious community as well.

God, and it is fundamentally a life committed to a certain kind of "public," even "political" engagement. Even the churches them- selves are, during the world, a "public" matter for their adherents, the mundane sustenance of which they work out by conciliar engagement with one another. This can sound gentle, but it need not be; conflict, debate, and murkiness happen not only on the boundaries of the faith, but also within the community of the faithful itself. Politics is our destiny in heaven, but it is also our fate during the world. Hence the Christian churches can form congregants in the right way – the church can be "the church" – only by being "evangelical"; and that means being public in the proper way.

This fact should not surprise us. After all, Christianity promises a polity. The trajectory from Genesis to Revelation is from garden to city, from nomads and farmers to urbanites; a consummately political community is our destiny, and the political language of the "kingdom" arguably plays a more profound and more encompassing role in Scripture than does the domestic language of "family," or even of "marriage." Christianity always embodies a dynamism towards publicity, an evangelical movement into the world. This, of course, has been one of the main theological "discoveries" of the past century. From the "social gospel" and "Christian realism" through "liberation theology" to "radical orthodoxy," again and again theologians have discovered and rediscovered – from Scripture, from tradition, from the signs of the times, and from their own and others' lived experience of the faith in the modern world – that Christianity *is* fundamentally public, properly political, and hence in some sense properly committed to a more abundant and more abundantly "worldly" life.

But this recognition has not been matched by any larger response by the people of God. To the contrary, the last century saw the increasing privatization of Christian belief (at least in advanced industrial democracies) and the disappearance of a vigorous public framework for faith, which has led believers into a Babylonian captivity to idolatrous patterns of life, work, and consumption. These patterns are diagnosed by Augustinians as various versions of the archetypal sin of *privatio*, of retreat into the self, securing our lives against the painful turbulence of the ultimate publicity, *coram Deo*.[52]

---

52. In this way we avoid the dubious tendency in much recent theology to blame our condition on our recent history. While our apprehension of the virtues is

As an antidote we should see public engagement as a furnace within whose fires we will be forged and tempered, until we show forth in our lives what we profess with our lips. Public engagement, gracefully undertaken, provides more than enough opportunities for <u>humility</u> and penance, recognition of one's sin and the sins of others, and a deepening appreciation of the terrible awe-fulness of God's providential governance of the world. Indeed, involvement in public life today may itself increasingly need some such ascetical discipline. Jeffrey Isaac has suggested that the benefits of contemporary public life will be minimal, fragmentary, and deeply compromised, and any proposal for civic engagement must confront these facts before disappointment turns to cynicism. Civic engagement will be "limited, partial, and frustrating. Learning to live with these frustrations, and persist without resentment in spite of them, may prove to be the most important civic virtue of our time" (2003: 147). Actually, he does not go far enough: we must learn to live with these frustrations, of course, but we should also learn *from* them; and our learning is our instruction into the theological virtues of faith, hope, and charity.

Conclusion

We feel public life's importance, but do not grasp what it properly is, for we are captive to a distorted image of politics in consumeristic terms. Many have said as much; but an Augustinian theological analysis offers more than further diatribe. It identifies the root problem as a despair of public life, a despair which is just one species of the apocalyptic escapism that is the root of sin. And our hope lies in the opportunity we have not yet lost, the opportunity to rediscover an idea of politics as rooted in love more primordially than in fear.[53] The cultural despair of politics is in important part caused by the contemporary political imagination's desire not to acknowledge the political importance of those longings, so a program of public

distorted by the current configuration of public life, the root cause of their distortion in apocalyptic directions lies not in "modernity" but in the Fall; to suggest that they are due fundamentally to local historical conditions is to surrender to the same apocalyptic temptations we are excoriating.

53. Several perceptive political thinkers have suggested such a rediscovery; see Kahn 2004, Fukuyama 1992, and Cowen 2000 for (very diverse) examples.

engagement that is partly built around such acknowledgment can offer a more vital and viable approach to politics than recent options allow. And such a program is found in faithful, hopeful, and loving Christian witness in public.

Part II details this program by explicating the civic and ascetic value of the three theological virtues' manifestation in public life, arguing that the virtues both organize and complicate Christians' engagement in fruitful ways. Furthermore, understood ascetically, the virtues attempt to enliven human capacities that we in our sin, and our culture in its corruption, wish to freeze, lock in place, kill. The virtues are intrinsically unstable and self-transcending, stretching on toward the goal. So while the chapters focus on the virtues, they mean thereby to identify what the virtues are fitting us for – a practice of endless beginning, of inhabiting our destiny as a new creation. Here virtue theory serves soteriology. We are being trained to bear the weight of the glory that has been prepared for us. But we are trained for that by using the world, in both its tantalizing proleptic communion and its awful moments of tragic and painful estrangement, to cultivate a deeper sense of longing for what the world cannot provide.

Each chapter puts one virtue in dialectical engagement with the most interesting (secular and religious) proposals regarding public life. It identifies the peculiar difficulties in public life that challenge our deepening appropriation of the virtue; then it shows how our ascetical inhabitation of that virtue can be enriched through proper engagement in public life, and how in turn our manifestation of that virtue contributes to civic life. Chapter 4 discusses faith – with the question of the proper character and extent of commitment to the civic realm. How should Christians have faith in public life? How should Christian faith qualify that other, civic faith, and how should their engagement sharpen and enrich their inhabitation of Christian faith? Chapter 5 addresses hope, as regards the proper character and extent of "prophetic criticism," the right sort of skeptical alienation from one's civic order. Given that a healthy polity requires its citizens to possess vital critical and skeptical faculties, what sort of stance of criticism is appropriate, and how can Christian hope shape and motivate such skeptical alienation? Furthermore, how can such hopeful yet critical engagement enrich Christians' inhabitation of eschatological hope? Finally, Chapter 6 discusses love, through addressing the proper quality of engagement one should seek with one's fellow citizens in the struggles of public life, and the role of Christian love therein. Given that public life necessitates working with others, what sort of relations should Christians expect to have with those others, and what is the value (immanent and indirect) of those primarily "public" relations? How should Christian *caritas* enable, enrich, and when necessary restrict these relations, and how will those operations of *caritas* in the public arena deepen Christians' appropriation of *caritas* itself? Answering these questions will help show both how Christians should inhabit a pluralistic public sphere in ways functional for that sphere, and how Christians should understand the spiritual training they will undergo through their civic involvement – how, that is, that engagement will help fit them to be citizens of the kingdom to come.

4

Faithful citizenship

How can faith operate in public life? If faith properly signifies our attachment to some community or end, some "ultimate loyalty" that cannot be prised away from a concrete historical narrative and material community, how can people possessed by one such loyalty affirm another one as well? And how in turn can faith be enriched by public engagement? Many think faith in public is properly impossible, both because faith assumes a capacity for deep and persistent conviction incompatible with the fluidity and radical voluntariness of contemporary society, and because the presence in public life of those committed to retaining such deep and persistent convictions is bad, both for public life and for believers. This chapter argues not only that there is a fruitful role for faith to play in public life, but that properly faithful engagement in public life is conducive to the deepening of participants' faith as well.

Today however, faith is a politically fraught term. For the state demands a certain kind of faith as well, and it is a jealous god. One of the oldest and deepest criticisms of Christianity is that it stymies true civic commitment. From Rome to Rousseau, and beyond to Nancy Rosenblum, those who find themselves most profoundly committed to the political order continually worry that those with other attachments and loyalties may find themselves torn between them in ways that damage their attachment to the civic good. But the opposite worry is real as well. Christianity can too easily become merely a device for commitment to the polity, a too tight confusion of faith and politics, leading either to a collaborationist Constantinianism, which invariably adulterates the faith, or a theocracy that moves in quickly totalitarian directions.[1] One way or the other, then, many thinkers on politics and religion have been troubled by the hazards of being faithful in public.

Thus it is curious, and not a little ironic, that today religion is looked upon by some as a source, and perhaps the most powerful source, of civic commitment. Many social thinkers, especially "communitarians," seem to think of religion as a good thing – but good because of its functional value as encouraging social cohesion. Many would agree with William Galston when he argues that "the greatest threat to children in modern liberal societies is not that they will believe in something too deeply, but that they will believe in nothing very deeply at all" (1991: 225). And they would affirm Wilson Carey McWilliams's argument that "the great faiths have something to teach the Republic about the metaphysics of civic morality . . . Facing a politics defined more and more by oligarchy and indifference, American democracy has worse things to fear than faith" (McWilliams 2003: 156–7). Many faithful citizens look hopefully on such renewed openness. We might call this the "Eisenhower strategy," for its general attitude is encapsulated in Eisenhower's (in)famous claim, "our government has no sense unless it is founded in a deeply felt religious faith and I don't care what it is." It has not gone away since Eisenhower; in a poll conducted in January 2001, of those who wanted religion to have a more influential role in America, 76 percent of them said they didn't care which religion it was.[2]

But in fact this strategy is a temptation, for its openness to religion is a trap, a false friend, taking away the liberty of religion to be religion – dismissing the ambivalences marking the relationship between religious and civic commitment, and implicitly subordinating faith's tendencies towards comprehensiveness and ultimacy to the immanent demands of the political community.[3]

1. See Nicholls 1989. Those who casually toss about the term "Constantinianism" should stop until they have confronted the powerful revision of the received story by Hal Drake; see Drake 2000.
2. For Eisenhower see *New York Times*, December 23, 1952. For a wonderfully puckish source-criticism of this quip, see Henry 1981. Perhaps Eisenhower knew his Gibbon, who famously claimed that "the various modes of worship which prevailed in the Roman world were all considered by the people as equally true; by the philosopher as equally false; and by the magistrate as equally useful" (1995, I: 22). On the contemporary statistics see Farkas *et al.* 2001.
3. See Fish 1999: 254.

It permits talk of "faith" in public life but only at the cost of surrender to a Procrustean mutilation: religious faith can "contribute,"
in some vague way, to democratic discourse, so long as it stays
within boundaries and does not destabilize the structures of the
preset political order – that is, so that it always dances to the tune
set by the immanent civic order.

Most of the arguments for the legitimacy of faith in public life
succumb to such Eisenhowerian temptations, and idolatrously
accept some immanent description of societal well-being as their
summum bonum. Most such arguments gain what plausibility they
have with their intended (and effectively, if not yet explicitly,
secular) audiences only by subtly undermining the reality-encom-
passing ambitions of the religious faiths they putatively defend.
Stanley Fish finds this even in the arguments of self-proclaimedly
"religious" thinkers "who set out to restore the priority of the good
over the right but find the protocols of the right – of liberal proce-
duralism – written in the fleshly tables of their hearts" (1999: 262).[4]
Such thinkers impose finally Procrustean frameworks on religion's
place in public life.

So theorists are captive to such Eisenhowerian mindsets; but
religious practitioners are far less obedient. Such believers often
engage in religious political action that is, to recall Jason Bivins's
helpful phrase, "politically illegible" – menacingly opaque for those
working with the received political vocabulary of the mainstream
(2003: 10). And states tend not to look fondly on what they cannot
understand. Again, they are jealous gods, bureaucracies with theo-
cratic pretensions, hungry for their citizens' unquestioning obedience. Hence thinkers like Rousseau and Tertullian are, to some
degree, right: an ineliminable animus exists between Christian faith
and totalizing civic commitment of the sort that is the grativational
tendency of political states. Neither readily allows its demands to be
subordinated to the other. The struggle between Jerusalem and
Washington is perpetual in this dispensation.[5]

---

4. See S. D. Smith 1995: 68: "Theories of religious freedom seek to reconcile or to
   mediate among competing religious and secular positions within a society, but
   those competing positions disagree about the very background beliefs on which
   a theory of religious freedom must rest." For a response to Smith's challenge,
   see Guinn 2002.
5. For a different theological account of the enmity between religious and civic
   faith, see Kraynak 2001.

Still, this is not a reason for theorists to despair, or for believers to retreat to the hinterlands, buy lots of guns, and have many children whom they dress in homemade clothes. For the contemporary liberal state is at least theoretically more accepting of limits on the demands it makes of its inhabitants than previous political structures have been. Contemporary democratic polities permit religious citizens opportunities for faithful citizenship undreamt of in other, earlier, political dispensations. Nonetheless, we must keep aware of both the inevitable entropic tendencies of states toward absolutism. Even self-professedly secular political thinkers are alert to these dangers. Speaking civically, how might we use the opportunities of democratic participation to counteract the dangerous effects of polities' inevitable idolatrous tendencies?

Commitment to the Christian faith reveals and keeps before our eyes the endlessness of political activity, its fundamentally provisional and accidental character. Public engagement should be faithfully undertaken, given certain minimal conditions, as part of the larger mode of ascetical and evangelical engagement with the world today. But such engagement teaches us that political institutions must not be the object of ultimate faith, and so should be affirmed only in a qualified way. Yet they must be so affirmed, again on grounds of faith, in order to encourage citizens both to be genuinely engaged and also to recognize the "mundaneness" of any particular political dispensation. But we cannot speak only in a civic register. We need a properly theological argument for why such civic engagement is good for faith, on its own terms – why, that is, such engagement is ascetically as well as civically fruitful. We need a theology of public engagement, a theology of citizenship – a vision of the relationship between Christians' commitments to their earthly polities and to the kingdom of heaven.

This chapter explores one such theology of faithful citizenship. It does so in three stages. First, it identifies two emerging proposals for responding to democracy's discontent – "communitarianism" and "civic republicanism" – explaining how these proposals attempt to recover "the political," and thereby to affirm that real political life is possible today. It next suggests that these proposals urge us to rethink the central political concept of "sovereignty," and shows how we might do that. Finally, it develops an Augustinian Christian theology of citizenship that offers both a fruitful model of faithful civic engagement, and a promising picture of how such faithful civic engagement will be ascetically fruitful for believers.

Beyond liberal political theory

While much of what passes for "liberal political thought" today does not help us address the challenges we currently face, some thinkers appreciate these challenges. They try to address them by appeal to a more capacious sense of what politics might be than liberal theories allow. For these thinkers, politics is a human good in a way that the received liberal pictures have a hard time acknowledging.[6] There are at least two ways in which this insight can be developed. "Communitarians" harness the energies of politics as a powerful force for community cohesion and thus for a group's self-identity, typically in modernity through the concept of the "nation." "Civic republicans" use those energies not simply for communal but also for individual purpose, as part of a belief that politics is a constitutive part of the good life, one in which we must participate in order fully to flourish. Neither of these accounts is wholly satisfactory, but each captures worthwhile insights. Communitarianism can see the problems we face, and it suggests an attractive way to respond to them, but it finally turns the ideal of community into an idol. Civic republicanism avoids this problem and is thus more attractive still, but its fixation on wholly immanent this-worldly goods makes it prone to temptations of fanaticism and apocalypticism.

We can do better than either. Like them, we can affirm the value of commitment as a way of recognizing the longings manifest in political life. But we must also recognize, with a properly understood liberalism, that all human community in this world – which is all any political community can be – is inevitably a "failed church," and to ignore its failure threatens to tempt us toward idolatry.[7]

The communitarian proposal

Communitarians aim to offer a vocabulary for a richer account of politics, or at least make such a politics' absence more palpable,

6. See Berkowitz 1999 and Polletta 2002.
7. I borrow this phrase from Robin Lovin, though he would probably disagree with the use to which I put it.

in order to help us re-energize the public moral consensus that is their goal. Building on a root description of the problem as civic disaffiliation, communitarians suggest we need to recover a language to affirm a vibrant civil society – a kind of model Tocquevillean polis of volunteer organizations, town meetings, and knitting circles, all doubling as latent political discussion groups – and that attention to cultivating civil society promises to reinvigorate civic discourse and public culture in crucial ways.[8]

Ironically, the state has the central role to play in this picture. While initially the language signified the broad dispersal of power and political sovereignty among a multitude of heterogeneous social organizations (e.g., professional guilds, associations for civic betterment, and the like), today – after Rousseau, the Romantic nationalists, and Hegel – it is invoked as a necessary tool for social unity, the mediating device whereby the "ethical substance" of the nation, what Rousseau called the "general will," was articulated and secured. And the state returns the complement: civil society is an energizing force for the state, and "the central purpose of the state is to construct ethical unity within the modern context" (Beem 1999: 227).

This view has its advantages. In an age suffused with concern about apathy and anomie, the need for fellow feeling is fundamental, and the nation seems the most appropriate focus for constructing such fellow feeling. But it only seems natural. First of all, incantations of the idea of civil society ignore the material conditions underlying its demise, such as the changing nature of work and of private leisure time.[9] Secondly, as scholars of nationalism argued, social identities are fundamentally artificial, and should not be granted unquestioned legitimacy. Here recent liberal critiques of communitarianism, as not only fundamentally nostalgic but practically disastrous, have teeth. There is such a thing as bad civil society – racist groups, exclusionary country clubs, and other associations that corrode the common good.[10] And third, communitarians share

---

8. See Glendon and Blankenhorn 1995: 278–81, Portes 1998, Hann and Dunn 1996, Ehrenberg 1999, Arato and Cohen 1992, Seligman 1992, and Rotberg 2001.
9. See Kumar 2001, Chambers and Kymlicka 2002, Edwards and Foley 1997, J. Cohen 1999, Kim 2000, Walzer 1998, and Seligman 1995.
10. See Chambers and Kapstein 2001, J. Cohen 1999, Rosenblum 1998, and Hoffmann 2003.

too much with liberals; they still believe that there is some sort of finality to the political process, that it is finally a technological process, with some final *telos* being a unified nation. Like many contemporary liberals, communitarians dream of a worldly condition without politics.

Christians have further reasons to suspect it, because this vision can actually subvert religion in society – in part precisely because of the particular way it values religious commitments. Communitarians typically appeal to religion as a device for thickening social bonds and strengthening civic associations, cultivating the "habits of the heart." Yet even civically, there is a tension between what this theory dictates and what actually happens to religions too tightly tied to the civic order; socio-politically, any such intentional association will eventually undercut religious faith's power.[11]

The "communitarian" inclusion of religion in civil society often tends towards the monotheism of the state – a nationalist idolatry that makes religion serve some immanent end. Yet recognizing that danger does not license a retreat into liberalism, for communitarians rightly insist that humans long for true community. All political entities are failed churches, faulty attempts to replicate the body of Christ. Any useful vision of politics must recognize and respect this longing even while it helps us resist its dangerous tendencies. Rather than thinning out the telos to be attained, we may want to rethink the idea of a *telos* to politics at all. The possibility exists of another route for reimagining politics after liberalism that may help us do just that.

The civic republican strategy

Complexly intertwined with communitarianism lies another vision of political life, which we may call "civic republicanism." Just as with communitarian and liberal thought, civic republicanism is manifold and diverse.[12] But even generically it captures insights to which we must attend.

---

11. There is an enormous literature on civil religion. See Shanks 1995, Bellah 1974, and especially Deneen 2005.
12. The challenges (brought, for example, by E. Nelson 2004) to talking about civic republicanism as an ideal-type are too fine-grained to worry me here.

For civic republicans, political life is most valuable not for its institutional outcomes (as liberals assume) or its solidaristic social effects (as for communitarians), but rather for its more immanent rewards for citizens. On this account public life lets us realize the fundamental good of participating in public life for a full human life.[13] As Hannah Arendt argued, political action creates agents as well as ensuring a vibrant political community. "Political freedom, generally speaking, means the right to be a participator in government, or it means nothing" (1963: 221). But their strategic goal, the end to which they understand that project to be oriented, differs from communitarians, for its *telos* is fundamentally positive, individualistic, and immanent. The end of such participation is authentic self-rule, the "positive" liberty of political virtue. Civic participation both flows from virtuous formation and further trains us in the virtues. While civic republicans fear moral corruption, typically through commercialism, they are more deeply motivated by a positive vision of human flourishing. Unlike both liberals and communitarians, republicans see actual political structures as secondary efflorescences of the character of the polity's citizens. Questions of obedience are fundamentally secondary to questions of participation.

This is not a recipe for anarchy; republican theorists have deliberated thoroughly about what institutions enable real political life to flourish. Sometimes they endorse a fundamental populism, such as they imagine in the direct democracy of the Athenian assembly; sometimes they detail a populism mediated through institutional "channels" for political life, such as the constitutionalism favored by thinkers such as Cicero and the American Founders. Either way they seek structures that function as anti-structures – systems that shake up rather than channel political authority, and thus keep things unsettled (or at least regularly unsettle them, though even that latter "regularity" is accepted only begrudgingly).[14] In contrast to communitarians, civic republicans see "civil society" as a lively,

---

13. See Gibson 2000, Pettit 1997; and for a critique see Millar 2002: 146–7.
14. There is a powerful strand of civic republicanism that endorses the state as unproblematically the goal of a virtuous citizenry, and is willing to use religious rituals and language to magnify the state's sacrality for citizens; but this strand of republicanism seems to me to be least usefully distinctive from communitarianism; for more see Wright 2005.

because perpetually disrupted, political order. Far from being the furnace in which a national identity is fused, politics ensures that no civic consensus gains a stultifying grip on the body politic. Political engagement does not make the nation; it makes *citizens*, political agents who are not somnolescently dependent upon the social largess of the government (where "government" includes also the hegemonic force of the opinion of their fellows), and thus who do not succumb to tyranny.

The key task for such a republicanism is the sustenance of a rich and vital civic order that will infuse political life with sufficient heterogeneity to resist the structural ossification and political arteriosclerosis that inevitably ends in the "naturalization" of political authority in the hands of some over against others. The political equation expressed in Lincoln's "Special Message to Congress" in 1861 captures something of this republican mindset; Lincoln says therein that government is always either too strong for people's liberties, or too weak to sustain itself. We should want a state that is always threatening to decline, for if we do not have that, the state is growing in power, which is typically worse. The ideal is not unity of national purpose (though such is not the anti-ideal either – national unity is not inevitably a disaster whenever it appears), nor is such unity necessary for the full realization of our individual humanity; the ideal is the citizenry's genuinely moral autonomy, an autonomy that is always at least distantly imperiled by society's "immanentist" urges, its desire to focus on the here and now as the *summum bonum*.

Communitarians' form of civic critique centers around their concern for apathy; apathetic disengagement is the problem, they feel, and the state must work hard to encourage engagement. Republicans, by contrast, worry not about apathy but about tyranny and luxury, which lead to oppression and, ultimately, slavery. This is the core motivation of their political criticism. For republicans, the state makes an unceasing if implicit claim on our obedience, merely by existing; and it is ultimately up to us to decide whether and how far we obey. But the state is ravenous for our loyalty, and it will always want more obedience than we offer. Ultimately this is bad even for the state, as it turns us from citizens into subjects. So part of our obligation to the state – which is also indirectly our obligation to ourselves – is to resist its siren song of infinite obedience. To borrow an idea from Ian Shapiro, the best strand of civic republicanism imagines democracy not so much as a political structure as an "ethic of opposition," a means to resist the abandonment of responsibility that political structures tend inexorably to encourage.[15] Such an ethic reflects a deep skepticism about political structures; as William Galston says, quoting Jon Gunneman, "the liberal state, like any state, is not and cannot be fully legitimate," and the degree to which most thinking persons feel vaguely scandalized by that idea is a sad metric of the perverse success, in our society, of a corrosive civic complacency (Galston 1991: 117).

This republican picture is not what typically goes by the name of "politics" in our culture; but that may not be a bad thing, for, as we have seen, such "politics" largely refers to the hegemonic and bureaucratic management of our lives by other people. And its intrinsic attractions are manifold and profound. It offers a picture of politics that is not tied to the idolatry of a rights-bearing individu-alist privatism or to that of a group-based communitarianism, while seizing elements of both for its own purposes. Of course, such a strategy may drive civic life perilously close to anarchy. But its basic insight is sound: politics is what we make of it – and we are what it makes of us.[16]

Such a view could be quite welcoming of religious citizenry, for such citizens' faith helps challenge the state's perpetual desire for a too thorough worldliness, by constantly reminding citizens of a "beyond" to which they should attend.[17] It conceives of that beyond in an immanent moral or civic vernacular, but structurally it is analogous to Christian transcendentalism, and so has resonances with Christianity. But civic republicanism is as much a challenge to Christians as it is a help. Christians can take from civic repub-licanism its affirmation of civic participation as the primary public good, its suspicion of all attempts at political closure, and its insistence that explicitly political structures are fundamentally

---

15. See Shapiro 1990: 266: "Democracy's principled hostility to hierarchy and to claims of political expertise ... makes it uniquely attractive as a system of political organization ... Democracy as I describe it is better thought of as an ethic of opposition than a system of government." See also Shapiro 2003. A similar position is that of J. Stout 2004.
16. Thanks to Catherine Oliver for this formulation.
17. See Deneen 2005, Hatch 1989, Morone 1998, and Sandel 1996: 320-1.

secondary to and derivative of what politics is really about – namely, civic participation. But Christians find in republicanism a dangerous immanentism, a ruthless insistence that whatever goods are to be found through politics are found in the here and now, in the flow of time itself. Christians see this immanentism as the root motor driving two problems vexing even the most interesting republican positions, namely fanaticism and apocalypticism.

Many republicans want commitment to the republic – the immanent "public thing" – to be as absolute as any communitarian would. Indeed, individual republicans must be finally absolutely committed to the greatness of their *patria*; to borrow from Machiavelli, they must love their city more than their souls. The idea of an "open-minded" republican, or a "relaxed" one, is unthinkable given the commitment republicanism demands. Ironically, traditional republicanism is both highly individualistic and highly authoritarian, emphasizing a vigilant citizenry but one whose vigilance abases itself before the god of the city. This absolute commitment, coupled with the republicans' philosophy of history, gives republicanism its tragic fatalism. Individuals must bind their fates to the wheel of history, and they are helpless to stop the wheel from rolling with them on it. Yet ironically, that this is a tragedy can be appreciated only by those outside the republican mindset. On their own terms, as Augustine said about the Roman republicans, they have no grounds for complaint, for they receive the reward that they sought (*DCD* 5.15–17). They are tragically mute and deaf. Fanaticism is a tragedy, but it cannot be seen as such by fanatics.

Along with this temptation towards fanaticism, and internally connected to it, republicans also face the problem of perpetually slipping into apocalypticism. They are always tempted to presume that now, this time, at last, they have built a political order that will finally escape the Polybian cycle of birth in virtue, growth into greatness and glory, and decay through luxury into slavery and collapse. But because this cycle is identical with history itself, they thereby become enemies of history, warriors against time, hoping that history has reached its end in their republic, and trying to convince themselves that it really has.[18] (There is something awesome about our human capacity, throughout history, repeatedly to

18. See Pocock 1975 and Shapiro 1990: 169–72, 211.

convince ourselves of something like this – sometimes even in full historical knowledge of the ultimate futility of such fantasies.) Republics may sound like they have transcendent goals, like the sacralization or sanctification of the nation; but the sacrifices they demand, the martyrs they make, for the sake of glory or fame are ultimately reduced to immanent (and ultimately narcissistic) ideals because of the apocalyptic frame within which they are conceived.[19]

Civic republicanism offers many insights. Christians can appropriate its affirmation that the primary good of politics is civic participation, its concomitant resistance to the idea of the state as an ultimate good, its challenge to the reification of authority, its recognition that "politics" cannot be escaped, and its emphasis on the prime necessity of cultivating robust political virtue in its citizens. But Christians should resist the apocalyptic idea that the immanent goods of politics are humanity's ultimate goods, as civic republicans often claim. Christians ought not to be sheer civic republicans, not because they do not agree with its critiques of the state, or because they do not recognize the Polybian cycles, but because they affirm that such cycles are not the final end, that there is something "beyond tragedy." Indeed, more thoroughly than civic republicanism allows, Christians should see politics as endless but worth engaging in anyway, in order to help cultivate real human virtue and piety. Christians have good reasons to refuse to be trapped in immanence; and in refusing this, they can offer a different, perhaps purer republicanism, one purged of its immanentist leaven.

Reconceiving sovereignty: faith in but not of politics

In sum, then, we are in an interesting and possibly promising position. We see beyond the assumption that politics is a device to make government a form of service industry. And we can appreciate the somewhat problematic communitarian recoil from that, and the more constructive, though still problematic, civic republican alternative. To do better, we should move towards a "theology of citizenship" that places republican themes within a

19. For an interesting analogous criticism of republics, see Shapiro 1990.

larger framework of Christian ascesis. Christians affirm the communitarian insistence that community has theological valences, while also exploiting the republican insistence on the endlessness of politics. Politics is endless, both in the vulgar temporal sense of perpetually unfinished, like a running sore, and in the more properly philosophical sense of refusing to see any distinct and discrete "end" for politics or political activity outside of the eschatological logic of Christian redemption. Politics, during the world, neither moves in some natural cycle, nor possesses an intrinsic end. Yet public engagement is not optional; it is simply never justified immanently, but has a transcendent legitimation. Political life as we experience it today is not the proper form of public life – it is an ersatz practice, at least as much a way of coping as a means of grace, an inescapable activity that is, like everything else, a mixed blessing.

Our theological account can begin where there is at present a felt absence – around the concept of "sovereignty" itself. If, as some argue, we live in a "post-secular" era (Coles 1997: 8), it is because we live in an era that has begun to resist reflexive obeisance towards all immanent – that is, modern – sovereignties, even the post-Ockhamist sovereign autonomous subject (itself derived from Ockham's doctrinally and conceptually dubious picture of a wholly voluntarist God). What is political community when the ideal of immanent political sovereignty is absent – when faith in a transcendent sovereign replaces the keystone of sovereignty with an open-air skylight?

The most interesting and detailed recent vision of Christian commitment to political life is offered by Oliver O'Donovan. O'Donovan argues that Christians worship God in obeying the political authorities, and that such obedience is the acme of the political realm. But this account is flawed because it obscures the role of *citizen* in politics: where Christian citizens are needed, O'Donovan promotes Christian subjects. *Pace* O'Donovan's account, the political order remains, until the eschaton, far more "unredeemed" than he allows; hence political life can never finally be a matter of simple obedience. As a counter to O'Donovan, we will sketch a "Christian republicanism" that tries to avoid the dangerous immanentism inherent in secular civic republicanism.

Recovering traditional sovereignty

For O'Donovan, "politics was changed by the Incarnation" (2001: 139). It brought the political powers into the economy of salvation. But these powers are not *redeemed* – their ties straightened, their shirts tucked in – and then allowed into the heavenly City of God; rather, they have now been subjugated, their false sovereignty broken, and the authorities and their subjects reminded that they are fully in debt, for their authority, to the Triune God. This reminder should make the authorities and their subjects understand their political behavior along the model of how they obey the divine. For O'Donovan, that is, politics must be understood as a form of liturgy, worship, and the church's particular political mission is evangelical: "If the Christian community has as its *eternal* goal, the goal of its pilgrimage, the disclosure of the church as city, it has as its *intermediate* goal, the goal of its mission, the discovery of the city's secret destiny through the prism of the church" (286).[20] Because of this task of mission, understood as the ever deepening "Christianization" of the whole society, the church has a "political" valence, and in support of its missionizing activity it can call upon the power of the state (217–18). What we today call "politics" should be understood as a form of mission, an extension of the mission of the church. After all, it is the church, and not the "nation," that bears the seeds of the true, eschatological, political form: "The church never was, in its true character, merely the temple of the city; it was the promise of the city itself" (285). In the end, the "desire of the nations" is for the nations to be overcome, disintegrated, and reconstituted in the church.

On this account, politics is "*the theatre of the divine self-disclosure*" (82), the arena in which we most fundamentally witness (to) God's glory. Set in this theological context, the tradition's concept of authority is remote from both poles of the modern dichotomy of "state sovereignty" and individual sovereignty (81); authority is the possession neither of the sovereign nor of the people, but is a gift from God for the good of both.[21] This is not in any way simply a

---

20. Unless otherwise noted, page references throughout this section are to O'Donovan 1996.
21. The similarities with Augustine's understanding of authority should be clear; but O'Donovan equally suggests that Augustine "smudged over" the "sharp distinction between political and pastoral tasks" (202).

divinization of political power. Quite to the contrary: in this vision, the church teaches the state to be humble, in large part by teaching it to acknowledge God as the only sovereign, and to recognize that all sovereignty, including its own, is a *potestas alienatum*, borrowed from the divine (219). But this equally means that that borrowed sovereignty is really *very* powerful; and that we should recognize in it the will of God.

The power and value of this account cannot be gainsaid. There is something refreshing and right in O'Donovan's brisk rejection of the "customary affectation of dismay at the supposed quietism of this picture" (147). And his assault upon the pieties of contemporary political life always provokes thought. He resists the idea of civic engagement as an absolute good (225) and he dismisses the idea of modern democracy as "strictly a fiction" (270), for democracy

> must always amount to the creation of a special political class which differs from other ruling classes in other forms of polity not by being representative (for they too are representative) but by having its representative status clarified by stringent electoral procedures ... The attempt to give substance to the notion of universal rule ... is not what is important about Western democracy. (269–70)

Because of this, he criticizes accounts of politics that do not acknowledge the primordiality of authority, that depict "political responsibility in a vacuum" (17).

O'Donovan is right that too often we settle for the nostrums of "liberty" without really thinking through its deep meaning. But his focus on authority, and on the idea that the political realm is most fundamentally one in which we apparently passively *witness* the glory of God, does, after all, seem problematically quietistic. For him, in the end, the essence of politics lies in the act of *obedience* to authority, and authority in our world inevitably possesses a religious cast. It is not simply that the fundamental political act is that eschatological moment when, at the name of Jesus, every knee shall bow; it is that political obedience today is legitimate only as a form of worship. In consenting to the state, you consent to God.

How has he reached this point? He begins by arguing that the basic political problem is authority – or rather, the lack of a workable concept of authority in modernity. While "authority is the nuclear core, the all-present if unclarified source of rational energy that motivates the democratic bureaucratic organizations of the Northern hemisphere" (16), in the "northern democracies" there seems no way to acknowledge the necessity, and even the good, of authority; instead all we hear, and all we seem able to speak of, is the knee-jerk and massive suspicion of authority (16–18). Political authority mediates our good to us in an "alienated and alienating form," to be sure, yet it remains *our* good (31). But to recognize it we need fundamentally to recover a more adequate picture of politics. Part of our problem here is fundamentally philosophical, rooted in our lack of any adequate "ontology of human freedom," which would reveal our anxieties about obedience to be the result of our bad voluntarist inheritance (30–1). But correcting our philosophy is not enough; more than simply downloading the right theoretical software into our heads, we must sketch a *"normative political culture"* (230) in which authority has a workable place.

All this is meet and right. The invisibility of authority in contemporary political culture is quite problematic, as others have noted as well.[22] But O'Donovan's preemptive dismissal of the tired pieties of modern politics does not really avoid the problem here, for the complaint against him is not fundamentally political but theological. Ultimately his problem is not his bracing dismissal of delusions about the realities of modern democracy – a dismissal that differs from many political scientists only in its vehemence – but rather his assumption that that dismissal leaves only a premodern picture of power for any possible politics. I agree we must beware a "liberal" account of "democratic faith" as a substitute for the church (219); but is there no space between a politics built around obedience to concrete authorities and one built around anarchic individualism? We need a picture of authority more supple than this dichotomy allows.

O'Donovan is obstructed from so imagining an alternative by his implicit understandings of "rule" and "power." In a sense "rule" is his principle concept; as he says, "It is not clear how we can see political authority as conferring freedom, rather than taking it away, unless we have first learned to think in terms of a rule that is salvific" (127). But he does not really think through the concept of "rule" – to uncover a deeper theological sense of it – in the same

22. See especially Seligman 2000.

way that he rethinks "authority." To do that, he would also need to
rethink the concept of power that lies behind his concept of rule.
And, ironically enough, he seems simply to accept an essentially
secular picture of rule itself. For O'Donovan, to have proper
authority, to rule rightly, is to wield the power to have others
voluntarily obey you. But is this an adequate concept of power,
either politically or theologically? After Arendt's mediations on the
difference between "power" and "violence," and the many liberationist theologies' insistence on empowerment as a reality for the
whole populace, it is hard to accept such a monochromatic picture
of power. O'Donovan's failure to expand his understanding of
power infects his understanding of politics, causing him to identify
it too totally with the concept of ruling.

This failing is caused by his too sanguine picture of political order $\ast$
in this world, driven by his too immanent and "realized" account of
sanctification: Christ's redeeming power works here and now, and it
works on the political order itself. O'Donovan too tightly joins
together heaven and politics, the kingdom of God and the kingdom
of this world. He makes the eschatological kingdom of God too
much like a this-worldly political entity, and the political structures
of this world too much like the kingdom. These assumptions
undergird his excessively confident assessment of prospects for a
contemporary Christendom. So to do better than O'Donovan, we
must rethink his concept of rule, which involves rethinking his
understanding of Christ's presence in history.

As regards the consummation of the kingdom, O'Donovan
assumes a stronger than warranted continuity between our worldly
anticipations and the supra-worldly satisfactions that await us. By
suggesting that Christ's effect is largely accomplished, O'Donovan
obscures the possibility that our current vision of salvation may be
revealed to be problematically provincial, too tightly tied to our own
limited perspective in space and time. Salvation is not fundamentally a condition of obedience or consent, but of liberation. To
describe it most fundamentally as consent is to encourage too
complacent a continuity between what we are called to accept here,
during the world, and our ultimate destiny. But this, as I said, suggests a bit too easily that we can "read off" of our current condition,
with some confidence, what our properly sanctified lives will be

like. And this seems highly dubious, not to mention potentially dangerous soteriologically.[23]

Secondly, as regards worldly life, O'Donovan conflates political structures with divine ordering. It is less clear than O'Donovan thinks that Christ redeems not only the world, but the political order itself. Christ has certainly changed everything, but not by baptizing the structures of *ordo* established east of Eden. This resistance need not move, as O'Donovan insinuates, towards a vision of the political authorities as demonic "powers," nor does it compel us to urge Christians to flee to the church as the only alternative: the church is no more pure in this life, no more a haven of righteousness, than any other institution. Furthermore, O'Donovan's confidence is too generally determinate; he is unwarrantedly confident that we can know the determinate shape of today's world from the Gospels. We should rather affirm a more open-ended eschatology, one that encourages us to affirm more vigorously that we know neither the day nor the hour of Christ's coming. If politics has truly changed because of the Incarnation, it has done so in ways that do not lessen our need to understand ourselves, and the rest of the world, as under a judgment we do not fully, and cannot fully, comprehend.

Construals of our current condition and our ultimate aim should differ from each other more dramatically than O'Donovan's account allows. We can do better by determining how Christians should exercise authority, and participate in political sovereignty, without succumbing to the idolatry of identifying God with the political structures they inhabit. To determine this we must answer two questions. First, how should we inhabit authority, in order best to remind ourselves that we undertake that inhabitation in fear and trembling, and to signal to others that we recognize the difference between the office we occupy and the person we are? Second, how should we properly acknowledge political authorities, devolving into neither anarchic resistance nor robotic obeisance? Help in answering the first question can be found in Augustine's own thought and example. Help in answering the second can be found in

---

23. This is an epistemological, not an ontological, point; it is our comprehension of the continuity that I challenge, not the continuity itself. The continuity is real; but it will be properly visible only from the perspective of redemption, not before.

civic republicanism. Both appropriations, we will see, turn on returning to and thinking through our received understanding of sovereignty. We turn to these topics next.

Augustinian politics: an endless secular republicanism

In thinking about authority we do well to turn to Augustine's thought. Certainly Augustine was in no sense a democrat, egalitarian, or populist. But his thought was very complex and chagrined about the nature of human authority. If participation is fundamental to Augustine's overall thought, how can we develop it for our purposes?

We saw earlier that Augustine can offer us at best indirect help. But such indirect help as there is, is considerable. First of all, Augustine's basic socio-political analytic apparatus is decisively shaped by republican concerns and concepts. His critical analysis of the moral state of society derives heavily from earlier Roman republican sources, and he agrees with them that a society's civic health is determined largely by its moral health.[24] This gives rise to Augustine's assessment of culture, which is essentially that Christians should oppose chaos and immorality (which is simply chaos internalized). Given this latent "civic republicanism" in Augustine, we can generate the following argument. In our setting, Christians are well advised to care about the civic order for negative reasons, for fear of what it might become – and what, by extension, it might do, in a degenerated state, to the character of its inhabitants. Because the contemporary drift of civic life, as we have argued, is towards the corrosion of citizens' character, Christians should be involved in civic life to resist its slide in consumeristic directions – which corrode both real politics and the prospects for proper Christian character formation.

Furthermore, his thought is surprisingly anti-elitist, in ways that help us develop a theology of faithful citizenship that is recognizably Augustinian both in contour and in content. Augustine's anti-elitism is most visible in his theology of grace, which is, in

---

24. See, e.g, his use of Ciceronian civic republican rhetoric in his correspondence with Nectarius, *ep.* 90, 91, 103, 104. More generally see Inglebert 1996: 399–592, esp. 502.

R. A. Markus's felicitous phrase, a "defense of Christian mediocrity" against monastic virtuosi elites of various sorts, most notably the Pelagians. On the one hand, no real perfection is available in this life, so the highest aims of the most rigorous Pelagians are impossible, and reflect a delusionary and sinful self-understanding. On the other hand, he thinks asceticism is not something pursued exclusively in the monastery; ordinary *rudes* – the unlettered "great unwashed" of his congregations – need be no further from the life of struggle than the most rigorous monks, and when presented with the opportunity Augustine expected them to treat their suffering in properly ascetic ways. Asceticism was for him not something some select group undertook for the rest of us; it formed the shape of the Christian life in general. (Indeed, Augustine delivered sermons on the ascetical opportunities – even the obligations – available to the *rudes*.) This anti-elitist "popularizing" of asceticism was far from Luther's "priesthood of all believers," of course; but it does stand in some affiliation with it, however distant.[25]

Alongside this anti-elitism, Augustine's analysis of sin made him deeply ambivalent about the prospects for solid human authority. He typically hedged his theoretical arguments for authority with an insistence on the importance of a scrupulous and meticulously self-critical attitude on the part of the authority himself; furthermore, his actual behavior as an authority was often self-subverting and self-critical in ways that made his contemporaries (both those of his own rank and those "beneath" him) uncomfortable, and his theological descendants un-Augustinian, precisely to the degree that they forgot his example and relaxed into claiming an untroubled authority. Augustine's theocentricism does not finally support all this-worldly authoritarianism, but aims to subvert it. This can be seen even in his early defense, against the Manicheans, of the rightful role of authority in inquiry; far from presenting an apologia for authoritarianism, his account of authority in texts like *de magistro* is meant to secure an appropriate place for authority while acknowledging the impossibility of any human ever fulfilling the office of "author." Augustine's insistence on the need for explicit authorities is really an appeal to humility on our part when faced

25. See Markus 1990a, Cooper and Leyser 2000, Leyser 2001, Mathewes 2002c, and Cavadini 2004. More broadly see Salzman 2002.

with authorities of the past, not an arrogation of power and pride into the office of bishop. He emphasizes the fundamental importance of participation by the whole community. Differences in rank and function among humans shrink to insignificance when compared both with the common task set before us – the task of coming to praise God – and with our common condition of being sinners. When placed in the context of ancient accounts of authority, Augustine's account is remarkable for how it recognizes that all human *imperium* stands under the judgment of a transcendent *dominium* that always escapes perfect representation.[26] In his view, a truly "prudent" authority accepts the burden of authority with fear and trembling, for to be an authority is to become an instrument of God in an altogether new way – and it means that one must seek constantly to understand how God is using one to advance God's purposes.[27]

This prudent authority is visible in Augustine's understanding of how humans "borrow" divine authority in teaching, and in all issues of authority *simpliciter*. How can one prudently be an authority, when one knows one's own sinfulness and one's temptations towards *superbia*? This was a problem Augustine struggled with, both theoretically and existentially, throughout his life. Augustine knows the power of *auctoritate* in his culture, both by witnessing its impression (at times quite literally) on himself as a pupil, and by his own exercise of it as teacher and master. But he came to see that all such authorities, inasmuch as they attempt to grasp authority, fail to grasp it: they both fail to grasp the concept of authority (and hence fail to understand themselves as vessels through which authority works and so fail to understand the inner nature of authority itself) and they fail actually in their self-proclaimed project, to become the *fons et origo* of their own authority (and are thus engaged in a futile task which likely works to stymie

---

26. See Griffiths 1999: 69, 161–4, Doyle 2002, and T. Martin 1998 and 2005; see also the work on Augustine's concept of church, e.g. Harmless 1995, Leyser 2001, and Schlabach 1994. On the question of toleration in premodern thought, see Laursen *et al.* 1998.

27. For a magisterial example of this see Augustine, *sermo.* 13. In fact it is at least possible that it was the textual enactment of this vision of authority in the *conf.* that provoked Pelagius' famous hostility to that text upon first hearing it – that his theological disapproval was secondary to his social-pedagogical disapproval. See Mathewes 2002c and Cavadini 2004.

their proper exercise of authority). The classical Greco-Roman vision of stern authority, with its apparent marble confidence in the controlling hand of the master, was cunningly subverted by God's uncanny providence. In fact, insofar as people have any real authority, they have it from someone else, not just socially (by the grace of etiquette and deference) but also more deeply ontologically. Augustine saw this early on, in his confrontation with the Manichees, and it is the deep point behind his claim, in the early dialogue *de magistro*, that Christ is ultimately the only teacher, and we are all at best "occasions" for learning, but not ourselves instigators of it. Recall Augustine's discussion of his own education in the *confessiones*: education does things to the students that neither students nor teachers fully comprehend, and plants seeds that neither can control.[28] Authority is legitimate only on theological grounds; because sin disorders human society and human individuals, authority can ultimately be grounded only on divine authority, and all human authority is borrowed, and should be exercised humbly and with hesitation and the constant confession of the authority's own weakness. In all these ways Augustine's account suggests how to inhabit authority in fear and trembling.

Civic republican thought can help as well, particularly in its challenges to the reification of authority and its recognition that "politics" can never be settled. But Christians ought to resist the civic republicans' idea that the immanent goods of politics ("glory," say, or "fame") are the ultimate goods. Civic republicanism's emphasis on participation, and its sense that there is more value in political engagement's indirect goods than in its direct benefits, resonate with Christians, who can develop these ideas through their understanding of liturgy. As O'Donovan argues, the fundamental Christian act – the act that serves as a paradigm for all other acts – is worship, the communal liturgical devotion to God. But worship is not fundamentally an act of mere obedience to a God of alterrifying sovereignty; it is proleptic participation, through Christ, in the endlessly self-giving love of the divine *perichōrēsis* which is our eschatological destiny. Conceiving of politics as a form of liturgy lets

28. See *conf.* 1 and, later, the example of Alypius being warned away (futilely) from the games by an offhand remark of Augustine's, an event that Augustine did not intend to apply to Alypius (*conf.* 6.7.12). For more on this, see Mathewes 2003.

us see politics as a properly soul-forming activity – but, *contra* O'Donovan and civic republicans, in a thoroughly non-immanentist, anti-apocalyptic, eschatological manner.

Christianity's relation with civic republicanism is ambivalent. First of all, elements of a republican mindset saturate the history of Christian political thought.[29] More basically still, the "logic" of basic Christian theological claims support radical challenges to all forms of political sovereignty when they present themselves as "settled" and not contingent.[30] But traditional republicanism, both as a political philosophy and as a political reality, is at odds with Christian commitments. Again, the most obvious danger of civic republicanism is its tragic affirmation of immanent good as the ultimate aim of politics. As Augustine said, the civically virtuous have had their reward (*DCD* 5.15). In contrast, Christians see the republican affirmation of immanence and self-rule as merely one more species of apocalypticism, a bad orientation towards our existence in time that needs to be diagnosed and critiqued. They can take a more relaxed attitude regarding concerns about the decline of civic decency and civic community because they do not identify their good with any particular civic order. They can render republicanism more radical by underscoring the wholly indirect goods of political life, fully purging its immanentist leaven. They do this by keeping a firm grip on the difference between an eschatological imagination and an apocalyptic one, and by holding on to the former while holding off the latter – and thus incarnating a distinct way of inhabiting temporal existence.

For Christians, "political life" is endless, in two senses. First, it is endless in having no goal, no end; it has no fundamental, immanent purpose of its own, and any political program that reaches for a more than provisional purpose fundamentally misconstrues the nature of its project, and threatens to set up a political idol that it will expect all, ultimately, to worship. It may have tactical aims, and micro-purposes – such as the ordinary stuff of political life, legislative activity, campaigns for workers' rights, fair wages, changes in criminal law, etc. – but none of these should gain total theological

29. See Pocock 1975, Thompson 2005, Black 1997, Walzer 1970, Hill 1991. For connections between republicanism and millennarianism in early America, see Hatch 1977, R. H. Bloch 1988.
30. See Tanner 1992 for a similar argument.

sovereignty over Christians' imaginations. (The impetus we feel towards assuming that politics has such a purpose is due to its participation in our properly transcendent longing for the eschatological community.) Christians engage in politics because they cannot do otherwise, but they do not understand themselves to be doing messianic work thereby.

Second, political life is endless in that it should seek no closure or stasis: the goal is to keep it unsettled, resisting closure. This is as true in terms of the "spheres" of life that can become political as it is of the idea that there could be an "end" of politics in history. Any realm of human life can become a topic of political debate, and there is no temporal cessation of political concerns. Political life is supposed to be unsettling, not calming; disturbing, not reassuring; a pilgrimage, not a homestead. Nor is it simply politics' accidental character that is a function of sin; rather, politics itself, and the form of life that requires politics, is our lot only because of sin. It is a way of coping, recognizing our need to cooperate with people often quite unlike us. It is an inescapable mode of life in which we ought to be engaged, until the eschaton, but it is not one that we ought to expect to enjoy.[31]

This may sound pessimistic. But it is not – it makes politics proleptic play, and thereby makes palpable the theological longing that communitarians recognize in it, but republicans deny. Refusing to grant politics its own "proper" sphere makes public life just one more aspect of the true life we are trying to live – the true life of communion with God and our neighbor. So conceived, the ultimate aim of engaging in political life is not to seek the republicans' closed *telos* of self-rule, but rather the open-ended, un-teleological *telos* of securing for us the relative stability, during the world, to participate in the endless ecstatic praise that is our ultimate end.

The recognition of transcendence does not devolve into an otherworldly escapism, because it trades on no perniciously dichotomizing dualism between this world and the next. Politics is not what we do "here," in some sort of semi-autonomous "sphere" as an antechamber to heaven, where we will do something fundamentally different; there is only one sphere, and that is God's creation. There is no fundamental qualitative difference between

31. See Polletta 2002.

what the church *qua* church does now and what it will do in paradise, and the dualism of "this-worldly" versus "otherworldly"
structures is overcome in principle; but, *contra* O'Donovan, there is
an infinite qualitative difference between Christians' current participation in divine joy and their delight on that eschatological
morning.

How should Christians act civically in ways faithfully alert to that
difference? To begin to answer that question we should address the
fundamental danger of instrumentalizing faith for civic order. We
turn to that now.

Faithful citizenship: resisting immanence

The dangers here are large. Much of modern life is profoundly
inimical to real belief or disbelief; our economic, social, and cultural
environment encourages us to eschew strong conviction. Genuine
faith is sticky and entropic, and can bind us to people and positions
in ways that make life in market societies – which reward ease of
attachment and detachment – difficult and awkward. Furthermore,
phenomenologically speaking, conviction needs concentration;
and in our world such concentration is becoming increasingly difficult to achieve, much less sustain. We are continuously pushed
towards the kind of compartmentalization and "multitasking"
that corrodes our integrity, and increasingly lack the time or
silence needed to cultivate the disciplines (such as patience and
obedience) required by the capacity for genuine belief.[32] Finally, life in
our hyper-complex and often self-contradictory societies strongly
encourages the cultivation of a self-distancing cynicism and ironism
which, whatever their value as defense mechanisms, are deeply problematic modes of inhabiting public life and politics.[33] Contemporary
society is a rocky ground on which the seed of faith finds it hard to
gain purchase.

But the problem here is not finally historically contingent, but
perennial. Our (self-described) need to be fully in charge of ourselves –
to be in control – encourages us to "loosen" our attachments to one

---

32. See Berger 1979, Gergen 1991, Wuthnow 1998a, Carter 1994, Sennett 1998, and
   C. Smith 2005.
33. See Sloterdijk 1987, Bewes 1997, and Chaloupka 1999.

another and our beliefs. Ironically, our desire for control, manifest in the governing ideas of preference and taste, represents us to ourselves as less self-controlled than ever before, as we are captive to the tyranny of our whims, slaves of our passions.

Of course, as Chapter 1 argued, everyone in fact does live out of some core confidences, insofar as they have an identity (even if their core conviction is that they refuse such convictions). So the danger is not radical skepticism *per se*, but a superficiality in which we simply never directly reflect upon our act of believing. In this ignorance we fall into a deluded response to our condition, a pose, the pose of knowingness.[34] We assume we fully understand what we say we know; or rather, because "assume" invests our act with too much self-consciousness and agency, we never think about what we know at all. We refuse to see the depth of mystery "behind" our confidence. What we take to be both knowing and doubting are really strategies of avoiding thinking about faith, avoiding the riskiness central to it. There is an enormous tension between what we tell ourselves we know, and the realities to which our "knowledge" refers – what Václav Havel calls the "tension between the living experience of meaning on the one hand, and its unknowableness on the other" (1989: 152) – and we tacitly acknowledge that tension by frequently changing our opinions about things, deepening them or simply tossing them overboard. But we avoid confronting the fact, or investigating the implications, of how frequently our beliefs change, and so those changes do not become significant, and are not incorporated into a rich narrative of growing in wisdom about the flimsiness and shallowness of our knowledge. We do not admit we live in history, and are thus ourselves ongoing projects; we would rather die than change, so we try to avoid having real beliefs, rather than confront what it would mean to have faith, and especially its implications for who we are. We cannot stand live questions, and because such questions are part of life, we try hard not to be alive at all. We presume to epistemological purity, a condition of having fully realized one's goals, no longer needing to question, to exist in time. Our knowingness has apocalyptic pretensions, tempting us at every moment to think we know, at last, the way we will at the end of history.

34. For more on this "knowingness," see Lear 1998 and Phillips 1996.

Our explicit convictions are analogous to a crust of ice of unknown thickness covering an abyssal sea that we must cross.[35] Yet only faith itself can teach us the danger that it faces, by teaching us the real fragility of our grasp on our faith, and the profundity of its grasp on us. (Just as Barth said that only Christians sin, we can say that only true believers know the shallowness of their faith.) Faith teaches us this by forcing us to confront both how and how much we rely on our faith; it thereby helps us become more fully eschatologically minded beings.

But how does it do this? How can we capture the dynamic energies, both intellectual and psychological, of true belief? How do we cultivate faithfulness?

The practice of suffering faith

To see how to cultivate faith we must understand what it properly is. Faith is complex, and possession of it is ambiguously related to conscious human agency. One's faith is the deepest thing about one, the most profound orienting guide in life; and yet at those foundations, Christianity has claimed, we find a struggle between belief and unbelief, righteousness and unrighteousness. In this life faith is never fully realized, incompletely apprehended in the "now," existing as we equally do in the "not yet."

Because we exist in this tension, our inhabitation of faith takes time, and because it takes time, it is best understood not simply as an epistemological state, but as a way of life, a spiritual practice. It is difficult, so we must labor to achieve it, and it is painful, so when we achieve it we are in a certain way suffering. But this suffering is simply a way of inhabiting the world in a rawer fashion than before – a way of attempting not to avoid or sugarcoat the real and painful changes that the world continually forces upon us. Suffering is part of Christianity's fundamentally kenotic, non-apocalyptic orientation in the world, best understood, not as a fully realized satisfactory answer to questions that we have been self-consciously asking ourselves all our lives, but rather as an orientation to a reality which gives us "fullness of life."

---

35. So Christians cannot claim any copyright on this faith; for corollaries see Phillips 2001b, van Fraassen 2002, and Elster 1993.

What is the nature of proper Christian faith? The first thing to note is faith's stabilizing power, its capacity to organize and orient our life plans through its affirmations. Cognitively, faith is often a matter of finding a history for ourselves, of telling a story about ourselves that gives us a comprehensive narrative; affectively, it is a way of understanding and affirming some loves or commitments in ways we were not doing before, ways that begin to harmonize our various affections. This cognitivity and affectivity are mutually reinforcing: by rendering the story of "how I got to be the way I am" more intelligible, these cognitive transformations deepen our affective commitments, while this affective transformation reduces the discomfiting dissonances among our attachments and valuations, and hence renders more luminous and intelligible our cares and commitments.

Every organizing "faith" has these marks. But Christian faith is more complicated in its concreteness. Its stability is leavened by a deep dynamism and open-endedness, for Christians confess a loving and free God, whose plan is not yet accomplished and whose ways cannot be fully known. Hence this faith implies an active disbelief, the decisive renunciation of certain idolatrous claims, and also challenges the faithful's achieved understanding of those propositions that they affirm.[36] Christian faith resists apocalyptic conclusion, and cultivates an eschatological attitude toward it, by continuing to question and by remaining open to those who would question it. Growth in faith is inevitable, and should work towards a deeper narration of our lives, a narration that depicts us as pilgrims, journeying towards a goal whose reality is only partly apprehensible to us before we reach it. In our youth we believe and go where we will; but with age we discover that our beliefs take us where we do not want to go. To be not a "true believer" but truly a believer is always, in this life, to be enduring, to be discovering the narratibility of our lives, and thereby how we will participate, in integrity, in eternity. The soul's ascetical struggle to be faithful is one of resisting its own sinful desires for closure, cessation, and death in favor of participating in God's endless ecstatic love of the world. Where once we sinfully feared the naked exposure that faith's ascesis leads us toward, in graceful faith we come to see it as

36. See Morse 1997.

another mode of wonder and awe at God's will. Faith – or the conversion and reordering of the soul to which our term "faith" really refers – is in no way a conclusion; it is only the beginning.

This faith is not a matter of tepid agnosticism or an indifferent skepticism, but a passionate seeking after, driven as it is by the desire for deeper knowledge, and not the skeptical shrugging off of that desire.[37] Nor is this primordially a voluntary act; there is no hyper-voluntary "leap of faith" because we are always already "faith-full," always already committed to worldly confidences in ways we do not know. We seek after because we are sought, because we are called out by name. Christian faith offers us a grounding and an identity, to be sure, but only by anchoring us, our cares and our narrative, in something "beyond" ourselves. In this way faith is ecstatic in its very nature; indeed, properly speaking our faith itself is not our own but "borrowed," as with the first principles of *sacra doctrina* for Aquinas. We have faith because God keeps faith with us, because God gives us faith.

Nor is faith apprehended merely negatively, the absence of conclusion; it has positive content as well, apprehended in hope. Hope informs the content of our faith, the knowledge it gives us. Faith is not inflexible or impervious to criticism; it knows (hopefully) that other voices speak God's will, and that it is good to listen carefully to them. Furthermore, faith has hope that its deeper sense is yet to be revealed. Hope reveals our faithful knowledge's temporal dimension; it infuses our knowing with a "not yet," with a resistance to the delusion that we know anything completely, even the most mundane things. This is true because we are sinners, of course, but it is also true because nothing yet bears the full weight of its eschatological glory. (The wonder we feel, from time to time, at the transfiguration of the mundane is in this way a proleptic foreshadowing of what we will see in the eschaton.) As Jürgen Moltmann says, even our most homely metaphysical concepts are eschatological, prophetic, "pro-visional" (1975: 270). Hope teaches us to see all things, in Adorno's phrase, in the light of redemption. This is especially so concerning particularly religious knowledge: "Theological concepts do not give a fixed form to reality, but they are expanded by hope and anticipate future being. They do not limp

37. See Turner 1995a and Davies 2001.

after reality and gaze on it with the night eyes of Minerva's own, but they illuminate reality by displaying its future" (Moltmann 1975: 36). Hope is the source of our reasons, yet it also relativizes our reasons eschatologically.

But faith is affected not only by hope, but also by love. Faith's loving energy makes the faithful person seek to share her faith with others, out of care for them. This care takes many forms. But the faith that God is in charge, and the deepening sense of the detailed contours of God's sovereignty, coupled with the hopeful and grateful confidence that this sovereign God is a *loving* God, coalesces in an energized concern for others that opens faith to others' counter-claims and checks on oneself, compassionately and kenotically.[38] Hence as hope vexes all pictures of the mind as a camera, love opposes all presumptions that the mind is fundamentally self-sufficient. Most of our faith comes from others; and our knowing occurs in a larger community of knowing and unknowing. The believer is part of a communal project – not of individuals acquiring true beliefs, but of a community collectively moving through time towards understanding.

Together, hope and love help shape faith into a confessional practice. *Confessio* was originally a public, legal term. The confession of faith is not so much a revelation of some otherwise private, subjective inner world, but a commitment to a particular public stance, and to a particular eschatological community. And it is not fundamentally an act or an achievement – the exhibitionism of modern television talk-show confessions – but rather an acknowledgment, the public acknowledgment of our common condition as those on the way of faith, wounded by God and now led forward in our lives by another.

The confession of faith is a communal confession of a common faith, the church's faith in which all participate. *We* believe, and often even our doubts and questions can be asked best in communal ways, so that the inquirer is not the solitary mind, but rather the community as a whole.[39] It does not impose on others, but invites them to share, and recognizes a common ground with others, a common ground on which we can then go on with our public

---

38. See Davies 2001.
39. See Pettit 1993, Norris 1998, and Burton-Christie 1993.

things. As such, confession is an act of love. But love also shapes faith by being the motive for its confession. Our faith is what matters to us; it is what we most want to be. And so when we show ourselves to others, we inevitably show them, if they know us long enough, our faith. Faith cannot be kept a secret; it must be shown. And what faith grasps is that God is love, that love is the fundamental character of the world; it acknowledges this in blossoming, not in the recitation of certain dogmatic formulae, but rather in works of love, the first of which is grateful praise. As such a dynamic and open-ended mode of responsive and ecstatic praise, this confessional faith is akin to philosophical wonder and Christian prayer – an awed, joyful apprehension of the basic truth of reality.

When we understand faith ascetically, then, we see it as a confessional practice and a form of prayer, ending in doxological wonder. But wonder is not faith's only practical implication. Faith confesses that God is infinite – not a brick wall into which we ultimately smack, but an endless expanse into which we journey ever more deeply. It also affirms that history is significant, that it "matters" in a way that is not finally "undone" or cancelled out in paradise. The end is not the same as the beginning. Furthermore, because this faith is inspired by a living God, and because it is inhabited by a people who know their sinfulness, it resists our apocalyptic, instrumentalizing, and technological attitudes towards the world, and instead promotes an ethics of reconciliation, an ethics of relinquishing control, of refusing to try to tell things what they are, and accepting that God will tell us, through them, just what they will become.

In these ways proper Christian faith exhibits the soul's ascetical struggle to resist its own sinful desires for closure, cessation, and death in favor of participating in God's infinite, endless ecstatic love of the world; it reveals the endlessness of our inquiry into God and God's love, the dynamic turbulence of our inquiry into God.

Faith in public: confessing faith beyond identity

Given this general picture of faith, how might faith be publicly manifest in ways that enrich public life? Simply put, faith helps us resist the magnetic agglomeration of power and authority by the institutions of the *saeculum*, in order more fully to share with one another genuinely public community by responsibly confessing our convictions. Faith helps us live more fully public lives by resisting our political institutions' tendencies to foreclose the ambiguities and ambivalences of real public community.

As we saw earlier, the state is a jealous god. But that is just one more reason why we must not allow it to become the only fact of civic life. The state implicitly presumes to be the ultimate arbiter of public life, and the ultimate topic of it. But both of these assumptions are false. In democratic societies, the state is simply the condensation of popular sovereignty, so the people finally govern; and while various proposals for and evaluations of the state's actions certainly occupy most conversation in public life, that conversation concerns society's public life as a whole, not just the explicit work of the state. The "public" and the (narrowly, "literally") "political" do not coincide. We should resist what Michael Taussig has called the "state fetishism" of modern political life (1992: 119–46). The state does not determine the properly public, and we must not identify the "public sphere" with the legislative process, or what you can say in public schools, or what the law allows the government to fund. That frame is far too constraining; a fixation on the state, and on what the state recognizes as public matters, renders invisible some of the most interesting movements in public life.[40] (Thus the political mobilization of conservative Christians was well advanced before it began to achieve legislative victories in the 1980s; Jim Crow era African American civic life, out of which the civil rights movement of the 1950s and '60s sprang, was never recognized as part of American public life, and is only now being studied as an example of what civic life can be and can do.) The nation-state is both too small and too large for many of the most important problems facing us today, problems such as the environment and globalization on the one hand, and how to mobilize local civil society on the other.[41] We must remind ourselves and the state to

---

40. Again, see Bivins 2003 on the "political illegibility" of many religious movements in public life.
41. Clearly, citizenship in some nation-state is not a prerequisite for a political life. The modern bureaucratic state is absolutely necessary to manage the complexity and galactic size of the global forces bearing down upon us and sustaining us in our societies every day. But it can also hinder us in realizing the goods of politics, because its "administrative logic" clashes with the collective, open-ended deliberations intrinsic to ground-level public life. See

acknowledge the gap between the state's vision of the society it governs and the reality of that society itself.

Furthermore, religiously faithful citizens, Christian and otherwise, are committed to a "higher" community, and so they inevitably resist the monotheism of the state, an idolatry to which republicans are susceptible.[42] More particularly, Christian faith encourages civic engagement, but also recognizes the limits of nationalism and all forms of identity politics, demanding that we distinguish between all the identities, all the "faiths" that we currently inhabit, and the faith that teaches us that our identity is only eschatologically achieved.

Many churches possess substantial, though latent, resources in their traditional political behavior that could encourage their faithful towards this kind of civic participation.[43] But these churches today typically do not see their civic programs as more than acts of purely optional, merely individual "charity"; they lack articulate ways of talking about their behavior in terms of their being both citizens and believers. The Roman Catholic Church has done a remarkable job of articulating an integrated vision of life, with encyclicals and the various bishops' statements; but their congregants, at least in the West, seem less able to do so. Most Mainline Protestants, and many of their church bodies, think that they are best able to serve public life by being sites of opportunity for public discourse, rather than participants within such discourse; so they offer themselves as crucial nodes in civil society, fundamental because they offer spaces – networking spaces, "bridging" spaces for citizens to meet and work together in public, open spaces for people who would not have other opportunities to meet. But this approach confines civil society within the horizon of secular life, and thus renders it fundamentally needing to be addressed within that horizon.[44] Finally, evangelical Christians seem haphazard in

Benhabib 1999: 728. For discussions that connect these challenges with the supposed decline of the Westphalian state system, see Paul 2004, Buchanan 2000, Krasner 2001, Scharpf 2000, Strange 1996, and Fukuyama 2004.

42. Wilson Carey McWilliams has it right: faith "counsels us ... not to expect from the Framers' extended Republic a warmer brotherhood than it can afford" (McWilliams 2003: 157).

43. See Wuthnow 1998b, Gill 1999, and McGreevy 2003.

44. See Jacobsen 2003, and Evans and Boyte 1986, on the need for "free spaces" – "free" in sense of not beholden to any particular or specific political agenda – to help organize and mobilize for political action. For evidence that churches

their civic engagement, and have not yet developed a "social gospel" of their own; limited by their lack of a rich ecclesial and social imagination, they often end up with remarkably imbalanced and partial accounts of religious civic engagement, when they are engaged religiously at all.[45]

For all their engagement with civil society, then, most Christians support it fundamentally as an addendum, an "alien work" whose reality does not internally flower from the logic of their own existence, either as citizens or as believers. And their churches suffer from a theological aphasia when they try to think about why it would be good theologically for them to participate in civic life. This aphasia renders them civically mute – that is, unable to speak in a thick and comprehensive language about the overall ordering, character, and purpose of the society as a whole. And when church authorities attempt directly to intervene in public life, they typically do so clumsily, in ways that seem to try to exploit spiritual authority for partisan political gain. Whatever the short-term advantages such interventions may bring one's chosen political candidates, it tends over the long term to blunt the effectiveness of religious participation in public life.[46] In both their silence and their speaking, they implicitly accept the master frame of the civil religion of the state or secular civic order without offering the radical challenge to that order that they should. They practically admit civic life's

---

offer such space for community activity and organization, and generally provide many social service programs, see McCarthy and Castelli 1998, Independent Sector 1988, and Cohen and Jaeger 1997. This last report notes the remarkable fact that 91 percent of the congregations under study (113 randomly selected congregations) offer community services, and 81 percent of the beneficiaries of those services are not members of those congregations.

45. See Lichterman 2005 and C. Smith 1998 and 2000.

46. Of course bishops should speak out, *as* bishops, on matters they consider central to their faith, and they finally have the right to decide what is central. But the danger of such interventions is that, unless they are tied to a long-term and systematic campaign of public intervention, they simply get folded into the vision of a wholly secular political struggle. It is certainly appropriate for bishops to talk about these things; but to do so only when a pro-choice (but personally anti-abortion) Roman Catholic is running for president smacks of mere Machiavellianism. And it is certainly appropriate for the Methodist Church to have views about whether its congregants should go to war; but to offer the occasional statement without addressing the larger geo-political context in a sustained way simply sounds like it is trying to jump on the anti-war bandwagon. Churches that act in these ways sound sinister, bullying, or pathetic, and effectively harm both their own causes and their societies' civic life. For an earlier version of these worries see Ramsey 1967 and 1988.

importance, but cannot fully explain its import in a satisfactorily theological manner.

This encourages congregants to assume that the energizing sources for actual participation in public life are fundamentally *non*-theological, that they must come from elsewhere than their churches and religious life; but this simply reinforces the general sense that civic engagement is one more "personal choice," one more lifestyle option, fundamentally a matter of sheer individual taste. This is problematic because it forgets that such participation may well be a duty to oneself and the community. Even more, it effectively discourages the sanctification of ordinary life, and hence is in profound tension with the deep encouragement of the full participation by the laity in the full work of these churches.[47]

To do better, the churches should be involved directly in the conversations that comprise civic life, articulating to the whole community, in richly theological terms, a comprehensive civic vision. (The Roman Catholic Church has a vision, but one that does not resonate with many believers nearly as fully as it should.) In so doing they will give an account of the purposes of politics that should underwrite their congregants' commitment to the common life as a theological task, and not simply a civic one.

An example of this more fruitful approach is not hard to find. Take poverty: even on the narrowest definition of "charity" – say, in their concern for impoverished, homeless, and unemployed in their communities – these churches work for political changes that make those "lost people" more visible and more a topic of direct public concern. Indeed, simply paying attention to the lived reality of impoverishment is political; a crucial part of the problem that the poor face is the blindness on the part of privileged groups to the real nature of poverty – the difficulties of living on the minimum wage, the difficulty of finding work you can commute to, of getting healthcare for those in your care (both elderly and young), of finding regular and secure childcare, even the compounding difficulty of simply making any of this unavoidably visible to those who are blissfully unaware of it. The churches' work on poverty is important, then, not simply for the direct legislative changes they may or may not achieve; more basically, it is valuable as a way to help us all

47. See Galston 2004 and Hatch 1989.

stay aware of the reality of poverty in a society where it is easily shunted off to special offices of the government (after all, over the last half-century, the state has become the largest source of social assistance), and by doing so, help all citizens live more fully in the reality of the world we inhabit, by recognizing those whom we so easily make invisible. Furthermore, in working with others – not simply with the marginalized members of society, but with other civic groups, secular and religious, committed to their empowerment – they are not only engaging in direct civic activity; by attempting to politicize these marginalized populations, they are encouraging them, and others, to become fully participating citizens as well.

This will make the state nervous, as the state tends to promote its own monotheism – the pretension that the state is the only important reality in public life. There may be worries that churches are seeking converts, or seeking a theocracy, in so doing. But if Christian citizens are faithful in their work with their fellow citizens, they will be living witnesses that this is an ungrounded prejudice. The goal of such action is not to install a permanent ecclesial ideology but rather to resist the inevitably immanentizing entropy endemic to all human realities.

An example may be useful here; how faith challenges "identity politics" will serve as one. Christian citizens face a profound problem in contemporary civic life, of being faithful without pigeonholing themselves as simply one more interest group. Many Christians, especially those to whom their faith seems most fundamental to their existence, are prone to falling into this trap. (I keep waiting to hear someone call himself or herself a "Christian-American"; I keep waiting to hear the hyphen.)

Yet while religious conviction may be a kind of identity politics, the converse is also true: identity politics is a kind of faith ascription as well. And all such public professions of faith, purportedly secular or patently religious, tend both to particularize and to polarize. Any such profession particularizes because it offers a more determinate picture of the person professing the faith; and it polarizes because it tacitly contrasts the believer with her or his audience. Recognition of this dynamic motivates many worries about religion in public: perhaps faith is inevitably a fractious force in public life, because it inevitably undercuts the possibility of actual association, expecting too much genuine existential communion, setting the bar too high for others to join in projects with the believer.

But what goes unnoticed in such cases is that such a profession of faith is also bad for the identity of particular believers, because of how they themselves understand their faith claims. Most believers do not know how to present their commitments in non-apocalyptic terms, in a way that invites their interlocutors into a conversation about the meaning and validity of those commitments. They thus become trapped into defending a particular understanding of their commitments at a particular time, and cannot allow themselves to acknowledge any change in these convictions. Their faith ossifies; their identity becomes apocalyptically fixed.

Of course, such apocalyptic identity ascription is a temptation felt by all citizens, religious and non-religious. And in a way identity politics is all we seem able to manage today; the modes of self-presentation dominant in contemporary public life encourage us to present ourselves either as too shallow to offer much of substance, or as too inflexible to collaborate and bargain. Public life is caught between too slippery superficialities and too enclosed and militant ethnic, nationalist, and religious particularisms – between what Benjamin Barber (1996) has called the hostility of "McWorld" and "Jihad." What is it about our condition that tempts us towards a rigidly dogmatic mode of public self-presentation?

Identity politics is fundamentally a defensive and protective strategy, normally used to secure a group whose existence as a group is perceived to be under threat. Such a strategy may be needed at some points and for some people or groups of people.[48] But it inevitably has damaging effects, for it closes us off from one another. It both expresses a genuine longing for community and flirts with a temptation towards a fantasized purity of the "we," an exclusive particularism where the other is written off as not part of the group. But no empirical identity is as seamless as identity politics claims, and we are all always already implicated in each other in ways that identity politics cannot handle.[49] Hence the central problem with identity politics is not with its "thickness" but with the

48. See Boyarin 1994: 242: "that which would be racism in the hands of a dominating group is resistance in the hands of a subaltern collective." And see Shelby 2005.
49. See Orlie 1999 and Boyarin 1994: 228–60.

impermeability and inflexibility of the boundaries it promotes; it cannot recognize the real complexity at the base of people, their occasional implication in several different "identity groups."[50]

The costs of the false confidence thus purchased are great, including a decline in self-knowledge, a narrowing of our proper inheritance, and a further weakening of the associative ties we feel with our fellow citizens and neighbors. You are never more than a representative of your identity; in public, I speak as a Christian, or as a gay white male, or as a gay black woman, or as a Jew, but I never quite speak as me, as the particular person I am, in public, let alone as one who is yet to be determined. Ironically, "identity politics" is anything but, for it severely narrows its adherents' identities and effectively suffocates their capacity to participate in broad-based political action.[51]

Theologically speaking, Christians ought to see such identity politics as reflecting our fallen desire for a fully accomplished, apocalyptically realized identity, one that "at last" knows what it is and inhabits that identity exclusively. And Christians should resist it. Identity is not a suit of armor we wear; part of our identity as humans is our desire for encounter with and exposure to others.

Christian faith may offer a helpful model of presenting oneself in public. This faith is inherently deeply transgressive, breaking across clearly marked identity groups, and so seems a good candidate for resisting too solid identities. It is theologically transgressive in its content, for it embodies the hope that a new shoot can be grafted on to the root of Jesse, that Christians can be adopted into a Jewish covenant; and it is metaphysically transgressive in its mode of expression, for it exploits – one might almost say "deranges" – Greek philosophical categories to convey its deeply un-Hellenic message. Furthermore, elements of Christian faith can work explicitly to resist our cultures' tendency to place that faith in the category of ascriptive identity. In particular, its properly eschatological character dramatically challenges what we can call the "apocalyptic ascriptivism" inherent in identity politics. When we confess our faith, we do not yet fully know what we are affirming, and hence we

---

50. For an interesting feminist argument that approaches this claim, see Okin 1999.
51. See the discussion of the "exclusion system" in Volf 1996: 57–98. See also Anderson 1995.

do not yet know who we are, or who we will be when we are finally called before the judgment seat. And in the interim, we should "wear" this identity in a non-defensive, "confessional" manner – welcoming conversation and dialogue, queries about what one believes, challenges to the coherence of those beliefs, and outright direct attacks on the particular objects of faith as well. People who believe differently than ourselves often have much to say that we need to hear, even as regards our central religious convictions; we should meet them with an openness that warmly welcomes them to assess our convictions. After all, they are already part of the "we" in which we condescendingly seek to include them.

Properly inhabited, such a faithful citizenship embodies genuine civic engagement, engagement skeptical of the dichotomy of seamless unity or utter disagreement assumed throughout so much of our public life. Through it we witness to our complexity, as Melissa Orlie puts it, "not appeasing the desire for pure difference but challenging its delusion ... the problem [we face] is not so much difference itself but the desire for unmixed difference, the desire for a purity that, because it does not exist, can only be forcefully pursued and insecurely achieved" (Orlie 1999: 146–7). In being such a witness, and thus challenging the delusion of the desire for pure difference, one undertakes the theologically evangelical service of witnessing to one's faith, as well as the civically virtuous service of modeling good citizenship.

"Faithful citizenship" of this sort will certainly find resonances and alliances with others who use other, non-Christian strategies to achieve a similar end, and through this strategy Christians can work with them. Many non-Christians are committed either to the common tactical goals of public engagement, and/or to the larger strategy of increasing public engagement itself, and especially members of other religious traditions have much of power to contribute.[52] Christians should always seek those allegiances out, for both theological and civic reasons. Nevertheless, the eschatological hope Christians have for the kingdom of God will probably not be the explicit basis upon which to organize alliances, even though it is precisely the faith produced by that hope that leads Christians to

52. See, e.g., Boyarin 1994, R. M. Smith 1997, Markell 2003, and Villa 2003.

seek out such alliances. Such a "convergence" of our "associational plurality" cannot be reasonably anticipated (Isaac 1997: 142–3).

Again, that is not to say that no alliances can be had. Indeed, even the received liberal democratic concept of citizenship is useful, for it is intentionally not a totalizing concept. Liberal democratic societies affirm that a person's identity is not exhausted by the political ascription "citizen"; the recognition of individuals' inviolable core, captured in the notion of "privacy," always allows the individual to be more than their civic role. (Here is where liberal notions of citizenship can usefully complicate more muscular republican ones.) And because this notion of privacy is detached from *any* form of communal identity – political, social, ethnic, religious, what have you – it also secures individuals against the latent totalizing claims of any association or identity they possess. Indeed, the liberal dialectic between "public citizen" and "private individual" is practically useful against identity politics, for we can always attempt to appeal to people as citizens – members of something more than their identity enclave – in order to begin to prise their self-consciousness apart from an apocalyptically narrow self-ascription. Faithful Christian citizens will accept as part of their practical tasks the encouragement of all citizens to such practices of existential ascesis – of recognizing that they are more than their place in social life.

But only as part. An ineliminable tension remains between Christians' faithful citizenship and more mundane forms of civic engagement, and Christians should not delude either themselves or their fellow citizens into hoping for a too simple unity. Christians should stand in deep and complicated relationship to the liberal notion of privacy, acknowledging its latent theological affirmation of the dignity of individuals while decrying its bleaching effects on communal identity and its anomie-inducing effect on individuals' sense of self.

Christians' faithful citizenship is perhaps most distinctive in its acknowledgment that our identity is not fundamentally an individualist identity but is most primordially communal. The church must be recognized as a community, but not identified with the political community. The model of citizenship proposed here certainly focuses on individuals' attitudes, and works on their dispositions, to mold them in a Christoform manner; but it does so only in order to encourage people to participate in a particular sort of community, the kingdom of God, and to understand themselves as always already formed by and in complex relation to some particular ecclesial community. The thought that Christians can undertake these practices largely alone as virtuosi of the faith is simply symptomatic of the atomistic individualism so pervasive today. Christians cannot be the sorts of individuals they should be outside of some church. To put it more strongly and perhaps more accurately, even on a sociological level, churches remain among the few cultural institutions that can still help us become the sort of people we should be.

This is not simply a nice, pious cliché. In our societies it is difficult to be the sort of people we ought to be, for we are often permitted to live in deep indifference to one another. And churches are just the sort of places where real differences can interact. This point is made nicely by Robin Lovin, who once described his church as "a group of people that includes a couple of welfare mothers, a commodities broker, two or three Filipino nurses, and a Filipino schizophrenic who carries a three-foot-high doll" (in Neuhaus 1989: 127; see Hauerwas's reply on 129). This vision of communion, running against the grain of our social divisions, suggests something of the power of the churches for social life. In such communities, people gather in groups that attempt expressly and harmoniously to connect multiple, complex, and diverse personal histories, rather than treat them as monolithic fetishes or inflexible distinguishing marks; and such are just the sorts of communities that can enable a rebirth of a real politics.[53] And the churches, whatever their failures and frailties today, remain one of the very few institutional spaces in modern societies where we may occasionally run into people who are not clones of ourselves. (Certainly academia, for all its talk about diversity, remains a remarkably homogeneous place in every way.) One civic task for Christians is, quite simply, to keep showing up in those spaces, and from them to go out of them, manifesting the kind of identity they find best suits them, the identity of people for whom there is neither Jew nor Gentile, master nor slave, male nor

---

53. This entails a certain populism, a subdued resistance to the typical intellectual bemoaning of the loss of "public intellectuals" as a specific class of people; see Bertram 1997.

female, but only children of God and citizens of the kingdom of heaven.

But that civic task does not exhaust the meaning of civic engagement. It has ascetical and pedagogical implications as well. The lessons learned in civic engagement can help Christians cultivate the kind of virtues whereby they will better become citizens of the kingdom of heaven. The next (and last) section of this chapter sketches just what that means.

The ascesis of faithful engagement

How can faith be cultivated through public life? The crucial clue lies in an important irony regarding faith. For the deep complaint of many is that faith expressed publicly is estranging. The unprovability of faith, its flagrant indifference to apologetic defense, is part of its scandal when presented in public: it seeks community, but when it is expressed publicly to those who do not share it (and to some who do) it can well be estranging, reminding us of what is, in this dispensation, our fundamental separateness from one another. To those who claim to be "without" it, or those who profess another faith – or even those who share the same faith but believe it in a different way – a "faithful" person inevitably appears, at least in part, as cruelly tantalizing, from a minuscule but unbridgeable distance, as if faith were hermetically sealed.[54] The same loving faith which turns us towards one another also highlights and accentuates the apparently ineliminable differences and distances estranging us from one another. How should we go forward from this tension?

The trick, in fact, is not to "go forward" from it, but instead to inhabit it as profoundly as we can, and to accept the disappointment it inevitably produces. This is no counsel of despair, however; a loving faith seeks to work from its given reality, and that reality is marked by manifold forms of estrangement. Only by authentically living in this estrangement can faith be cultivated. All a loving and hopeful faithfulness can do is seek to begin to share itself with

---

54. This estrangement is experienced not only by believers but by those who do not share their faith; for a nice example of what this feels like from the perspective of one being confronted with evangelization, see Frykholm 2004: 10.

others, to bring us closer – even if the first step in that process is
backwards, in the form of recognizing differences and disagreements long denied, not least to ourselves. All it can do is begin in the
present; and our present is disfigured by brokenness.

H. Richard Niebuhr's account of a non-defensive confessional
approach to belief can help us here. Niebuhr worried that faith, if
employed as a device for control, would inevitably subvert one's
engagement with others, the world, and ultimately God, rather than
enable or deepen it. And he saw this not simply, or even primarily,
as problematic for human conversation; he saw it as more disastrously a matter of violating the divine–human relationship,
denying human sinfulness and divine sovereignty:

> Such possessed revelation must be a static thing and under the
> human control of the Christian community .... It cannot be
> revelation in act whereby the church itself is convicted of its
> poverty, its sin and misery before God. Furthermore, it cannot be
> the revelation of a living God; for the God of a revelation that can
> be possessed must be a God of the past. (1941: 30)

Instead, Niebuhr proposed that faith begin confessionally, with a
non-defensive explication of itself, confessing "how one sees
things," and then waiting faithfully on the other to reply, hoping
that that reply would enrich one's faith, and with the respectful love
that sees the other as deserving such non-defensive engagement.
Here faith is not fundamentally a shield of arrogance, but a doorway
of humility into one's living existence. Manifesting faith in this way
demonstrates both that we do not know our convictions fully and
that we wish to learn more about it, both marks of true faith. To be
faithful in public, then, is nothing more than to be properly faithful.

Attempting authentically to inhabit such a confessional faith
reminds us repeatedly of how deeply we are alienated even from
ourselves, during the world. We neither fully inhabit our present
understanding of our faith, nor fully possess our final faith. We do
not fully inhabit our present faith because we can sympathize, and
likely resonate with, some suspicions about it; and we do not yet
possess our final, fully realized faith because an honest self-assess-
ment shows us how flawed and flimsy our grasp on faith now is.
Again, the self is an eschatological achievement. Proper faith,
authentically undertaken, vexes our sinful pretensions towards
perfectly and completely inhabiting any single identity, during the

world. Engagement in public life reinforces this ascesis; public life repeatedly reminds us of the peculiarities of our own convictions, and of our understanding of the obligations they impose upon us, in ways that make our convictions seem increasingly, not implausible, but dubiously defended, at least by us. In this life we are always more than our expressions of what we are; that is a vexation for us now, but it is also a promise of our coming integral glory.

Furthermore, speaking communally, such a confessional faith reminds us that we are not self-subsistent, but that we need others to understand even ourselves. Public life reveals how much we rely both on the trust, commitment, and general "good faith" of others, and on the larger belief system in which we are embedded (as faith in "tradition" is a trust in the witnesses of tradition). But our pretensions toward apocalyptic identity cannot be replaced by the apocalyptic identity of our community, for the community as a whole is unclear about what it believes – whether that "community" be our church or our nation. Here our longing for community is also revealed as an eschatological longing, inevitably only partially realized during the world.

Some might worry that this account domesticates faith, draining away its determinate content and radicality, and replacing it with a vague affirmation that "things are OK." This is a fair worry. There is an irreducible dogmatic confidence to faith; the faithful's world looks different from the non-believer's, and any account of faith must accommodate its determinateness, its "now" as well as its "not yet." But despite its legitimacy, this worry does not see that faith, precisely in its determinate content, generates an intrinsic indeterminacy. It does so simply by being honest: we do have determinate knowledge of God, but ours is in no way a comprehensive knowledge. It is no disgrace to faith to allow that God is intrinsically infinite and doing a new thing, and that the determinate knowledge God gives us, God just keeps on giving. We cannot "round off" our knowledge in a nice neat summative judgment.[55] Besides, claims that one's knowledge of God is fundamentally conclusive or absolutely determinate are not only theologically unseemly, but also dangerously apocalyptic and ascetically malforming. They encourage an identity politics of faith, reducing faith

55. See Milbank 1997: 7–35, Lash 1990, and Turner 1995a.

to a form of knowingness, a presumptuous clarity about what one believes, a clarity that is both an expression of impatience and a form of sloth, an unwillingness to imagine that one's views could yet develop or change over time. To presume that our faith gives us some grip on the general contours of God, and that this general shape will be filled in only by the details revealed in the eschaton, mistakes the nature of our hopeful faith, and the character of the God by whom and with whom we are called, like Jacob, to wrestle.

In these ways, faith is revealed to be a matter of enduring; and faith engaged in public is a particularly pronounced site for such endurance.

Conclusion

Two questions present themselves to us next. First of all, how is this resistance to an improper secular sovereignty actually manifest in political action? This is what Chapter 5, about hope, will discuss. Secondly, how can such a "faithful witness" still express a form of genuine caring about the political community and those particular people who comprise it? Is this a real form of concern abut politics, or just an instrumentalization of it? Answering this worry will be the concern of Chapter 6, about love.

5

Hopeful citizenship

Consciously or unconsciously, the eschatological thinking of the present day is determined by the messianic visions of the nineteenth century and the apocalyptic terrors experienced in the history of the twentieth century. What hope can be justified, once we wake up out of the messianic dreams and resist the apocalyptic anxieties?　　　　　Jürgen Moltmann, *The Coming of God*

How should hope shape Christian citizens' public engagement? Today hope has become just one more empty word in public life. Keep hope alive! Hope is on the way! Believe in a little town called Hope. These are not even clichés any more; they are simulacra of clichés, too aware of their own cheesiness to pretend to anyone that they could be believed. Today, hope has succumbed to cynicism. But not long ago, hope motivated public action in real and powerful ways. In America it was essential in the civil rights movement; in Central and Eastern Europe it motivated, in part, the campaigns against the Soviet bloc in the 1980s. What happened? Can we be hopeful today?

This is not in fact a merely pragmatic question; it is properly theological. For hope is always needed and always something we do not properly possess. It is a divine dynamic in which we may, through grace, participate, but which we try perpetually, in sin, to control. Our need, and our lack, are especially visible in public life, where our need of hope is accentuated because of the many frustrations that lurk therein. After all, public life is fraught with an inescapable and inevitably resentment-generating tension – a tension between the indelibly moral cast of politics and the pragmatic compromises that political life frequently forces upon us. We enter into public life confident that there is not only an effective way but a *right way* forward, and that the point of politics is to advance that right way. Yet it often comes about that reality vexes that confidence, and they find themselves compelled to compromise their convictions in order to achieve some moiety of the right as they see it, while trying not to betray their most treasured convictions; or they find themselves redefining what a previous version of themselves would have seen as a betrayal or as a compromise; or they find that their ideals do not succeed in carrying the day among other political actors and deliberators, or they find that those ideals, at least as they understood them, fail to pass the tribune of reality (as even they acknowledge it to be) when they are put into practice; or they discover themselves to be far less righteously motivated than they thought they were (which will cause them, if they are even minimally reflective, to rethink the particular importance of their moral convictions in the psychic economy of their motives); or they may become thoroughly disillusioned and come to believe that morality – their own and everyone else's – was, is, and always will be nothing more or other than a smokescreen for other, less pretty motives. In this way, public engagement inevitably places our professed ideals in palpable contradiction to our real actions, a pressure that inevitably produces ever-deepening resentment for those engaged in public life.[1]

To counteract this resentment, we need hope, which helps us survive the brutalizing banalities of public life's relentless immanence, its bruising way with our plans and expectations. To think about hope in public, we can turn to the prophets' calls for the transformation of the present order. Hence, where Chapter 4 sketched the contours of a faithful citizenship, and thus how to be properly committed to the civic order, this chapter asks something like the opposite: how to be properly estranged from public life – how to be present in and for public life yet without accepting the given protocols of that life. How can Christians be prophetic critics

---

1. The thoughts expressed here draw from the work of Bernard Williams and Isaiah Berlin.

of the contemporary, routinized civic order? And how should they understand such critique as a richly religious endeavor?

Contemporary laments for prophetic critics and public intellectuals are platitudinous, but they have a point.[2] Public discourse needs vibrant critical voices. It is hard to see those voices today, and our public life suffers for it. But Christians have particular cause to be worried, for they are religiously obliged to be witnesses, prophets, to offer imaginative alternatives to the fallen social structures in which they find themselves, thereby reminding society of the ideals to which it ought to aspire. Absent some such language, the churches cannot make their members into the Christian witnesses they are called to be.[3] The churches, and civil society, need some language in which to voice criticism, and yet we seem increasingly to lack anything that has much traction on precisely those patterns of behavior that we should resist.

But the challenge is deeper than this because, in another way, American public life today offers too much explicit critique. We live in a "culture of critique" – a public culture where critique, suspicion, and paranoia largely exhaust the sphere of public discourse.[4] It is not that "the argument culture" is especially personally nasty or toxic, but that "critical" public discourse powerfully exhibits many of the problems facing contemporary civic life in general.[5] It suffers from a failure of critical affirmation, because it rejects the "moral analysis of culture," inquiry interested in helping us intelligently and self-consciously inhabit our culture (Gunn 1985: 109).[6] While contemporary cultural criticism offers many invaluable concepts for illuminating and understanding the relations of social norms to (potentially unjust) structures of power, it remains trapped in bare reiterations of simple critique. It thus ignores the question of how we should respond in reality to our implication in the present's injustices. We lack ways simultaneously to criticize *and* affirm;

2. See West 1982 and 1988, W. Brown 1995, Wolfe 1996, McCarraher 2000, Posner 2001, and Lilla 2001. More generally, see Darsey 1997.
3. See Tanner 1997.
4. See Shannon 1996.
5. I agree with Alan Wolfe's critique of the sort of global complaints expressed in Deborah Tannen's work about the "argument culture." See Wolfe 1996: 203, 208–10, and Rescher 1993.
6. See S. K. White 2000: 151, Dickstein 1992, Krupnick 1986, Unger 1977: 266–8. For a precedent situation, see Stern 1961.

instead, we simply bewail without offering constructive alternatives, or merely defend without acknowledging and addressing the fundamental flaws in the position defended. The problem does not lie in individual critics' failure of moral nerve, but in the *habitus*, worldview, and vocabulary generally assumed by all of us when we attempt to engage in civic and cultural critique. This "culture of criticism" leaves untheorized its own mode of cultural engagement – that is, critique – as a practice of contemporary life. Contemporary cultural criticism is not too critical, but rather not critical enough. It has no critical theory of itself.

Theological analysis is more illuminating still, for the dominant forms of cultural criticism today are structurally apocalyptic, interested more in passive spectatorial prediction than in committed proposals, driven by revulsion at and recoil from the world, and hubristically confident in having – at last! – found the true code for interpreting the world. We need a more eschatological form of criticism – one acknowledging that the world is corrupted but not utterly lost, and hence still tragically significant for our existence, in a condition whose extension is indeterminate yet which is radically contingent.

Such a rich Christian "hopefulness" best emerges from a context of vibrant religious community. Speaking theologically, while we emphasize the churches' prophetic obligations, we cannot ignore the priestly vocation, of teaching the people of God how to witness, in praise and thanksgiving, to Christ. After all, the most powerful example of prophetic critique in twentieth-century America – namely, the civil rights movement of the 1950s and '60s – manifests quite clearly the importance of ecclesial preparation. It was only because the African-American churches had been developing powerful "counter-publics" to the Jim Crow "public" of the post-Reconstruction South, and had been organizing and training their congregants for half a century, that the early victories of the civil rights struggles were won. Hopeful citizenship, that is, requires a certain kind of community to sustain it.[7]

While there are non-Christian analogues of this hopeful citizenship, this chapter explicates an Augustinian political theology of

---

7. See Marsh 2005. I thank Douglas E. Thompson and Charles Marsh for conversations on these matters.

hopeful citizenship, anchored in a hopeful "hermeneutics of charity" that resists the cynicism of despair. This theology of hopeful citizenship begins with a prophecy – a diagnostic critique of contemporary critical cynicism – that shows how an Augustinian account of evil as the perversion of naturally good desires accommodates contemporary critics' insights, by seeing the failures and malformations they identify as themselves rooted in (and comprehensible in terms of) natural desires. Critique thus becomes a constructive and therapeutic project. So understood, the kind of diagnostic criticism exposited here can intellectually sustain a broader practice of hopeful citizenship.[8]

The chapter proceeds in three steps. First, it details this crisis of critical affirmation in terms of intellectuals' general failure to offer a credible "post-utopian" hopefulness, and identifies the root problem as their failure to present a picture of evil and our implication therein (on both the societal and the individual level) that can comprehend the profundity and complexity of the challenges that subvert all utopias, without overwhelming our capacity to affirm goodness; their failure here reveals the critics' captivity to a crisis of cynical despair about the goodness of the world. The chapter next sketches the theoretical basis for such a realistically hopeful critical stance, building on the hermeneutics of charity found in Augustine's *City of God*. Finally, it offers a programmatic picture of how this recovered hopeful critical stance helps sustain a larger practice of hopeful citizenship, a practice that contributes both to Christian citizens' participation in their polity's public life and to the churches' formation of their members as eschatologically minded pilgrims during the world.

The contemporary crisis of cultural criticism

We begin by anatomizing and diagnosing the problems hindering contemporary cultural critique. "Prophetic critique" today is tempted towards fundamentally reactionary spectatorial sneering. Such cultural criticism embodies an escapist apocalyptic recoil from the world, brought on by a crisis of hope about the world's goodness. To support these claims this section dissects several examples

---

8. For a similar view, see Darsey 1997, esp. 117.

of such cultural criticism. Then it seeks an explanation for the current lamentable state of cultural criticism in the current conditions of its practice. But while such a "material analysis" is suggestive, it is incomplete; for deep cultural, axiological, metaphysical and even theological problems vex contemporary cultural criticism, problems that must be addressed on a deeper level.

Secularized apocalyptic pseudo-Augustinianism

I begin by sketching an Augustinian analysis of and response to a major recent position in critical theory, that offered by Michael Hardt and Antonio Negri in their much discussed book, *Empire*.[9] *Empire*'s conceit is that our condition is analogous to Christianity's encounter with the Roman Empire, in ways that can inform a strategy for action today. And yet, for all its analytic sophistication, the book is finally a Manichean apocalyptic prophecy masquerading as a work of socio-cultural analysis.

"Empire" signifies the heterogeneous and conflictual forces of contemporary capitalist society – the whole constellation of structural forces too complex and widespread to be captured by the concept of "the state" as it has been imagined in this Westphalian era, structural forces that are completely suffused by market concerns. Their account of "Empire" has two facets. On the one hand, they offer a nuanced Foucauldian account of power as capillarial: Empire's rule is pervasive and inescapable, yet invisible, suffusing all our relations, even those we have with ourselves, and they trace the varieties of commodifying pressure those forces bring to bear on all aspects of life. It creates our subjectivity through the highly complex and incessant exchanges of capital, which constitute our very reality. There is no outside to Empire in this sense, nothing remaining beyond its commodifying grasp – least of all us (58, 186–90, 196). Yet on the other hand, Empire is a paper tiger; it is empty at the core, its "corruption is simply the sign of the absence of any ontology" (202; cf. 62, 389), and so Empire is always parasitic, indeed vampiric, on humans' real productivity and creativity; as *nihil*, it

---

9. Hardt and Negri 2000. Page references to this book are embedded parenthetically in the body of the text. Their more recent work, *Multitude* (2004), makes no advance on these problems.

cannot create the power it needs to survive. Hence something ontological inevitably "pushes back" against Empire's vampiric depredations; it contains within itself its own demise: "the function of imperial power is ineluctably linked to its decline" (361).

What should we do in this situation? Hardt and Negri offer a variety of apparent practices in which we should engage: circulation, "miscegenation," the fundamental practice of "saying no." But more importantly, they prophesy a "new social body" (204), which will emerge as Empire's self-constituted "other," a social form they label as the "multitude," and which will evolve from itself a further social structure called the "posse" (408). This posse will enact an entirely immanent, this-worldly theurgical practice which will empower its members and help them realize the goods they seek. They admit that their proposals are, after all, "rather abstract" (399); their analysis of the "posse" is nothing but a frustratingly vague prediction.

But the sheer abstractness of the proposal is not the fundamental problem; what is, is the fact that the abstractions are for them more ultimately real than the empirical realities they inhabit. They remain devotees of the old Marxist saw of "historical inevitability," simply one more version of modernity's immanent apocalypticism, the belief that we have finally cracked the code of history. This is what allows them to append to wildly optimistic prophecy utterly despairing critique:

> Imperial corruption is already undermined by the productivity of bodies, by cooperation, and by the multitude's designs of productivity. The only event we are still awaiting is the construction, or rather the insurgence, of a powerful organization ... We do not have any models for this event. Only the multitude through its practical experimentation will offer the models and determine when and how the possible becomes real.
> (411)

The ultimate optimism of this picture – the precise character of which we will examine in a moment – is not what is most noteworthy about this passage. What is, is the way that this account simply punts on practical prescriptions: "Only the multitude ... " One is reminded of *Waiting for Godot*; the model is not coming today, but it will surely arrive. It *must* arrive. This is socio-political analysis in the mode of plate tectonics, so remote from concern for human agency that there is no need for intentional action; all we need do is wait around for the inevitable demise of the status quo. Salvation is coming – and we can know it – but we ourselves are merely spectators, witnesses of its advent.

At first glance this fundamental emphasis on witness and waiting is not necessarily, at least on religious grounds, problematic. An "advental" element characterizes many religions, particularly Christianity; and our recommended Augustinian account is guided by theoretical insights, and emphasizes our fundamental passivity before these events, in ways apparently similar to Hardt and Negri. But in fact there is a large difference between the two. First of all, their view is far more purely passive than Christian eschatology because it is intelligible only through events that have not yet occurred. Their history and the narrative gain their meaning wholly through an understanding of history as determined totally from a projected future. There are no events of eschatological anticipation; no Christ-event provides a foretaste, epistemologically and ontologically. The whole narrative is a loan taken out on an at present completely hypothesized, utterly unrealized future. Furthermore, this apocalypticism is thoroughly post-Foucauldian, built around the paranoia that all are implicated in the corruptions and subversions of an all-encompassing web of power (well, all except themselves in their role as analytic prophets). It is a conspiracy so immense that we all may be a part of it. In fact we *are* the problem: they have naturalized evil, and so cannot find a way to talk about our responsibility for it. We are helpless before Empire. Of course, helplessness in eschatological terms is not bad; but the problem here is that this helplessness is existentially premised on a deep and paralytic despair of ourselves improving or struggling against this web of "power," an abdication of responsibility for it – which makes theirs fundamentally spectatorial and escapist. As Mitchell Cohen suggests, "one senses that Hardt/Negri's concern is ontological tantrum rather than alternative politics" (2002: 23).[10]

This does not discount the fundamental utopic optimism of their prophecy of Empire's demise. But the optimism that motivates their revolutionary pronouncements is truly utopian, grounded in nowhere; it is fundamentally hydroponic, unrooted in anything but

10. More generally, see Wolfe 1996: 109–10.

the artificial nutrient brew of their own theory. It is a desperately deliberate, willful utopianism. It exemplifies an ethics of inarticulacy. It suffers from an aphasia about the possible grounds for hope. Their very utopianism, that is, reveals that they have no real hope.

Yet they are not to be pitied for their hopelessness, but condemned. They have refused hope and take refuge in an escapism underpinned and camouflaged by their structural pessimism. We are victims; all we have to do is survive – we do not have to be transformed. Their picture is deeply complacent. Instead of talking about the complicity of all in the structures of power and domination, they straightaway turn to a language of opposition, and more specifically of enemies. The focus is on blame: knowing who the enemy is, is the "first question of political philosophy today" (210–11). But even this language plays no functional role for them, even as a tactical device to mobilize opposition to those one labels as enemies; instead it functions to *de*mobilize, by locating those in need of fundamental change as others and not oneself. By resisting any recognition of complicity, not only are they wrong; they refuse one of the psychologically most powerful ways of undertaking social change.

Here is where the charge of Manicheanism goes deepest. Their account is fundamentally Manichean, not most deeply in implying any dualism (they rarely get to the point of talking about the positive pole of any such dualism), but rather in the complacent, otherworldly, and escapist mentality they speak out of and encourage in others. They offer what Gillian Rose once called "a counsel of hopelessness which extols Messianic Hope" (1996: 70).[11] Hence, for all their interesting allusions to Christian religious figures in their work, and especially Augustine (who is their model as a theorist of Empire [205–7]), their account is quite different. We must look elsewhere than in Hardt and Negri to see how that can be accomplished.

It would be a mistake to think that we can simply translate Hardt and Negri's arguments into a Christian vernacular for all to be well; indeed, many recent theological accounts of politics rely on a

11. See also Wolfe 1996: leftist critics suffer from an "increasingly tired conservativism" and an enthrallment to ideology (34), their anti-realism is really the desire to "express romantic longings" (38), and their "utopian speculations serve as a substitute for their missing social science" (87).

similar pessimism to legitimate a fundamentally renunciatory and escapist attitude towards public life. An example of this is William Cavanaugh's very powerful program (one to which this book is much indebted). For him, the church ought to embody a counter-polity to unmask the simulacra of politics offered by the secular state, which is inescapably a demonic structure. Yet Cavanaugh's depiction of this counter-polity is reactionary against, reductive of, and parasitic upon the very state structure he takes the church to oppose.

His most complete argument for this is visible in his book *Torture and Eucharist* (1998). There he uses the story of the Roman Catholic Church's travail under the Pinochet regime in Chile as a prism through which to understand the Christian churches' struggles to have a political voice in the contemporary world. But by taking the Pinochet era as his object of study, Cavanaugh has too clear-cut an enemy; he uses the Pinochet regime to normalize a grotesque manifestation of the state, insisting that this is the *telos* of modern political life in general. (The same can be said with some of the recent resurgence of work on Bonhoeffer; too often people seem to want to draw easy analogies between living in Nazi Germany and living in any modern state.[12]) His assertion that torture is the epitome of the "imagination of the state," is extremely reductionist. The modern state has been of great use to religious groups – protecting them not only from the state itself, but also occasionally from other citizens. Framing a political vision fundamentally as an ethic of opposition to the modern state sets oneself too narrow a project for a true politics.

Furthermore, in many non-totalitarian societies – as Hardt and Negri (among others) note – the state is no longer the central problem. I am not being merely more sanguine about our situation; I mean that the complex of threats challenging Christian life in advanced industrial societies may be importantly different than those facing Chileans under Pinochet. How could this account apply to non-totalitarian, post-industrial democracies such as our own? To reply that such societies are "only apparently" not totalitarian is flagrantly to ignore fundamental differences in the conditions

---

12. For an insightful discussion and analysis of hyperbolic claims of this sort, see McClay 1994.

distinguishing, say, California from East Germany. Cavanaugh's expressed politics are of the *Catholic Worker* sort; but his most obvious political allies in the fight against Big Government are far from supporting these political commitments. What about consumerism? What about global capitalism? What about our culture of entertainment? A picture of modern politics as basically torturous not only obscures the realities at hand; it also offers defenders of the status quo the easiest possible way to dismiss whatever concrete concerns the critics might present.

Cavanaugh seems to recognize this, but his suggestive language of "eucharistic counter-politics" remains disappointingly undeveloped.[13] In a situation in which political structures are generally seen to be fundamentally illegitimate or absent, the churches may offer an "alternative polis." But in this dispensation churches do not normally take the role of the state, and only in extreme circumstances of political catastrophe (totalitarian dictatorships, the Dark Ages, contemporary sub-Saharan Africa, etc.) should it take up the state's central tasks. Most of the time the churches will not expend their energies in being a counter-state, but rather in attempting to shape its members for citizenship in a kingdom that is yet to come – in part (as this book is arguing) by instructing them on how to be involved in public life in this life, an involvement which will inevitably engage state structures in complicated ways. To be blunt, the church must not get caught in a narcissistic mimetic rivalry with the secular state, for it has bigger fish to fry; its horizon transcends that of any earthly kingdom, and its agenda must be set on fundamentally different terms. Cavanaugh's failure to see this is symptomatic of the more general failure of religious intellectuals today.

The (academic) culture of (cynical) critique

Of course, there are many very good reasons for a fundamentally hostile stance towards our contemporary commodified world. A

---

13. He himself suggests ways beyond this negative political theology, when he argues that the church is "founded on a disappearance" (1998: 281), and offers a discipline of dying (271) and an alternative economy of pain (280). But he does not develop these ideas. I think Cavanaugh's problems here simply manifest the difficulties attending to what Graham Hughes (mis-)labels "church theology"; see G. Hughes 2003: 222, 225–33.

radical perversity lies at the roots of contemporary culture, and there are good reasons to fear that the culture does not realize its fundamental insanity. As Marshall Sahlins suggests,

> The whole cultural organization of our economy remains invisible, mystified as the pecuniary rationality by which its arbitrary values are realized. All the idiocies of modern life from Walkmans and Reeboks to mink coats and seven-million-dollar-a-year baseball players, and on to McDonald's and Madonnas and other weapons of mass destruction – this whole curious cultural scheme nonetheless appears to economists as the transparent effects of a universal practical wisdom. (1993: 12)

How did we get this way? The answer lies in the curiously partial way in which the forces of modernity have "denaturalized" our condition. Let me explain.

The decisive characteristic of our age is the growing knowledge of *contingency*, our deepening belief in the artificiality of all arrangements, our increasingly preconscious recognition that the world does not have to be organized or constituted the way it is. This recognition of increasing contingency – this recognition of our condition's radical non-naturalness – becomes reflexive (in Anthony Giddens's sense) when we realize that even modernity is not a necessary, inevitable, or monolithic process. There are as many ways to be "modern," to cope with the knowledge of contingency, as there are people; modernization need not be associated with secularization, rationalization, global homogenization, denationalization, renationalization, postmodern giddiness, or antimodern anomie – though it can be associated with any of these. What it essentially is, however, is the growing knowledge that things do not have to be this way, and the effects of that knowledge on ourselves and our societies. (This, for example, is the idea that the oft-heard claim at which "everything is political" gestures – even though those who utter it never stop to think about the claim's reflexivity.[14]) "Nature," as a concept, is growing increasingly vestigial; as Frederic Jameson puts it, "Postmodernism is what you have when the modernization process is complete and nature is gone for good" (1990: ix). All that is

---

14. For a very helpful discussion of the dangers and seductions of such apocalypticism, see Yack 1997.

solid melts into air; everything we once assumed was natural has become contingent.[15]

Well, *almost* everything. For inevitably not everything can be up for grabs; humans need some stable ground from which to see all else as contingent. The central remaining source of stability, which provides the language in which we increasingly understand our actions, is the language of economics. Modernity's denaturalization has taken over everything *except* the market; there the tides of contingency arose and broke against the sea walls. We grant market metaphors the privilege of literality, letting them shape our social relations, pressing us to transform all our interactions into economic transactions, to translate all value into cash value. We face an increasingly commodified world, even religiously. The increasing economization of our lives suggests that institutions not immediately subservient to this economic system will change to serve that system, or become increasingly vestigial.[16]

Confronted by this "mystified" insanity, the first task is to resist; we must unmask, and by unmasking critique, what "goes without saying." This is why cultural theory is dedicated to the task of critique, to rendering uncomfortably obvious the non-inevitability, the non-naturalness, of these taken-for-granted economizations of everyday contemporary life. Such critiques have their place. They always have; the practice of unmasking has roots more ancient than modernity. It is present in Amos's critique of the "cows of Bashan," or Plato's critique of the poets in the *Republic*.

But it is peculiarly central to modern thought. As Kant said, "our age is the age of *kritik*" (1965: 9); a similar critical estrangement was, after all, the foundational move of Descartes, and as Montaigne made clear, it is basic to anthropology and ethnography as well.[17]

---

15. See Harvey 1990, Beck *et al.* 1994, and Cronon 1995. I do not want to discard the idea of nature entirely; while I am suspicious of "natural law" accounts, I find the moral realism to which they aspire finally inescapable for any adequate ethic. See Lieberman 1998 and Fukuyama 2002.

16. For the history of the triumph of economic discourse, see Hirschman 1977. For a general account of the origins of this "economic ideology," see Dumont 1977. On the limitations of economic frameworks, see Kuttner 1997. On academics' surrender to these views, see Hauptmann 1996 and Green and Shapiro 1994. On religion and the economy, see M. F. Brown 1997 and Roof 1999.

17. See Geuss 1981, Hulliung 1994, Koselleck 1988, and Yack 1986. For a discussion of the decisive impact of the "resistance experience" upon postwar European (and by extension American) intellectual life, see Wilkinson 1981: 261–79. For a study of more recent roots of this, see Stephen 1998.

The concern with criticism, so commonly assumed to be a "new" concern, thus seems to be as old as modernity – which is to say, as old as the valorization of "newness" itself.[18]

But while "critique" is intrinsic to modern consciousness, contemporary cultural theory offers an almost exclusively, caustically cynical voice in its engagements with culture. Contemporary criticism proceeds without attention to any possible positive picture. It has chosen most primordially to oppose; it refuses to express any responsible critical act of affirmation and affiliation, choosing instead to make the best the enemy of the good. Intellectual engagement becomes essentially a practice of resistance, a way to refuse hegemonic ideologies' mythologized consolations, exploding the pieties of contemporary life with critical demolition charges, then slipping away into the night of postmodernist rhetoric.[19] Critique needs some distance from what it is critiquing, for leverage's sake; but resistance without a positive vision of resistance's purpose becomes mere reactionary posturing.[20] Intellectual discourse has become not only narcissistic, but fundamentally cynical and self-hating, aiming for a theoretical *auto-da-fé* of self-consumption. Alan Wolfe puts this well: "The romantic rebel ... is not really a rebel against society, however much he may disdain society's conventions, for his hostility, which can easily turn into self-hatred, serves no particular end and certainly not the end of social reform, but becomes an excuse for its own self-perpetuation" (1996: 43). Contemporary critical theory, that is, all too often simply is its discontents, its "critique" merely an exquisitely sophisticated form of cynical griping.[21]

It is too easy to wag our fingers at this cynicism; in many ways our cultural condition breeds it today. Intellectuals are marginal to the

18. On Montaigne's work as supporting a profound quietism, see Toulmin 1990. Alan Wolfe suggests that the theoretical romanticism of contemporary cultural criticism is rooted in its origins in the discipline of anthropology, with its essentially anti-modernist, pro-pastoral, Rousseauean perspective (1996: 29–30, 40).
19. See Gunn 1985: 60, Asad 1993: 265, Surin 1989, Santner 2001: 56ff.
20. One might say that the problem is the same one that Nietzsche diagnosed as the "will-to-truth." Indeed, as Bernard Yack argues, even Nietzsche is still in thrall to the will-to-knowledge, despite his realization that it is a trap. See Yack 1997: 112.
21. For good discussions of this cynicism in practice, see Cushman 1997 and Bartov 2002.

workings of contemporary society. They inhabit a perpetual intellectual stand-off, one endemic to the hypercomplexity of modern civilization, in which we need to manage the self-contradictions inherent within our beliefs by having different regions of them in constant intellectual opposition to one another.[22] Furthermore, the hothouse environment of academia encourages a skewed valuation of difficulty as a good in itself, and hence unhelpfully distorts the thinking of those caught up in it.[23] Intellectuals affirm their stance of "alienation" as a methodological technique, "an aura of innocence and moral disinterestedness" meant to "distanciate" their objects of study – to make it seem strange, no longer taken for granted, hence visible in its distinctness.[24] As Gerald Graff suggests, this approach legitimates intellectuals' alienation by presenting critique as a replacement for more direct political action – but this only ends up reinforcing the aroma of *ressentiment* their work exudes, the justification for their importance becoming a sort of "consolation prize for letting others run the world" (1989: 246). Over time, such static critique curdles into preening cynicism, and the "critique" becomes little more than a hodgepodge of sneers and metaphysical whining, the opium of the intellectuals.

But contemporary cultural criticism's cynical cul-de-sac is not simply due to structural compulsion, etiological survivals, or esoteric epistemological technique. It is also rooted in a profoundly negative assessment of human society in general. As James Darsey puts it, "Our distrust of prophets is really a reflection of a profound distrust of ourselves and our ability to tell true from false" (1997: 209). Contemporary cultural criticism suffers from melancholic despair, a despair expressed in and reinforced by simplistic pictures of the human condition and the human predicament.

Contemporary critical theory's problem lies in a "moral ontology" that depicts the world as fundamentally and inescapably morally compromised, wherein the only kind of viable moral stance is the stance of total critique, fundamental negativity.[25] One cannot know what the good would be, for any such claims to "knowledge"

22. See Sloterdijk 1987, Perl 1989, Bewes 1997, Chaloupka 1999, and Brint 1994.
23. See Isaac 2003: 88–9 and M. Warner 2003.
24. See Siebers 1988 and Pels 2000. On marginality, see Walzer 1987 and Moore 1986: 48–71.
25. On "moral ontologies," see Taylor 1989.

would invariably be revealed as the clever positioning of oneself (or the interests that one represents) for a power-grab over against others. Contemporary radicals have "no faith in their own righteousness" (Darsey 1997: 206); all they can do is gesture indirectly at goodness and justice, while focusing direct critical attention on rooting out the particular injustices that exist in every direction. Critics give lip service to the good, but their main duty lies in exposing the oppression of power.

But this confidence about identifying evil is actually a mask for a profound despair. Indeed, the issues are of a properly metaphysical character, relating to deep concerns about the ultimate status of evil, concerns shared by contemporary culture as a whole. As Andrew Delbanco has put it, "a gap has opened up between our awareness of evil and the intellectual resources we have for handling it" (1995: 3). Most contemporary thinkers want to resist this language and rephrase the problem in more banal vocabulary. But such revisions only obscure the profound and intractable character of our problems, which are not fundamentally a matter of simply contingent (and hence fixable) social conditions or psychological malfunctions, but are of a properly ontological profundity. Our sense of the basic felt wrongness of the world is inescapable in this life; we must acknowledge it without deceiving ourselves that it can ever be conclusively overcome. Whether described in the language of psychosis, sinful idolatry, or commodification, the root problem is the experience of a wrongness in the world so fundamental that it cannot be fixed – and yet a wrongness that, simply in *being* so palpably wrong, is not *natural* to reality. The root difficulty provoking critical theory, that is, is the classic problem of evil.[26]

Some theorists partly recognize this, but they fail properly to address it because they refuse to grasp the problem in its full depth.[27] They try to replace the term "evil" with the term "power." But such cynicism is ultimately superficial, for it refuses to think down to the roots of their resistance to injustice and oppression. In doing so, they not only inevitably fail even in the partial tasks they

26. See Mathewes 2001a.
27. For example, see Edmundson 1997: 62, Siebers 1993: 68–70, and Isaac 1997: 41–58.

set themselves; they also are condemned, like characters in Dante's *Inferno*, to endless repetition, endless critique, because they have no grounds to affirm. Ironically, their very insistence on the "contingency" of human existence, which underpins their resistance to "metaphysical" thinking about evil and associated categories, forbids their confronting the possibility that reality, in this dimension, could be radically otherwise than it is. They refuse to countenance the idea that evil might not be a necessary and inescapable fact about the world; they refuse to imagine that evil and suffering might be contingent. They despair that what we call evil in fact does reveal the truth of history and the world, that the world is finally *not* scarred by sin, but is in all relevant ways "naturally" riddled by evil. Contemporary critical theory's cynical disbelief in evil, then, is born out of a certain kind of despair: for them, any affirmation of the world's fundamental goodness threatens to generate a dangerous complacency that will subvert the necessity of critical attention. And this is what it means, in part, to lack hope.

This refusal to reflect on evil is not only a tragedy for contemporary cultural criticism; it is part of a larger despair into which much of contemporary culture has fallen. Paradoxically, perhaps, the idea of evil captures something fundamental about reality by being fundamentally hopeful – that is, by affirming that realities such as malice, suffering, and injustice do not tell the whole truth about reality, but are in some way partial, perhaps even accidental, to the ultimate nature of reality itself. At its heart, then, the problem is a religious one, and it admits only of a religious response. We turn to that next.

Augustinian cultural criticism: the hermeneutics of hopeful charity

Augustine's thought offers substantial resources for a superior proposal. In his most extended act of cultural criticism – the *City of God* – we can discern a general strategy for today. When we do so, what we find is a hopeful charity: a mode of interpreting the world that sees love as the fundamental interpretive fact, because it is the fundamental ontological fact, but whose vision is qualified by the soberly hopeful recognition that such a truth can be fully proven and "redeemed" only eschatologically.[28] This will be easier to apprehend once we have a perspicuous grasp on Augustine's strategy.

Augustine's ideology critique in de civitate Dei

Though Hardt and Negri identify with Augustine's critique of the Roman Empire, that earlier critical engagement proceeds in a way quite different, because more generous and forgiving, than that of *Empire*. Augustine's "ideology critique" of the Roman Empire's ideology of *gloria* is built around his conception of sin, which depicts sin as a perverted ordering of originally good loves. Here critique is more than a nihilistic iconoclasm, more than a ritualized and fetishized "unmasking" of evil; it attempts to identify the injustices and absurdities riddling imperial Roman culture, and to resist their deforming powers, through a hermeneutics of charity – that is, by attempting charitably to understand how one could inhabit this worldview.

We cannot comprehensively display the scope of Augustine's program of cultural criticism in *City of God*. From its title forward, it is truly the most Cecil B. DeMille-esque of theological texts: the widest of wide-lens Panavision cameras would need a tracking shot of several hours' duration simply to encompass the entire cast of characters whose antics comprise the work's raw matter. Its hyper-magnificence also makes it, ironically, a paradigmatically Roman text, for greatness and glory were two of the linchpins of Roman value. Men and women did amazing things on no basis more material than the shame they might suffer were they not to do them, and the glory they might attain if they did them. There is something truly awesome – something worth honoring – about what J. E. Lendon calls the Roman "Empire of Honor" (Lendon 1997).

Augustine agrees. His response to this ideological web is not simply condemnatory. He sees its real value in keeping the Empire together, in keeping order, even as he bemoans its absolute commitment to merely superficial goods. He is extremely sensitive to

28. For two examples that approach such a view without ever fully showing what it would look like, see Shannon 1996 and McCarraher 2000. For examples of this project in Augustinian garb, see Dodaro 1991 and 1994; but his more recent 2004a study is far more comprehensive and adequate. Another fruitful, if partial, attempt is Schuld 2000.

the ambiguities present in a system ruled by honor and glory, to how those ideals can motivate and secure, and how they satisfy the basic human need to evaluate ourselves and our world – and how that project of valuation easily warps into a disastrously powerful motivation for acts of horrific evil.

Given this, Augustine's rhetorical strategy for confronting the ideology of *gloria* is simple. He does not renounce that language; that would suggest that it was purely a fabrication of evil, which is ontologically and theologically impossible. Instead, he suggests that it is itself a fallen and fragmentary perversion of the true and proper language of human evaluation. For Augustine, it is not that honor or glory are bad things to pursue, but that they have been pursued improperly, crucially because we do not know the ultimate reference of honor or glory, the one to whom honor and glory are due. The Romans are mistaken, not in the fact *that* they have organized their lives around honoring, admiring, and loving, but in *what* they have organized their lives around loving. They have loved Rome, or themselves, and sought the glory of the city or the person, when they should have loved God and sought God's glory.

He makes that purpose clear in the work's first word – namely, *gloriossissimam*, "most glorious" (*DCD* 1.*praef.*).[29] He immediately turns that word to a surprising new use, referring not to Rome but instead to "the city of God," the blessed company of the elect. Here we see his rhetorical strategy's core: not to renounce the language of Roman glory, but to wrest it from its previous uses and turn it to new contexts; or, better yet, to show how Christ's life, death, and resurrection have already "wrested" that language back; or, best of all, to show how Christ's story demonstrates that fallen humans have failed to wrest that language away from its proper use in the first place, to the extent that their own misuses of it remain "warped," always tending to spring back towards the arc of their

29. I use the Bettenson translation most of the time, and I note all departures from it. Later references to the work are embedded parenthetically in the main body of the text. For a very nice discussion of the first sentence of *DCD*, and in particular the *distensio* it means to evoke in its readers, see Fitzgerald *et al.* 1999: 13–15. See also Conybeare 1999: 72–3 on how Augustine "interrogates the concept" of *gloria* in *DCD* 5.12 forward; compare this with Dodaro 1994: 91–3. More generally, see Schindler 1990, O'Donnell 1980, and Dodaro 2004a. It is worth noting that in the first two books of *de officiis*, Cicero criticizes *gloria* severely, but not radically; so Augustine had some antecedents in the classical world for his strategy, though he took it in surprising directions.

proper use, always retaining, despite our best efforts to obliterate it, some memory of their true meaning.[30] It is a strategy of conversion, not of opposition.

The work's first ten books unpack this strategy, captured in his famous claim that Roman virtues are really "splendid vices." He appreciates the effectiveness of Roman ideology in shaping its citizens. The Romans' "unbounded passion for glory, above all else, checked their other appetites . . . It was this greed for praise, this passion for glory, that gave rise to those marvelous achievements" (5.12 [Bettenson 197]). While it is not true virtue, glory-seeking effectively (albeit partially) mimics it; those who employ virtue "in the service of human glory . . . are of more service to the earthly city when they possess even that sort of virtue than if they are without it" (5.19 [213]).

This strategy both acknowledges the pragmatic effectiveness of Roman ideology and offers an immanent critique of it, comparing it with its own antique practice and noting how it falls short. Drawing on the civic republican tradition in Roman historiography, he argues that contemporary Roman *mores* are far from the frugal and virtuous ideals of their ancestors, despite their self-proclaimed continuity: "In early times it was the love of liberty that led to great achievements, later it was the love of domination, the greed for praise and glory" (5.12 [198]).[31] Yet neither does Augustine accept the Roman republican historians' nostalgia for a long-ago age of real purity; for Augustine, history has always been like this.

The fact that these values were fundamentally superficial and unstable meant that the system tended over generations to misshape its inhabitants. Roman critics (particularly the Stoics) noted this; but Augustine goes further than they in diagnosing deep anthropological reasons for this tendency to decay, identifying a "slippery slope" between desire for glory and desire for domination – the *libido dominandi*, the "lust for domination" that is simultaneously the "dominating lust" of which he speaks at the very

---

30. Augustine was quite self-conscious about doing this; as he argues in DDC, it is entirely appropriate for Christians to take whatever of value they find in other peoples' beliefs and "baptize" that language for their own purposes. (DDC 2.40.60.)

31. See also 2.18–19, and Inglebert 1996: 399–592. For a general discussion of the shape of Augustine's language of immanent critique, see Lawless 1998.

beginning of the work (1.*pref.*; 5.19). So for example Augustine saw Cato's suicide not really as a mark of greatness, but as revealing a petty petulance at Caesar's possible glory were he to pardon Cato (1.23). And what was true individually is equally true on the level of groups: even class warfare was conducted more out of a desire for victory than out of any interest in equity and morality (2.17). Roman ideology, then, provided a problematic form of power. The benefits of the system are impermanent, "worldly." God gives temporal goods to those seeking temporal ends; but once those immanent aims are achieved – if they are achieved (for there is no protection against moral luck) – they have received their reward in full. Temporal victories are impermanent, hence the Romans' rewards were as well (5.17, 15).[32]

This is a powerful immanent critique, but it is more than that. For Augustine offers the single proper "principle" by which to interpret history: Christ. But this is not fundamentally an abstract, ahistorical, denaturalized critique. For Augustine, every event of history is in itself homogeneously ambiguous, with one exception – the life, death, and resurrection of Christ, from which the rest of history gains meaning. Our ideals must be found ultimately beyond history's record of slaughters and depradations (2.21); we can find them only eschatologically, in God, and in the proleptic manifestation of Jesus Christ. Christ offers a route beyond immanent criticism but yet still fundamentally not otherworldly.

In Christ we can see that while the Romans' virtues are impermanent, they should not be simply dismissed; just as the Roman language of honor betrays its proper meaning in every misuse, the splendid vices "shadow," significantly mimic, the real virtues attainable by Christians. The Romans' pseudo-virtue is even useful for Christians, because it gives a perverse *exemplum* for the citizens of the city of God, both promoting humility in Christians and provoking them to outdo the Romans' stories (5.16). Hence Augustine compares Brutus' killing of his sons with the story of Isaac and Jacob and ultimately the figure of Christ: Christians do "not ... kill our sons, but reckon among our sons the poor people of Christ," and thereby exemplify the virtues of the City of God in comparison to the

---

32. As R. A. Markus has argued, Augustine is the great demythologizer of late Roman *imperium* (1970: 55, 173). See also Lambert 1999.

Romans (5.18 [Bettenson 211]). Indeed, even on Rome's terms, the City of God does better, for its virtues contain the pagan virtues: "Rome is outshone by the Heavenly City ... where victory is truth, high rank is holiness, peace is happiness, life is eternity" (2.29).[33] The point is not to renounce the Romans' virtues, but to show them to be merely "perversions" of true virtue, imitations of the real thing; this lets us see what we really are after, and undeceive ourselves about possessing them at present (or really, "possessing" them at all – for it is better to say that we are "possessed" *by* them, as we are possessed by love). In this way, Augustine offers an "ideology critique" of the Romans' valorization of "honor" and "glory" that affirms the energies attempting to come to expression in these concepts, while also fully recognizing – and indeed sharpening – the critique launched against them by civic moralists and pagan philosophers.

What makes possible Augustine's incisive diagnostic critique of Rome's empire of honor? It is his hermeneutics of charity, which bears psychological, metaphysical, and theological significance. *Caritas* has a psychologically integrating power that reveals its metaphysically world-affirming implications by understanding itself as theologically a participation in God's love for the world, converting the world back to God. Civically this hermeneutics engages others by seeking communion with them. And one seeks such communion through confessional openness. This is at heart affirmative, inhabiting (and creative of) the "public sphere," insisting that things of this world should matter to us and manifesting in one's own life just such care for those things. Furthermore, it must be participatory, involving our whole lives in the activity of cultivating a "world" that is fit for human habitation. Finally, it must be responsible, accountable to others for its claims and willing to be corrected when it errs.[34]

---

33. Bettenson (87) mangles this passage, inexplicably translating *ubi* as "instead," instead of as "where."

34. For a partial antecedent to this argument, see Bathory 1981. Bathory suggests that "Augustine argues that man's most fundamental nature – when recognized – leads him to politics" (164). But Bathory argues that Augustine's work led him to offer a practical proposal towards politics, which is concerned with "the common good" and securing of individual "freedom," though Bathory says disappointingly little about what he takes those terms to mean. In contrast, I think that more basic than any practical proposal was the ascetical-affective revolution Augustine sought to realize in our orientation towards the world.

There is no promise of happiness in this. Not only will our engagement with the world never be wholly joyful, not only are there good parts and bad parts, but the good and the bad overlay each other, so that cultural existence will be forever mixed. We can anticipate only an eschatological satisfaction; in the interim we must be patient, and be presently tutored by our dissatisfactions, "trained by longing" for the end (*in Io. ep.* 4.6). During the world, we can enjoy our happiness only in hope: we are happy in the future, but in this life there is properly speaking no happiness; we only endure. This condition of suspension, of waiting, is hard to take, but it is our condition, and any attempt to end it by telling a story that claims fully to possess our ultimate end is dangerously premature.

Augustinian cultural criticism: irony beyond cynicism

What practical program of cultural engagement does this hermeneutics of *caritas* entail? Essentially it offers a vision not finally of resistance or renunciation but of transfiguration. This entails significant changes in the social structures that sustain the "culture of critique's" own most particular cultures, which are largely within university, and not ecclesial, settings. In many ways the modern university's isolating division of labor, and the whole university's isolation from the larger world, supports a deeply bureaucratized and even consumerist culture that undermines the cohesion and integration needed to cultivate the rich intellect. But this is a spur to alertness, not a warrant for despair; there is no one monolithic academic culture, but a complex network of tensions and outright contradictions that can be played off one another. Most directly, Augustinian cultural critics can help resist the isolating compartmentalization of contemporary academic-intellectual life by emphasizing the integrative character of intellectual activity. Intellectual life pressures its inhabitants towards over-specialization and obscures the vision of inquiry as a whole; Augustinians help resist this by emphasizing inquiry's ultimate focus on the whole human project, and its practical aim of joining individual scholars together in common cause. Furthermore, participation in the hermeneutics of charity urges us to transform academic culture towards a more fully engaged – that is, argumentative and dis-putatious – community than it presently is. Conflict is a crucial element in authentic engagement during the world, one whose reality is not avoided by being denied.[35]

We are conflicted, both within ourselves and with one another, and it is better to acknowledge and try to confront those conflicts, ultimately with the aim of reconciliation, than to avoid them. As Chapter 3 argued, one central motif of much Christian theology is the reconciliation of othernesses, and it is precisely by coming to embody this task of reconciling othernesses that Christians come more fully to inhabit their faith. Of course we should not reject critical vigilance; but it seems unlikely that an Augustinian stance is especially susceptible to Pollyannaish mystifications. "Suspicion" is a useful and wise thing to have, and we ought always to be more than a little skeptical to claims of moral integrity or earnestness, particularly when they emerge from the principalities and powers. Yet this critical vigilance is not sheer pessimism, nor is it cynicism, nor is it a straightforwardly "realistic" or potentially paralytic "tragic" vision; what is most central to it is an ironic apprehension of the complexity of our condition. It affirms that things are never as good, or as bad, as we think.[36] Irony is an inherently complex form of thought, recognizing multiple levels of meaning that contradict one another, and whose contradiction opens up a further, not fully articulable insight into the mysterious, awesome, and perhaps properly terrifying truth that we must act without knowing what our actions will ultimately "mean." In this way irony participates in an eschatological mindset as opposed to an apocalyptic one. Such irony has a positive energy, for it is grounded on a dynamic and destabilizing hope; as R. A. Markus says, this hope "is a permanently unsettling force, seeking to prevent social institutions from becoming rigid and fixed, always inclined to treat the *status quo* with suspicion" (1970: 169). Augustinians embed this critical skepticism within a larger enframing affirmation of the good of the created order, an affirmation which many contemporary cultural critics would likely find inexpressible, even if they resonated with it. We are not authors of our stories but characters within them, and while we must try to discern what is going on, in order most appropriately to respond to it, the fact that we exist within our

35. See Mathewes 1999, MacIntyre 1990, Jones and Paulsell 2002, and Webster 1998.
36. See Wolfe 1996: 50.

stories means that the ironies of our involvement and our attempts at understanding that involvement will only mount, and never fully be resolved.

Our entrapment in this condition is what makes cynicism so tempting today. How can we resist it? We can say either too little here, or too much. So to say too little: the contemporary intellectual crisis of hope is in fact a choice people make, a decision they make to accept that cynicism. It is not the natural, inevitable fate of the intellect in the modern age. Yet the counter to this choice is not another choice – that would be equally an attempt to impose one's will on the world, just one more version of the will to power. We cannot counter the critics' despair with sheer exercise of will or the power of positive thinking. Instead, we must do something altogether different: to look and see. We can inhabit this vision of the world not by activity at all but by passivity – by a change in vision, by looking up from our ceaseless labors and seeing that the world is good, and that it merits hope. This hope is not Hardt and Negri's hope in an ultimate, but at present wholly promissory, utopia; it is grounded not simply in an indeterminately distant future, but in the affirmation of the fact that suffering is not the ultimate truth of the world even at present; that lies will finally, albeit eschatologically, be overcome by the truth; and that, even if these things do not today occur with anything like regularity – even if they occur infrequently enough to seem the exception that proves the rule – they are in fact the rule, the *regulus* of the world.

What would it mean, what would it change, were we to inhabit that hope?

Critically hopeful citizenship

We now turn to how this vision can become incarnate in a larger practice of hopeful citizenship. How should such critical hope fund engagement in public life? And how can it be cultivated by public engagement?

"Hope" is an ambivalent political virtue. It can suggest a kind of political anesthetic, a societal pressure-release valve, the force whereby poor and oppressed peoples are paralyzingly consoled when a realistic assessment of their situation would generate the sort of anger necessary for real change now. But hope also seems politically mobilizing. Hope gives us the power to imagine a world quite different than the one we inhabit – and that act of imagining can be the first step towards creating that world. As Slavoj Žižek puts it, in his inimitable (and who would want to imitate it?) style, "in order effectively to liberate oneself from the grip of existing social reality, one should first renounce the transgressive fantasmatic supplement that attaches us to it" (2000: 149). Václav Havel recognized this regarding the resistance movements in Eastern Europe, which culminated in the revolutions of 1989; all the "small hopes" of local change are anchored in the "deep, inner hope that is not dependent on prognoses, and which was the primordial point of departure in this unequal struggle" against Soviet totalitarianism (1991: 186). <u>Hope, then, seems both dangerous and necessary.</u>

Yet today it is a responsibility that seems difficult to fulfill, as we saw above, for our culture is in important ways hopeless, with cynicism as its consolation. And Christian accounts do no better. Our age in general has failed to keep in tense balance hope's immanent and transcendent dimensions. Reinhold Niebuhr, for example, treated hope almost as an anesthetic, like a scotch at the end of a hard day at work. Niebuhr's work is often criticized for exploiting the Christian faith to underpin a kind of "muscular" involvement in society, for ends that are never explicitly articulated but that seem to be fundamentally conservative and stabilizing, or "realistic." His account of hope seems to support that interpretation; for in some way Niebuhr's account is really about providing a kind of high-ampere yet moderating motivation for men in power – as he put it, "The final wisdom of life requires, not the annulment of incongruity but the achievement of serenity within and above it" (R. Niebuhr 1952: 63). This desire for "serenity" can sound dangerously Stoic, confusing hope with a willfulness that is not really hope at all. Niebuhr's work focused, in potentially problematic ways, on how to understand and inhabit the humble, chastened, and yet energized confidence in and hope for action in the *saeculum*. There are of course other elements of his thought more thoroughly resistant to a problematic desire for control; and even the language of "serenity" above is troubled, however inadequately, by being contrasted with "the annulment of incongruity." And there is a "pessimistic hope," that one does some good and yet also recognizes that partiality will always have its way with us, that in this

✳ world we are not released from the contradictions of history until the end of history. Yet we must recognize that "Christian realism" has sometimes confused reality with the status quo, and has hence been too resigned to the way the world presently is; witness Niebuhr's doubts about the wisdom of the civil rights campaigns of the 1950s, which were effectively that perfectionist energies were being applied too directly to a sordid world.[37]

Other Christian accounts of hope have other lacunae. Liberationist accounts seem all too confident in their knowledge of the course of history and in how we should respond to it. If Niebuhr's account of hope ties it to an Ecclesiastes-ish resignation about vanities, liberationist accounts move too far towards an easy messianism.[38] (Their historical affiliation with Marxism is not essential to their theology, but it does highlight their messianic proclivities.) Since the historical contradiction of their political expectations in 1989 and forward, and the increasing practical contradiction of their social assumptions in the Third World's turn away from liberationist "base communities" and towards Pentecostal and evangelical movements, such theologies have largely retreated to the academy. But it seems that their immanentism forbids their rejuvenation as such.[39]

In contrast to the suffocating immanentism of Niebuhrian accounts, and the hyperventilating immanentism of liberationists, the influential position of John Howard Yoder (1972) seems a calming breath of fresh air. For Yoder, politics as an immanent project must be simply renounced, for we have a better vision of politics modeled for us by Jesus, and this politics is not really about organizing life in this world, but is instead a matter of already living, albeit adventally, in the kingdom. On this view, justice is reserved until the last judgment, and attempts to realize actual justice in this world are impious attempts to usurp God's power. The kind of public activity one should engage in is best understood finally as witness, being salt and light, a leaven in society (but to what end?); a

---

37. On Niebuhr and the civil rights movement, see Lasch 1991: 386 ff. and Polsgrove 2001.
38. A fine example of this is found in Gutiérrez 1988: 92–5, even though the work also evinces a fairly naive apocalyptic progressivism (e.g. his claim that "the social praxis of contemporary humankind has begun to reach maturity" [30]).
39. I have learned much from Bell 2001.

witness that does not expect real goods to be realized in the current dispensation. This proposal has many attractions, but ultimately it recapitulates the "church versus world" dichotomy that we should transcend, as captured in its implication of rebellious powers or demonic structures standing over against God, and the apocalyptic metaphors of spiritual warfare are inadequate for understanding our situation during the world.[40] Furthermore, the account never really gets around to offering a vision of existence during the world as a sacramental and proleptic participation in the coming kingdom, and so renders obscure the nature of our existence, however "advental," in the world today. This account differs radically from liberationist accounts in emphasizing the non-immanent nature of the kingdom; but also, like the liberationists, it does not confront the conditions of our lives during the world so much as suggest that Jesus offers us a way to avoid those conditions.

To do better than these, we must explore what hope is, in order to see how more fully to inhabit it. Hope serves simultaneously as a powerful goad and support for public engagement, a radical chastening device for resisting our temptations towards apocalyptic political expectations, and a powerful and profound icon of the largely indirect ultimate significance of political life itself – as an icon, indeed, of our whole existence in this world. Hope mobilizes and empowers by giving us a capacity for vision; but it also transcends politics by chastening our idolatrously immanentist expectations for politics, and by seeing all iconically, as signs of a greater kingdom to come. We can have hope because, and only because, we live in a "hopeful" world; hope is more an ontological reality than it is a psychological one – an ontological reality that encourages a certain style of inhabiting time in advental anticipation.

This section first discusses hope's disconsoling character, how it renders us open to the eschatologically new throughout our lives. Then it explores how a hopeful politics can be civically mobilizing, while still disconsoling political expectations as regards the durability and ultimacy of their "this-worldly" success. Finally it suggests how public life can help us practically cultivate this hope.

---

40. For more, see Chapter 6 below.

The practice of disconsoling hope

We begin by contrasting hope with some seemingly similar attitudes. Preeminent here is the language of optimism or pessimism. Hope is neither of these; as R. A. Markus puts it, "optimism and pessimism are equally alien to [hope's] eschatological transcendence, and to the historical agnosticism which is its correlative" (1970: 166). Hope is not optimism; it is not a matter of forecasting, divination, or spiritual meteorology – forms of positive prognostications about the world's fate. Hope and optimism have different attitudes towards our condition as inevitably anticipatory creatures. Optimism takes that anticipation and "leans" on it as a way of organizing its present life; it relies on a determinate picture of the future in justifying its actions now. It is fundamentally a willed disposition, projecting a sunny disposition on to the future. And it is inevitably a reflection, mirroring back that sunniness on to our faces in the present. Hence it is really about justifying what we do now in terms of what will come later. (The willed character of optimism also illuminates the psychology of illusion and wish-fulfillment: illusion is less a matter of seeing something that is not there than of not seeing what is there. Humans can will themselves to ignore realities in a way that they cannot simply imagine *ex nihilo* things that are not there.) Optimism, that is, never escapes the orbit of subjectivity. Hope sees optimism as fundamentally *praesumptio*, the prejudgment that imposes our sense of what we expect on to the future. As such, optimism presumes that everything will stay the same as it presently is; it pictures time as closed, a cycle of episodes whose contours do not ask of us any radical change. It is a form of spectatorial sloth, of unwillingness to participate.[41]

Yet hope is not fatalism either. While hope acknowledges what happens, it does not approve of everything as it currently appears to us. It realizes that a hasty acquiescence to appearances is not realism, but yet one more form of the false consolation of complacency – the

---

41. See Havel 1989: 150–1. Havel contrasts this with "genuine faith," by which I take him to mean something more like "trust," and thus at least continuous with hope. Interestingly, Moltmann offers a similar critique of too optimistic "presentative eschatologies" as exemplifying an "*eschatologia gloriae*," not really eschatological at all; better to have a more fully Pauline "*eschatologia crucis*." See Moltmann 1975: 158–9.

consolation, again, of knowing that one has a full grip on the picture, that one knows what is happening. Hope is patient with what it disapproves of. It does not accept it, it makes no effort to disguise its non-acceptance and hence does not collaborate with it, but it does not attempt to force itself on reality. Patience entails a certain humility and openness to the course of history. As Václav Havel puts it, patience can express itself in waiting, though this waiting is positive, "a state of hope, not as an expression of hopelessness ... This kind of waiting grew out of the faith that repeating this defiant truth made sense in itself, regardless of whether it was ever appreciated, or victorious, or repressed for the hundredth time" (1997: 104). Hope is patient with unknowing; it does not allow its wishes to construct a fantasy of what will happen next.

Both optimism and fatalism differ from hope by being attempts to escape our condition of accepting "the new" that time constantly delivers to us (or delivers us to). They are modes of avoiding our existence as recipients of time. But they cannot fully succeed, so they must try to grapple with the new in ways that allow them to ignore or avoid their inescapable vulnerability to it. In them, we attempt to inhabit history in a slothful manner, by convincing ourselves that we are not inhabiting it at all. They express our desire to control history, to tell ourselves what history is, so that we no longer have to worry about what history will do to us. As Moltmann says, "Modern philosophy of history has in fact the character of a philosophic, enlightened millenarianism: the 'ending of history in history' is, as in the old religious millenarianism, its goal" (1975: 264). Yet this historiographical urge, so deeply characteristic of modernity, is not simply modern; it expresses a reflex deep in human being, a sinful reflex that it is part of hope's vocation, during the world, to help us resist.

We can supplement this intuition by a brief sketch of the Christian phenomenology of hope – the hope that, Christians proclaim, all inchoately feel, and that Christians come incrementally articulately to inhabit. This "hope" is not a purely subjective attitude, portable across contexts; hope is always situated, a response to some context (Marcel 1962: 30).[42] To say "I have hope" is not simply

---

42. See also Havel 1997: 238: "The primary origin of hope is, to put it simply, metaphysical ... hope is more, and goes deeper, than a mere optimistic

to report on one's inner state, but also to suggest something about the world one understands oneself to inhabit. It is not most fundamentally a matter of voluntary action or self-expression, an audacious act of reckless courage, of imposing one's will in the face of an empty and pitiless universe. Hope calls attention, not to itself, but to the world – to how the world can change. These are secondary to the basic experience of hope, which is in a way the humble acknowledgment of a revelation, a recognition, as Václav Havel put it, of "the world as something – a unity, a set of values – that is a source of hope, a reason for my sacrifices (as they are so nobly called), a repository for the true meaning of my actions" (1989: 129).[43] Another characteristic of hope is its sense of solidarity. To be hopeful is to not be alone, to realize that we are not abandoned. Hope itself often feels other to us, an alien and involuntary fact we do not choose, but acknowledge; it is not argued for, but confessed. As despair can be an act of betrayal, so hope is a confession of loyalty. Furthermore, hope need not be merely an individual acknowledgment; it can also come to us in community, indeed as community in a certain way. Hope's solidarity is not just a solidarity with the source of hope; it also urges us towards solidarity with others as well.

Hope is thus not a matter of the will or decision; it is assent, participation, cooperation – being "in tune with the world," in Joseph Pieper's phrase.[44] This is a form of activity based on a fundamental passivity or receptivity; we accept the sheer givenness of hope, and work from it.[45] We can call it "responsive receptivity," a matter of finding oneself in the rhythms of history, of recognizing that those rhythms give one one's being, and that one cannot "step outside" of them. To hope is not simply or finally an interior state of mind or psychological disposition; it is a mode of assenting to

inclination or disposition of the human mind"; it is anchored in "humanity's experience with its own Being and with the Being of the world."

43. His larger argument concerns the importance of an "absolute horizon" of value; see Havel 1989: 152: such hope, while not necessarily elicited phenomenologically by any object or set of objects in the world, yet still speaks to a basic sense of "at-home-ness" in the world, and so remains ontological in my sense.

44. See Pieper 1999.

45. For Marcel, hope is cooperation, not initiatory action; yet we do "act" in some way, this is what makes hope a virtue we can exercise.

participation in the rhythms of history. Our hope is secondary, our response to that, or whom, by which we are called.

Still, this hope has an intelligible core, however vague it may be. We know that the promise of the "new creation" that St. Paul speaks of is a resurrection, not a fundamental rupturing or disjunction; our present condition and our eschatological consummation are crucially continuous. Hence there are trajectories and vectors of the promise that are apprehensible even now. There are reasons for hope, though they may be too general and underdetermined to turn into predictions.[46] Because both continuity and rupture mark the consummation of Christian hope, complacency is impossible, and there is no steady way to move forward in stable progression; but while there may be no fair and easy road to heaven, yet we are on the way towards it, however divagating that track may be, and we may participate proleptically in the consummation even now. We cannot tease out of our partial participation in hope a determinate metaphysic; but our hope does participate in such a metaphysic, even though we cannot, *in medias res*, fully comprehend it. Hope is still on the way, in no way yet "accomplished." Perhaps, as Karl Rahner has suggested, it will never be concluded – perhaps we will still have hope, indeed perhaps we will only truly have hope, in the kingdom on the eschatological morning. Perhaps hope is part of the *epekstasis*, the infinite ingoing into God, that Gregory of Nyssa spoke of in his *Life of Moses*. Hope commits us to certain ontological affirmations; from within the perspective of hope, we can see that we have hope because we live in a hopeful world.[47]

What would it mean to inhabit such hope, to "live in hope"? How does it shape our knowledge, our behavior, our very mode of being? This hope is and must be for us a whole way of life, one that is fundamentally ascetic. Hope is an ascetic practice because it involves resisting the temptation to judge, to sum up, in order better to prepare ourselves to inhabit what our desire for judging shows us we want, prematurely, to possess even now.[48] Hope is not knowledge, but the recognition that all "knowledge" we have now stands under a radical eschatological judgment.

46. See also Polkinghorne 2002: 30–4, on the intuitions underlying hope.
47. See K. Rahner 1966, and Gregory of Nyssa 1978 on *epektasis*.
48. See von Balthasar 1988b.

To acknowledge this hope is not simply to accept a changed perception of the external world; it changes our self-understanding. We are, in a way, different people to ourselves when we hope. Hope engages us in the world; in contrast to a fundamentally spectatorial optimism, hope is always involvement, participation in a process or ongoing reality.[49] Indeed, it is a communion with openness, with a "living God." Hope is a mode of inhabiting time – indeed, it is the mode of inhabiting time, of genuinely accepting time *as* time – as new, as the advent of unprecedented events that come to us unbidden and unanticipated, for it acknowledges that time is open, that it is given to us and thus not ours to control. To live in hope is genuinely to live in history; and, as Jürgen Moltmann has said, to live in history is to live in an event still open to reality: "Only as long as the world is not yet sound and whole, only as long as it is open towards its truth and does not yet possess it, can we speak of 'history'" (1975: 265). Hope is always newly discovered; it knows it cannot expect, and so it does not try, to "know already" how everything will turn out all right. Hope must finally transcend our desires, must allow that it is not a hope, finally, for what we want – even though we may want what we hope for, our hope does not grasp its object under the form of our desire.[50] Hope is liberatory because it recognizes that time is liberatory.

Hope's patience, its openness to the new, enables realistic vision. This may be surprising; many suspect that hope, and especially religiously rooted hope, *blinds* us, that it distracts our attention away from reality, because it "always already knows" what will happen, and so never attends to the realities before it. But some of those most profoundly sensitive to the concrete sufferings and injustices faced by others, as well as by them themselves, often confessed that their sensitivity to suffering, their inability to ignore it as "just the way the world is," comes from the hope that the world is not meant to be this way.[51] In fact, whereas optimism and pessimism impose one's expectations on to the future and thereby on to the present,

---

49. On the distinction between spectatorial optimism and participatory hope, see Marcel 1962: 33–5, and von Balthasar's critique of "epic" theologies in 1988a: 20.
50. This is the deep truth behind the Orthodox attempt to appropriate the Stoic language of *apatheia*; see Marcel 1962: 53, 66, and R. Williams 1989a.
51. This is how Ignacio Ellacura, a Jesuit martyred in El Salvador in 1989, used his hope; see Hollenbach 1996: 15–16.

hope renounces such impositions, and is shriven of those illusions. Hope is visionary, more interested in the end than in the means to the end; it is the virtue of the inventor, not of the technician (Marcel 1962: 51–2). Because it is visionary, it recognizes that it does not see the way to salvation; hence it does not delude itself that it may not know the goal, but at least it knows how we will get there. Hope has no need to obscure the cracks and flaws in our lives or in the world; it has no need to delude itself that everything is currently all right, that everything is the way it should be. It is liberated from the lie of normality, and sees with an eye unimpressed by the desperate pleading of the present to be accepted as acceptable. It sees things "with all their flaws and ready for redemption" (Moltmann 1975: 269). To have hope, as Havel says, "doesn't mean closing one's eyes to the horrors of the world – quite the contrary, in fact: only those who have not lost faith and hope can see the horrors of the world with genuine clarity" (1989: 141). Because it is shriven of the illusion that the world is complete and closed, because it is liberated from the refusal to await the truly new thing, hope can see. Indeed, one can say that, in one way at least, hope just is that liberation, a capitulation to vulnerability towards the new.

Hope is not only provisional but pro-vocative, in two senses. First of all, hope provokes action. It is not simply an inner state. No one who is hopeful can resist participating in the hopeful world that has been disclosed to them. Second, the action hope so provokes is fundamentally vocative, linguistic and even evangelical, expressing thanks to the hopeful world and seeking to lead others to apprehend that hope as well. Hope not only seeks to participate in the new world, it seeks partners in such engagement; and before all else, the hopeful soul wants to help them see as it does. So it expresses itself, bringing to articulation its view – and hoping to connect, to articulate, with the listener thereby.

Yet despite this engagement, hope is never manically proactive; even in its most dynamic and rapid action, it always feels itself as patiently responding to the prior and absolutely active call of God. Hope's activity, that is, is fundamentally characterized by patience, deliberateness, and watchfulness. But this does not make it timid, for such patience is as relentless as the call to which it responds. To be hopeful is most fundamentally to wait – to wait on the Word from beyond oneself, the Word that many words have taught you is coming, to wait to be surprised by it, to be delighted and overjoyed at the new thing.

Yet this waiting is not rigor mortis, but the tensed vigor of waiting for life abundant. Hope teaches us to inhabit the condition of natality, of birth. "The believer is not set at the high noon of life, but at the dawn of a new day, at the point where night and day, things passing and things to come, grapple with each other" (Moltmann 1975: 31).[52] Hope helps us to see ourselves as beginning, as participating in the new thing that God is doing; thus hope encourages us to act with the piety of the new.

In all these ways, hope is not just a mode of inhabiting time; it is a form of suffering, of ascesis, disciplined vulnerability to change, change that shapes the hopeful soul in ways that render it ever more appropriately vulnerable to reality, and thus to God, in anticipation of the infinite "changing" of the *epekstasis* that is our eschatological destiny. Hope is thus a practice, a disciplined and complex structure of socially established and cooperative human activity, organized purposively.[53] To us in our sinfulness it is also an acknowledgment of necessary suffering – to suffer the inevitable shocks that time constantly gives to our presumptuousness. Yet it is not a simple activity, for it begins with passive receptiveness, and is a way of existence that precedes our superficial, hyperactive, choosing selves.

But we should not deceive ourselves that we altogether want this life; for to be alive is to not know what will happen to you, to not be in control. And there is a consolation to being a corpse: nothing worse can happen to you. In resurrecting us, hope tells us that we are not our own, and so tells us that our acts bear significances we cannot yet perceive. Hope fills us with the chilling disconsolation that we know not what we do, and we know not what we are, or will be. Thus there is in peculiarly Christian hope an element of terror. The presence of this terror is a clue that shows how hope can enrich public life, and how engagement in public life enriches our inhabitation of hope as well.

---

52. See also E. Bloch 1986.
53. I borrow, with slight modifications, this definition of "practice" from Kelsey 1992: 118.

Eschatologically hopeful citizenship

Hope's civic contributions begin with its power to mobilize people's energy for civic change, and its power to enable people to resist change. Hope is politically mobilizing both because of what it negates and because of what it affirms. It affirms the legitimacy of the inchoate assent to the world that is part of every human's existence. But it also opposes the various stultifying deceptions we collectively tell ourselves in order to dull or numb that affirmation. Hope's power, that is, lies as much in its resistance as in its recognitions. In both ways it resists our "worldly" temptations towards a wholly mundane understanding of our world and especially of our civic order.

Hope is both realistic and fantastic, true vision and powerful imagination. Hope is vision because it sees clearly the true situation and resists illusion's attempts to anesthetize the intellect. The obscurities we face come from imposing our will on our vision, interposing our wishes and our needs. When these drop away, we see clearly.[54] Its vision is a matter of fidelity, of refusing the seduction of living unthinkingly "in the lie," of not giving in to a certain kind of political-psychological sloth, or living in death. (Yet note how this resistance, once accomplished, seems astonishingly easy and simple.)

Yet this resistance to the lie is not simply a matter of clearsightedness, it is also a powerful act of imagination: for we know that we are not meant to be this way. Hope empowers in part because of the vividness of the dreams it gives us; their very vividness, the ease with which they arise and the force with which they present themselves to us, give us a sense of their palpable plausibility for our world. Hope helps us imagine a "counter-polis," an anti-politics of the mind, and by imagining it we work to transform reality closer to the image of our imagined world.[55] This is not to say that eschatological change is possible, but something like the opposite: that it is through hope that we know that no political order in this life is apocalyptically final.

---

54. On the power of waiting as creative and rooted in purposefulness, see Vanstone 1983: 104–5 and Milosz 1981.
55. See Kenney 2002.

Furthermore, hope offers us not consequentialist but immanent goods. The energy of hope is not a utopian loan, a promissory note from some realized paradise in the future. It is not that our hopes can be confirmed and hence validated by the millennium, much less that our hopes are devices for hastening the end's arrival; the eschaton is present proleptically in our current hope. In hope we do not act for the future, but for the present, for the present good that hope delivers. Hope is oriented towards the future, but more by reaction against the dead hand of the past than by any sense of some easy future resolution of our problems. Our hope is due not to our prediction of some future configuration of history but to the nature of being itself, both stretched out temporally and gathered in eternity. As Havel says,

> Only the infinite and the eternal, recognized or surmised, can explain the no less mysterious phenomenon of hope ... humankind's sense of something that transcends earthly gratification – a belief that such a fate, or such an apparently hopeless act of courage, whose significance is not easily understood, is recorded in some way and adds to the memory of Being. (1997: 239)

Finally, we should purge a last error from our understanding of hope – the assumption that hope is exceptional, unusual, only an occasional state or mood in contrast to our routine acquiescence, our everyday condition of insensibility and indifference to hope. So it may be, for us; we may be so habituated to the status quo that we feel only the most occasional moments of hope for something else to punctuate our routines, as a needle of flashing silver stitches a brilliant yellow stretch through a dull gray cloak. But this reveals not the truth of hope, but our captivity to sin. Hope is not the exception but the rule, the basic *regulus* on which our existence is built; it is resigned acquiescence in the status quo that we should properly see as odd, abnormal. The true, hopeful way of life is, as Glenn Tinder puts it,

> a way of waiting for, and so far as possible furthering by means of attentiveness and speech, the coming of a community so complete that the alienation and ignorance which are the primal considerations of history would be dissolved. For Christians, the prophetic stance is not willful or subjective or fainthearted. It is an attitude of settled receptivity to the Word which will not return to

God void but will accomplish the thing for which it was sent.
(2000: 240).[56]

Here we see what makes hope so ambiguous a presence in public
life for non-Christians. For, mobilized politically, hope can fall into
the trap of believing its own press clippings, so to speak – it may
encourage us to become arrogant and complacent, encouraging the
worst sort of political zealotry and megalomania. This charge certainly has force. Many of the greatest revolutionaries become terrible oppressors once in power; and honest and wide-minded
reformers, once elected, often become inflexible tyrants. What can
hope do to resist this tendency? Can hope, that is, be politically
chastening? Can it make us doubt our predictions, can it trouble our
agendas, and in general work as a leaven not to weaken our will-
power for action, but rather to weaken our confidence that we can
foretell the outcome of our action?

Properly Christian hope confounds our worldly expectations in
two distinct ways. First, it is deeply chastening. Hope does not
promise that our hopes will be realized but rather that the will of
God will be accomplished, so there is always a slight gap between
our concrete expectations and its promised end, a gap which
encourages us always to be open to the new, without deflating our
energies for action. But secondly, this hope encourages us always to
see beyond the immediate worldly political goals that we pursue,
and appreciate the iconic character of our political engagement – its
insistence that political ends are not in themselves adequate, or
finally complete, but that they always tell of deeper aims beyond
themselves in the eschaton.

This "hope" may sound to us escapist and otherworldly. But this
suspicion reflects the despair we feel at being (we assume) wholly on
our own – unsponsored by the universe, with our hopes and longings simply expressions of what we would like to be true. We do not
believe we have any right to hope. The audacity of Christian hope
lies in its semi-immanence, how it tempts us with its tantalizing
possibility. And if we – when we – "surrender" to its temptation,
we will not have willed this surrender but simply ceased to attempt
to seize control for ourselves. We do not achieve hope, we

56. See Vanstone 1983, 103: "The experience of waiting is the experience of the
world as in some sense *mattering*." See also Heschel 1962 and Walzer 1985.

acknowledge it, because it is inextricably part of a complex theological project: the ongoing, always only just-begun practice of expressing gratitude for the gratuitous gifts of a loving God.

Nonetheless, while this Christologically grounded and formed hope is distinctively Christian, analogues to it are available outside the Christian tradition. It can be a kind of humanistic affirmation – not a subjectivism that glorifies humanity, but a recognition that the dignity of human agency entails that we live within a moral order, even as we can revolt (and have revolted, and thus are revolting) against that order. Albert Camus and Hannah Arendt held something like this, as did Joseph Brodsky and Zbigniew Herbert; and Adam Michnik and Václav Havel do so today as well.[57] Hence this could be a genuinely "catholic" hope, creating a rhetorical or strategic opening to all "persons of good will;" yet for those who inhabit it, it remains irremediably and inexpungeably theological. Because its concrete hopefulness cannot be detached from theological warrants, it is intentionally difficult for its adherents to diminish, forget, or ignore disagreements with their allies even as they work together.

Such hope offers a kind of critique, with real socio-political power, because it flows from the larger communal practices of the ecclesial community. If we have hope at all, it springs from prayer, prayerful action, and prayerful reflection upon such action.

A historical example of this may help. In the fourth and fifth centuries, various Christian bishops created a new social category, the category of "the poor." These bishops used scriptural interpretation – largely in their sermons, the most overtly "public speech" of bishops at that time – to bring into view the reality in their cities of an enormous underclass of people who were the poor. But the bishops were not freestanding intellectuals; they had become aware of these people, and realized their plight, because of the church's practices of caring for all who need help. Of course, their development of this language was also connected to their own awareness of their growing moral, social, and political authority, and their realization that they were coming to be seen as the "protectors" of their cities, or as the stewards of their cities' saintly protectors. Nonetheless, before the bishops did this there was no

---

57. For more academic exemplars, see Novak 1989 and J. Stout 2004.

sociological category of the poor in late antique cities, but only "the crowd"; whereas once they created this vocabulary, "the poor" emerged as a real cause of social concern and interest. Furthermore, the ascription of "the poor" became more fundamental than that of "citizen" at this time – a human being's impoverishment is a more important fact about her or him than whether she or he is a member of the same political community as you yourself are. The bishops had noticed that the received political languages of their day obscured realities that church practices made palpable for them; and they changed that language in order to render that reality more fully visible.[58]

What sort of concrete practices do we have, then, that might serve as the anchor from which a systematic hopeful critique can emerge? Quite a few, actually. Within national boundaries, the churches are deeply concerned with just-wage campaigns, education concerns, family issues, peace marches, environmental activism, helping the homeless, and addressing the diverse concrete problems our societies face. Internationally, they have been committed to mission work of various sorts; concerns about Third World debt relief, transnational and interreligious dialogue and understanding; and "domestic-international" concerns such as migrant labor, the sanctuary movement in the 1980s, and questions of international justice as they arise in concerns about church investments. This is quite a various list of concerns, to be sure, but they all have at their heart a basic conviction – namely, that people are more than their place in the systems they inhabit, more than their functions in various social, economic, and political networks. Insofar as such networks attempt to offer exhaustively immanent languages for describing the world, and for valuing all things within it, they are false and deceptive, and must be critiqued. And such criticism is what the church is called to be and do.[59]

In all such patterns of practical and expressed ecclesial dis-comfort, several tactical insights are repeatedly emphasized. We should acknowledge the need, value, and legitimacy of social structures, but we must not grant them their apocalyptic preten-sions. We must recognize the limits to the systems we inhabit – to

58. See P. Brown 1992 and 1997, Davis 1996, Daley 1999, and Holman 2001.
59. See Jenkins 2002 and Hertzke 2004.

the political form of the modern nation-state, to the economic form of liberal market capitalism, and to the socio-cultural form of liberal individualism, among others. But we best recognize these limits, not simply by proclamation, but by witnessing to what gets lost when these systems ignore their own limits. This applies to language as well. The absolute hegemony, in some churches' campaigns for social justice, of the language of rights and of individuals as fundamentally bearers of rights, may be problematic; such language ought to be enframed explicitly and intelligibly within a language of children of God, which gives them positive moral force. (We should care about children of God, but people with rights we can just leave alone.) Both conservatives and liberals suggest that "rights talk" may be socially valuable when embedded in a rich moral vocabulary; but it may be socially destructive when we rely on it alone.[60] It should not become an idol.

Certainly these may be nice strategies for political engagement, a critic might say; but how, precisely, do they manifest the virtue of hope? How does this laundry list of practices reflect the churches' hopefulness? Most directly, behind all of them is a recognition that our world is more than these systems allow it to be – though that "more" cannot be exhaustively articulated in the present dispensation. Human beings and their actions transcend their bare literality, and the eschatological hopefulness of the churches emerges in part through their refusal to take the nation-state system with ultimate seriousness. What the state lays claim to is not its proper possession; it is on loan, as it were, from the heavenly kingdom, and, sooner than the state thinks, that loan will be called due.

This eschatological hopefulness has several implications. As regards our political concepts, this hopeful attitude towards public life persistently presses beyond the contractual language of the state towards a deeper, covenantal language. We do not know fully what our obligations are, we are not fully in control of them. Citizenship is not a simple contract, drawn up between fundamentally autonomous interlocutors; it bespeaks a larger relationship, a commitment that begins in the here and now but inevitably extends back in

---

60. For progressive worries, see Ignatieff 2001 and Saletan 2003; for conservative worries, see Glendon 1991 and Shapiro 1999.

time, as we take responsibility for our polity's past, and across political boundaries, as we see political divisions as ultimately not final divisions. While civic membership in some polity here is essential, it is ultimately, for believers, derivative; our primary citizenship, and the primary meaning of citizenship *tout court*, is theocentric: our citizenship is in heaven. The churches recognize the limits of political citizenship, by critiquing nationalism, and by demanding care beyond worldly citizenship – through the sanctuary movement, care for migrants, transnational understanding, etc. And political states will be held eschatologically accountable to these standards, and found wanting; a fundamentally negative judgment of God upon the pretensions of Caesar stands beneath all the churches' other proclamations, a *basso profundo* counterpoint to the higher notes. To recognize the value and necessity of such civic commitment alongside its non-ultimacy: that is what Christian hope demands. Inevitably, this understanding of citizenship ironically invests more in the concept than any worldly polity will want to allow – in large part because the investment is beyond that worldly polity's control.

This insistence on the covenantal character of citizenship highlights the dispositional transformation that eschatological hopefulness encourages in us as well. Through it, we become better "readers" of the language of politics. Many offer apocalyptic readings of "the signs of the times," but such readings are implausible to the extent that they are confidently determinate, for they refuse to leave space for the surprises that the future inevitably holds. Hence there are very, very few Cassandras, and even their batting averages are always disappointingly low. The claim that "we should have foreseen it" is often not an attempt at browbeating self-abnegation so much as another attempt at consoling ourselves and convincing ourselves that "the new" never really happens, that history bears its own meaning immanently within itself, that there is no suprahistorical Lord steering its course, that all we will find there is more of the same. But whatever the future will be, it is unlikely to be that. We are not called on to be prognosticators; we are called on to be hopeful. Hope has a hesitancy about it – a hesitancy regarding its expectation, not of the new, but of our capacity to comprehend the new, at least before the eschaton. The new is the secret center of history, its hidden heart, and it is a heart we can never, in this dispensation, comprehend and penetrate. A proper Christian hope cultivates the capacity that the shepherds should have had – the capacity to be joyfully surprised.

It is in this capacity that we see the core disposition of hope displayed. For hope is, most simply, the conviction and affective anticipation that there is always yet more coming, and the more will not be more of the same, but will be genuinely new, genuinely unpredictable from what has come before. And this hope can never stop at being merely local, merely a minor hope: it is all or it is nothing. As David Novak says, the hope the world "needs for its very survival can only be the hope for its final redemption" (1989: 156). This is an insight both terrifying and exhilarating. And it is in this exhilarating terror that we see not only hope's ultimate civic message, but also its deepest ascesis. We turn to that next.

The ascesis of hopeful engagement

So hope is about not being in charge. It does not promote political zealotry, fanaticism, or any of the other apocalypticisms which constantly tempt us. It resists our longing for closure, which is itself induced in us by our despair, our lack of confidence in God. Hope is about learning to endure, to live in a world where we are not in charge, where not even how our words are heard is under our control. Yet this hope makes us joyful because it liberates us: to think of the judgment of hope, its chastening, as in any way fundamentally condemnatory or damning misunderstands both hope and the God who gives us hope.

A proper hope seeks a middle ground between the too complacent apocalyptic immanentism of the resigned or self-righteous, and the too complacent apocalyptic escapism of the embittered or smug. It anchors this view on its theology of history and creation, on its claim that history is not finally literally legible, but only sacramentally so. Neither immanentists nor escapists can capture the true longings of humans, which inevitably transcend the mere immanent satisfactions or anesthetics they advertise. God has made us for Godself, and our heart is restless until it rests in God, so no worldly dispensation is adequate. Yet this dispensation matters; the violations and injustices here are not simply accidental or immaterial, and its joys and sorrows will finally be taken up into God and transformed into their full reality.

During the world, hope is our mode of recognizing our *distensio*, our experience of tantalizing incompleteness that we confess we exist in at present, yet proclaim will be healed in the eschaton – and we must recognize both our own incompleteness, and the way that it tantalizes us. We recognize the profundity of what John Cleese's character in the movie *Clockwise* says: "It's not the despair I mind, it's the hope I can't stand." The hope we can barely stand is indeed what we must endure; and it is God's hope, not primarily ours at all. In hope, we refuse to cease suffering, and look instead to find ways to deepen our attentiveness, both to hope's tantalizing visage and the reasons we need it so desperately.[61]

How can this hope be deepened by public engagement? The answer is straightforward: by being vexed. In public life, history's recalcitrance to our expectations is most visibly, even glaringly, displayed; our actions never have quite the effect we command them to have, and so our engagement with "worldly matters" inevitably involves our losing control of our fate more than gaining control of it. Hope is deepened by being repeatedly recalled to the tension between that fact and our continuing confidence that history's ultimate destiny is what we partially and provisionally glimpse today in joy. Engagement in public life can work as a graceful brush fire, clearing away the choking undergrowth of our indulgent delusions so that we can know the consequences of our choices.

This is not a little ironic. We think of hope as deeply comforting, encouraging, and empowering. But it is not simply sweetness and light – not to us, not as we are presently (de)formed. It is also equally deeply a judgment on our anxiety and the consequence of that anxiety, namely our desire to delude ourselves into believing that we know what will happen. It is shrivening and chastening, because it reminds us constantly of the impurity of our intentions – the leaven of hypocrisy, excessive self-interest and self-righteousness that accompanies our every word and deed. Hope forbids and implicitly condemns any too determinate expectations of the coming order. For all the talk about "empowering" people to engage in

61. Again, see Bell 2001.

public life, what actors in public life repeatedly report is a deepened sense of their own smallness, of the complexities of the issues involved and the power of unforeseen and unforeseeable accidents and consequences – their power to warp one's actions. This is not only a fact about modern public life either; as Sophocles and Thucydides teach, even 2,500 years ago, it was in public affairs that nemesis was most palpably present.

Yet hope's chastening does not demoralize or de-energize, because it is governed by affirmation. Indeed, hope is liberating precisely *as* judgment, for it frees us from the fantasy that we are in control, and lets us use the enormous psychic energies dedicated to sustaining that fantasy for other, more fruitful tasks. It is the angel announcing the good tidings, announcing the birth of the new; and we are made new in and by that annunciation.

Still, hope's liberation almost always wears the face of a judge for us, at least at first. For, like beauty, hope is the beginning of terror, and we should appreciate its terror. By "terror" I mean that, even though we do not know what hope promises us – even though in hope we stand in a way beyond knowledge, resisting its claims to complacency – we know that hope will change us, in ways that we do not fully understand, and indeed in ways that we do not, at present, fully wish to understand, much less undergo. Hope is ultimately an action upon us, and the recognition that further such action is forthcoming. Now, in our sin, we fear change, and see it as a threat. But we will not be allowed to gird ourselves and go where we will; another will gird us and take us where we do not want to go. Mercy it may be, in the end; grace it may be, in retrospect; but today, to creatures such as we are, grace and mercy can easily evoke terror. This does not deny that there is some part of us – we may affirm it as the better part, though even that affirmation is only partial – that does feel the silent thrill of hope, that grasps the unimaginable joy that would come from this hope being true; this part helps us not to drown in terror, and gracefully offers us a path besides repression or capitulation, towards acknowledgment. To those who have seen a glimmer of hope, the whole world hums with the coming transformations; and all our will to deafen ourselves to it cannot finally fully hold out the noise. This struggle between our fears and God's hopeful grace is the deepest ascesis of hope.

In public life, this struggle with terror is most clearly manifest through hope's prophetic dimension. Politics is constantly tempted towards the sinful prescription of self-sufficiency, towards the presumption that politics' goals are legitimately immanent and self-enclosed ends in themselves – that somehow the sphere of the political or the "social" has an integrity and coherence of its own. Hope works against this complacency by insisting, obtrusively, that our politics falls short of our hopes, in two distinct ways. First of all, it falls short on its own terms: the poor are not clothed, the hungry not fed, the homeless not housed, the righteous not rewarded, the wicked not punished. It is an essential part of the prophetic imagination, itself grounded in hope, to remind us, as did Amos, of the covenant we continually fail to keep, of the need for justice to flow like a river, and righteousness as a mighty stream. But this call for justice is only one prophetic task. God has demands on us beyond justice; God wants more of us than simply to play fair. Prophetic hope challenges the pretension that humans are fundamentally aiming at ends achievable by politics at all – that humans' ends are fundamentally this-worldly. Hope calls politics beyond itself, and reveals politics' ultimate inadequacy.[62] Hope calls us beyond the mundane, and reminds us that our lives are not simply about the outcome of our actions, but that they flourish most profoundly in conversation and communion with a God whose ways are not our own. But that public life is insufficient does not imply that it is irrelevant. Politics is one way God speaks to us; beyond its mundane literality, worldly action has an iconic character. We see all semiotically, and we act as *semeia*, signs of God. This is how Abraham Lincoln, in his Second Inaugural Address, "read" the Civil War as God's judgment on the people of the United States, "North and South," as punishment for their collective complicity in the sin of slavery. Along with justice, then, the prophets insist that public life has a destiny beyond justice; but it is a destiny that will transfigure our mundane life, not renounce it.

Public life for Christians, then, when properly undertaken, inevitably leads to contemplation of the mysteries of providence, the sovereignty of God, and the cultivation of the holy terror that is

---

62. This is yet another place where the "natural" versus "supernatural" contrast has no role in this Augustinian account.

integral to true piety. By hopeful engagement in public life, that is, the public sphere itself becomes the forum for an ascetical inquiry that it cannot itself, in this dispensation, comprehend. By so gracefully enduring hope, we are better shaped more fully to receive God's grace.

There is one more dimension of the ascesis of public life to investigate: love. We turn to that next.

6

Charitable citizenship

But the state of grace this natural act requires,
Have we the natural strength for it?

Molly Peacock, "There Must Be"

We have now seen how the theological virtues of faith and hope can inform a general picture of civic engagement, a "liturgy of citizenship." But what about love? Augustinian theology sees love as the fundamental theological, ontological, and psychological truth about reality. Is love also politically and civically fundamental? How can it operate in the public realm?

Many thinkers seem to think that what politics does *not* need is love. They reverse Clausewitz's dictum: politics is the continuation of war by other means, and as such it must be carefully managed and controlled. Politics is precisely the realm where we manage to accommodate each other without asking for passionate investment in one another. To invite private passions back in is to court disaster.

That we appreciate these concerns is the signal achievement of the tradition of liberal political thought, from Hobbes and Locke forward. Out of an often salutary fear that a more ambitious political scope will lead to endless fratricidal conflict, this tradition urges us to quarantine existential questions, and to limit the political to those matters that (more or less) directly concern the public good.[1] There is much wisdom in this aversion. But it begs the question of whether or not such ambitions can be fully purged from public affairs, whether fear and other negative motivations are

---

1. See Hirschman 1977.

sufficient to secure political order. Many argue that alongside such negative motivations, political thought must acknowledge equally primordial positive desires, for fame, honor, and glory, and most preeminently the desire for communion, the power of love.[2]

When such arguments are made, liberalism's salutary skepticism about love gives way to a deeper, more properly metaphysical, suspicion about love as part of our world – a skepticism that love can only be an accidental and episodic reality. This skepticism is something any human feels, from time to time. But this book does not share this doubt. At its heart – as part of the core of the Augustinian construal of the Christian vision itself – lies a deep and abiding emphasis not just on love but on joy and delight; eye has not seen, nor ear heard, the joys awaiting us in God's kingdom. Hence this theology gives pride of place to joy, to the idea that we are made to delight. Humans are created for the purpose of pur- poselessness – for God's delight, and our own.[3] This book's focus on joy provokes this most profound reflexive skepticism about and resistance to Christian claims about love. And it is primordial: it is not contingent upon "liberalism" or "modernity" or "secularism," but such doubts are simply part of the human makeup, after the Fall, during the world. Here we must directly confront our innate skepticism of the idea that humans are made for joy.

To confront it, however, we must work through the political challenge, the immediate political problem with love. Public life is typically understood to corrupt love, because it curdles the ideals we bring to public life, and makes us cynical by embroiling us in end- less conflict, which is antithetical to true love. After all, inevitably in politics, one makes enemies. Political life is extremely complex, with many realities tangled up with one another, and humans are

---

2. This is a larger tradition than that "liberal political *theory*" that I discussed in the Introduction to this Part II. My complaints about contemporary theorists do not directly apply to this larger tradition of liberal political thought, though (as will be clear) I think there are concerns about this latter, larger, tradition. See Mendus 1999 and Kahn 2004 for discussions of how love appears in the most unlikely of places in liberal political theory.

3. See O'Donovan 1996: 181–4 and Barth 1961: 375: it is "astonishing ... how many references there are in the Old and New Testaments to delight, bliss, exultation, merry-making and rejoicing, and how emphatically these are demanded from the Book of Psalms to the Epistle to the Philippians." C. S. Lewis has much to say here as well; I discuss it in the Conclusion to the book. I thank William Werpehowski for bringing this passage to my attention.

potently habitual, tending to favor those interests they have favored before; hence, regular patterns of support and opposition inevitably appear among members of every polity. One finds oneself regularly opposed to someone else on issue after issue – sometimes on issues that seem quite disconnected to one another, sometimes even on issues where your previously professed positions might have led you to expect alliance. It can even come to seem that the opposition between you and the other is the reason for the position you take: sometimes you may find yourself taking a position simply because it is the position opposed by your opponent (or at least not the position she or he has taken). Sometimes enmity can seem a conventional political shorthand. Sometimes it can actually be that shorthand.

In some situations, such opposition can mellow into a rivalry, with respect communicated across the aisle of political difference. But such regular opposition more often results, not in an appreciation of one's opponents, but in a deepening animus towards them: you shift from finding yourself opposing them on various issues to finding yourself opposing *them*. What began as a set of discrete policy disputes is transformed into a cosmological dualism; the person who once was offering a different though legitimate view on some issue or other now becomes invested with an almost diabolically perverse desire to thwart not just your favored legislation but *you*, especially "you" in the form of the ideals you espouse, the hopes and dreams you have for your polity. They become your enemy. At its most sophisticated, the process can float entirely free from concrete historical people and become attached to metaphysical abstractions that may manifest themselves in people but that are not ultimately captured in them. (Think of the demonization of "liberals" or "neocons" in contemporary American politics.) Here the energies of your psychic economy have made such "opponents" into such. You have, indeed, made your enemy.

Typically responses to this fact have been twofold. One response demonizes the reality of conflict, and hence of real engagement in public life. This response makes "the best" the enemy of "the good," and so effectively urges us, even if it would never admit this to itself, to flee politics. There is something ironic about this, for it is precisely such anti-political thinkers who most vociferously protest that "everything is political." As was argued earlier, this is essentially a second-order ideological or mythological claim: it is not really speaking about reality but about how we should orient ourselves towards reality, and for them we should orient ourselves towards reality by shunning it.

The other response fantasizes that a conflict-less politics is possible, that there could be a "politics of sincerity" or a "politics of meaning." We may call such thinkers "cosmopolitans"; such thinkers urge political commitment to a political community fully inclusive of all humanity. This view insists that the presence of conflict is not essential to the world, and posits, either as practically achievable or as regulative, an ideal cosmopolitanism as political program.

Critics of cosmopolitanism argue that such views reveal that their adherents have no idea of what politics really is. First of all, the critics say, real politics is about tension and conflict between firmly held positions, and it can play a fruitful constitutional role by separating powers and setting them in potential tension. Conflict may be good for the polity even as it is bad for its members; public virtue may breed private viciousness. Furthermore, the critics continue, insofar as cosmopolitans imagine that they can deliberate about political issues while genuinely and effectively considering the interests of all humanity, they have succumbed to the megalomania of universal sincerity – imagining others in a way that seeks a universal "we" and so effaces significant differences among people. To imagine that such a program could be practically viable can stymie our current political action, and vitiate our political character, because it tends towards demonizing enemies and instrumentalizing friends. The cosmopolitan is an intoxicating, flashy, and fizzy drink, not a productive political program.

Christian realists agree with the above critique of treacly cosmopolitanisms. But they then find similar charges directed their way too. Sometimes these criticisms are framed formally as one, about the confusion of "religio-moral" and "political" categories. But basically it is a material critique: the critics suspect that Christians' faith in a politics of love simply reveals Christianity's equally intoxicating cocktail of naïveté, *ressentiment*, bad faith, and slave morality.

Yet Christianity's love commandment can be interpreted in another way. Jesus did not deny that enemies exist; he called upon us to love our enemies. And he followed that call up with the demonstration of what he meant in the pattern of his own life and death.[4] It is easy to read that command as proposing a strategy to undo all enmity, but perhaps that is more wishful thinking on our part than what is really being proposed; perhaps instead the proposal is that we accept that we will have enemies, but that we refuse to grant that the enmity we share is all we share with one another. Augustinian Christians see themselves as developing this suggestion by allowing that politics is continuous with war (after all, Augustine himself said something like that) while still insisting that that whole phenomenon is still governed by the divine will and, yes, divine love, and so can remain within the realm of communion. (Here is where arguments that war can be waged in love are interestingly illuminated.[5]) Even some deep-thinking secular thinkers suggest that politics has a communal trajectory that cannot and should not be expunged.[6] Nonetheless, if politics is a potential site for communion, even Christians should allow that it is quite a curious form of communion – a cruciform communion, as it were. What sort of communion is this, and how far, in this life, can it be realized as such?

This chapter attempts to answer that question. Its argument is straightforward. We must acknowledge the ineradicable presence of conflict in public life, despite the general avoidance of this fact in political theory. So the chapter turns to the best secular account of such conflict, namely, "agonist" political thought. But simply acknowledging conflict is not enough; such acknowledgment must explain why conflict appears to us *as* conflict – as a tension that seems problematic to us – and that requires us to think about communion, and the meaning of love. Hence the chapter argues that agonism ultimately succumbs to a naturalizing despair regarding the inescapability of conflict, thereby losing its grip on the contingent character of political reality. An Augustinian proposal offers a richer account of conflict, because it shows us how a psychology built on love understands conflict as a struggle over loves. So the chapter concludes by arguing that this account offers a more thoroughly agonistic, engaged, and genuinely charitable

---

4. See Vanstone 1983.   5. See O'Donovan 2003.
6. See J. Stout 2004, Allen 2004, and (in a slightly critical way) Markell 2003.

vision of citizenship, a vision with civic benefits for the public and ascetic benefits for believers. Civic engagement motivated and informed by such a divinely charged love is open to the full range of civic possibilities in ways that more self-proclaimedly "worldly" accounts are not, because through it we can acknowledge that our deepest political ambitions, during the world, will only ever be realized proleptically. By doing this, Christian citizens become equipped to accommodate the full range of challenges public life sets its participants, in a way that trains them more fully to show forth in their lives the love that they profess with their lips.

The agonist proposal

The most promising thinking about these matters is the work of recent political theorists who offer what they call an "agonistic" alternative to liberal political theory. Inspired by thinkers like Nietzsche and Carl Schmitt, agonists argue that the first truth of politics is that it is founded not on some set of just principles, but rather on endless struggle and power. This is not a license for mere brutality towards one another, but an acknowledgment that real engagement, undertaken with the best intentions, will inevitably take the form of a struggle. Someone will always lose, and the right never rests wholly with the side that wins. Agonists see the fundamental political project as the fostering of disagreement, debate, and conflict among groups and within them. They do this not out of some perverse or demonic desire for conflict, but rather because they believe that fostering such disagreement encourages the full participation of all members of society in the ongoing construction of their society. Agonists think this offers two benefits. First, such agonistic engagement brings conflict within the licit sphere of "the political" and thereby reduces its propensity to whirl out of control. Second, it brings to the surface the tensions and conflicts latent in any and every social identity, and hence resists the necessarily oppressive trap of fixed and stale identities. Agonistic engagement is an end in itself, not just a means to other ends; the point of politics is not simply to settle on policies, but at least equally significantly to unsettle both the status quo of the social consensus and the individual participants in that consensus, as far as that is possible.

The agonists are worthwhile interlocutors because of their central thematic concern – the role of conflict in politics – and because that concern leads them to engage positions usually ignored by political theorists, most notably religious positions.[7] But that engagement reveals a larger, and more problematic, psychology and ontology. They are ideologically committed to an "ontology of conflict" that pictures reality as an archipelago of alterities, and that does not allow them the freedom to step back from conflict's immanent self-presentation to see its true character. Still, to see this we must appreciate their insights.

Agonism's attractions

Unsurprisingly, agonists define themselves against an opponent – liberalism. They argue that received liberal theory is so concerned about the possibility of conflict that it sacrifices the possibility of legitimate contestation in order to pursue the chimera of perfect social peace. For Chantal Mouffe, John Rawls's political liberalism "tends to … [expel] any legitimate opposition from the democratic public sphere"; for Rawls, "a well-ordered society is a society from which politics has been eliminated" (Mouffe 2000: 14, 29, 31).[8] Agonists see liberals as profoundly conservative; their opposition to conflict effectively protects the social and individual structures of the status quo against destabilizing radical critique.

In contrast, agonists see pluralism as a happy part of our condition, one worth fostering. This pluralism begins at the bottom. Individual persons are not the solid autonomous Westphalian states in miniature that liberals assume them to be. Identity and difference are cathected inside the self, so that a too secure identity is first of all realized only through an enormous amount of psychic violence, and kept in place only by a larger intersubjective political economy that radically restrains our capacities to explore and/or inhabit the mutifarious psychic energies we actually are.[9] What looks like innocuous ordinary socio-politics is, for agonists, an enormous

---

7. For examples of such sustained engagement, see Connolly 1999, S. K. White 2000, and Coles 1997.
8. Mouffe makes the same complaint against so-called "deliberative democrats," who she thinks destroy real pluralism; see 2000: 46–9, 55, 81–2, 91–2.
9. See Connolly 2002b.

self-imposed attempt to repress our actual polymorphousness in order to impose clear and stable individual identities on ourselves. The central question for agonists is not how to design structures for resolving political conflict, but rather how to induce enough people to start disagreeing with one another, and with themselves, in order to cultivate thick and contentious dispute.

Agonists begin with the axiom that society is non-natural, a human artifact whose reality is significantly a product of human decisions, not of inevitable natural structures. There is no "natural" or even necessarily eternally best way to organize society; its nature is always ultimately up to the people who inhabit it.[10] Complete consensus is both impossible and undesirable. Modern states' actions are so complex and comprehensive, their citizens so diverse, that every decision cannot but exclude some dissidents. This dynamic of inclusion and exclusion is essential to political life: "every discourse, even one filled with words like 'fair' and 'impartial,' is an engine of exclusion and therefore a means of coercion" (Fish 1999: 223). Because of this, political life should be carried on in full acknowledgment of the essentially fabricated and inevitably conflictual nature of political order. As Mouffe puts it, we must resist "the sacralization of consensus," and "the closing of the gap between justice and law that is a constitutive space of modern democracy"; we must "constantly challeng[e] the relations of inclusion-exclusion," in order both to resist the rigor mortis of some particular political configuration and to ensure that political life remains able to welcome the genuine novelty of other new voices and the inevitable changes that come from living into an ever new future (2000: 10, 32, 113).

Some might worry that such an agonism is just a recipe for violent anarchy, but such worries assume that argument is the same as combat. Not so; agonistic disagreement is not a reversion to some sort of state of nature, but a political achievement, requiring skills and dispositions that must be learned. Acknowledging the inevitability of conflict and exclusion does not entail any celebration of violence; instead, such acknowledgment helps resist conflict's tendencies to turn bloody. In contrast, political theories for which radical challenge to its fundamental political framework is

---

10. See Mouffe 2000: 103. For a similar analytic approach, see D'Agostino 1996.

unthinkable (sometimes, as in Jürgen Habermas's proposal, quite literally) are more prone to a much greater danger of violence.

Agonists believe we can begin to imagine a non-violent political struggle by thinking not in terms of enemies, but in terms of adversaries; in imagining the "us" versus "them" dynamics inherent in political life, as Mouffe puts it, we should "construct the 'them' in such a way that it is no longer perceived as an enemy to be destroyed, but as an 'adversary,' that is, somebody whose ideas we combat but whose right to defend those ideas we do not put into question" (2000: 101–2). By so imagining our opponents as engaged with us, not in an ethical dispute about what is morally good, but rather in a political dispute about what is politically the best thing to do, we resist the temptation to subsume politics into the ethical project of "the recognition of the Other," and instead imagine the political as a realm of debate and dissent relatively free of the anxieties and aggressions we invariably bring to our moral projects (129–40).

Obviously agonism is an intensely interesting and potentially fruitful way of looking at politics. It offers a vital and exciting way of thinking about political life outside the forced teleology and illusory idealism of much political thought. Engagement in the agonists' project could help revivify Christians' civic participation, as it would engage them in the project of explaining themselves to their fellow citizens (and to each other – for, after all, not all "Christians" will align on the same side of any position).

But agonism is not finally satisfactory. It has its own internal problems, and even if it did not, it would stymie Christian attempts to appropriate it. Indeed, it is more interesting and useful as a provocation to Christian political thought than as a template. I say why next.

Agonism's problems

In the end, agonism does not so much transcend the dominant liberal political approach as repeat its profound difficulties. For all its trumpeting of the inescapability of conflict, agonism finally aims via such acknowledgments to contain conflict, to be as magisterially (and managerially) non-partisan as liberal political theorists purport to be. Ultimately agonism's ambitions are incoherent: like theorists such as Rawls, it still wants to be the referee, offering a theory of politics capable of accommodating and organizing the conflicts among the very divergent political positions present in any society. But this very focus on accommodating conflict, and including all possible viewpoints, is premised on a prior exclusion of any positions that would imagine politics in radically different terms. Agonism is what happens when academic elites recognize the contestability of their positions but still hold on to the hope that there can be an essentially neutral and descriptive political philosophy within which such contestations can occur. In so hoping, they fall, as Stanley Fish says, into "the theorist's most rarefied temptation, the temptation of thinking that recognizing the unavoidability of politics is a way of avoiding it" (1999: 233).[11]

Return to Chantal Mouffe's distinction between adversaries and enemies. The hope is that this distinction will contain conflict within acceptable levels. But in itself this is just an assertion, with all the violence that entails. Mouffe attempts to manage conflict – to secure the stability of the basic framework within which conflict can occur, before entering into conflict. Again, Fish puts this well: while agonists believe in "openness to revision," and argue "that some forms of organization are more open to revision than others," they fail to recognize

> that openness to revision as a principle is itself a form of closure, not at all open to ways of thinking or acting that would bring revision to an end. "Openness to revision" is an internal, not an absolute, measure; it is relative to whatever understood exclusions – and there will always be some – give the politically organized space its shape. (1999: 235)

Where agonists claim to offer "a political philosophy that makes room for contingency," Fish argues, "contingency is precisely what you can't make room for; contingency is what befalls the best laid plans of mice and men – and that includes plans to take it into account or guard against its eruption" (237). Agonism remains crippled, like the liberal theories its advocates want to supplant, by being essentially a strategy based around a root fixation on the problem of conflict, and how best to accommodate it: "The

11. Agonism's fundamental similarities with liberalism in this regard are nicely brought out in the exchange between Flathman 1998 and Macedo 1998.

assertion that forms of order and stability are always provisional is equivalent to the assertion that values are plural and nonadjudicable. Both are offered as reasons for withdrawing from conflict" (239).

This failure is connected to another: agonists assume a moral psychology that is interestingly self-contradictory, as is revealed in their treatment of the relevance of individuals' commitments, their concerns and interests, to politics. Agonists cannot take our commitments seriously enough. On their picture, there is a certain phenomenological "lightness" to our grip on our commitments, as if they could be easily jettisoned; but, as Fish puts it,

> if the clash of values is irremediable and if the forms of order (and thus the configurations of 'us' against 'them') are continually shifting, it is best not to insist too strongly on the values you happen to favor or the forms of order you prefer. If everything is up for grabs, why grab anything with the intent of hanging on to it? (Fish 1999: 239)[12]

In fact this "lightness" is just what our real commitments do not have. Paradoxically and ironically, such theorists "back into" affirming this too thin understanding of our "commitments" because of their presumption of our commitments' very intransigence and intractability; for them, it is madness to expect that our commitments can be changed or commensurated, and so we must be resigned to that. (There is, in this way, a deep Stoical resignation, even despair, at the heart of the agonists' political ontology; recall, from Chapter 3 above, William Connolly's despair of actually changing anyone's mind.) They depict our commitments as permanent interests, "objectively" given in our constitution and fundamentally unquestionable. Hence agonists also take our commitments too seriously, accepting them as absolute and inflexible, fixed for ever in ways we must accommodate, and cannot hope to change.[13]

Furthermore, the agonists exhibit a persistent resistance to rendering explicit any commitment to justice, to giving a reason why

---

12. Fish 1999: 239. Note the similarities with Sandel's critique of Rawls's anthropology (1982: 154–65).
13. See Lieberman 1998 and Frankfurt 1988. See also Hirschman 1977; this is where the Enlightenment's turn to inflexible "interests" as opposed to more plastic "passions" may have deleterious consequences.

the inclusion of all, or the encounter with the other, is worthwhile, beyond the simply pragmatic (and metaphorical) one of relieving psychological (and social) tension. This manifests a moral-theoretical aphasia – Charles Taylor's "ethics of inarticulacy" once again – and suggests that their vocabulary for understanding human behavior, the vocabulary of conflict, cannot capture their own motivations for seeking to engage others.[14]

Ultimately, the vision of politics they offer entails certain dubious ontological assumptions. Like the liberal theorists they disparage, the agonists never actually theorize conflict, never actually analytically investigate and unpack the appearance of conflict to see how deep down it goes; instead, they simply assume it as the bedrock fact from which all political thought must begin, and, like the liberal theorists, they offer what is essentially a protectionist response to conflict, one aimed at ensuring that it does not become too dangerous. But agonism can only ensure this containment of conflict – or, rather, convince itself that it can ensure it – if, like the liberal theory it attempts to supplant, it makes us not *too* tied to our aims, willing to renounce them for the sake of the agon. And that is manifestly false to human psychology. By fixating on conflict, agonists back into asking humans to be the kind of creatures we cannot be, and so attempt (again) to "solve" politics before anyone actually begins to engage in it.[15]

In being resigned to the fact of conflict, ironically they also naturalize and domesticate it, with deleterious effects for the anthropology and ontology of conflict. Anthropologically, the naturalization of conflict demands that we anesthetize ourselves to it. If conflict is natural, our reflexive resistance to it – our incomprehension and stuttering inarticulateness before it – is itself unnatural, a hysterical, superfluous, and ultimately melodramatic overreaction. We should renounce all hope or imaginative possibility of some sort of ideal absolute harmony, and some sort of final reconciliation of all with all; we should mistrust our basic discomfort with conflict. But such a practice of mistrusting our intuitions encourages us ultimately to doubt our ability to tell right from

---

14. See Coles 1997: 194 and Taylor 1989.
15. Here criticisms of postmodern thinkers' "ontology of violence" (such as Milbank 1990b) are on to something.

wrong. Furthermore, our conviction of the accidental character of conflict can at times make us work hard to overcome it. Not only does such a naturalization encourage human temptations towards an enervating pessimism and despair; it also stands in manifest tension with the agonists' own insistence that patterns of human interaction are radically contingent, always open to contestation and reimagination.

Speaking ontologically, by trying so to naturalize and absolutize conflict, such accounts homogenize and domesticate it, and ignore the extremes to which it can go. As conflict is basic to the world, on their view, it cannot really be fundamentally opposed to the structures of the world itself. All conflict is ultimately the same sort of thing; there is not, on this view, the rich spectrum of different sorts of conflicts, some "manageable" by us, others not. This constrains our understanding of conflict, and hinders our response to it. Sometimes politics does lead to war, and some of those wars – not many, but some – are just. The agonists' "construction of the category of adversary" avoids the fact that sometimes we face enemies, and we must not allow the concept of adversary wholly to eclipse that of enemy. Occasionally good and evil do appear in the political sphere, and some forms of political argument are simply right or simply wrong. It is just a fact that some political programs may not be the objects of legitimate contestation, or understandable support, and it is unrealistic to imagine that people should not operate with ethical motivations in the political realm. The agonists' particular vision of politics as a sphere of "conflict" wholly distinct from the realm of the ethical may be a salutary warning for most of our political engagements, but it cannot be allowed the privileged place of metaphysical dogma that agonists seem to want to grant it, for it forecloses the possibility that politics may be more important, both positively and negatively, than we normally experience it as being.[16]

Agonism has considerable insights, but profound limitations; and both come from its unremitting focus on surfaces and appearance. It recognizes the ineradicability of conflict in this life, and acknowledges that conflict goes "all the way down," into our inmost selves. It realizes that public engagement can help move us towards a deeper and more capacious authenticity. But essentially it fails

16. This parallels Milbank's critique of the "policing of the sublime" in 1990b.

because it cannot see beyond the surface of public life: agonism is too trusting of public life's self-expression. Agonism's very attempt to capture the essence of politics, by focusing on politics' "surface expression" of conflict, domesticates that conflict, and cannot acknowledge the real psychological complexity of the self, and in particular the possibility that some parts of the self are more "real," less transcendable than others. It thus fails to see beneath that surface, and refuses to acknowledge *both* the desire for engagement and the fact that desire can be vexed – the twin realities that collectively constitute the reality that the agonists' emphasis on "conflict" too crudely attempts to encompass. For good and ill, agonism is finally a superficial account.

The priority of charity

Agonism's insights are better transplanted into an Augustinian account, which sees love, and not struggle – and thus communion, and not alterity – at the heart of the universe. Such an account offers a love-centered ontology that can make more sense of our interest in and commitment to one another. Love better understands the morality of public life because it can illuminate, better than agonist accounts, the phenomenological imperative to recognize the other person *as* an other person, an "other me." It thereby can make intelligible the fundamental political acts of respecting the other and recognizing that his or her voice is irreducible to one's own. Love, in brief, makes sense of the conversation that constitutes public life.

But agonism's internal difficulties are not the only reason our proposal cannot simply swallow it whole; it also directly challenges the idea of an Augustinian political engagement because agonism challenges the idea of a loving politics. In addressing it, we must fully confront the challenges facing an emphasis on love in public life.

Some agonists argue that Christians, like all moralizers, are likely to expect too much from political action because they expect properly moral outcomes therefrom. For such critics, Christians are dangerous because they fantasize an ideal world without violence, and so necessarily disdain this world, and the actions necessary for its sustenance, in ways which corrode our attachment to it. Despite (or even within) Christians' acknowledgment of the inescapability of violence in this-worldly politics, especially through the doctrine of sin, they typically retain a theoretical idealism, believing that there is some sort of "pure community" whose existence, now or eschatologically, bears, in some ambiguous way, on the sordid and sloppy realities of life in this world. This idealism presses Christians towards demonizing their opponents in dangerous ways, for to disagree with their plan is to place oneself firmly in the camp of evil. Agonists argue that this moralism invariably arises from and in turn reinforces an otherworldly, nay-saying *ressentiment* that poisons Christian participation in worldly affairs – and poisons Christians against other participants in the public sphere. Moralism, that is, is just another version of escapism.

Others develop the accusation of "idealism" differently, arguing that Christians treat politics with too little seriousness. They do not believe that Christians will sincerely participate in such an agonistic and pluralistic conversation at all, given that their aim inevitably is (or should be) the conversion of other participants; under the guise of politics Christians are secretly playing another game, seeking converts, not conversation partners. Christianity seems essentially just the sort of "final" discourse that agonists cannot countenance; its dogmas are incontestable, and thus would only resist the deliberations agonists would cultivate. This ultimate unseriousness is finally the weakness of slaves, who know they cannot win and therefore reject the game before it even begins.

These challenges are profound, and reward serious reflection. But they are not new; for while agonism may sound very avant-garde, in fact it has deep roots in the very pagan *mythos* that Augustine set himself against throughout his career. Hence it is no surprise that Christians possess considerable resources with which to respond to this challenge. Precisely because they *are* worrisome – because they find a place within Augustinian Christian political thought – they help to rethink the distinctively Augustinian understanding of public engagement.

In fact, the critics do not fully realize the depth of their disagreement with Christianity, because they do not understand what Christians ought to be all about. The worries misconstrue what "winning" is for Augustinian Christians, as well as the sort of "struggle" they understand themselves to undertake. For believers, conflict is not the most basic fact about human society; conflict is merely the symbol (and the symptom) of the reality of our disordered loves. The struggle of politics can be a struggle for conversion, conversion of one's loves and the loves of one's interlocutor. This interpretation of political conflict reimagines it as a conflict about our loves. Augustinians argue that agonists typically oppose "love" and "conflict" too comprehensively. Charity and agony have something interesting in common: love itself is the ultimate form of struggle, and struggle is unintelligible apart from love. Ironically enough, then, Augustinian Christians are more "agonistic," more playful and more valuing of politics, than more "secular" thinkers can be.

To show this, Augustinians must show that they can accommodate the reality of conflict during the world and in the self even more comprehensively than do the agonists. They do so because they have a pessimistic anthropology, not a pessimistic ontology, and because their account of sin as disordered loves precludes its adherents from demonizing their opponents. To see this we must first explain how the reality of conflict can be adequately captured in an Augustinian schema, and then, second, talk about how such a schema more appropriately depicts human political psychology.

An alternative Augustinian cosmology

Agonism and Augustinian Christianity propose fundamentally different cosmologies. Agonists, assuming ontological conflict, tend both to naturalize and to domesticate conflict, and thus to render perplexing agonism's simultaneous insistence on the primordiality of conflict and on the obligation to recognize the otherness of the other. Augustinians think reality is not most fundamentally the blind, billiard-like collision of Leibnizian windowless monads; conflict is fundamentally secondary to the real harmonies of being which underlie it. Hence, teleologically, this account affirms that we can genuinely encounter others, not just butt up against them. This emphasis on love, perhaps paradoxically, more readily comprehends the profundity of conflict while also refusing to "naturalize" conflict.[17]

17. My thoughts here are shaped by Santurri 1987.

It is worth explicitly noting the radical character of this alternative. This Augustinian cosmology is rooted in the cosmological revolution undertaken by Judaism and Christianity on their inherited Ancient Near Eastern roots, a revolution that rejected the received view of the cosmos as formed in an agonic struggle between two (or more) divine entities, replacing it with a cosmology of a single monarchic Deity from whom creation has tragically and inexplicably swerved. Conflict is real, but the crucial "violence" has already occurred, once and for all, in sin and in God's "overcoming" of our sin – which is actually not a second act of God, but simply God's refusal to allow us to complete our attempted violence of original sin. Yet the profundity of this picture has been obscured by its superficial familiarity. Many of the root myths of the universe, the worldviews from which Christianity borrows many of its concepts – such as the concept of virtue – are agonistic, fundamentally conflictual; Christianity's claim to transform them is quite radical, and we should appreciate that fact more thoroughly than we typically do.[18]

So Christians will oppose the agonists' naturalization of conflict, for reasons discussed earlier. But the interpretation of conflict, which induces them to resist this naturalization, does not deny conflict's reality, but offers a picture of harmonious community, the idea that reality is "at bottom" marked by order, against which conflict stands out as disharmonious dissent. This picture helps us recognize the desirability of genuine communal harmony, which is a political motivation quite different from the motivation of fear for what we might lose.

Recognition of this prompts another agonist challenge to Christianity, namely that it idealizes harmony to a degree that effaces the real and palpable fact of conflict in the universe. But such charges ignore the role of the concept of sin for Augustinians (which we discuss below). More profoundly still, such charges misconstrue Christians' basic expectations of political engagement, by characterizing it in immanent terms as hope for the this-worldly realization of the kingdom of God. This fails to appreciate the eschatological character of the Augustinian Christian position. Admittedly, all too often in history, Christians have pursued

18. See Forsyth 1987, Mathewes 2001a, and H. R. Niebuhr 1963: 106–7.

presumptuously apocalyptic socio-political programs; but properly speaking, Christian hope's eschatological orientation condemns such desires for any final ending in time. Christians should not want to "win," because Christ has "already" won. Because of Christ's victory, Christians should not conceive of either history in general or politics in particular as essentially agonistic, essentially a struggle or a war; it is rather a pilgrimage. Thus, against those who see conflict as necessarily and essentially violent, governed by a zero-sum logic, Christians can imagine and approach moments of conflict in the eschatological conviction that "losing" and "winning" need not be objects of ultimate concern.

Precisely because Augustinians see reality as more primordially about communion than conflict, they can also articulate why "care for the other *as* other" is politically important. The need to respect the otherness of others is palpable. One excruciating, maddening fact about public life is that others, with other views, are *tantalizingly* rational – that is, they seem amenable to reasoned conversation and dialogue, but effectively seem dedicated to vexing consensus. When confronted with these experiences, agonism can see such experiences only as opportunities either to rework the self, or simply to turn away from the other as not worth the effort; and it is hard to tell when to do the one or the other. In contrast, Augustinian political love manifests something quite like a certain kind of political respect, of seeing another as another you, another self. As Robin Lovin suggests, while improper love can smother the object of its attention, incorporating him or her into one's own narcissism, proper love can be politically restraining: "the best evidence that I have achieved some understanding of what love requires is that I can talk about the good of others in terms they can recognize" (1995: 200).[19] In Augustinian terms, this is connected to the idea that love is akin to vision, to seeing the truth about someone. Love is fundamentally an affirmative recognition of an other; to love is fundamentally to will that the other be – for it is the being of the other that gives you delight. Love, properly inhabited, fundamentally respects the other's alterity – and when someone does not

19. I thank Eric Gregory for this reference. For good discussions of the complexities of love in warping our vision of others – and yet the inescapability of love as motivating us – see A. L. Hall 2002 and Ferreira 2001.

respect that otherness, this failure of respect is most fully comprehensible as a failure of love.

Love's close connections with play illuminate this attention to the
other, and through it we can also understand, better than we can
through agonism, the various dimensions of the encounter with the
other. "Play" may sound frivolous, but in fact there is a deep
theological tradition that speaks of God as playing with the world.
In fact, the idea that God delights in, plays with, and enjoys the
world suffuses the Bible; in Proverbs, Wisdom says that "I was by his
side, a master craftsman, delighting him day by day, ever at play in
his presence, at play everywhere in the world, delighting to be with
the sons of men" (Proverbs 8:30–1).[20] Play is the activity and mode of
receptivity prompted in the playing self by its delight in the activity
at hand and in its partner in play. Play requires an other to play, an
otherness-in-relation-to-oneself, an otherness appropriately related
to oneself, in the ways necessary for both of you to understand the
rules of the game you are playing. And play requires the self to be
"other" too, in the sense that the self is expected to go outside of
itself and "into" the game, in something like ecstasy. So understood, love is the primordial form of play – an activity of ecstatic
delight with and towards others.

Play and ecstasy make agonists nervous; they are a bit too much
for them – too dangerous, too vulnerable. But of course the otherness that such ecstasy describes is precisely what the agonists posit
at the heart of the self, the idea that selfhood is not a unitary phenomenon; and so their discomfort here has no theoretically
respectable basis in their thought. Some might worry that "play"
suggests too superficial, too frivolous an approach. But it need not:
play is actually a form of risky engagement, one that reveals the
vulnerability of love, implicit in play's necessarily genuine openness
to the other. Here critics will naturally doubt that the language of
risk is doing much real work. Certainly charitable engagement will
not jettison its faith; so how risky, the agonists ask, can it truly be?
No less risky than the agonists' more typical Nietzschean approach
aims to be – and indeed, much more risky than their approach
actually manages to be.

20. See Pieper 1999, H. Rahner 1972, and Huiziga 1955. I am grateful to Patrick D.
Miller for calling my attention to this passage.

How is this so? In what does this "putting one's beliefs at risk" consist? It certainly does not mean "jettisoning one's faith," if that means trying to be an unbeliever, or attempting to hold all one's skeptical convictions at a skeptical distance, or being willing to jettison them at the first sign of an interlocutor's discomfort. That is not real engagement, it is play-acting. It is impossible totally to doubt one's own framework, because that framework undergirds the very vocabulary for the activity of doubting that would call it into question. Every intellectual framework that the human mind can inhabit has some "outside" that it cannot, and sometimes actively will not, theorize; the only question is whether the framework's adherents recognize that fact. So-called "open-minded" people have a very hard time imagining what it would be like for them to become blinkered fundamentalists; sometimes you can actually see the revulsive recoil from such an imagined future in their faces as they try to contemplate it. We simply cannot saw off the branch we are sitting on; and if we think we are doing that, it is only because we were never sitting on that branch at all.[21]

Rather, what this "riskiness" means is being willing to put one's beliefs "into play" – that is, to offer them to the other as a means of shared understanding – a way for the two (or more) of you to understand the conversation. (For example: in a discussion of capital punishment, you say, "Well, in my tradition we talk about the need for justice always being framed by mercy.") If you do this, and do it in a non-defensive manner, and if your interlocutor allows this interpretation to "play itself out," and you do too, you will find that your beliefs are no longer simply yours, but have become something like "common property." (Your interlocutor replies, "Yes, mercy – but mercy to whom? To the murderer? To the victim? To the

---

21. Stephen White's powerful and illuminating *Sustaining Affirmation* (2000) is a good example of such an approach. His account of what a "weak ontology" is (14–15), and of its contrast with a "strong ontology" (6–8), merely delays the ontological question, pressed in different ways by thinkers such as Alasdair MacIntyre and Richard Rorty, as to the final ontological status of such "weak ontological" claims: are they fundamentally imagined, or do they speak to something real? For more see Fish 1999: 235: "[the agonist] thinks that some forms of organization are more open to revision than others. What she does not see is that openness to revision as a principle is itself a form of closure, not at all open to ways of thinking or acting that would bring revision to an end. 'Openness to revision' is an internal, not an absolute, measure; it is relative to whatever understood exclusions – and there will always be some – give the politically organized space its shape."

victim's family?") And when you receive them back they may be slightly changed, modified here and there by the other's handling of them, out of her or his (or their) own irreducible perspective and previous experience. Allowing one's beliefs to go on such public pilgrimages will invariably make them more complex. But such "complication" of one's beliefs pre-dates anyone's possession of them; both theologically and historically, Christian faith is not parochially local or fundamentally narcissistic, but is always already cracked open to, and involved with, alternative modes of being. What is more disturbing is that this kenotic publication of one's beliefs may mean that after they have become public, they change so profoundly that you cannot recognize them any more. When our convictions meet reality, reality challenges us in ways we cannot control.

How can one relativize one's own beliefs? Rather than attempting to do it in language that looks to have pretensions to philosophical neutrality, Christians should employ the unapologetically local and particular dialect of Christian faith, particularly the importance of humility due to our own sinfulness and God's inherent transcendence. Openness to change is not a matter of placing a fundamentally external theoretical control on our beliefs, but rather it emerges organically from within the account, from the inside out. Furthermore, *pace* the agonists, this risk can be only indirectly accepted. As we saw, the attempt to "prepare to risk everything" is always an impossible task. There is no possible way to do it, and the attempt to do so invariably comes down to one more attempt to control what is put at risk. Any attempt directly to theorize one's own dissolution, or one's self-understanding's dissolution, is impossible; such dissolutions can be narrated retrospectively, but cannot be pre-emptively anticipated. The most we can do is leave open the possibility of a radical departure from Christian belief. But because this is an intra-Christian account, it cannot and need not theorize its own dissolution, especially because it cannot formulate an account of how it could be rejected.

Such risk is analogous to our experience of being in love. We cannot from within love imagine love's dissolution; but we can acknowledge that it is possible, and that attempts to secure our "loving selves" against its possibility will end up destroying the very thing we are attempting to secure – namely, those loving selves.

Love, to be love, simply must be vulnerable to change of the sort that can destroy it.

To respond to this Augustinian challenge, agonism's defenders must do two things. First, they must show how their proposal for a change from talk of "enemies" to talk of "rivals" can be done, and is not really different from Christian love. Secondly, they must also show how one can actually make that transformation in one's affections. There is something alchemical about the change, something more assumed than actually analyzed. Augustinians acknowledge the mysteriousness of the change, which they ascribe to grace; agonists may need something akin to that to be realistic, even by their own lights.

Agonists might respond by going on the offensive. For love is quite a dangerous ingredient in public life. And appeals to it can sound glib and simplistic. But what about the inevitable delusions, the inescapable projections of self-interest – what, that is, about the ineliminable presence of self-love in human affairs? How do Christians practice and secure the permanent presence of self-critique? How do they avoid falling into the trap of self-righteous purity, and the demonization of their opponents, that their convictions would seem to encourage? It is precisely because love is so powerfully charged, agonists conclude, that it should be kept out of the political realm.

But, Augustinian Christians reply, the fact that something is complicated and partly contradictory does not speak to whether or not it is part of reality. And love, with all its attendant dangers, just is part of reality; indeed, it is the deepest part. To imagine that one can simply "expel" it is to fall into the most outrageous of illusions, and to imagine that one can, over time, learn to restrict one's passions so that ultimately love is removed is only to defer the outrageousness one or two steps. Augustinians attempt to capture the complexity inherent in love by using a further concept, derivative from love: the concept of sin. Thus while the basic Augustinian Christian metaphysics is fundamentally optimistic, its anthropology is practically pessimistic. We turn to this next.

An alternative Augustinian psychology

Like agonism, Augustinian Christianity does not assume that the self is stable, whole, or complete. Far from it; in this life any coherence is a mark of grace, and a proleptic participation in the final integrity when we will be made whole by standing before God. But where agonists see the constitution of the self in terms ultimately of conflict and tension, Augustinian Christians understand the self as formed by its loves. Love better captures the self-unsettling character of politics, in a way that agonism's emphasis on "provisionality" and "openness to revision" misses; it better accommodates the present mutability, contingency, fragmentariness, and incompleteness of the self by interpreting the self as only eschatologically integral.

The prioritization of love entails a deeper and more hopeful interpretation of conflict as well, as captured in the symbolics of sin. Like agonists, because they see conflict as rooted in human psychology, they acknowledge that conflict is more than merely incidental, hence ineliminable during the world. Yet unlike agonists, they characterize conflict in psychological and anthropological, not ontological, terms, so that conflict does not reflect humans' ultimate estrangement from one another. This hope in our ultimate community has profound political significance. Violence is not fundamental to politics. During the world, we live east of Eden; but that should not obscure the essentially non-violent character of the cosmological vision Christianity expresses. Sin, and thus conflict, is a fundamentally secondary concept, derivative of love.[22]

22. The complexities of this approach to violence are often overlooked, but can be glimpsed by looking at Augustine's understanding and justification of coercion. He is often accused of supporting theocracy because of his endorsement of the use of violence. But it is worth remembering that Augustine was unique in offering a justification of violence and coercion in his time; other Christian thinkers did not think the use of force was theologically troubling (see Bowlin 1997). Furthermore, the character of his justification of force was not at all theological or, more specifically, evangelical; he never thought souls could be won for Christ by the edge of the sword. Violence is part of the worldly economy; it is not used for religious aims, such as gaining converts. On his understanding, coercion was, rather, an essentially political act, one expressly concerned with the stability of the civic order. It took the form of religious coercion (and forced conversion) only because it responded to the danger presented by people who understood their religious identities to be necessarily and violently opposed to that order. In Augustine's world, it was the Donatists who offered an explicitly religious warrant for violence (or engaged in religiously motivated violence without condemnation by their leaders). Augustine's justification of the necessity of force was made wholly on nonecclesial civic grounds; he wanted them "converted" – which meant forced to publicly repent their views, as they disparaged the "Catholics" for having done in the past – in the hope that such experiences would undercut the righteous zeal fuelling their violence (see N. Wood 1986: 46-8).

Understanding conflict in terms of love has several distinct advantages in shaping public engagement. When one engages opponents, the concept of sin compels us to seek an explanation for their behavior, not in sheer perversity or nefariousness, but in terms of goods to which they are committed – and with which we can feel at least some flicker of affiliation. Demonization of one's opponents is made very difficult on this scheme, because we assume some ultimate continuity between their psychological-motivational structure and our own. (Indeed, Augustine doesn't even "demonize" the demons themselves; instead he employs this psychology to understand, as best he can, their revolt against God, and describes them more in a pitiful language than in a language of righteous justice.)

Furthermore, this psychology forbids us from imputing too pure motives to ourselves. All our actions have the taint of an illegitimate (because self-aggrandizing) self-interest; so even when we fight against people whose programs repulse us, those struggles or crusades do not recursively permit us to whitewash our motives or our souls. The language of sin and love strongly encourages us always to see ourselves as flawed, imperfect, perpetually open to correction and inevitably in need of improvement.

Collectively, this acknowledgment of our complicity in sin and the concomitant acknowledgment of the attractions of our opponents' programs, whether or not they are explicitly "political," means that we must remain perpetually vulnerable to the real attractions and plausibility of others' views. This will deepen our patience and humility, permitting us more honestly to acknowledge the chaos of genuine but pluriform goods we find in our world, without either simply impatiently stipulating (as "liberal pluralists" do) that this welter of goods just is the way the world finally is, or allowing this plurality to dismiss our longing for unity or coherence, as agonists expect. We will not be the ones to resolve, and thus end, the world's complexity.[23] Throughout history the same basic problems will remain, because we will remain. Eden is lost to us for ever. And good riddance, *felix culpa*: what lies ahead of us in the heavenly city is greater than that over-plotted garden ever was.

---

23. This eschatological imagination can identify the essential continuity of apocalyptic longings and utopian fantasies as equally impatient desires to bring the kingdom of heaven to earth on our own terms. This impatience is visible in much liberation theology; see Gilkey 1975 and McCann 1981.

In these ways, among others, public engagement can change, even purify not only our views but our presentation of our views. But Augustinian Christians do not just have a richer and more complex concept of conflict; they have a richer notion of what politics can be about. A true politics will be a sacramental politics – a politics that ✳ understands that political action has a meaning and significance "beyond" its literal meaning. What such a politics would look like – what gifts it would bring to our public life, and how it offers a fruitful ascetic practice for Christians – is the final topic of this chapter.

A charitable citizenship

An Augustinian Christian account does not simply meet the well-defined needs of secular thinkers; it also challenges the conceptual terms whereby those thinkers understand the contours and content of public life. It does that most clearly in talking about a politics based on love. Many worry that an account of politics built around love will ineluctably pressure us towards a kind of communion that often seems impossible and even dangerous in public life. Augustinian Christians both agree and disagree with this statement. Certainly such a political account will urge us to acknowledge the reality and inescapability of our longings for such communion; but these longings reveal that politics is motivated by a desire that it cannot itself comprehend, the desire for communion. (Here is where those who recognize the "cosmopolitan" trajectory of politics are right.) Politics is teleological, but its goal is not achievable by us; its achievement will come like a thief in the night. Just as the self will be only eschatologically realized, so political community aches for a communion that will be realized only in the koinōnia of the kingdom of God.

Such a politics not only better comprehends the reality of conflict than does agonism; its faith in the possibility, and its hope for the reality, of communion are both civically and ascetically fruitful. Civic engagement motivated and informed by love is thus open to the full range of civic possibilities in ways that more self-proclaimedly "worldly" accounts are not. Augustinians can affirm a playful politics, one that cares about public life in a certain way less than we otherwise would, for we realize that our political ambitions, during the world, will only ever be realized proleptically (and then very occasionally). This recognition also, albeit paradoxically, allows Christians also to care about it more: love better understands public life's ambition, because it recognizes the dimension of longing for real communion that suffuses it, and respects that longing for what it is. It asks less of politics immanently, but expects more of it eschatologically.

Furthermore, in its vulnerability to the turbulence of public life, this account disciplines Christians more fully into the love they proclaim. And Christians need as much help as they can find to be disciplined into the love they profess. For our contemporary individualist and consumer culture offers us ways of behaving and desiring that are profoundly inimical to true Christian love. Our individualism has largely instrumentalized and privatized talk of love and so cannot see its public face. Coupled with our own sinful tendencies towards radical self-interest, this produces a powerful tendency towards a privatized consumerist eroticism – an affective orientation towards the world that sees the world as a collection of consumable objects meant to satiate our individual appetites. We imagine love as a particular kind of self-focused satisfaction, based on what Wendell Berry (1990: 38) calls our "fundamentally ungenerous way of life," our captivity to a theology of endless (in several senses) acquisition. We imagine "joy" in terms of *more*: more of what we want, an infinite supply of equally disposable, perhaps interchangeable goods and pleasures. This fixation on more offers no space to challenge our desires themselves – to ask whether those desires will ever be satisfied on the terms they propose; it simply assumes that more is better.[24]

But true love is what we receive before it is what we give, and because it is not properly and privately ours, it is both deeply public and radically non-consumeristic. Love orients us toward others by teaching us how we are properly affected by those others – how we properly apprehend their value and how that apprehension helps us come to a better, less self-aggrandizing, assessment of our relative significance. Love is a passion, an attentive orientation towards reality. As a passion, we experience it as a kind of suffering. And as a passion, it is not most fundamentally a punctual emotion; it never goes away. We endure love, just as it endures. It is in love's endurance, even in public life, that we undergo our ascetical training.

We will discuss this by expositing what Augustinians take love to be, paying special attention to how it is usefully related to concepts of play and joy. Then we will suggest how such love can be deepened and enriched through public engagement. I conclude with some thoughts about how this love in public may be, not just a rehearsal, but a distant, partial, and proleptic participation in God's love for creation.

The practice of enduring love

Statements such as the above sound absurd today to most political thinkers, and probably to most contemporary people more generally. Certainly they sound a bit romantic and idealistic; and where they do not meet rejection on cynical charges of "romanticism," they meet blunt incomprehension on charges of fantasy. This incomprehension is related to a larger incomprehension of what we might call the passive affections – joy and happiness. We believe we must work in order to earn leisure, work in order to merit delight, work to deserve to enjoy; enjoyment is an end-point to be attained, a vacation from the "real world," not a basis from which to work. Love is not a gift, because we think no such gift is possible. There is no such thing as a free lunch; instead, we imagine we must earn everything. In our self-understanding, we accept a framework governed wholly by purposiveness, means-ends reasoning which is focused on meeting our anxious, grasping needs. Our vocabulary is so infected with an instrumentalizing economic ideology that it affords us little leverage from within itself to imagine a world organized not around work, but instead around joy. We have a hard time imagining that a life lived in delight is anything but shallow; we can admit we need relaxation (or "down time") under the misnomer of "frivolity," but this renders joy a parody of what it really is. Our age makes it hard to sustain the belief that a desire to be happy is an appropriate desire by which to guide one's life. As Adorno famously put it, "it is impossible to write poetry after Auschwitz" (2003a: 162). Pleasure seems a scandal to us.[25]

Here we touch on our most fundamental suspicion of joy: the worry that such a focus on joy is escapist, luring us away from confronting the hard facts of our lives and of real existence. But the character of proper Augustinian love involves deep engagement with the world, profound participation with God and the church, and a fundamental insistence that the love and joy here described are not a conclusive event, but rather an inaugural one, oriented towards always once more resetting the self towards being born again. But to understand all this we should get clear on what we mean by "joy" and "play" first.

We can begin by distinguishing joy from both frivolity and amusement. Frivolity is the attitude of the modern aesthete, whose genealogy stretches from Walter Pater and Bloomsbury to Richard Rorty and Jacques Derrida. It aims to help its adherents endure the boredom that they see as the fundamental condition of life – to defeat superficiality by an even more shallow superficiality. While this aestheticism means to resist the dominant insistence on the purposefulness of life, it only reinforces it by retaining the endlessness of life, both as of infinite duration (in the literal sense of lacking any boundaries or structure) and as of lacking any overall goal. Frivolity is never quite able to forget its own inadequacy, and so ends up offering itself its own ironic knowingness as a consolation prize; but this consolation turns out to be cold comfort.[26] The mode of being of the aesthete, then, is that of diversion and distraction, what Pascal called *divertissement*.[27] But this diversion is

25. See John Milbank's intriguing attempt to distinguish between a "negative" and "positive sublime" in Milbank 1997: 7–35. See also W. Steiner 1995 and Scarry 1999. I disagree with those who claim that our problem is rooted in our careless assumption that we have an "infinite" theological desire, which creates an infinite dissatisfaction with the world; this is a form of "worldliness" that this chapter is meant to oppose. For similar secular accounts, see Goodheart 1991 and Lear 1998: 80–122.

26. See Sontag 1966. Sontag's essay inaugurated a new style of thinking which eschewed the "hermeneutics of depth" and the tone of high moral seriousness of thinkers such as Lionel Trilling, in favor of playfulness and a "light" touch; it began a transvaluation of critical values in a Nietzschean direction that yet remains trapped in the logic of capitalism and shopping (see Ross 1989: 147, 151, 169–70).

27. On *divertissement*, see Pascal 1966, esp. § 136. See also Rosen 1987: 71–3, which criticizes Derrida for frivolity, as opposed to Plato's "serious play." And see

merely a form of boredom driven to desperation, attempting to escape its mode of life. While the need to escape is right, this diversion moves the aesthete in the wrong direction, as it were – further into the ephemeral and transient, a realm that they can never fully inhabit. Frivolity, thus, is anxious despair masquerading as action and indifference.

If frivolity is an essentially superficial form of activity, amusement is the fundamental passivity cultivated in a society of media (and especially television) consumers. This passivity, however, is anything but inert. Amusement is equally ephemeral, equally transient, and equally reflects an essentially nihilistic attitude towards the world: constantly switching channels, the "amusee" seeks little but a momentary distraction, one provided wholly by the flickering pictures, ever changing yet never satisfactory, on the screen. Such amusement seems obligatory in our culture – what Jean Baudrillard calls a "fun morality," an oddly Kantian-deontological maxim to be happy (1988: 49).[28] Similarly, Robert Wuthnow, a social theorist no one will confuse with Baudrillard, argues that the contemporary belief in the "gospel of happiness" creates a religious situation that is deeply inimical to the proper apprehension of the Christian message (1997: 90–8). The experience of receiving the cultural command or obligation to "be happy," far from obligating us to do anything, merely licenses us to avoid doing anything real. The inert lassitude of amusement, camouflaged by the appearance of activity in watching, reveals not so much a desperate sense of endlessness to life as a stubborn refusal to begin it, a passive-aggressive rejection of connection to the world. If frivolity is our form of angst and despair, amusement, that is, is the contemporary manifestation of sloth.[29]

Joy differs from both amusement and frivolity just as love differs from despair and sloth. Both manifest bad relationships to time. To seek amusement is ultimately to avoid time, in favor of a form of ontological titillation; but joy and love plunge us into time and the

---

MacIntyre 1984: 24ff. for a discussion of the "aesthete" as a modern type. On boredom see Raposa 1999 and Svendsen 2005.

28. Note that this need not deny that actual needs exist, but just that "consumption, as a concept specific to contemporary society, is not organized along these lines" (1988: 47).

29. See Postman 1985 and Harris 2001.

world, recklessly. The aesthete's frivolity is finally self-referential, but the joyous soul roots its happiness outside of itself, in the eternal love that is God. This is why Augustine thinks joy is possible in this life only through hope (*DCD* 19.4). It promises a participation in the kingdom, when we will participate in God's absolute view of each of us as lovable, without letting us think that during the world we ever have more than an inkling of what that will be.

That last thought is important: joy does not rest content with the world. Joy does not seek satisfaction, equity, or indeed any form of adequation to the world. It does not seek sufficiency; that is not its point. Joy is always already excessive, always already super-abundant, and so is traduced by looking finally for a payoff or balance. Joy is a form of quite literally ecstatic play, which moves the self ever more deeply into the rhythms or, as Augustine would say, the *ordo* of creation. To enjoy the world is to not expect it to meet our needs; it is to play with, by playing in, the world. In going outside oneself in this playful ecstasy, one does not leave oneself behind, but rather one enters more fully into participation with the world. And we play with the world because God plays with it; in using the world we are enjoying it and loving it quite literally *in* the way that God loves it – we are participating in God's being-for the world. In using the world we are loving it; and in loving the world we are becoming deified. To realize this is to realize that the "enjoyment" of God need not entail that the "use" of the world denigrates created things; rather, it consummates them.[30]

Play is, phenomenologically speaking, most fundamentally receptive, even passive. In play, the subject is taken out of itself and plays a game "larger" than itself. The language of play may too easily be heard as self-starting, as if we must take the first step, must make the first move, begin the play. But no: part of the vertiginousness we experience in play is that we cannot know if we primordially play or rather "are played" by the game – we cannot know which is prior (ontologically, not chronologically) to which, and there are moments when we really do seem fundamentally secondary to the playing in which "we find ourselves." Play, and the joy that accompanies it, reveals the ontological truth that we are not our own, that our being is more primordially tied up with the rest of

30. See Hauerwas 1983: 146–51.

creation than we typically imagine. We are fundamentally recipients of reality, more given than giving, in a way difficult for our typical subjectivist self-understandings to admit. When we play fully – when we are truly "captivated" by a game – it is impossible for us, in later reflection, to describe our experiences in subjectivist terms; for we are enraptured, caught up in it, and in a way we gain our determinate being in and through the game. This quieting of my own desire, this quieting of my subjectivity, teaches me that I am not the author of this story, that my perspective on the world is not the only one, and that there is a far truer perspective that is not mine to inhabit. So understood, play is as much a form of witness as ✳ it is participation, and it provides us with a deeper way of understanding ourselves as "acted upon" more than acting; it deepens our ability to reflect upon ourselves, and hence makes us more humble, and more able to love.

In inhabiting this love, we come to acknowledge that our habitual solipsism is simply self-deception. Our love of others, and especially our recognition and acceptance that they have plans and agendas beyond our own immediate interest in them, oppose our desire for control, as we simply recognize their own agendas, and perhaps even come to imagine ourselves in their place. This love, that is, is both kenotic and agapic – attending to the other as another, someone genuinely other than oneself, not just a screen upon which to project one's own agenda, nor simply a bit player in a story fundamentally about oneself. This loving engagement shows us that we are deceiving ourselves about the extent to which we care about others; in fact, we care about others far more than we let ourselves believe. For in play we come to see this love as part of who we really are, perhaps the deepest part of who we really are. It is the other-directedness of our being, our strong desire for communion with another as the consummation of our own selfhood. We can call this mode of being ecstatic, for in it we are brought "outside of ourselves," into something – a "court" – where we play with another. Play's ecstasy leads one to come to see the other as my destiny; but this other is a living other, and so I cannot determine the love too totally – I must remain open, "agape" for the other, fundamentally receptive. Nonetheless, this receptivity cannot be understood as permission for sloth or laziness. Yes, the other is free, and so I must wait on her or his self-giving to me; but I should cultivate the longing for them. Furthermore this longing does not just flap loosely like the end of a rope out over an abyss, hoping for its far end to be caught by another; it is a longing *for*, elicited from the first by a determinate object.

So understood, play is a foundational attunement towards creation as a whole, a dialogical mode of being whereby we most fundamentally "meet" the world as the day that the Lord has made. So understood, the concept of "play" is intimately tied up with the plausibility of a unitary idea of "the world," and with seeing the world as significant beyond its literal presence, as sacramental. Play is always in important respects defined, delimited, and enframed by boundaries; the precise phenomenological confusion we feel of self and play could not exist if we could not imagine a mode of existence outside of play. Play is simultaneously serious and joyful, and it can be both only by allowing the players to be both immersed in the play and able, sacramentally, to "see beyond" it.[31]

Here again we meet the deep connections between love and play, married in the activity of God's loving playfulness with (or playful love for) the world. To see the world *as* a world, and to see its sacramentality, means we see it as God sees it, in a sense with God's eyes. So understood, play is actually a proleptic form of participation in God. We play because God plays, and we "play" by being proleptically taken up in God's play, which we will only properly possess in the eschaton. We can love because we are loved: this is God's orientation; God plays with the world in this way, using it to mean more than what it is in itself, while still treating it with real seriousness. Seriousness, even somberness, is embedded within playful joy; God accepts the crucifixion, yet does not allow death to have the last word, but takes up death into God's self and transcends it without erasing it or otherwise undoing its reality.[32] The person whom Hugo Rahner called "the grave-merry man of play" can exist,

---

31. Taylor 1989: 211–302, Lash 1988, and Lear 1990. For a sympathetic critique see Soskice 1992.
32. This is not to deny the complexity of God's vision, nor is it to ignore the question of the relation between joy and power which God's will manifests in Scripture and which exemplary theologians of the Christian tradition (up to and including twentieth-century theologians such as H. Richard Niebuhr) have always discerned. See H. R. Niebuhr 1989. Compare this theological vision with Bernard Williams's discussion of the ancient gods' "profound lack of style" in 1993: 165.

and the attitude of joyful play as a general comportment towards the world is in fact a viable orientation, because it is not most basically our orientation, but God's, and God allows us to participate in it through the liturgical discipline of the form of the community of God, the church. It is a mode of life meant to allow us to apprehend God's act of "Eastering in us," as Gerard Manley Hopkins put it (1986: 118): to recognize and inhabit our lives as gifts from a loving God whose central expectation of us in response to the gift of our life is that we join in the "work" of delightfully loving and joying in creation *as* Creation, as a gift of sheer gratuity.[33] Such a mode of life sees others as partners in joy and seeks them out as such, and so expects to be surprised by joy, by moments of true communion, rather than seeing all as a grim grey task to be undertaken. And the communion so experienced, albeit proleptically, is not simply a this-worldly community, something tidily confined in the *saeculum*; it is none other than the divine *perichoretic* community of the Triune God, in Godself and in God's gratuitous creation, sustenance, and salvation of our "worldly" reality. The "play" we speak of here is love inflected by faith and hope, a dynamism within and between God and between God and God's creation. It is not only that we are able to do this by God's urging; in fact, in doing it we are simply participating in what God has been doing all along, in what God has been all along. This is the final ascesis of love: that it recognizes that we are not primordially playing but instead are being played, are actors in the divine drama that is the essence of God's being God.[34]

When we understand this, we understand that our lives themselves are sacraments, that we ourselves are finally God's speech, not our own, and that public engagement is inescapably an attempt to participate in the divine work of exultation and glorification – and for us, deification. It is in short to see the entire universe, Creation as a whole, as a liturgy; as Peter Berger says, it is

> a vast liturgy in praise of its creator. It was created for this purpose and it *is* this purpose. This liturgy includes all human beings who have

---

33. See H. Rahner 1972, Lash 1988, R. Williams 2000, and Pieper 1999.
34. It is clear that this vision of play and glory and drama is related to the work of von Balthasar; but it is also available in the work of Reformed theologians like Calvin, Edwards, and Barth. The convergence on this issue of the most "ornate" and the most "spare" strands of Western Christian thought is no accident.

> been brought to this understanding and ... it also includes those who praise God under strange names. The cosmic liturgy includes the living and the dead, and it includes the angels and all beings in this or any other world. If Christianity is true, then the one who affirms this truth must necessarily join the community of praise. (1992: 186)

In this we see the ultimate destiny of the world, a destiny of praise and glory. The essential shape of such a way of life is eucharistic. The Eucharist provides, as David Ford says, "a condensation of the Christian habitus" (1999: 140), in three ways. First, the power of the elements to bear their transubstantiation in the ritual – however that transubstantiation is understood to occur – reveals to us the sacramentality of creation, its latent capacity to bear the eschatological weight of glory for which it is destined. Second, we can "accomplish" the ritual itself only proleptically; this is not a "satisfactory" dinner, but instead each meal should make us more hungry for the heavenly banquet that awaits us at the eschaton. And finally, the end of the Eucharist reveals the "reversal" of agency that has been effected in the meal; for in it we are not the primordial eaters, we are the eaten, consumed in the meal and incorporated into the body of Christ. As such, it is a training in being responsive, in being more acted upon than acting, in receiving before we give.

Yet even in the Eucharist, during the world, we must keep alive the eschatological tension necessary lest a proper "sacramental piety" become, as Reinhold Niebuhr put it, "a source of a particularly grievous religious complacency" (1949: 242). The Eucharist offers genuine participation in God, but it is participation both as an immanent nourishment and as an instrumental orientation towards life during the world. It both confronts us by challenging us ascetically to review and assess our desires, and welcomes us by affirming the ultimate goal of these desires.[35] In all this the Eucharist teaches us how to inhabit time, in three dimensions. First, as regards the present, experiences of complete, apocalyptic, desire-ending satiation are impossible. To seek such satiation in the world is apocalyptic; it is to expect the resolution of all tensions in a world where such tensions mark all our existence until the eschaton. (In fact, since eschatological desire is not one built upon a palpable "lack," in the eschaton it will be "satiation" itself – as the cessation into stasis

---

35. See Ford 1999: 145, 164–5.

of the dynamism of desire – that will "cease," having been revealed as a bad (worldly) interpretation of who we are called to be.) Instead, we should anticipate, experience, and recall our moments of joy not so much as immanently apprehensible, carrying their significance like a density inside themselves, but rather as foretastes of something to come, a fugitive fragment from another age. Such an experience helps us both by gifting us with itself, and also by reminding us that this present age is *not* where we are made fully happy. Insofar as joy in this sense is love, we can love now only because we will love fully in the eschaton. Second, as regards the past, what we are "re-membering" is not just ourselves, indeed not primarily ourselves, but rather the communal history of the body of Christ. In this activity of re-membering in "recollecting" the church, we enter into the communal dance of *perichōrēsis*. We "remember" ourselves in Christ and the church.[36] The Eucharist is a communal celebration, not a collection of atomic individuals. Third, as regards the future, this act of remembering is not an attempt at concluding, not summing up our lives, but rather finding a new way to begin in and from them. The key is the way one keeps in mind the full length of one's life, remembering always that one is larger than the particular moment and yet equally limited, "rounded off" in both death and birth. This is not a strategy so much for *memento mori* as for *memento natali*. Life is not finally about learning how to end, how to commit suicide; rather and more fundamentally, it is about learning how to accept being begun.

This picture provokes in us two questions. First, how does Christians' loving action in public affect the public in ways that enrich it, even as it makes nervous those who do not share this commitment to loving action? Second, how does such loving action help cultivate Christians' deeper apprehension of love itself?

Love in politics: longing for communion

What the critics identify as reasons for worry about love in public life are actually, when properly identified, love's advantages.

---

36. This is always a proleptic "remembrance," as well as one carried out in the shadow of the cross. For more on what this means for understanding ourselves as existing in time, see Mathewes 2003.

Through them, Christian citizens have a notion of what politics could be which is richer than immanentists allow. Augustinian Christians' eschatological faith lets them treat politics as not ultimate, and conflict as not absolute. They therefore harbor hopes for politics that extend beyond the grim zero-sum vision of agonists. They can imagine it as a site for conversion, for the further transformation of all participants during the long waiting for the realization of our longings. Public engagement motivated by love encourages an attitude, not of anxious grasping after control, but of a kind of responsive and non-anxious playfulness. The civic witness so provided is considerable.

For agonists this is terribly dangerous. They worry that such a "playful" vision of politics occludes politics' central reality, namely, the nature of serious give and take for real stakes – what Max Weber called the murky and painful "slow, powerful drilling through hard boards" (2004: 93). This is a reasonable worry. Can Christians really care enough about politics to be truly political, or are they always going to be interested in politics for merely instrumental reasons? Will Christians give up on politics if it gets too difficult or morally compromising, no matter the import of the stakes? Does this vision of politics invest it with the wrong sort of importance so that it actually ends up rendering real politics disappointing and unfulfilling, and hence undermines Christians' desire to engage in it?

The proper response is to challenge the stark either/or choices that these critics impose. The language of "seriousness" captures important truths about politics, but also imports a certain portentousness that we should resist. Politics can have its full and real significance without our granting it more importance than it merits. One of the perpetual dangers of engagement in public life is that its demands can be magnified in our imagination to the occlusion of other considerations. We should leaven our genuine though proximate commitment to political ends with a confidence that "all will be well." But politics can never change the ultimate truth about the world – that what we say and do would become the sum of what there is. Politics is not God, and the contingent configuration of history does not bear the ultimate meaning of history immanently in itself.

This is a deeply liberating vision, releasing us from the terrible presumption of acting as if we were the ultimate guardians of what goodness the world has. Indeed, it is precisely Christianity's capacity to see beyond the this-worldly horizon of the agonists' self-proclaimed "political" vision that allows Christians to value rightly the political conflicts as political, and not of ultimate significance. As Rowan Williams says,

> The only reliable political leader, the only ruler who can be guaranteed to safeguard authentically *political* values (order, equity, and the nurture of souls in these things) is the man [*sic*] who is, at the end of the day, indifferent to their survival in the relative shape of the existing order, because he knows them to be safeguarded at the level of God's eternal and immutable providence, vindicated in the eternal *civitas Dei*. (1987: 67)[37]

With this charitable confidence, Christians can use politics in ways not recognizable as legitimate from within a purely this-worldly "political" perspective.

Christians will "use" politics for more than simply negotiating public perplexities and cultivating the common good. Beyond those aims, they will use political engagement in a manner analogous to the agonists: as a way to unsettle and disrupt routinized patterns of behavior, though they characterize those patterns, and justify their disruption, in terms different than the agonists'. Properly undertaken, public engagement can be a struggle for conversion, conversion of one's loves and the loves of one's interlocutor, without ceasing to be genuinely political – without, that is, luring our interest and attention away from the immediate immanent concerns of the matter directly at hand.[38]

What do play and risk do to and for public life? How can play enrich, enliven or at least render less grim and gloomy public engagement? A playful politics will manifest itself in public life through a greater sensitivity to the dialogical character of public life – the inescapable facts of compromise, bargaining, negotiation, etc., in public affairs. But this playfulness is not simply useful in getting us to accept the facts of politics. It also seeks out others to play with; it welcomes others. And love sees others not as enemies only but as fellow humans, neighbors. The general attitude derived

---

37. See also O'Donovan 1987.
38. The agonists' primary response to this proposal – namely that it annihilates the real "political" character of politics – is, by their own lights, a contestable political argument.

from this will be one that reaffirms the joy of the other and the good of play even when public life can seem suffocatingly immanent.

This picture of love as play captures something close to liberalism's deepest insight, better than many professedly liberal accounts do. That insight is the reality that stands behind our experience of respect – the fact that we recognize that the heart of each individual is finally inviolable by others. Liberalism misframes this insight by developing it into the philosophical view that the value of politics is wholly negative, securing a space of "privacy" where the self is left fundamentally alone by the larger community to pursue its own good. "Privacy" may seem an odd description for this most public of facts, this longing for communion, but it is all that liberalism can offer in the way of capturing its meaning. While such a view is, during the world, a useful pidgin or *modus vivendi* language for negotiating some of our public affairs, it is eschatologically inadequate and impoverished, and cannot be allowed to stand apart from the eschatologically deferred divine judgment against it. In contrast, our love-centered account, culminating in play, escapes that frame, and instead offers a rich ground on which we can make sense of the phenomenological respect we should have for one another.

This will not be much comfort to those agonist critics who worry about Christians treating politics too lightly. They will see such "play," and the proposal to see politics as a site for working on ourselves, as both deeply narcissistic and done in bad faith, fundamentally disparaging and dismissive of politics' genuine significance. For them such an attitude inevitably weakens our ability to work for the sort of radical political changes we need. Augustinians respond that this is not bad faith but right love: the critics' worry bespeaks not their greater disillusioned "realism" or post-Marxist savvy about the consolatory comforts of theoretical or metaphysical dogmas. (Such savvy was not invented by Marx or other moderns; they invented only the conceit that they invented it.) Instead, its oddity is due precisely to the critics' *un*realism, to their stubborn enthrallment to a bit of ideological dogma: namely, the dogma that any such attitude of ultimate "indifference" or "relaxation" inevitably dissipates our political energies. And it is well past that dogma's expiration date.

What do I mean when I call this view ideological dogma? I mean it retains its plausibility for us not by its repeated verification by reality, but due to its function in sustaining an overall worldview. For when one compares it to reality, it clearly falters. When one thinks of the great political struggles of the twentieth century, what springs to mind are episodes such as the US civil rights campaigns of the 1950s and '60s, or struggles against oppressive regimes in the British Raj in India, apartheid South Africa, Pinochet's Chile, and the communist regimes of Eastern Europe. In all of these, the presence of religious bodies expressly committed to presumably "otherworldly" values was essential to the movements' contemporary success and relative peacefulness. Despite the slanders often launched at "otherworldly" motives, critics can point to no comparative set of successful movements informed and/or led by those with thoroughgoing "immanent" orientations; and even if they could point to some examples, they would still be faced with the problem of explaining how otherworldly values did not, in the cases enumerated above, eventuate in the failings their ideology would lead them to predict.[39]

So Christian love, as an expressed liberation from public life's immanent demands, may help public life by caring about it less. But equally, if paradoxically, Christian love knows that it must care more about public life than that life allows itself to do; public life has a particularly significant role to play in the economy of salvation, as a site of proleptic participation in our eschatological destiny. How can this be so? After all, this account acknowledges the mournfulness of public life as it is presently constituted, in our fallen world. But its ability to acknowledge this mournfulness is crucial. This mournfulness has cause, for public life does not want to be simply itself; it wants to be more: it wants to reach communion. Or rather, we who engage in public life want it to be more: the longings that motivate us to seek community, that lead us into public life, extend beyond the horizon of that life. We have desires that we cannot properly immanently name. But Christian faith can name them. And this is the last major contribution to public life that this Augustinian proposal provides.

---

39. For an early attempt by a traditional intellectual to work out the implications of this, see Michnik 1993. It remains a relevant book in part because, sadly enough, there are few other works similar to it. See also Casanova 1994 and Marsh 2005.

In so naming it, Christianity gains access to several insights that would otherwise go imperfectly recognized. First, it allows us to give voice to a fact about politics that is otherwise hard to acknowledge: public life is frustrating. Many who acknowledge that it is difficult do not see the profundity of this fundamental phenomenological fact. There is, as I said above, something suffocating in the relentless immanence of the petty minutiae that constitute public life. But more than these local accidents there is a deeper frustration, the frustration of our hope for something more, something that public life cannot itself even name, so we must name the tension and anger latent in public life without naturalizing it, but allow it to be what it is – a negative reminder of what public life wants to be.

Such an interpretation allows us to recognize public life's "sky-light," as it were – its desire for more than it can achieve, its longing for real communion. Through it, we can challenge contemporary public life's own vocabulary of immanence and transcendence, for the communion that it seeks is both immanent and transcendent – a communion of one with another, but a communion that is more than simply our final, exhausted agreement to allow the world to be run in a particular way. The communion sought is captured in Paul's description of our ultimate situation before God and our neighbor, when we will stand "face to face" with them. Indeed, even in this life it will sometimes be realized. Real community can happen; miracles can occur; politics can eventuate in something more akin to a wedding or a festival than an election. We can never forget that the "proleptic" character of real communion means that, some-times, actual communion can happen.

This merits further consideration. One of the great failures of much secular political thought is its ultimate embarrassment at the reality of such longings, and its stuttering inarticulateness at those moments when those longings may actually be partially realized. We need to accept it, name the longing, and be joyful in it. Doing so is not only more honest; it may also help us come to change our basic vision of the shape and nature of "politics" in our world.

This vision of politics as potentially a site of communion meets its ultimate challenge, in our time anyway, in the fact that our political imagination is at its root still captive, by and large, to a deep terror of what politics might create. There are three basic imaginary cen-ters available, I think, to political thought today, represented by certain dates. One can imagine the shape and prospects of politics out of the experience of revolution, out of the experience of the mob, swamping civilization; this is the experience of 1789 and 1917.[40] On this view the basic task of politics is resisting the mob, the crowd – of stopping it before it begins to riot. The basic political emotional stance for this account is fear – fear of the mob; this drives the account to develop in the way that it does. This is, I suspect, the majority view of politics.

Alternatively one might begin from the basic emotion of cynicism. Here the fundamental political object to be confronted is not the crowd but "the system," the network of bureaucratic government and corporate control that invests our society at all levels with its capillarial powers. This approach begins not from revolution but from the failure of revolution to be revolution, its co-optation by the forces it thought it was opposing. In a way, if the previous vision of politics sees the mob from above, out a window, this one sees, from within the crowd, the people in the window, obscured by the haze of teargas. Here the experience is of 1968. Typically, again, it is not the experience itself – at least not the Czech experience of 1968 – but rather the way that experience was remembered and gained determinate shape over time, often by events decades later. Here the experience was not just of revolution defeated, but of revolution frustrated from within, of revolution co-opted. The basic task of politics here is unclear, but in some way the basic political task, developed to its extremity by Foucault, is to show people the truth of The Who's song "Won't Get Fooled Again" – "say hello to the new boss, same as the old boss." This view is probably the main minority view of what politics really is.[41]

But there is a third possible vision, a deeply minority vision, one rooted in the experience of 1989. In this case there was a real revolution (and it was even televised!), and while it never of course achieved the millenarian goals some set for it, it incontestably managed, in most of Central Europe at least, actually to be a good thing. This vision of the world begins not from the crowd, neither seeing it from above nor being in it from below, but from what must

40. Needless to say, it is not the actual experience of those events, but the way those events have been communicated to us through the *Wirkungsgeschichte* of their interpreters, from Burke forward. See Mayer 2000 and Buford 1992.
41. See Bewes 1997.

come before the crowd gathers, if the crowd is not to devolve into a mob: the long, slow work of creating the kind of culture of civic commitment – a culture that knows what it wants, and how it can get it (and what it must not do if its goals are to be possible at all). Given that civic culture, the crowd becomes something more than the crowd: it becomes a unity, a people, a united will. For this view, the basic task of politics is to find out how such civic commitment can be fostered, and then to foster it.

These are three basic "mythologies" of politics and public life today. Our *mentalité* is still so captive to the first two that it will remain almost impossible, for some time, for us to imagine that the third might be possible. But in fact I believe it is true, or at least bears truthful lessons that we need to hear. By and large the world of political thought is still governed by cynicism and fear; and these need at least to be complemented, and perhaps ultimately to be subordinated, to the basic idea that politics has enormous promise for us. And politics' promise is found not only in the republican ideal of self-rule, but also in the properly theological vision of communion.

For this Augustinian proposal it is axiomatic that we all – to some degree, at some resonant level, however faint – feel this desire for communion. It is the unity behind the civic republicans' expression, "we the people"; it is the integrity of Rousseau's idea of the general will; it is the unity that haunts the "multitude" of Hardt and Negri; it is even the unity behind (quite far to the back of) the notion of a fully legitimate liberal state for liberal political theorists. But Augustinians see this political vision as such a political vision only at the same time as seeing that it is *more* than political. For it is the idea, ultimately, of "Thy kingdom come" – the final and most holy vision of humanity, the Beloved Community. That is to say, all of these are imperfect and incomplete and inadequate, because the real political community, the prototype that taunts our reality, is the *perichōrēsis* of the Triune God. Christians should never simply say "kingdom come" but "*Thy* kingdom come, *Thy* will be done"; it is not our kingdom, but God's, in which Christians are members through Christ.[42]

42. All of this is nicely put in Ricoeur 1965: "The theme of the neighbor ... effects the permanent critique of the social bond" (108), because "the meaning of the encounter [with the neighbor] does not come from *any criterion immanent to history*" (109). Therefore, "it is [theologically transcendent] charity which

This vision can never be fully realized in this life, never fully or finally articulated. But it can never be *less* than that longing either. And we will be enraptured by it, so long as we are political beings. One of Augustine's greatest contributions on this score is just to say not only that it will never be realized, but that we cannot deny its presence in our lives or its power over history. We need to look up from our labors in public life and see – be still and know – a force that governs history and has a destiny in store for the world.

Not very many non-Christians, perhaps especially secularists, will fully resonate with this view. But many will find aspects of it not uncongenial. Many of the faithful of other religions will be fellow travelers in this. And many non-religious citizens will recognize the usefulness of having this vision of the prospects of public life available in the public realm. There will be times when a politics of love can find secular allies for concrete, finite causes; but the truth is that the alliances, for such explicitly eschatological goals, will be quite few and far between. From the secularists' perspective, the contribution this vision makes is simply having the counterweight of its idealism available, to oppose the soul-crushing frustrations and cynicism that are so often a part of public life. This vision can enrich public life, but, unfortunately, most secularists, at least today, will not be able to see its intrinsic attractions.

But whether or not non-Christians will appreciate it, Christians themselves must ultimately be convinced that such a loving engagement will be ascetically productive for their religious lives. The next and last section sketches an argument to that effect.

The ascesis of loving engagement

If we have faith in God as sovereign, and if we have hope that this sovereign God is in charge of the course of history, so that we need not be anxious about the future, then we may engage in public life in a new way. Simply put, loving engagement in public life, undefensively and genuinely undertaken, ascetically shapes us by forcing us consciously to inhabit the tension between love of God, love of neighbor, and love of self. Its inner logic participates in the

governs the relationship to the *socius* and the relationship to the neighbor, giving them a common *intention*" (109). See Marsh 2005.

eucharistic patterns of transformation that structure our life as a whole. And so such engagement teaches us to see all as playing parts in a divine drama, in the heavenly chorus, full participation in which is our ultimate destiny.

Public engagement aids our ascesis in several ways. It brings us up repeatedly against the stubborn, bare there-ness of the people we meet in public life; it teaches us again and again the terrible lesson that there are other people, other ideals, other points of view that we can see and appreciate, even if we cannot inhabit them and remain ourselves. Much of the time what we call "corruption" is not our victimization by political realities, but our impatient decision, when we are confronted by the exposure of our ideals as self-interested, to affirm that self-interest as the most we can say – not to ask the deeper question of why our ideals are vexed. In this life we see one another, and not only God, always in a mirror darkly; our vision is always obscured by ego, haste, distractions, and the bare fact of the velocity of change over time. And this is so on both sides; we always present skewed and partial views of ourselves to one another and to ourselves, and those self-presentations are likely to change from one day to the next. (This is why clarity and stability of expressed interest in public life are so appreciated.) In this way, genuine, loving public engagement is a check and vexation against our selfish proclivities towards instrumentalizing those others, or part of ourselves.

Furthermore, this engagement teaches us the difference between being idealistic and being loving. Far from being related, love and idealism are in one way deeply opposed. Ideals are ours, and so are inevitably indexed to our self-righteousness; love is about seeing the other. When we discern the distinction between ideals and loves, we can see how loving engagement may be ascetically useful. Public life is not about the imposition of our ideals on others, or theirs on us, but about living with other people. And as the basic experience of charity's working in our lives is found in the ongoing work of our being purged of our temptations toward instrumentalization, we find that a genuinely loving engagement deepens and accelerates that practice of purgation. Our fate during the world is to live in the tensions of love of self, love of God, and love of neighbor, not to deny or repress them; for it is in these tensions, and in our training in longing for a day when they are not in tension, that we find our deepest ascesis. When public engagement is ascetically effective, it aids this purgation.

But public life's check on our egocentric instrumentalization is not the only work it does. It also offers the torturously tantalizing prospect of a "yes" alongside its many "no's"; it offers the prospect, which can emerge at the most surprising times, of genuine contact and communion across the most profound chasms, the most intractable disagreements. Other people's presence is not simply a check on our own pretensions; it is also the gift of themselves to us. Apprehending this gift requires a change in perception that the gift itself may provoke; and such a perceptual change may have larger implications still. For when we begin to see others as not part of our story, we then begin to see them as part of a larger (and for Christians, divine) story, and then finally we come to see ourselves as part of that story as well, as authored by another; we come to see others and ourselves in iconic terms, as significant of God's glorification, of the holy liturgy of creation itself. Indeed, this change in perception is inevitable for properly loving engagement.

The combination of affirmation and contradiction that is the heart of loving public engagement should come as no surprise; it merely reflects the Eucharist's dialectic of confrontation and welcome, which is the central dynamic of love's work on our hearts *tout court*. In it, we come to see how public life is simply one more facet of existence in which love expresses itself as play; play is already close to being played, so by seeing love in terms of play, we come to see ourselves as being played by God. Metaphors of drama, following von Balthasar, may be useful here, but perhaps ones drawn from music are more evocative; just as singing teaches us alertness and responsiveness, skills that are essential to our training in Christianity, so we may say that similarly, proper engagement in public life requires of us similar virtues, and so may be analogously ascetical.[43]

Public life is not just a pallid rehearsal for heaven, then, or a hollow simulacra of real life, but is itself a proleptic participation in the loving liturgical song of praise sung by the saints in paradise. And in and through our loving public engagement, we find ourselves called to serve in the choir of God's glorifying chorus, even if

43. See Ford 1999: 125.

we at best only dimly and in a mirror know what the whole is doing; and we come to undertake the proper ascesis of loving engagement, by coming to participate playfully, in tune and in time, in God's action in, and on, the world.

Conclusion

This vision of loving engagement not only offers the rudiments of an adequate answer to the agonists' challenges; it also shows how a Christian vision of civic life offers a real alternative to the more pessimistic "liberalism of indifference" by which so many thinkers – Christian and non-Christian alike – today remain bewitched. For it imagines that the basic challenge of political life is not simply adjudicating conflicts between people into permanently endurable stalemates, but the proper ordering of our loves into harmonious polyphony – albeit a polyphonic harmony only eschatologically attained, let alone resolved.[44] In a sense, as we have seen, contemporary liberal political theory and agonism share a common despair, a despair of politics being more than the negotiation of solitudes. The vision presented here offers a quite radical alternative to it.

The theology of citizenship it reflects is clearly controversial. It may seem wildly optimistic on sociological grounds, both to those Christians more dubious about political life, and to those (Christian and non-Christian) more suspicious about Christian involvement in it. It may seem perilously optimistic on more philosophical grounds, in its assumption that we are most deeply constituted by our loves, and that those loves are fundamentally excessive, amenable only to eschatological organization and realization. There are serious worries about this position that cannot – in this dispensation, at least – be answered or resolved; they can only be endured. And they contain much wisdom that all pilgrims, during the world, should heed. Politics will never, in this dispensation at least, be simply a means of joy (and not only will politics never be wholly joyful, not only are there good parts and bad parts, but the whole of any part will never be simple joy). Good and bad overlay each other, so that the results of public life, and the practice of it, will be forever mixed.

44. See Cowen 2000.

We must insist on this complexity, not its complete corruption, and on the possibility that good can come out of our being political in this way, however difficult the path may be. Difficulty is our lot in this life, during the world.

Ultimately, however, Christians' acceptance of the complexities, ambiguities, and simple difficulties of life during the world is predicated on the affirmation that something exists beyond the world, that makes us recognize the world as not the ultimate frame of our lives. It is in this beyond that we have faith; it is for it that we hope; and it is because of it that we are given the strength to love. How should our longing for this "beyond" shape our lives here and now? The conclusion to this book offers some final remarks directly on that topic.

Conclusion: The republic of grace; or, the public ramifications of heaven

> There we shall be still and see, see and love, love and praise. Behold what will be, in the end to which there will be no end!
>
> Augustine, *de civitate Dei*

What if heaven really were our destiny? What would that mean for how we should live now, during the world? This is the question that this book has tried to answer. It is an intelligible question to us – to all humans – in part because of our intuition that the world as we have it, the world in its simple immanence, is not a fully satisfactory reality, an adequate habitation for our hopes. This intuition begins as a vague discontent, an apprehension that our ordinary experience of the world today is wrong, incomplete. It gains determinate positive content in Christianity's claim that our destiny is gratuitous, that there is life beyond death for us – indeed, that all creation is similarly gratuitous. Heaven, it seems, is not only our destiny, but the world's as well.

How should that conviction shape life during the world? It may seem in tension with this book's argument that Christianity has as its fundamental dynamic a movement towards deeper engagement with the neighbor and creation, as well as with God. But the conflict is more apparent than real. For this dynamic gains its particular determination by Christianity's radically eschatological orientation. The meaning of history itself is determined in Christ, and Christ has come, but his first coming only inaugurated the end times, only began the definitive determination of history; so we await the second coming, the *parousia*, as the ultimate revelation and thus determination of the meaning and significance of history, of our lives, and of God's purposes. Grace, and perhaps especially grace understood as the presence of the Holy Spirit in and among believers, is the true *res publica*, the true "public thing."

Nonetheless, while the conflict is more apparent than actual, a real tension exists here. For in talking about grace, we are tempted to describe it as what lies outside of the structures of cause and effect that constitute creation. It is only a short step from that exteriority to talk that warrants concerns about "otherworldliness." So in talking about the political ramifications of grace, we are brought again back to the tension latent in otherworldliness. Hence the deep roots of this proposal do, in fact, put powerful pressure on the usual understanding of public engagement, pressure of a sort that profoundly shapes Christian public engagement. In truth, this tension lurks at the heart of Christian thought more generally, and not only as a problem, but as a promise of what is to come. Here at the end of this book, I want to see what insights derive from this most fundamental tension. Here we explore how heaven is publicly significant not only in the eschaton but even today; how, that is, a vision of life that is so fundamentally eschatological can also be so profoundly pro-creation as to shape a distinctive and powerful form of public engagement – yet a form of caring about the world that might not make "the world" fully comfortable.

Kairos and ordinary time: the dialectic of public life

Christianity does not simply project its hopes for public life upon the world by force of will. It sees intimations of its vision in the tensions between transcendence and mundaneity, revolution and inertia, continuity and discontinuity, that riddle public life. Such tensions are visible to any moderately self-reflective participant in public life. They give public life its dialectical quality.

An example is not hard to find. Much of politics, as it exists today in this impatient, petulant, risibly sin-riddled world, is waiting. We wait at rope lines for candidates to pass; we wait for election returns to arrive late at night, faces pale in the sterile glow of TV screens; we wait while a canvasser reads us his talking points on the phone, or urges us to support her candidate on our doorstep. Less obviously we wait for our friends and family and neighbors and co-workers and new acquaintances to enumerate, in what often seems to us inexplicably, narcissistically meticulous detail, why their chosen candidate or cause is obviously the only right one, wondering all the while where to begin in disputing their whole way of seeing the world. Sometimes we must even wait for our own minds to make up their opinions on issues we feel we need to have a view on *now*, if not yesterday. And always we wait to see – with fear and trembling if we are pious and wise – whether the political causes we supported ultimately turn out the way we hoped they would turn out. (Usually this means waiting to find out how, precisely, we shall be disappointed.) Much of public life is spent enduring interminable time, when time itself drones on.[1]

And then, sometimes suddenly, everything changes. Everything seems to happen all at once: deliberation ends, the ballots are cast, the votes counted, decisions made, the new thing emerges. The old order – which seemed so solid, so firm, so unchanging – is swept away. Public life is a disconcerting concatenation of *kairos* and ordinary time, with jarring shifts from one to the other, a kind of wild oscillation between "now" and "not yet."

Much recent political theory can be seen as a series of attempts to obscure or deny this tension, the dialectical character of public life. The violence of these temporal disjunctions is taken by some to prove that democratic rule is strictly speaking a myth; that elections are too limited, too punctual a device for properly affirming public rule; that the control so exercised by the populace over their government is too flimsy to be described as self-rule. And yet, again and again the people shock their overlords; they vote down referenda urged on them by the governing elites, or approve them in the face of politicians' determined opposition; they elect men or women of the people or throw the bums out of office, upsetting the table at which the cloistered politicians were working out delicate bargains. When this happens, of course, the pooh-poohers of popular rule then suggest that it simply demonstrates that the people have too much power, are too undisciplined, dangerously unconstrained in their political wills – that whimsy and outrage rule the day; that after all what we need is less democratic governance, or less "direct" governance (which comes by and large to the same thing), and more

---

1. For more see Vanstone 1983.

mediation by elites, tempered in the brutal forge of academia. Such is the strategy of much liberal political theory. Still others will say that such experiences demonstrate not that democracy is dangerous but that all power is exercised this way, that "democracy" so understood is really the brute exercise of power, with nothing to do with fairness. From Thrasymachus to Machiavelli to Carl Schmitt, such nihilistic approaches have always been with us.

So it was said 200 years ago; so it is said today; so shall it be said a hundred, a thousand years hence. The very variousness of the charges tells against their veracity. And the antiquity of the accusations suggest that they embody clichéd reactions, running down well-worn rhetorical grooves, rather than actual new thinking on the part of their enunciators.

There are secular critics who recognize this, such as Jeffrey Isaac, William Connolly, and Benjamin Barber. Augustinian Christians share these criticisms, but they also look with sympathetic understanding and even pity upon such secularist animosities at the *saeculum*, and the escapism that these animosities reflect. They understand why public life might make secularists so disturbed at its revolutions. They appreciate the concerns such secularists have about how its vicissitudes can manhandle our plans and break apart our best hopes. They too see how dangerous can be the power of the crowd. But they see these tendencies as dangers and temptations, not inevitabilities, so they think that secularists who fixate on them are thereby blinded to the goods that public life enables, and they diagnose this blindness as expressive of a sort of escapism, the illusion that such engagement can somehow be avoided. Behind and beyond these temptations they see engagement in public life as a refining fire whereby our lives and our communities are hammered into something greater than they would otherwise become. In this way, Augustinians understand the debate about the viability of public life as just one more version of the struggle against escapism, albeit camouflaged in a secular vocabulary, and they respond appropriately thereto.

Apocalyptic escapism

Escapism is neither a temptation only in public life, nor a temptation only for ingrown secularists. It is at least as palpable, and yet more vigorous, in contemporary religion, particularly in its apocalyptic varieties. In the West, many Christians especially find it tempting. Indeed, a great deal of Christian religiosity today, perhaps especially in America, is possessed by such apocalypticism.

This is presented quite vividly, for example, in the "Left Behind" novels. The "Left Behind" series is the most popular "religious fiction" in America since World War II; indeed, they are among the bestselling novels of any sort in America since World War II. The series has been criticized for its problematic political, cultural, ethical, and religious attitudes.[2] But few recognize how its cultural philistinism, political isolationism and xenophobia, and overall consumerist parochialism are underpinned by what, from this book's perspective, is the most fundamental, and properly theological, problem: a profound and abiding escapism, a confusion or despair about the nature of creation itself and its role in God's salvific providence.

This escapism is manifest in the series title, and is latent in the hostility towards anyone even slightly different than the white, upper-middle-class mentality of its authors. But it appears most profoundly in the Manicheanism beneath the series as a whole – the idea that the world itself is wrong, fundamentally bad, and that our condition as "worldly" is a mark of our fallenness – a Manichean attitude that reveals an animus at ineliminable aspects of human life: temporality and materiality. In the series, time is not itself a positive gift to be received; it can only be tolerated, or bulled through, for it is simply a waiting around for something to happen. (One might say that, without the *divertissement* of the ominous antics of the anti-Christ, and the theatricalized hysterics of the Last Days, the series' characters would simply drop dead of boredom.) But the animus is still more palpable in the series' account of damnation, in which hell is wholly a matter of material suffering. Consider the following, from the (almost) climactic encounter of the armies of the anti-Christ with the returned Jesus:

> Tens of thousands of foot soldiers dropped their weapons, grabbed their heads or their chests, fell to their knees, and writhed as they were invisibly sliced asunder. Their innards and entrails gushed to

2. For critiques of the apocalypticism expressed therein, see Boyer 1992 and 2005, and Cook 2004. For a different view, see Frykholm 2004. Frykholm argues that readers use the books in ways opposed to what their authors seem to intend; but that simply bespeaks the bankruptcy of the series' worldview.

> the desert floor, and as those around them turned to run, they too
> were slain, their blood pooling and rising in the unforgiving
> brightness of the glory of Christ. (LaHaye and Jenkins 2004: 226)

Here, flesh itself seems to have been congealed suffering all along –
frozen pain, waiting to thaw into its natural liquid state of agony at
the name of Jesus.

The novels' deep animus toward our worldly condition reflects a
disappointed recoil from the world, a presumptuous disappointment that the world has let us down, has not met the desires we
brought to it. "Left Behind" is not unique in expressing this: phar-
macology, our favorite TV shows, all are forms of the oldest technology humans have, the technology of avoidance, *divertissement*,
ways of convincing ourselves that we are in control of creation, in
charge of time. It may be that apocalyptic temptations are so
available to us today just because we are so comfortable in this life,
just because we have a hard time appreciating our proper
estrangement from it. The root cause of our problem may be, then, a
comfort-provoked failure of imagination, reflected in insufficient
attention to the otherness of God, and hence to the contingency of
our given order. Perhaps we simply cannot imagine a destiny radically better than anything the world, as we find it, can offer.

This failure of imagination lies at the root of our susceptibility to
the various escapisms, secular and religious, that confront us, today
and every day. But can we offer an alternative?

Augustinian eschatology against apocalyptic escapism

From the outside, this book's proposal may seem sympathetic
to the worldview of "Left Behind." After all, it suggests that we should
understand ourselves as existing during the world, and see this life as
a training in suffering and endurance for the next. Is this not just
another, albeit more sophisticated, species of apocalyptic escapism?

No. Quite the contrary: this book's Augustinian eschatology and
that of "Left Behind" are exact opposites, revealing radically different estimations of worldly life. In the books it is the saints who
escape the world, who get to heaven. But for Augustine, it is
the sinful who get "raptured" from the church, not the church that
is raptured from the sinful; on this view the sinful are the truly

escapist.[3] Augustine's own eschatological reflections developed in crucial respects as a critique of the Christian churches' apocalyptic temptations, and the struggle against the human proclivity towards escapism and avoidance – manifest in believers and non-believers alike – has always been one of the fundamental tasks of theology.

We can see this difference displayed in the contrast between the picture of hell in "Left Behind" and Augustine's in Book 21 of the *City of God*. There Augustine argues that while hell is material, it is not hell *because* it is material, but because the damned are attached to their materiality in the wrong way; they make it their absolute, their god. After all, materiality is not a fundamental ontological category, as if the world were fundamentally composed of "matter" and "spirit"; it is simply one stage of the gradual continuum between God's absolute Being and the *nihil* that lies "outside" what God ordains to be. Hence it is not the damned's flesh that is the proper locus of suffering, but their souls (*DCD* 21.3); it is not the world that is the problem but our expectations of it (and by extension of ourselves) – what we demand that it (and we) be.

On an Augustinian reading, then, the eschatology of "Left Behind," and its picture of the world as the locus of sin, simply reveal one more strategy of the sinful soul, longing for evasion. But escapism cannot simply be condemned; it must be replaced, and so this book's strategy has been an indirect one, coming to grips with the disappointment that motivates escapism rather than simply assaulting it. We should not look to have our desires satisfied, but look instead to see what prompts them – to look first not at the world, but at God, and at what God wants for us, proclaimed in and through Christ and the churches he inaugurated. When we have understood God's purposes for us, we can see the world anew, and see it as not ultimately what we think of as "the world" at all, but as part of God's ongoing gratuitous gift of Creation, in and through which (but not from which) we have our being. Our redemption is not found in an escape from our created condition, but a final, full, and endless reception of the gift of Creation itself. Today, during the world, we live east not only of Eden, but of Creation itself – oblique,

---

3. See *DCD* 20.19: "until the mystery of iniquity, which is now hidden inside the church, departs from the church." I thank Kevin Hughes for bringing this to my attention; see K. Hughes 2005a: 104 n. 52.

off-center, eccentric. We must come to see our world as the *old* world, waiting to be transformed into the new, and ourselves – the aged and withered, the tired and cynical – as those who are always being reborn as little children, infants in God's graceful tutelage. As Miroslav Volf puts it, "Unlike the present world, the world to come will not be created *ex nihilo* but *ex vetere*," out of "the old" (Volf 2000: 92). As in the Incarnation and the Eucharist, there is a continuity, a mystical continuity between old and new – a transubstantiation of creation, if you will, a union of two natures, in which life takes in and redeems death. The resolution of our story comes not most fundamentally by renunciation – the renunciation of escapism or the renunciation of our very temptations toward escapism – but by transfiguration and reception.[4]

This theological claim lies at the base of Augustine's disagreement with both thoroughgoing secularists and thoroughgoing apocalypticism. Against the former, Augustinians affirm the real continuity (and hence relevance) of putatively "otherworldly" concerns with this-worldly ones, and insist that we not suppress or ignore humans' transcendental longings. Against the latter, Augustinians affirm the real continuity (and hence value) of "worldly" matters with otherworldly realities, and insist that we not indulge in our (already too powerful) temptations toward escapism. For Augustinians, this world is pregnant with redemption, groaning in labor, bearing the weight of glory.

This theological vision entails not only a metaphysics of continuity, but more precisely an ontology of natality, wherein beginnings are more fundamental to being than endings. The new, and beginning, is real, yet it implies no rupture with our life before; it has a continuity with our present condition. We have everything backwards – we are moving not towards conclusion but towards truly beginning. As Franz Rosenzweig puts it, the Christian is the "eternal beginner" (1985: 359); and for Christians, the fundamental ontology of the world is describable as "being born again" – a form of existence oriented toward an ever deeper beginning. We *are* saved from something, but what we are saved from is fundamentally a bad version of ourselves, our solitude, our isolation. And what we are given is life abundant – life that has properly, at last, begun.

---

4. See Schmemann 1973 and P. Miller 2000, esp. 163–4.

Called to the feast of the kingdom of God

The church is that structure wherein we try to live out this habitus of natality. While our inhabitation of it is provisional, we do see in it (or in our understanding of it) some intimations of this most proper mode of our being. The church, as Augustine says, seeks the end without end (*DCD* 22.30). And it does so fundamentally musically, embodying a musical form of being – in the sense that music is the fundamental experience of receiving the gift of time.[5] The church is the singing society of the redeemed, in pilgrimage during this life, towards that time when it will join in the full choir of the saints, its song finally and fully underway, unrestrained.

How is this *habitus* of natality inhabited today? David Ford gives an important clue when he says that the "Christian vocation can be summed up as being called to the feast of the Kingdom of God. The salvation of selves is in responding to that invitation," so that we have "a responsibility to respond to an invitation into joy" (1999: 272). The metaphor of "feast" signals three dimensions of that calling – how we are to relate to ourselves, to our neighbors and creation, and to God.

As regards oneself, here the struggle is to become what Ford calls a "singing self," one capable of "being loved and delighted in" (99). This is a struggle to come to see ourselves as fundamentally public: we are not fundamentally private, isolated, and disconnected monads, but part of a larger harmony, seen and loved by another, God, who in this love wishes us nothing more fundamentally than to be. And this is a struggle, for we fear being seen. To be seen is to be exposed. Too often the gaze is a gaze of judgment or condemnation. But what we do not see is that our "exposure" before God is not fundamentally an exposure to harsh condemnation, but an ennabling love. God's love and judgment are inseparable; God's judgment is rooted in nothing but God's love for us, and so when we seize this judgment without seizing this love, we do not imitate but perversely parody God.[6] We separate them by presumptuously usurping God's right to judge, while dismissing the love

---

5. See Ford 1999: 123.
6. For more see P. Miller 2000, esp. 165: "the encompassing rhetoric for the end [is] *consummation* rather than *judgment*."

that energizes and directs that judgment. And this is our despair. At heart we are self-condemned; we see ourselves, and judge ourselves thereby to have fallen woefully short of where we should be, and so we fear God's judgment as a simple extension of our own. But we must be shriven of this, our most fundamental prejudice, our prejudice against ourselves – a prejudice built on the enormous presumption to be able to see *sicut Deus*, "like God" – and renounce our attempt to seize our inheritance before it is due to us. When we are so shriven, we see that the gaze that we fear is not (as we think it is) the condemning gaze of the judge, but the merciful gaze of God. We see that our panicked activity consists fundamentally in our trying to be God, which means trying to judge ourselves. Instead, we should submit to God's judgment and hence to God's love. We must accept our publicity, our being seen, and through that discern our being loved. Because being loved is an affirmation of our being at all, accepting God's love for us as unmerited by us means accepting our "being begun."

The "singing self" is not alone; we sing with each other, and to each other, as well as to God.[7] The self is part of a choir, so that its being is simultaneously individual and communal. Once our fear of being judged has been named and crucified, living with the neighbor, in the church, we seek genuinely to see and to be seen. This is a phenomenological truth; in loving someone we want to see them exposed to us, we want to see them entire. As with our experiences of love here and now, so paradise will be all of us, with nothing hidden, involving the full disclosure of who we are and how God saved us from ourselves. In this disclosure the practice of confession will turn out to have been all along a practice of presence, of our presence for and before each other. Confession will turn out to be, in part, our proleptic participation in God's kingdom. In our recognition that we will be judged, and the activity of confession that that recognition provokes, we seek to be seen in our desire genuinely to be present. More than that, we seek to see one another, to stand in the warm glow of our neighbors' presences. We shall seek to see by trying, properly speaking, to recognize the neighbor,

7. See Ford 1999: 122 and P. Miller 2000: 169; for an analogous secular project, see Allen 2004: 88–9 on the symbolic expression through singing of a community's "aspiration to wholeness (not oneness)."

an act that requires mutual reciprocation. Love and vision regard our relations with others as well; to love someone is to want to see them, to see all of them, to adore them. Indeed, ultimately to see just is to adore; apprehension and adoration finally draw together.

Yet we will not see each other directly but in the refracted and reflected illuminating gaze of God. We will see, that is, through God. To see the neighbor, properly to see them, is to see them as infinitely valuable. As C. S. Lewis said, "There are no *ordinary* people. You have never talked to a mere mortal" (Lewis 1980: 39). This recognition is the basis of the ethical language of "dignity." It is also one crucial, but under-appreciated, source for the political language of democracy. To see our neighbors is the core of democracy; to recognize their value, not their "worthiness," but their value in God.

Naturally the respect for the other's dignity that is endorsed by this adoration is deeper, more profound, than democracy, and hence has a place in other political orders. But democracy can at times be a reinforcing form of Christian witness, because democracy itself can be a partial form of seeing the neighbor, an awesome vision of realizing our ultimate magnitude; it has the advantage of suggesting more distance between a person's position or "station" (in democracy, no one is stationary) and their proper significance. In recognizing the other as a genuine, living other – by seeing the other as the neighbor – we seek truly to see them. This core recognition of the other is what we call "respect," which in German is the far more revelatory word *Achtung* – attention – the way we elicit from one another, if we can hear the call, real looking at who we are. And this recognition both warrants our statements about human dignity and generates the political energies of democracy.

This is not an easy task, and it is certainly not what we do in everyday social life; in fact that life may seem to run better if we actually evade it. We so rarely see one another, seeing instead only the masks we place upon one another – stranger, neighbor, friend; child, parent, spouse; colleague, enemy, ally. All these are nothing but forms of cognitive avoidance, ways we negotiate the world in proximity to one another without ever actually asking, "But who, really, *are* you?" So much of our "knowledge" of one another is in this way little more than a technique for avoiding facing each other, confronting the *plenum* that each of us, in our molten quiddity, finally is. So social life can be strangely dissatisfying, even as it grows more efficient; and the dissatisfaction consists fundamentally in this, our tacit recognition that we actually want to see one another – or better, that each of us is worth seeing in ourselves for who we truly are.

Our solicitousness for our neighbor does not rest content in her or his bare there-ness. To see the neighbor is to see a mystery that transcends itself and iconically refers to the divine reality beyond it. The dignity of the neighbor is the glow of a divine purpose immanent within her or him, yet also not exhaustively immanent therein. To see the neighbor is to love the neighbor, and to love the neighbor is to be awed by and drawn to the other whose love for the neighbor anchors our own – namely, God. God loves each of us and knows us by name. In light of this, we seek the neighbor out as coparticipant in our proper task of adoring God.

What we are doing, understood as community and as individuals begun by God, is adoring God. But what is that heavenly adoration like What, that is, is this beginning? We have only the slimmest glimpses of it in Scripture and tradition; but what we can say is that our worshipful adoration of God will be endless and infinite – not the bad infinite of ceaselessness, which is really merely temporally extended stasis, but the truly infinite dynamism of everdeepening, ever widening, and ever heightening seeking into (not seeking "out for") God's infinite being. Here, "consummation" entails both achievement and dynamism. Aquinas captured this, in part, in his metaphysics of God as *actus purus*: the idea of God as wholly dynamic, without reserve, willing God's Trinity as love and Creation as the beneficiary of that superabundant love. Yet this dynamism, so complete, is also not a dynamism provoked by some need of something outside of it; in that way the activity is simultaneously a peacefulness, a restful exertion, an exposition of pure gratuity. Such restful dynamism is God's gift to us of self-presence, in the eschaton; as W. H. Vanstone puts it, the glory of God is an activity that leads to passivity, that "destines itself to waiting" in love (1983: 99). God's "completion" is not the cessation of temporal sequence, but its consummation, the fullness of life, of being and time itself.

And a form of this perfection is what God has destined for us as well; as God is, so shall we be when we live fully in God, in God's gratuitous gift to us of Creation. To see Creation for what it truly is,

God's Sabbath gift – a restfulness and peace which are not exhaustion but fullness of life and primacy of being – is to begin to live our true lives, to begin the process of living into a beginning without an ending.

At last, the first things

In the fusion of stability and dynamism of God as *actus purus* is the core idea of our experience of heaven – both rest and joy, resolution and commencement, the "Sabbath morning without an evening" – and also, unsurprisingly, the core idea of our experience of the presence of God. But the site of this sabbathing is none other than Creation – a new creation, to be sure, but again one born of the old, not a renunciation but a completion, not an annihilation but a resolution. We will see God walk, not in the cool of the day, but in the morning of the new creation.

What will that day, that eschatological morning, look like? What will we feel? What will feeling be, or for that matter understanding? We cannot know here, during the world. The best words we have for it are paradoxical, attempts to communicate the vexation of our comprehension, such as Augustine's claim that "busy idleness (*otioso negotio*) will be our beatitude" (*ennar.* 86.9).[8] But we can affirm now, in faith and hope, that such a beatitude exists; and we can, partially and proleptically, participate in it – in love – even today. C. S. Lewis well describes this faithful, hopeful, and charitable agnosticism:

> At present we are on the outside of the world, the wrong side of the door. We discern the freshness and purity of morning, but they do not make us fresh and pure. We cannot mingle with the splendors we see. But all the leaves of the New Testament are rustling with the rumor that it will not always be so. Some day, God willing, we shall get *in*. (Lewis 1980: 37)

And we shall get in; and then we will, at last, see God as all in all – see the Father, in Christ, through the Holy Spirit, and our neighbor; and through the Father, in Christ, our neighbor, our friend, our other self. Then, at last, shall we be fully joyful; then, at last, shall we be blessed; then, at last, shall we be we; and then, and only then,

---

8. See Griffiths 2001 for illuminating work on this.

shall our lives as beginners be fully given to us – not given over, handed over as Jesus was by Judas to the authorities, but truly given, with the giver in the gift, as Jesus gave himself to his disciples, even unto Judas, and through them the world – and our true lives finally begun.

But in the meantime, during the world, our task is to quicken to that longing, to sharpen our waiting on this advent: to be brave, be strong, stay firm in the faith, do all our work in love, and in so doing to long for the day when – and, best as we can in the here and the now, during the world, to accept the presence of the promise of that day as – we turn to one another, face to face, before the Father, through the Son, in the Spirit, and say: *venite adoremus*.

References

Abraham, William J. (1989), *The Logic of Evangelism*. Grand Rapids: William B. Eerdmans.

Adorno, T. W. (2003a), "Cultural Criticism and Society," pp. 146–62 in *Can One Live After Auschwitz? A Philosophical Reader*, ed. Rolf Tiedemann. Stanford: Stanford University Press.

(2003b), "Trying to Understand *Endgame*," pp. 259–94 in *Can One Live After Auschwitz? A Philosophical Reader*, ed. Rolf Tiedemann. Stanford: Stanford University Press.

Alexander, Jeffrey (2003), *The Meanings of Social Life: A Cultural Sociology*. New York: Oxford University Press.

Alison, James (1996), *Raising Abel: The Recovery of the Eschatological Imagination*. New York: Crossroad.

Allen, Danielle (2004), *Talking to Strangers: Anxieties of Citizenship since Brown v. Board of Education*. Chicago: University of Chicago Press.

Alston, William (1991), *Perceiving God: The Epistemology of Religious Experience*. Ithaca: Cornell University Press.

Ammerman, Nancy (1997), "Golden Rule Christianity: Lived Religion in the American Mainstream," pp. 196–216 in *Lived Theology in America: Toward a History of Practice*, ed. David Hall. Princeton: Princeton University Press.

Anderson, Victor (1995), *Beyond Ontological Blackness: An Essay on African American Religious and Cultural Criticism*. New York: Continuum.

Anscombe, G. E. M. (1958), *Intention*. Ithaca: Cornell University Press.

Anselm (1998), "On the Fall of the Devil," pp. 193–232 in *Anselm of Canterbury: The Major Works*, ed. Brian Davies and G. R. Evans. New York: Oxford University Press.

Aquino, Frederick D. (2004), *Communities of Informed Judgment: Newman's Illative Sense and Accounts of Rationality*. Washington: Catholic University of America Press.

Arato, Andrew, and Jean Cohen (1992), *Civil Society and Political Theory*. Cambridge, MA: MIT Press.

Arendt, Hannah, (1963). *On Revolution*. New York: Viking

Asad, Talal (1993), *Genealogies of Religion: Discipline and Reasons of Power in Christianity and Islam*. Baltimore: Johns Hopkins University Press.

(2003) *Formations of the Secular: Christianity, Islam, Modernity*. Palo Alto: Stanford University Press.

Auden, W. H. (1968), *The Dyer's Hand: And other Essays*. New York: Vintage.

Audi, Robert (1986), "Direct Justification, Evidential Dependence, and Theistic Belief," pp. 139–66 in *Rationality, Religious Belief, and Moral Commitment: New Essays in the Philosophy of Religion*, ed. Robert Audi and William J. Wainwright. Ithaca: Cornell University Press.

Ayres, Lewis (1992), "Between Athens and Jerusalem: Prolegomena to Theological Anthropology in *De Trinitate*," pp. 53–73 in *Modern Theology*, 8.1.

(1995), "The Discipline of Self-Knowledge in Augustine's *De Trinitate* Book X," pp. 261–96 in *The Passionate Intellect: Essays on Transformation of the Classical Traditions*. New Brunswick: Transaction Books.

Baer, Helmut David (1996), "The Fruit of Charity: Using the Neighbor in *De Doctrina Christiana*," pp. 47–64 in *Journal of Religious Ethics*, 24.1 (Spring).

Baier, Annette (1994), *Moral Prejudices*. Cambridge, MA: Harvard University Press.

Baker, C. Edwin (1994), *Advertising and a Democratic Press*. Princeton: Princeton University Press.

Balthasar, Hans Urs von (1988a), *Theo-Drama: Theological Dramatic Theory*, I, trans. Graham Harrison. San Francisco: Ignatius Press.

(1988b), *Dare We Hope "That All Men Be Saved"? With a Short Discourse on Hell*, trans. Dr. David Kipp and Rev. Lothar Krauth. San Francisco: Ignatius Press.

Barber, Benjamin (1988), *The Conquest of Politics: Liberal Philosophy in Democratic Times*. Princeton: Princeton University Press.

(1996), *Jihad vs. McWorld*. New York: Ballantine Books.

Barnes, Michael, SJ (2002), *Theology and the Dialogue of Religions*. Cambridge: Cambridge University Press.

Barney, Darin (2000), *Prometheus Wired: The Hope for Democracy in the Age of Network Technology*. Chicago: University of Chicago Press.

Barth, Karl (1957), *Church Dogmatics, Vol. I/1: The Doctrine of God*, trans. G. W. Bromiley *et al.* Edinburgh: T. & T. Clark.

(1961), *Church Dogmatics, Vol. III/4: The Doctrine of Creation*, trans. G. W. Bromiley. Edinburgh: T. & T. Clark.

(1975), *Church Dogmatics, Vol. I/1: The Doctrine of the Word of God*, 2nd edn trans. G. W. Bromiley. Edinburgh: T. & T. Clark.

Bartov, Omar (2002), "The Scholarly Profession and Extreme Violence," pp. 508–18 in *International Social Science Journal*, 174 (December).

Bathory, Peter Dennis (1981), *Political Theory as Public Confession: The Social and Political Thought of St. Augustine of Hippo*. New Brunswick: Transaction Books.

Batnitzky, Leora (2000), *Idolatry and Representation: The Philosophy of Franz Rosenzweig Reconsidered*. Princeton: Princeton University Press.

Baudrillard, Jean (1988), "Consumer Society," pp. 31–44 in *Selected Writings*. Stanford: Stanford University Press.

(1994), *The Illusion of the End*. Stanford: Stanford University Press.

Bauman, Zygmunt (1987), *Legislators and Interpreters: On Modernity, Postmodernity, and Intellectuals*. Cambridge: Polity Press.

(1999), *In Search of Politics*. Cambridge: Polity Press.

Bavel, Tarcisius J. van, OSA (1991), "Augustine on Christian Teaching and Life," pp. 89–112 in *Augustinian Heritage*, 37.

(1987), "The Anthropology of Augustine," pp. 25–39 in *Milltown Studies*, 19/20.

(1986), "The Double Face of Love in Augustine," pp. 169–81 in *Augustinian Studies*, 17.

Beck, Ulrich, Anthony Giddens, and Scott Lash (1994), *Reflexive Modernization: Politics, Tradition, and Aesthetics in the Modern Social Order*. Stanford: Stanford University Press.

Beckett, Samuel (1958), *Endgame*. New York: Grove Press.

Beem, Chris (1999), *The Necessity of Politics: Reclaiming American Public Life*. Chicago: University of Chicago Press.

Beiner, Ronald (1992), *What's the Matter with Liberalism?* Chicago: University of Chicago Press.

(1997), *Philosophy in a Time of Lost Spirit*. Toronto: University of Toronto Press.

Bell, Daniel (1988), *The End of Ideology: On the Exhaustion of Political Ideas in the Fifties*. Cambridge, MA: Harvard University Press.

(1996), *The Cultural Contradictions of Capitalism*. New York: Basic Books.

Bell, Daniel M., Jr. (2001), *Liberation Theology After the End of History: The Refusal to Cease Suffering*. New York: Routledge.

Bellah, Robert (1974), "Civil Religion in America," pp. 21–44 in Russell Richey and Donald Jones, eds., *American Civil Religion*. New York: Harper & Row.

Benhabib, Seyla (1999), "Citizens, Residents and Aliens in a Changing World: Political Membership in the Global Era," pp. 709–44 in *Social Research*, 66.3.

Bennett, Oliver (2001), *Cultural Pessimism: Narratives of Decline in the Postmodern World*. Edinburgh: Edinburgh University Press.

Berger, Peter (1979), *The Heretical Imperative: Contemporary Possibilities of Religious Affirmation*. Garden City: Anchor Press.

(1992), *A Far Glory: The Quest for Faith in an Age of Credulity*. New York: Free Press.

ed. (1999), *The Desecularization of the World: Resurgent Religion and World Politics*. Grand Rapids: William B. Eerdmans.

Berkowitz, Peter (1999), *Virtue and the Making of Modern Liberalism*. Princeton: Princeton University Press.

Bernstein, Michael André (1994), *Foregone Conclusions: Against Apocalyptic History*. Berkeley: University of California Press.

Bernstein, Richard J. (1983), *Beyond Objectivism and Relativism: Science, Hermeneutics, and Praxis*. Philadelphia: University of Pennsylvania Press.

Berry, Wendell (1990), *What are People For?* San Francisco: North Point Press.

Bertram, Christopher (1997). "Political Justification, Theoretical Complexity, and Democratic Community," pp. 563–83 in *Ethics*, 107.4 (July).

Betti, Ugo (1956), " The Queen and the Rebels," in *Three Plays by Ugo Betti*, ed. and trans. Henry Reed. New York: Grove Press.

Betz, Hans Dieter (2000), "The Human Being in the Antagonisms of Life according to the Apostle Paul," pp. 557–76 in *Journal of Religion*, 80.4.

Bewes, Timothy (1997), *Cynicism and Postmodernity*. New York: Verso.

Binder, Amy J. (2002), *Contentious Curricula: Afrocentrism and Creationism in American Public Schools*. Princeton: Princeton University Press.

Bird, Colin (1999), *The Myth of Liberal Individualism*. Cambridge: Cambridge University Press.

Bivins, Jason C. (2003), *The Fracture of Good Order: Christian Antiliberalism and the Challenge to American Politics*. Chapel Hill: UNC Press.

Black, Antony 1997, "Christianity and Republicanism: From St. Cyprian to Rousseau," pp. 647–56 in *American Political Science Review*, 91.3 (September).

Bloch, Ernst (1986), *The Principle of Hope*, trans. Neville Plaice, Stephen Plaice, and Paul Knight. Oxford: Blackwell.

Bloch, Ruth H. (1988), *Visionary Republic: Millennial Themes in American Thought, 1756–1800*. New York: Cambridge University Press.

Block, James (2002), *A Nation of Agents: The American Path to a Modern Self and Society*. Cambridge, MA: Cambridge, MA: Harvard University Press.

Bonhoeffer, Dietrich (1997), *Creation and Fall*, trans. Douglas Stephen Bax. Minneapolis: Fortress Press.

Bowlin, John (1997), "Augustine on Justifying Coercion," pp. 49–70 in *The Annual of the Society of Christian Ethics*, 17.

Boyarin, Daniel (1994), *A Radical Jew: Paul and the Politics of Identity*. Berkeley: University of California Press.

Boyer, Paul (1992), *When Time Shall Be No More: Prophecy Belief in Modern American Culture*. Cambridge, MA: Harvard University Press.

(2005), "Biblical Prophecy and Foreign Policy" pp. 107–22 in Claire Badaracco, ed., *Quoting God: How Media Shape Ideas about Religion and Culture*. Waco: Baylor University Press.

Boyle, Marjorie O'Rourke (1997), *Divine Domesticity: Augustine of Thagaste to Teresa of Avila*. New York: E. J. Brill.

Boyle, Nicholas (1998), *Who Are We Now? Christian Humanism and the Global Market from Hegel to Heaney*. Notre Dame: University of Notre Dame Press.

Bramadat, Paul A. (2000), *The Church on the World's Turf: An Evangelical Christian Group at a Secular University*. New York: Oxford University Press.

Bright, Pamela, ed. and trans. (1999), *Augustine and the Bible*. Notre Dame: University of Notre Dame Press.

Brinkley, Alan (1998), *Liberalism and Its Discontents*. Cambridge, MA: Harvard University Press.

Brint, Steven (1994), *In an Age of Experts: The Changing Role of Professionals in Politics and Public Life*. Princeton: Princeton University Press.

Brooks, David (2000), *Bobos in Paradise*. New York: Simon & Schuster.

Brown, Michael F. (1997), *The Channeling Zone: American Spirituality in an Anxious Age*. Cambridge, MA: Harvard University Press.

Brown, Peter (1988), *The Body and Society: Men, Women and Sexual Renunciation in Early Christianity*. New York: Columbia University Press.

(1992), *Power and Persuasion in Late Antiquity: Towards a Christian Empire*. Madison: University of Wisconsin Press.

(1995), *Authority and the Sacred: Aspects of the Christianization of the Roman World*. New York: Cambridge University Press.

(1997), *The Rise of Western Christendom: Triumph and Diversity, AD 200–1000*. Malden: Blackwell.

(2000), *Augustine of Hippo: A Biography*, rev. edn. London: Faber.

(2002), *Poverty and Leadership in the Later Roman Empire*. Hanover, NH: University Press of New England.

Brown, Wendy (1995), *States of Injury: Power and Freedom in Late Modernity*. Princeton: Princeton University Press.

Bruns, Gerald (1984), "The Problem of Figuration in Antiquity," pp. 147–64 in *Hermeneutics: Questions and Prospects*, ed. Gary Shapiro and Alan Sica. Amherst: University of Massachusetts Press.

(1992), *Hermeneutics Ancient and Modern*. New Haven: Yale University Press.

Buchanan, Allen (2000), "Rawls's Law of Peoples: Rules for a Vanished Westphalian World," pp. 697–721 in *Ethics*, 110.4 (July).

Buford, Bill (1992), *Among the Thugs*. New York: Norton.

Bull, Malcolm (1995), *Apocalypse Theory and the End of the World*. Oxford: Blackwell.

Burnaby, John (1938), *Amor Dei: A Study of the Religion of St. Augustine*. London: Hodder & Stoughton.

(1970), "Amor in St. Augustine," pp. 174–86 in Charles Kegley, ed., *The Philosophy and Theology of Anders Nygren*. Carbondale: Southern Illinois University Press.

Burnell, Peter (1992), "The Status of Politics in Augustine's City of God," pp. 13–29 in *History of Political Thought*, 13.1.

(2005), *The Augustinian Person*. Washington: Catholic University of America Press.

Burnyeat, Myles (1987), "Augustine and Wittgenstein *De Magistro*," pp. 1–24 in *Proceedings of the Aristotelian Society*, Supplementary Volume LXI.

Burrell, David (2004), *Faith and Freedom: An Interfaith Perspective*. Cambridge, MA: Blackwell.

Burton-Christie, Douglas (1993), *The Word in the Desert: Scripture and the Quest for Holiness in Early Christian Monasticism*. New York: Oxford University Press.

Butler, Joseph (1983), *Five Sermons*. Indianapolis: Hackett.

Campbell, Colin (1987), *The Romantic Ethic and the Spirit of Modern Consumerism*. New York: Blackwell.

Camus, Albert (1956), *The Fall*, trans. Justin O'Brien. New York: Alfred A. Knopf.

Canning, Raymond (1993), *The Unity of Love for God and Neighbor in St. Augustine*. Leuven: Augustinian Historical Institute.

Carney, Frederick S. (1991), "The Structure of Augustine's Ethic," pp. 11–37 in William S. Babcock, ed., *The Ethics of St. Augustine* JRE Studies in Religious Ethics 3. Atlanta: Scholars Press.

Carruthers, Mary (1992), *The Book of Memory: A Study of Memory in Medieval Culture*. Cambridge: Cambridge University Press.

Carter, Stephen (1994), *The Culture of Disbelief: How American Law and Politics Trivialize Religious Devotion*. New York: Anchor Books.

Cary, Philip (2000), *Augustine's Invention of the Inner Self: The Legacy of a Christian Platonist*. New York: Oxford University Press.

Casanova, José (1994), *Public Religions in the Modern World*. Chicago: University of Chicago Press.

Cavadini, John. "Simplifying Augustine," pp. 63–84 in *Educating People of Faith: Exploring the History of Jewish and Christian Communities*, ed. John Van Engen. Grand Rapids: William B. Eerdmans.

Cavanaugh, William (1995), "A Fire Strong Enough to Consume the House: The Wars of Religion and the Rise of the State," pp. 397–420 in *Modern Theology*, 11.4 (October).

(1998), *Torture and Eucharist: Theology, Politics and the Body of Christ*. Malden: Blackwell.

(1999), "The City: Beyond Secular Parodies," pp. 182–200 in Milbank *et al.*

Cavell, Stanley (1976), "Ending the Waiting Game: A Reading of Beckett's *Endgame*," pp. 115–62 in *Must We Mean What We Say? A Book of Essays*. New York: Cambridge University Press.

(1979), *The Claim of Reason: Wittgenstein, Skepticism, Morality, and Tragedy*. New York: Oxford University Press.

Certeau, Michel de (1992), *The Mystic Fable*, trans. Michael B. Smith. Chicago: University of Chicago Press.

Chaloupka, William (1999), *Everybody Knows: Cynicism in America*. Minneapolis: University of Minnesota Press.

Chambers, Simone, and Jeffrey Kapstein (2001), "Bad Civil Society," pp. 837–65 in *Political Theory* 29.6 (December).

Chambers, Simone, and Will Kymlica (2002), *Alternative Conceptions of Civil Society*. Princeton: Princeton University Press.

Chappell, David (2004), *A Stone of Hope: Prophetic Religion and the Death of Jim Crow*. Chapel Hill: University of North Carolina Press.

Chappell, T. D. J. (1995), *Aristotle and Augustine on Freedom*. New York: St. Martin's Press.

Charry, Ellen (1997), *By the Renewing of Your Minds: The Pastoral Roots of Christian Doctrine*. New York: Oxford University Press.

Clarke, Randolph (2003), *Libertarian Accounts of Free Will*. New York: Oxford University Press.

Claussen, M. A. (1991), "*Peregrinatio* and *Peregrini* in Augustine's *City of God* and the Image and Idea of Pilgrimage as a Metaphor for the Christian Life in the Early Church Fathers," pp. 33–75 in *Traditio*, 46.

Cloeren, Herman J. (1985), "St. Augustine's *De magistro*: A Transcendental Investigation," pp. 21–7 in *Augustinian Studies*, 16.

Clooney, Francis X. (1992), *Theology After Vedanta*. Stony Brook: State University of New York Press.

Coakley, Sarah (2002a), *Powers and Submissions: Spirituality, Philosophy and Gender*. Oxford: Blackwell.

(2002b), "Deepening Practices: Perspectives from Ascetical and Mystical Theology," pp. 78–93 in Volf and Bass 2002.

Cohen, Diane, and A. Robert Jaeger (1997), *Sacred Places at Risk: New Evidence on How Endangered Older Churches and Synagogues Serve Communities*. Philadelphia: Partners for Sacred Places.

Cohen, Jean (1999), "Trust, Voluntary Association, and Workable Democracy: The Contemporary American Discourse of Civil Society," pp. 208–48 in *Democracy and Trust*, ed. Mark E. Warren. Cambridge: Cambridge University Press.

Cohen, Lizabeth (2003), *A Consumer's Republic: The Politics of Mass Consumption in Postwar America*. New York: Knopf.

Cohen, Mitchell (2002), "An Empire of Cant: Hardt, Negri, and Postmodern Political Theory," pp. 17–28 in *Dissent*, 493 (Summer 2002).

Colburn, Forrest D. (2002), *Latin America at the End of Politics*. Princeton: Princeton University Press.

Coleman, John J. (1996), *Party Decline in America: Policy, Politics, and the Fiscal State*. Princeton: Princeton University Press.

Coles, Romand (1997), *Rethinking Generosity: Critical Theory and the Politics of Caritas*. Ithaca: Cornell University Press.

Collinge, William J. (1988), "The Relation of Religious Community Life to Rationality in Augustine," pp. 242–53 in *Faith and Philosophy*, 5.3 (July).

Connolly, William (1999), *Why I am not a Secularist*. Minneapolis: University of Minnesota Press.

(2002a), *The Augustinian Imperative: A Reflection on the Politics of Modernity*, new edn. Lanham: Rowman & Littlefield.

(2002b), *Neuropolitics: Thinking, Culture, Speed*. Minneapolis: University of Minnesota Press.

Constable, Giles (1976), "Opposition to Pilgrimage in the Middle Ages," pp. 125–446 in *Studia Gratiana*, 19.

Conybeare, Catherine (1999), "*Terrarum Orbi Documentum*: Augustine, Camillus, and Learning from History," pp. 59–74 in Fitzgerald *et al*. 1999.

(2000), *Paulinus Noster: Self and Symbols in the Letters of Paulinus of Nola*. Oxford: Oxford University Press.

Cook, Martin (2004), "Christian Apocalypticism and Weapons of Mass Destruction," pp. 200–10 in *Ethics and Weapons of Mass Destruction: Religious and Secular Perspectives*, ed. Sohail H. Hasmi and Steven P. Lee. New York: Cambridge University Press.

Cooper, Kate, and Conrad Leyser (2000), "The Gender of Grace: Impotence, Servitude, and Manliness in the Fifth-Century West," pp. 536–51 in *Gender and History*, 12.3 (November)

Cowen, Tyler (1998), *In Praise of Commercial Culture*. Cambridge, MA: Harvard University Press.

(2000), *What Price Fame?* Cambridge, MA: Harvard University Press.

Cox, Jeffrey (2003), "Master Narratives of Long-Term Religious Change," pp. 201–17 in *The Decline of Christendom in Western Europe: 1750–2000*, ed. Hugh McLeod and Werner Ustorf. Cambridge: Cambridge University Press.

Cranz, F. Edward (1972), "The Development of Augustine's Ideas on Society Before the Donatist Controversy," pp. 336–403 in *Augustine: A Collection of Critical Essays*, ed. R. A. Markus. Garden City: Anchor Books.

Crenson, Matthew A., and Benjamin Ginsberg (2002), *Downsizing Democracy: How America Sidelined Its Citizens and Privatized Its Public*. Baltimore: Johns Hopkins University Press.

Cronon, William, ed. (1995), *Uncommon Ground: Toward Reinventing Nature*. New York: W. W. Norton and Company.

Crouse, R. D. (1976), "*Recurrens in te unum*: The Pattern of St. Augustine's *Confessions*," pp. 389–92 in *Studia Patristica XIV*, ed. E. A. Livingstone. Berlin: Walter de Gruyter.

Curran, Charles E. (2002), *Catholic Social Teaching, 1891–Present: A Historical, Theological, and Ethical Analysis*. Washington: Georgetown University Press.

Cushman, Thomas (1997), *Critical Theory and the War in Croatia and Bosnia*, The Donald W. Treadgold Papers in Russian, East European, and Central Asian Studies. Seattle: Jackson School of International Studies, University of Washington.

Dagger, Richard (1997), *Civic Virtues: Rights, Citizenship, and Republican Liberalism*. New York: Oxford University Press.

Dalton, Russell J. (2000), "Value Change and Democracy," pp. 252–69 in *Disaffected Democracies: What's Troubling the Trilateral Countries?*, ed. Susan J. Pharr and Robert D. Putnam. Princeton: Princeton University Press.

Dalton, Russell J., Scott C. Flanagan and Paul Allen Beck, eds. (1984), *Electoral Change in Advanced Industrial Democracies: Realignment or Dealignment?* Princeton: Princeton University Press.

Davidson, Donald (1980), "How is Weakness of the Will Possible?" pp. 21–42 in *Essays on Actions and Events*. New York: Oxford University Press.

Davies, Oliver (2001), *A Theology of Compassion*. London: SCM Press.

(2004), *The Creativity of God: World, Eucharist, Reason*. Cambridge: Cambridge University Press.

Davis, Scott (1991), "'Ed Quod Vis Fac': Paul Ramsey and Augustinian Ethics," pp. 31–69 in *Annual of the Society of Christian Ethics*, 19.2.

(1996), "Philanthropy as a Virtue in Late Antiquity and the Middle Ages," pp. 1–23 in *Giving: Western Ideas of Philanthropy*, ed. J. B. Schneewind. Bloomington: Indiana University Press.

D'Agostino, Fred (1996), *Free Public Reason: Making It Up As We Go*. New York: Oxford University Press.

Daley, Brian E., SJ (1999), "Building a New City: The Cappadocian Fathers and the Rhetoric of Philanthropy," pp. 431–61 in *Journal of Early Christian Studies* 7:3 (Fall).

Darsey, James (1997), *The Prophetic Tradition and Radical Rhetoric in America*. New York: New York University Press.

Dawson, John David (2002), *Christian Figural Reading and the Fashioning of Identity*. Berkeley: University of California Press.

De Lubac, Henri (1969), *Augustinianism and Modern Theology*, trans. Lancelot Sheppard. London: Geoffrey Chapman.

Deane, Herbert A. (1963), *The Political and Social Ideas of St. Augustine*. New York: Columbia University Press.

Delbanco, Andrew (1995), *The Death of Satan: How Americans Have Lost the Sense of Evil*. New York: Farrar, Strauss, Giroux.

Deneen, Patrick (2005), *Democratic Faith*. Princeton: Princeton University Press.

Dickstein, Morris (1992), *Double Agent: The Critic and Society*. New York: Oxford University Press.

DiNoia, J. A. (1990), "American Catholic Theology at Century's End: Postconciliar, Postmodern, Post-Thomistic," pp. 419–518 in *The Thomist*, 54.3 (July).

(1993), *The Diversity of Religions: A Christian Perspective*. Washington: Catholic University of America Press.

Dionne, E. J., Jr. (1991) *Why Americans Hate Politics*. New York: Simon & Schuster.

Dionne, E. J., Jr. and John J. DiIulio, eds. (2000), *What's God Got To Do with the American Experiment?* Washington: Brookings Institution Press.

Djuth, Marianne (1990), "Stoicism and Augustine's Doctrine of Human Freedom After 396," pp. 387–401 in Schnaubelt and Van Fleteren.

Dodaro, Robert, O. S. A. (1991), "Pirates or Superpowers: Reading Augustine in a Hall of Mirrors," pp. 9–19 in *New Blackfriars*, 72.845 (January).

(1994), "Eloquent Lies, Just Wars and the Politics of Persuasion: Reading Augustine's *City of God* in a 'Postmodern' World," pp. 77–138 in *Augustinian Studies*, 25.

(2004a), *Christ and the Just Society in the Thought of Augustine*. Cambridge: Cambridge University Press.

(2004b), "Political and Theological Virtues in Augustine, Letter 155 to Macedonius," pp. 430–474 in *Augustiniana*, 54.

Doody, John, Kevin L. Hughes, and Kim Paffenroth, eds. (2005), *Augustine and Politics*. Lanham: Lexington Books.

Dorff, Elliot N. (2000), "The King's Torah: The Role of Judaism in Shaping Jews' Impact in National Policy," pp. 203–21 in Douglass and Mitchell 2000.

Doughtery, Richard J. (1990), "Christian and Citizen: The Tension in St. Augustine's *De civitate Dei*," in Schnaubelt and Van Fleteren.

Douglass, R. Bruce and Joshua Mitchell, eds. (2000), *A Nation Under God: Essays on the Future of Religion in American Public Life*. Lanham: Rowman & Littlefield.

Doyle, Daniel Edward, O. S. A. (2002), *The Bishop as Disciplinarian in the Letters of St. Augustine*. New York: Peter Lang.

Drake, Hal (2000), *Constantine and the Bishops: The Politics of Intolerance*. Baltimore: Johns Hopkins University Press.

Dreyfus, Hubert (1991), *Being-In-The-World: A Commentary on Heidegger's Being and Time, Division I*. Cambridge, MA: MIT Press.

Dubay, Thomas (1999), *The Evidential Power of Beauty*. San Francisco: Ignatius Press.

Dumont, Louis (1977), *From Mandeville to Marx: The Genesis and Triumph of Economic Ideology*. Chicago: University of Chicago Press.

Dunn, Richard (1970), *The Age of Religions Wars 1559–1689*. New York: W. W. Norton & Company.

Dyas, Dee (2001), *Pilgrimage in Medieval English Literature 700–1500*. Rochester, NY: D. S. Brewer.

Eberle, Christopher J. (2002), *Religious Conviction in Liberal Politics*. New York: Cambridge University Press.

Eck, Diana L. (2001), *A New Religious America: How a "Christian Country" Has Become the World's Most Religiously Diverse Nation*. San Francisco: HarperSanFrancisco.

Edmundson, Mark (1997), *Nightmare on Main Street: Angels, Sadomasochism, and the Culture of Gothic*. Cambridge, MA: Harvard University Press.

Edwards, Bob, and Michael Foley, eds. (1997), "Social Capital, Civil Society, and Contemporary Democracy," *American Behavioral Scientist*, 40 (March–April).

Ehrenberg, John (1999), *Civil Society: The Critical History of an Idea*. New York: New York University Press.

Ehrman, John (1995), *The Rise of Neoconservativism: Intellectuals and Foreign Affairs, 1945–1994.* Yale University Press.

Eliasoph, Nina (1998), *Avoiding Politics: How Americans Produce Apathy in Everyday Life.* New York: Cambridge University Press.

Elshtain, Jean Bethke (1981), *Public Man, Private Woman: Women in Social and Political Thought.* Princeton: Princeton University Press.

(1995), *Democracy on Trial.* New York: Basic Books.

Elster, Jon (1983), *Sour Grapes: Studies in the Subversion of Rationality.* New York: Cambridge University Press.

(1993), *Political Psychology.* New York: Cambridge University Press.

Emerson, Ralph Waldo (1957), *Selections From Ralph Waldo Emerson,* ed. Stephen E. Whicher. Boston: Houghton Mifflin.

Ertman, Thomas (1997), *Birth of the Leviathan.* New York: Cambridge University Press.

Eusebius of Caesarea (1976), "In Praise of Constantine," in *In Praise of Constantine: A Historical Study and New Translation of Eusebius' Tricennial Orations,* by H. A. Drake. Berkeley: University of California Press.

(1999), *Life of Constantine,* ed. and trans. Averil Cameron and Stuart G. Hall Oxford: Clarendon Press.

Evans, Sara, and Harry C. Boyte (1986), *Free Spaces: The Sources of Democratic Change in America.* New York: Harper & Row.

Everett, William Johnson (1997), *Religion, Federalism and the Struggle for Public Life.* New York: Oxford University Press.

Fabian, Johannes (1983), *Time and the Other: How Anthropology Makes Its Object.* New York: Columbia University Press.

Farkas, Steve, Jean Johnson, and Tony Foleno (2001), *For Goodness's Sake: Why So Many Want Religion to Play a Greater Role in American Life.* New York: Public Agenda.

Ferree, Myra Marx, William Anthony Gamson, Jürgen Gerhards and Dieter Rucht (2002), *Shaping Abortion Discourse: Democracy and the Public Sphere in Germany and the United States.* Cambridge: Cambridge University Press.

Ferreira, M. Jamie (2001), *Love's Grateful Striving: A Commentary on Kierkegaard's Works of Love.* New York: Oxford University Press.

Fiorina, Morris P., Samuel J. Abrams, and Jeremy C. Pope (2005), *Culture War? The Myth of Polarized America.* New York: Pearson Longman.

Fish, Stanley (1999), *The Trouble with Principle.* Cambridge, MA: Harvard University Press.

Fitzgerald, Allan D., O. S. A., Mark Vessey, and Karla Pollmann, eds. (1999), *History, Apocalypse, and the Secular Imagination: New Essays on Augustine's City of God.* Bowling Green: Philosophy Documentation Center.

Flathman, Richard (1998),"'It All Depends … on How One Understands Liberalism': A Brief Response to Stephen Macedo," pp. 81–4 in *Political Theory,* 26.1 (February).

Flood, Gavin (2004), *The Ascetic Self.* New York: Cambridge University Press.

Fodor, James (1995), *Christian Hermeneutics: Paul Ricoeur and the Refiguring of Theology.* Oxford: Clarendon Press.

Foley, Richard (1993), *Working Without A Net: A Study of Egocentric Epistemology.* New York: Oxford University Press.

Ford, David (1999), *Self and Salvation: Being Transformed*. New York: Cambridge University Press.

Forsyth, Neil (1987), *The Old Enemy: Satan and the Combat Myth*. Princeton: Princeton University Press.

Foucault, Michel (1981), *The History of Sexuality*, I, trans. Robert Hurley. Harmondsworth: Penguin.

Fowler, Robert Booth (1999), *Enduring Liberalism: American Political Thought Since the 1960s*. Lawrence: University Press of Kansas.

Fowler, Robert Booth, Allen D. Hertzke, and Laura R. Olson, eds. (1999), *Religion and Politics in America: Faith, Culture, and Strategic Choices*, 2nd edn. Boulder: Westview Press.

Frank, Thomas (1997), *The Conquest of Cool: Business Culture, Counterculture and the Rise of Hip Consumerism*. Chicago: University of Chicago Press.

(2004), *What's the Matter with Kansas?* New York: Metropolitan Books.

Frankfurt, Harry G. (1988), *The Importance of What We Care About: Philosophical Essays*. New York: Cambridge University Press.

Fredriksen, Paula. (1990), "Beyond the Body/Soul Dichotomy: Augustine's Answer to Mani, Plotinus and Julian," pp. 227–51 in *Paul and the Legacies of Paul*, ed. William Babcock. Dallas: Southern Methodist University Press.

Friedman, Lawrence Meir (1990), *The Republic of Choice: Law, Authority, and Culture*. Cambridge, MA: Harvard University Press.

Frykholm, Amy Johnson (2004), *Rapture Culture: Left Behind in Evangelical America*. New York: Oxford University Press.

Fukuyama, Francis (1992), *The End of History and the Last Man*. New York: Free Press.

(1999), *The Great Disruption: Human Nature and the Reconstitution of Social Order*. New York: Free Press.

(2002), *Our Posthuman Future: Consequences of the Biotechnology Revolution*. New York: Farrar, Strauss & Giroux.

(2004), *State-Building: Governance and World Order in the 21st Century*. Ithaca: Cornell University Press.

Gagnier, Regenia (2000), *The Insatiability of Human Wants: Economics and Aesthetics in Market Society*. Chicago: University of Chicago Press.

Gainsborough, Juliet F. (2001), *Fenced Off: The Suburbanization of American Politics*. Washington: Georgetown University Press.

Galston, William (1991), *Liberal Purposes*. New York: Cambridge University Press.

(2002), *Liberal Pluralism: The Implications of Value Pluralism for Political Theory and Practice*. New York: Cambridge University Press.

(2004), "Civic Education and Political Participation," pp. 263–6 in *PS: Political Science & Politics* (April).

Gamwell, Franklin I. (1990), *The Divine Good: Modern Moral Theory and the Necessity of God*. San Francisco: HarperSanFrancisco.

(1995), *The Meaning of Religious Freedom: Modern Politics and the Democratic Resolution*. Albany: SUNY Press.

Gardella, Peter (2003), "Pluralisms in the United States and in the American Empire," pp. 255–9 in *Religious Studies Review*, 29.3.

Gary, Brett (1999), *The Nervous Liberals: Propaganda Anxieties from World War I to the Cold War*. New York: Columbia University Press.

Geach, Peter (1977), *The Virtues*. Cambridge: Cambridge University Press.

Gergen, Kenneth (1991), *The Saturated Self: Dilemmas of Identity in Contemporary Life*. New York: Basic Books.

Geuss, Raymond (1981), *The Idea of a Critical Theory*. New York: Cambridge University Press.

Gibbon, Edward (1995), *The Decline and Fall of the Roman Empire*, 3 vols. New York: The Modern Library.

Gibson, Alan (2000), "Ancients, Moderns, and Americans: The Republicanism-Liberalism Debate Revisited," pp. 261-307 in *History of Political Thought*, 21.2 (Summer).

Gibson, Cynthia, and Peter Levine, eds. (2003), *The Civic Mission of Schools*. New York and College Park: Carnegie Corporation and CIRCLE, The Center for Information and Research on Civic Learning and Engagement.

Gilkey, Langdon (1975), "Reinhold Niebuhr's Theology of History," pp. 36-62 in *The Legacy of Reinhold Niebuhr*, ed. Nathan A. Scott. Chicago: University of Chicago Press.

Gill, Robin (1999), *Churchgoing and Christian Ethics*. Cambridge: Cambridge University Press.

Glendon, Mary Ann (1991), *Rights Talk: The Impoverishment of Political Discourse*. New York: Free Press.

Glendon, Mary Ann, and David Blankenhorn, eds. (1995), *Seedbeds of Virtue: Sources of Competence, Character, and Citizenship in American Society*. Lanham: Madison Books.

Glenn, John K., III (2001), *Framing Democracy: Civil Society and Civic Movements in Eastern Europe*. Stanford: Stanford University Press.

Goldfarb, Jeffrey (1991), *The Cynical Society: The Culture of Politics and the Politics of Culture in American Life*. Chicago: University of Chicago Press.

Goodheart, Eugene (1991), *Desire and Its Discontents*. New York: Columbia University Press.

Graff, Gerald (1989) "Looking Past the de Man Case," pp. 246-54 in *Responses on Paul de Man's Wartime Journalism*, Werner Hamacher et al., eds. Lincoln, NE: University of Nebraska Press.

Green, Donald P., and Ian Shapiro (1994), *Pathologies of Rational Choice Theory: A Critique of Applications in Political Science*. New Haven: Yale University Press.

Greer, Rowan (1986), *Broken Lights and Mended Lives: Theology and Common Life in the Early Church*. University Park: Pennsylvania State University Press.

Gregory of Nyssa (1978), *The Life of Moses*, trans. Abraham J. Malherbe and Everett Ferguson. New York: Paulist Press.

Griffith, R. Marie (2004), *Born-Again Bodies*. Berkeley: University of California Press.

Griffiths, Paul J. (1991), *An Apology for Apologetics: A Study in the Logic of Interreligious Dialogue*. Maryknoll: Orbis Books.

(1999), *Religious Reading: The Place of Reading in the Practice of Religion*. New York: Oxford University Press.

(2001), "Nirvana as the Last Thing? The Iconic End of the Narrative Imagination," pp. 17–36 in *Theology and Eschatology at the Turn of the Millennium*, ed. James J. Buckley and Gregory Jones. Oxford: Blackwell.

Guinn, David E. (2002), *Faith on Trial: Communities of Faith, the First Amendment, and the Theory of Deep Diversity*. Lanham: Lexington Books.

Gunn, Giles (1985), *The Culture of Criticism and the Criticism of Culture*. New York: Oxford University Press.

Gutiérrez, Gustavo (1988), *A Theology of Liberation*, rev. edn. Maryknoll: Orbis Books.

Habermas, Jürgen (1984), *The Theory of Communicative Action*, I: *Reason and the Rationalization of Society*, trans. Thomas McCarthy. Boston: Beacon Press.

Hadot, Pierre (1995), *Philosophy as a Way of Life: Spiritual Exercises from Socrates to Foucault*, ed. Arnold I. Davidson, trans. Michael Chase. Oxford: Blackwell.

(2002), *What is Ancient Philosophy?* trans. Michael Chase. Cambridge, MA: Harvard University Press.

Halberstam, Michael (1999), *Totalitarianism and the Modern Conception of Politics*. New Haven: Yale University Press.

Hall, Amy Laura (2002), *Kierkegaard and the Treachery of Love*. New York: Cambridge University Press.

Hall, Peter Dobkin (1984), *The Organization of American Culture, 1700–1900: Private Institutions, Elites and the Origins of American Nationality*. New York: New York University Press.

Halliburton, R. (1967), "The Concept of 'Fuga Saeculi' in St. Augustine," pp. 249–61 in *Downside Review*, 85.

Halter, Marilyn (2000), *Shopping for Identity: The Marketing of Ethnicity*. New York: Schocken.

Halttunen, Karen (1998), *Murder Most Foul: The Killer and the American Gothic Imagination*. Cambridge, MA: Harvard University Press.

Hammond, Phillip (1992), *Religion and Personal Autonomy: The Third Disestablishment in America*. Columbia: University of South Carolina Press.

Hann, Chris, and Elizabeth Dunn, eds. (1996), *Civil Society: Challenging Western Models*. New York: Routledge.

Harding, Susan Friend (2000), *The Book of Jerry Falwell: Fundamentalist Language and Politics*. Princeton: Princeton University Press.

Hardt, Michael, and Antonio Negri (2000), *Empire*. Cambridge, MA: Harvard University Press.

(2004), *Multitude: War and Democracy in the Age of Empire*. New York: Penguin Putnam.

Hariman, Robert, ed. (2003), *Prudence: Classical Virtue, Postmodern Practice*. University Park: Pennsylvania State University Press.

Harmless, William (1995), *Augustine and the Catechumenate*. Collegeville: Liturgical Press.

Harpham, Geoffrey Galt (1987), *The Ascetic Imperative in Culture and Criticism* Chicago: University of Chicago Press.

Harris, Daniel (2001), *Cute, Quaint, Hungry, and Romantic: The Aesthetics of Consumerism*. Cambridge, MA: Da Capo Press.

Harrison, Carol (2000), *Augustine: Christian Truth and Fractured Humanity*. New York: Oxford University Press.

Hart, Stephen (2001), *Cultural Dilemmas of Progressive Politics: Styles of Engagement Among Grassroots Activists*. Chicago: Chicago University Press.

Harvey, David (1990), *The Condition of Postmodernity*. Cambridge, MA: Blackwell.

Harvey, Paul B., Jr. (1999), "Approaching the Apocalypse: Augustine, Tyconius, and John's Revelation," pp. 133–51 in Fitzgerald *et al.*

Hatch, Nathan O. (1977), *The Sacred Cause of Liberty: Republican Thought and the Millennium in Revolutionary New England*. New Haven: Yale University Press.

(1989), *The Democratization of American Christianity*. New Haven: Yale University Press.

Hauerwas, Stanley, (1983), *The Peaceable Kingdom: A Primer in Christian Ethics*. Notre Dame: University of Notre Dame Press.

(2002), "Enduring, or, How Rowan Greer Taught Me To Read," pp. 199–213 in *Reading in Christian Communites: Essays on Interpretation in the Early Church*, ed. Charles A. Bobertz and David Brakke. South Bend: University of Notre Dame Press.

Hauerwas, Stanley and Will Willimon (1989), *Resident Aliens: Life in the Christian Colony*. Nashville: Abingdon Press.

Hauptmann, Emily (1996), *Putting Choice Before Democracy: A Critique of Rational Choice Theory*. Albany: SUNY Press.

Havel, Václav (1989), *Letters to Olga: June 1979–September 1982*, trans. Paul Wilson. New York: Henry Holt & Company.

(1991), *Disturbing the Peace*, trans. Paul Wilson. New York: Vintage Books.

(1997), *The Art of the Impossible: Politics as Morality in Practice*, trans. Paul Wilson *et al.* New York: Knopf.

Healey, Nicholas (2000), *Church, World, and Christian Life: A Practical-Prophetic Ecclesiology*. Cambridge: Cambridge University Press.

Heim, S. Mark (1995), *Salvations: Truth and Difference in Religions*. Maryknoll: Orbis Books.

Henry, Patrick (1981), "'And I Don't Care What It Is:' The Tradition-History of a Civil Religion Proof Text," pp. 35–49 in *Journal of the American Academy of Religion*, 49.1.

Hertzke, Allen (1988), *Representing God in Washington: The Roles of Religious Lobbies in the American Polity*. Knoxville: University of Tennessee Press.

(2004), *Freeing God's Children: The Unlikely Alliance for Global Human Rights*. Lanham: Rowman & Littlefield.

Herzog, Don (1989), *Happy Slaves: A Critique of Consent Theory*. Chicago: University of Chicago Press.

Heschel, Abraham (1962), *The Prophets*. New York: Harper & Row.

Heyd, David, ed. (1996), *Toleration: An Elusive Virtue*. Princeton: Princeton University Press.

Hick, John (1990), "The Non-Absoluteness of Christianity," pp. 16–36 in *Christian Uniqueness Reconsidered: The Myth of a Pluralist Theory of Religions*, ed. Gavin D'Costa. Maryknoll: Orbis.

Hill, Christopher (1991), *The World Turned Upside Down: Radical Ideas During the English Revolution*. New York: Penguin Putnam [1972].

Hirschman, Albert O. (1970), *Exit, Voice, and Loyalty: Responses to Decline in Firms, Organizations and States*. Cambridge, MA: Harvard University Press.

(1977), *The Passions and the Interests: Political Arguments for Capitalism Before Its Triumph*. Princeton: Princeton University Press.

Hoffmann, Stefan-Ludwig (2003), "Democracy and Associations in the Long Nineteenth Century: Toward a Transnational Perspective," pp. 269–99 in *Journal of Modern History*, 75 (June).

Hofrenning, Daniel J. (1995), *In Washington But Not Of It: The Prophetic Role of Religious Lobbyists*. Philadelphia: Temple University Press.

Hollenbach, David. (1996), "Social Ethics Under the Sign of the Cross," pp. 3–18 in *Annual of the Society of Christian Ethics*.

(1997), "Politically Active Churches: Some Empirical Prolegomena to a Normative Approach," pp. 291–306 in *Religion and Contemporary Liberalism*, ed. Paul Weithman. Notre Dame: University of Notre Dame Press.

Holman, Susan R. (2001), *The Hungry are Dying: Beggars and Bishops in Roman Cappadocia*. New York: Oxford University Press.

Holmes, George (1962), *The Later Middle Ages*. New York: W. W. Norton.

Holmes, Stephen (1993), *The Anatomy of Anti-Liberalism*. Chicago: University of Chicago Press.

Hopkins, Gerard Manley (1986), *Gerard Manley Hopkins: The Major Works*, ed. Catherine Phillips. Oxford: Oxford University Press.

Hout, Michael A., Andrew Greeley, and Melissa J. Wilde (2001), "The Demographic Imperative in Religious Change in the United States," pp. 468–500 in *American Journal of Sociology*, 107.

Hubbard, Moyer V. (2002), *New Creation in Paul's Letters and Thought*. New York: Cambridge University Press.

Hughes, Graham (2003), *Worship as Meaning: A Liturgical Theology for Late Modernity*. New York: Cambridge University Press.

Hughes, Kevin (2005a), *Constructing Antichrist: Paul, Biblical Commentary, and the Development of Doctrine in the Early Middle Ages*. Washington: Catholic University Press.

(2005b), "Local Politics: The Political Place of the Household in Augustine's *City of God*," pp. 145–64 in Doody et. al. 2005.

Huiziga, Johan (1955), *Homo Ludens: A Study of the Play Element in Culture*. Boston: Beacon Press.

Hulliung, Mark (1994), *The Autocritique of Enlightenment: Rousseau and the Philosophes*. Cambridge, MA: Harvard University Press.

Hunter, James Davison (1990), *Culture Wars*. New York: Basic Books.

(2000), *The Death of Character: Moral Education in an Age without Good or Evil*. New York: Basic Books.

Hütter, Reinhard (1992), "The Church's Peace Beyond the 'Secular': A Postmodern Augustinian's Deconstruction of Secular Modernity and Postmodernity," pp. 106–16 in *Pro Ecclesia*, 2.1.

Ignatieff, Michael (2001), *Human Rights as Politics and Idolatry*. Princeton: Princeton University Press.

Independent Sector, The (1988), *From Belief to Commitment: The Activities and Finances of Religious Congregations in the United States*. Washington: The Independent Sector.

Inglebert, Hervé (1996), *Les Romains chrétiens face à l'histoire de Rome: histoire, christianisme et romanités en Occident dans l'Antiquité tardive (IIIe–Ve siècles)*. Paris: Etudes augustiniennes.

Inglehart, Ronald (1990), *Culture Shift in Advanced Industrial Society*. Princeton: Princeton University Press.

Innes, Stephen (1995), *Creating the Commonwealth: The Economic Culture of Puritan New England*. New York: W. W. Norton.

Irvin, Dale T. (1994), *Hearing Many Voices: Dialogue and Diversity in the Ecumenical Movement*. Lanham: University Press of America.

Irvine, Martin (1994), *The Making of Textual Culture: Grammatica and Literary Theory, 350–1100*. Cambridge: Cambridge University Press.

Isaac, Jeffrey C. (1997), *Democracy in Dark Times*. Ithaca: Cornell University Press.
  (2003), *The Poverty of Progressivism: The Future of American Democracy in a Time of Liberal Decline*. Lanham: Rowman & Littlefield.

Isaac, Jeffrey C., Matthew F. Filner, and Jason C. Bivins (1999), "American Democracy and the New Christian Right: A Critique of Apolitical Liberalism," pp. 222–64 in *Democracy's Edges*, ed. Ian Shapiro and Casiano Hacker-Cordón. New York: Cambridge University Press.

Jackall, Robert, and Janet M. Hirota (2000), *Image Makers: Advertising, Public Relations and the Ethos of Advocacy*. Chicago: University of Chicago Press.

Jackson, Timothy (1997), "The Return of the Prodigal? Liberal Theory and Religious Pluralism," pp. 182–217 in *Religion and Contemporary Liberalism*, ed. Paul Weithman. Notre Dame: University of Notre Dame Press.

Jacobs, Alan (2001a), "Bakhtin and the Hermeneutics of Love," pp. 25–45 in *Bakhtin and Religion: A Feeling for Faith*, ed. Susan M. Felch and Paul J. Centino. Evanston: Northwestern University Press.
  (2001b), *A Theology of Reading: The Hermeneutics of Love*. Boulder: Westview Press.

Jacobsen, Eric (2003), *Sidewalks in the Kingdom: New Urbanism and the Christian Faith*. Grand Rapids: Brazos Press.

Jameson, Frederic (1990), *Postmodernism: Or, the Cultural Logic of Late Capitalism*. Durham, NC: Duke University Press.

Jasper, James M. (1997), *The Art of Moral Protest: Culture, Biography and Creativity in Social Movements*. Chicago: University of Chicago Press.

Jenkins, Philip (2002), *The Next Christendom: The Coming of Global Christianity*. New York: Oxford University Press.

Jenson, Robert (1997), *Systematic Theology, I: The Triune God*. New York: Oxford University Press.
  (2004), "On the Ascension," pp. 331–40 in *Loving God with Our Minds: The Pastor as Theologian*, ed. Michael Welker and Cynthia A. Jarvis. Grand Rapids: William B. Eerdmans.

Johnston, David (1994), *The Idea of a Liberal Theory*. Princeton: Princeton University Press.

Jones, L. Gregory (1990), *Transformed Judgment: Towards a Trinitarian Account of the Moral Life*. Notre Dame: University of Notre Dame Press.

Jones, L. Gregory, and Stephen Fowl (1991), *Reading in Communion: Scripture and Ethics in the Christian Life*. Grand Rapids: William B. Eerdmans.

Jones, L. Gregory, and Stephanie Paulsell, eds. (2002), *The Scope of Our Art: The Vocation of the Theological Teacher*. Grand Rapids: William B. Eerdmans.

Jones, Serene (2002), "Graced Practices: Excellence and Freedom in the Christian Life," pp. 51–77 in Volf and Bass.

Juergensmeyer, Mark (1993), *The New Cold War? Religious Nationalism Confronts the Secular State*. Berkeley: University of California Press.

(2000), *Terror in the Mind of God: The Global Rise of Religious Violence*. Berkeley: University of California Press.

Jüngel, Eberhard (1989), "The World as Possibility and Actuality: The Ontology of the Doctrine of Justification," pp. 95–123 in *Eberhard Jüngel: Theological Essays*, trans. and ed. John Webster. Edinburgh: T. & T. Clark.

Kahn, Paul W. (2004), *Putting Liberalism in Its Place*. Princeton: Princeton University Press.

Kant, Immanuel (1965), *Critique of Pure Reason*, trans. Norman Kemp Smith. New York: St. Martin's Press.

Kantorowicz, Ernst Hartwig (1957), *The King's Two Bodies: A Study in Medieval Political Theology*. Princeton: Princeton University Press.

Keller, Catherine (1996), *Apocalypse Now and Then: A Feminist Guide to the End of the World*. Boston: Beacon Press.

(1997), "The Lost Fragrance: Protestantism and the Nature of What Matters," pp. 355–70 in *Journal of the American Academy of Religion*, 65.2 (Summer).

Kelsey, David (1992), *To Understand God Truly: What's Theological about a Theological School*. Louisville: Westminster/John Knox Press.

Kenney, Padraic (2002), *A Carnival of Revolution: Central Europe 1989*. Princeton: Princeton University Press.

Kim, Sunhyuk (2000), *The Politics of Democratization in Korea: The Role of Civil Society*. Pittsburgh: University of Pittsburgh Press.

King, Anthony (2000), "Distrust of Government: Explaining American Exceptionalism," pp. 74–98 in *Disaffected Democracies: What's Troubling the Trilateral Countries?* ed. Susan J. Pharr and Robert D. Putnam. Princeton: Princeton University Press.

Kirk, Kenneth (1966), *The Vision of God: The Christian Doctrine of the summum bonum*. New York: Harper & Row.

Konrád, George (1984), *Antipolitics: An Essay*, trans. Richard E. Allen. San Diego: Harcourt, Brace, Jovanovich.

Krasner, Stephen D., ed. (2001), *Problematic Sovereignty: Contested Rules and Political Possibilities*. New York: Columbia University Press.

Kraynak, Robert P. (2001), *Christian Faith and Modern Democracy: God and Politics in the Fallen World*. Notre Dame: University of Notre Dame Press.

Krupnick, Mark (1986), *Lionel Trilling and the Fate of Cultural Criticism*. Evanston: Northwestern University Press.

Kumar, Krishan (2001), *1989: Revolutionary Ideas and Ideals*. Minneapolis: University of Minnesota Press.

Kuttner, Robert (1997), *Everything for Sale: The Virtues and Limits of Markets*. New York: Alfred A. Knopf.

LaHaye, Tim, and Jerry B. Jenkins, (2004), *Glorious Appearing: The End of Days*. Wheaton: Tyndale House.

Lakoff, George (2002), *Moral Politics: How Liberals and Conservatives Think*, 2nd edn. Chicago: The University of Chicago Press.

Lambert, David (1999), "The Uses of Decay: History in Salvian's *de gubernatione dei*," pp. 115–30 in Fitzgerald *et al.*

Lamberton, Robert (1986), *Homer the Theologian: Neoplatonist Allegorical Reading and the Growth of the Epic Tradition*. Berkeley: University of California Press.

Lane, Robert E. (2000), *The Loss of Happiness in Market Democracies*. New Haven: Yale University Press.

Laraña, Enrique, Hank Johnston, and Joseph R. Gusfield, eds. (1994), *New Social Movements: From Ideology to Identity*. Philadelphia: Temple University Press.

Lasch, Christopher (1991), *The True and Only Heaven: Progress and Its Critics*. New York: Norton.

Lash, Nicholas (1988), *Easter in Ordinary: Reflections on Human Experience and the Knowledge of God*. Charlottesville: University Press of Virginia.

Laursen, John Christian, and Cary J. Nederman, eds. (1998), *Beyond the Persecuting Society: Religious Toleration Before the Enlightenment*. Philadelphia: University of Pennsylvania Press.

Lawless, George (1998), "*Auaritia, Luxuria, Ambitio, Lib. Arb.* 1,11,22: A Greco-Roman Literary Topos and Augustine's Asceticism," pp. 317–31 in *Studia Ephemeridis Augustinianum*, 62.

(2000), "Augustine's Decentering of Asceticism," pp. 142–63 in *Augustine and His Critics*, ed. Robert Dodaro and George Lawless. London: Routledge.

Layman, Geoffrey (2001), *The Great Divide: Religious and Cultural Conflict in American Party Politics*. New York: Columbia University Press.

Lear, Jonathan (1990), *Love and Its Place in Nature: A Philosophical Interpretation of Freudian Psychoanalysis*. New York: Farrar, Strauss & Giroux.

(1998), *Open Minded: Working Out the Logic of the Soul*. Cambridge, MA: Harvard University Press.

Lears, T. J. Jackson (1994), *No Place for Grace: Antimodernism and the Transformation of American Culture*. Chicago: University of Chicago Press.

Lendon, John (1997), *Empire of Honour*. Oxford: Oxford University Press.

Levinas, Emmanuel (1969), *Totality and Infinity*, trans. Alphonso Lingis. Pittsburgh: Duquesne University Press.

Lewis, C. S. (1980), *The Weight of Glory and Other Addresses*. New York: Macmillan.

Leyerle, Blake (2004), "Monastic Formation and Christian Practice: Food in the Desert," pp. 85–112 in *Educating People of Faith: Exploring the History of Jewish and Christian Communities*, ed. John van Engen. Grand Rapids: William B. Eerdmans.

Leyser, Conrad (2001), *Authority and Asceticism from Augustine to Gregory the Great*. Oxford: Clarendon Press.

Lichterman, Paul (1996), *The Search for Political Community: American Activists Reinventing Commitment*. New York: Cambridge University Press.

(2005), *Elusive Togetherness: Church Groups Trying to Bridge America's Divisions*. Princeton: Princeton University Press.

Lieberman, Marcel (1998), *Commitment, Value, and Moral Realism*. New York: Cambridge University Press.

Lilla, Mark (2001), *The Reckless Mind: Intellectuals in Politics*. New York: New York Review Books.

Lischer, Richard (1995), *The Preacher King: Martin Luther King Jr. and the Word that Moved America*. New York: Oxford University Press.

Loughlin, Gerard (1996), *Telling God's Story: Bible, Church and Narrative Theology*. Cambridge: Cambridge University Press.

Lovibond, Sabina (1982), *Realism and Imagination in Ethics*. Minneapolis: University of Minnesota Press.

Lovin, Robin (1995), *Reinhold Niebuhr and Christian Realism*. New York: Cambridge University Press.

Lyotard, J. F. (1989), *The Postmodern Condition: A Report on Knowledge*. Minneapolis: University of Minnesota Press.

Macedo, Stephen (1993), *Liberal Virtues*. Oxford: Clarendon Press.

(1998), "Flathman's Liberal Shtick," pp. 85–9 in *Political Theory*, 26.1 (February).

(2000), *Diversity and Distrust: Civic Education in a Multicultural Democracy*. Cambridge, MA: Harvard University Press.

Macedo, Stephen, ed. (2004), *Democracy at Risk: Toward a Political Science of Citizenship*. Princeton: American Political Science Association.

McCann, Dennis (1981), *Christian Realism and Liberation Theology: Practical Theologies in Creative Conflict*. Maryknoll: Orbis Books.

McCarraher, Eugene (2000), *Christian Critics: Religion and the Impasse in Modern American Social Thought*. Ithaca: Cornell University Press.

McCarthy, John, and Jim Castelli (1998), *Religion-Sponsored Social Service Providers: The Not-So-Independent Sector*, Working Paper Series. Washington: The Aspen Institute.

McClay, Wilfred M. (1994), *The Masterless: Self and Society in Modern America*. Chapel Hill: University of North Carolina Press.

McCloskey, Deirdre (1994), "Bourgeois Virtue," pp. 177–91 in *The American Scholar* (Spring).

McDowell, John. (1992), "Putnam on Mind and Meaning," pp. 35–48 in *Philosophical Topics*, 20.

(1994), *Mind and World*. Cambridge, MA: Harvard University Press.

(1995), "Knowledge and the Internal," pp. 877–95 in *Philosophy and Phenomenological Research* 55.4 (December).

McGreevy, John T. (2003), *Catholicism and American Freedom: A History*. New York: W. W. Norton.

MacIntyre, Alasdair (1984), *After Virtue: A Study in Moral Theory*, 2nd edn. Notre Dame: University of Notre Dame Press.

(1988), *Whose Justice? Which Rationality?* Notre Dame: University of Notre Dame Press.

(1990), *Three Rival Versions of Moral Enquiry: Encyclopedia, Genealogy, and Tradition*. Notre Dame: University of Notre Dame Press.

McLynn, Neil (1999), "Augustine's Roman Empire," pp. 29–44 in *Augustinian Studies*, 30.

MacQueen, D. J. (1972), "Saint Augustine's Concept of Property Ownership," pp. 187–229 in *Recherches Augustiniennes*, 8.

McRoberts, Omar M. (2003), "Worldly or Otherworldly? 'Activism' in an Urban Religious District," pp. 412–22 in *Handbook of the Sociology of Religion*, ed. Michele Dillon. New York: Cambridge University Press.

McWilliams, Wilson Carey (2003), "American Democracy and the Politics of Faith," pp. 143–62 in *Religion Returns to the Public Square: Faith and Policy in America*, ed. Hugh Heclo and Wilfred M. McClay. Baltimore: Johns Hopkins University Press.

Mahmood, Saba (2005), *Politics and Piety: The Islamic Revival and the Feminist Subject.* Princeton: Princeton University Press.

Marcel, Gabriel (1962), *Homo Viator: Introduction to a Metaphysic of Hope*, trans. Emma Craufurd. New York: Harper & Row.

Markell, Patchen (2003), *Bound by Recognition.* Princeton: Princeton University Press.

Markham, Ian S. (2003), *A Theology of Engagement.* Oxford: Blackwell.

Markus, R. A. (1970), *Saeculum: History and Society in the Theology of St. Augustine.* Cambridge: Cambridge University Press.

(1990a), "A Defense of Christian Mediocrity," pp. 45–62 in his *The End of Ancient Christianity.* Cambridge: Cambridge University Press.

(1990b), "City or Desert? Two Models of Community," pp. 157–79 in his *The End of Ancient Christianity.* Cambridge: Cambridge University Press.

(1996), *Signs and Meanings: World and Text in Ancient Christianity.* Liverpool: Liverpool University Press.

Marsh, Charles (1997), *God's Long Summer: Stories of Faith and Civil Rights.* Princeton: Princeton University Press.

(2005), *The Beloved Community: How Faith Shapes Social Justice, from the Civil Rights Movement to Today.* New York: Basic Books.

Martin, David (1997), *Does Christianity Cause War?* Oxford: Clarendon Press.

Martin, Thomas, O.S.A (1998), "'An Abundant Supply of Discourse': Augustine and the Rhetoric of Monasticism," pp. 7–25 in *Downside Review*, 116.402 (January).

(2005), "Augustine and the Politics of Monasticism," pp. 165–86 in Doody *et al.*

Marx, Karl (1978), "For a Ruthless Critique of Everything Existing," pp. 12–15 in *The Marx-Engels Reader*, 2nd edn., ed. Robert C. Tucker. New York: W. W. Norton & Company.

Mathewes, Charles T. (1999), "The Academic Life as a Christian Vocation," pp. 110–21 in *Journal of Religion*, 79.1 (January).

(2000), "An Appreciation of Hauerwas: One Hand Clapping," pp. 343–60 in *Anglican Theological Review*, 82.2 (Spring).

(2001a), *Evil and the Augustinian Tradition.* Cambridge: Cambridge University Press.

(2001b), "The Hermeneutics of Charity and Original Sin: A Response to Gilbert Meilaender," pp. 35–42 in *Journal of Religious Ethics*, 29.1.

(2002a), "The Liberation of Questioning in Augustine's *Confessions*," pp. 539–64 in *Journal of the American Academy of Religion*, 70.3 (September).

(2002b), "Reconsidering the Role of Mainline Churches in Public Life," pp. 554–66 in *Theology Today*, 58.4.

(2002c), "The Career of the Pelagian Controversy," pp. 199–210 in *Augustinian Studies*, 33.2.

(2003), "The Presumptuousness of Autobiography and the Paradoxes of Beginning in *Confessions* Book One," pp. 7–23 in *A Reader's Companion to Augustine's Confessions*, ed. Kim Paffenroth and Robert P. Kennedy. Louisville: Westminster/John Knox Press.

Mayer, Arno J. (2000), *The Furies: Violence and Terror in the French and Russian Revolutions*. Princeton: Princeton University Press.

Mehta, Uday Singh (1995), *Liberalism and Empire: A Study in Nineteenth-Century British Liberal Thought*. Chicago: University of Chicago Press.

Mele, Alfred (1995), *Autonomous Agents: From Self-Control to Autonomy*. New York: Oxford University Press.

Melucci, Alberto (1989), *Nomads of the Present: Social Movements and Individual Needs in Contemporary Society*. Philadelphia: Temple University Press.

Mendus, Susan (1999), "The Importance of Love in Rawls's Theory of Justice," pp. 57–75 in *British Journal of Political Science*, 29.

Mennell, Susan (1994), "Augustine's 'I': The 'Knowing Subject' and the Self," pp. 291–324 in *Journal of Early Christian Studies*, 2.3.

Meyrowitz, Joshua (1985), *No Sense of Place: The Impact of Electronic Media on Social Behavior*. New York: Oxford University Press.

Micheletti, Michele (2003), *Political Virtue and Shopping: Individuals, Consumerism, and Collective Action*. New York: Palgrave Macmillan.

Michnik, Adam (1993), *The Church and the Left*, trans. David Ost. Chicago: University of Chicago Press.

Milbank, John (1990a), "The End of Dialogue," in *Christian Uniqueness Reconsidered: The Myth of a Pluralist Theory of Religions*, ed. Gavin D'Costa. Maryknoll: Orbis Books.

(1990b), *Theology and Social Theory: Beyond Secular Reason*. Cambridge, MA: Blackwell.

(1997), *The Word Made Strange*. Oxford: Blackwell.

Milbank, John, and Catherine Pickstock (2001), *Truth in Aquinas*. London: Routledge.

Milbank, John, Catherine Pickstock, and Graham Ward, eds. (1999), *Radical Orthodoxy: A New Theology*. New York: Routledge.

Millar, Fergus (2002), *The Roman Republic in Political Thought*. Hanover, NH: University Press of New England.

Miller, Char Roone (2001), *Taylored Citizenship: State Institutions and Subjectivity*. Westport: Praeger Publishers.

Miller, Patrick (2000), "Judgment and Joy," pp. 155–70 in *The End of the World and the Ends of God: Science and Theology on Eschatology*, ed. John Polkinghorne and Michael Welker. Harrisburg: Trinity Press International.

Miller, Vincent (2004), *Consuming Religion: Christian Faith and Practice in a Consumer Culture*. New York: Continuum.

Milosz, Czeslaw (1981), *The Captive Mind*, trans. Jane Zielonko. New York: Octagon Books.

Moltmann, Jürgen (1975), *Theology of Hope: On the Ground and Implications of a Christian Eschatology*. New York: Harper & Row [1967].

(1996), *The Coming of God: Christian Eschatology*. trans. by Margaret Kohl. Minneapolis: Fortress.

Moore, R. Laurence (1986), *Religious Outsiders and the Making of Americans*. New York: Oxford University Press.

Morone, James A. (1998), *The Democratic Wish: Popular Participation and the Limits of American Government*, rev. edn. New Haven: Yale University Press.

Morse, Christopher (1997), *Not Every Spirit: A Dogmatics of Christian Disbelief*. Valley Forge: Trinity Press International.

Mouffe, Chantal (2000), *The Democratic Paradox*. New York: Verso.

Muers, Rachel (2004), *Keeping God's Silence: Towards a Theological Ethics of Communication*. Oxford: Blackwell.

Murdoch, Iris (1970), *The Sovereignty of the Good*. London: Routledge & Kegan Paul.

Murphy, Andrew R. (2001), *Conscience and Community: Revisiting Toleration and Religious Dissent in Early Modern England and America*. University Park: Pennsylvania State University Press.

Murray, John Courtney (1988), "Is it Basket Weaving?: The Question of Christianity and Human Values," pp. 175–96 in his *We Hold These Truths: Catholic Reflections on the American Proposition*. New York: Sheed & Ward.

Nagel, Robert F. (2001), *The Implosion of American Federalism*. New York: Oxford University Press.

Nederman, Cary J. (2000), *Worlds of Difference: European Discourses of Toleration, 1100–1550*. College Park: Pennsylvania University Press.

Nelson, Daniel Mark (1992), *The Priority of Prudence: Virtue and Natural Law in Thomas Aquinas and the Implications for Modern Ethics*. University Park: Pennsylvania University Press.

Nelson, Eric (2004), *The Greek Tradition in Republican Thought*. Cambridge: Cambridge University Press.

Neuhaus, Richard John, ed. (1989), *Reinhold Niebuhr Today*. Grand Rapids: William B. Eerdmans.

Newey, Glen (2001), *After Politics: The Rejection of Politics in Contemporary Liberal Philosophy*. New York: Palgrave.

Nicholls, David (1989), *Deity and Domination*. London: Routledge.

Nie, Norman, and D. Sunshine Hillygus (2001), "Education and Democratic Citizenship," pp. 30–57 in *Making Good Citizens: Education and Civil Society*, ed. Diane Ravitch and Joseph P. Viteritti. New Haven: Yale University Press, 2001.

Niebuhr, H. R. (1941), *The Meaning of Revelation*. New York: Macmillan.

(1960), *Radical Monotheism and Western Culture*. New York: Harper & Row.

(1963), *The Responsible Self*. San Francisco: Harper & Row, Publishers.

(1989), *Faith on Earth: An Inquiry Into the Structure of Human Faith*. New Haven: Yale University Press.

Niebuhr, Reinhold (1943), *The Nature and Destiny of Man, Vol II: Human Destiny*. New York: Charles Scribner's Sons.

(1949), *Faith and History*. New York: Charles Scribner's Sons.

(1952), *The Irony of American History*. New York: Charles Scribner's Sons.

(1953), "Augustine's Political Realism," pp. 119–46 in his *Christian Realism and Political Problems*. New York: Charles Scribner's Sons.

Nisbet, Robert (1990), *The Quest for Community: A Study in the Ethics of Order and Freedom*. San Francisco: ICS Press.

Nolan, James L., Jr. (1998), *The Therapeutic State: Justifying Government at Century's End*. New York: New York University Press.

Noll, Mark (2002), *America's God: From Jonathan Edwards to Abraham Lincoln*. New York: Oxford University Press.

Norris, Kathleen (1998), *Amazing Grace: A Vocabulary of Faith*. New York: Riverhead Books.

Novak, David (1989), *Jewish–Christian Dialogue: A Jewish Justification*. New York: Oxford University Press.

(2000), "Mitzvah," pp. 115–26 in *Christianity in Jewish Terms*, ed. Tikva Frymer-Kensky, David Novak, Peter Ochs, David Fox Sandmel, and Michael A. Singer. Boulder: Westview Press.

Nussbaum, Martha C. (2001), *Upheavals of Thought: The Intelligence of Emotions*. New York: Cambridge University Press.

Nygren, Anders (1957), *Agape and Eros*, trans. Philip S. Watson. London: SPCK.

Ochs, Peter (2000), "The God of Jews and Christians," pp. 49–68 in *Christianity in Jewish Terms*, ed. Tikva Frymer-Kensky, David Novak, Peter Ochs, David Fox Sandmel, and Michael A. Singer. Boulder: Westview Press.

Ochs, Peter, and Nancy Levene, eds. (2002), *Textual Reasonings: Jewish Philosophy and Text Study at the End of the Twentieth Century*. Grand Rapids: William B. Eerdmans.

O'Connor, William Riordan (1983), "The *uti/frui* Distinction in Augustine's Ethics," pp. 45–62 in *Augustinian Studies*, 14.

O'Daly, G. J. P. (1977), "Time as Distensio and St. Augustine's Exegesis of Philippians 3, 12–14," pp. 265–71 in *Revue des Etudes Augustiniennes*, 23.

O'Donnell, James J. (1980), "Augustine's Classical Readings," pp. 144–75 in *Recherces Augustiniennes*, 15.

(1994), "To Make An End is to Make a Beginning," in *Augustinian Studies*, 25.

O'Donovan, Oliver (1980), *The Problem of Self Love in Augustine*. New Haven: Yale University Press.

(1982), "*Usus*, and *Fruitio* in Augustine, *De Doctrina* I," pp. 361–97 in *Journal of Theological Studies*, n.s. 33.2 (October).

(1987), "Augustine's *City of God* XIX and Western Political Thought," pp. 89–110 in *Dionysius*, 11 (December).

(1996), *The Desire of the Nations: Rediscovering the Roots of Political Theology*. Cambridge: Cambridge University Press.

(2001), "Deliberation, History, and Reading: A Response to Schweiker and Wolterstorff," pp. 127–44 in *Scottish Journal of Theology* 54.1

(2003), *The Just War Revisited*. Cambridge: Cambridge University Press.

O'Leary, Joseph S. (1985), *Questioning Back: The Overcoming of Metaphysics in the Christian Tradition*. Minneapolis: Winston Press.

O'Leary, Stephen (1995), *Arguing the Apocalypse: A Theory of Millennial Rhetoric*. New York: Oxford University Press.

Oliver, J. Eric (2001), *Democracy in Suburbia*. Princeton: Princeton University Press.

Okin, Susan Moller (1999), *Is Multiculturalism Bad for Women?* Princeton: Princeton University Press.

Orlie, Melissa (1997), *Living Ethically, Acting Politically*. Ithaca: Cornell University Press.
  (1999), "Beyond Identity and Difference," pp. 140–9 in *Political Theory*, 27.1 (February).
Pascal, Blaise (1966), *Pensées*, trans. with an introduction by A. J. Krailsheimer. New York: Penguin.
Patterson, Thomas E. (2002), *The Vanishing Voter: Public Involvement in an Age of Uncertainty*. New York: Knopf.
Paul T. V., G. John Ikenberry, and John A. Hall, eds. (2004), *The Nation-State in Question*. Princeton: Princeton University Press.
Peacock, Molly (1989), "There Must Be," p. 71 in *Take Heart: Poems*. New York: Vintage.
Pels, Dick (2000), *The Intellectual as Stranger: Studies in Spokespersonship*. New York: Routledge.
Perl, Jeffrey M. (1989), *Skepticism and Modern Enmity: Before and After Eliot*. Baltimore: Johns Hopkins University Press.
Perry, Michael J. (1999), *We the People*. New York: Oxford University Press.
  (2003), *Under God? Religious Faith and Liberal Democracy*. New York: Cambridge University Press.
Pettit, Philip (1993), *The Common Mind: An Essay on Psychology, Society and Politics*. New York: Oxford University Press.
  (1997), *Republicanism: A Theory of Freedom and Government*. New York: Oxford University Press.
Phillips, Adam (1996), *Terrors and Experts*. Cambridge, MA: Harvard University Press.
  (2001a), *Houdini's Box: The Art of Escape*. New York: Pantheon Books.
  (2001b), "An Answer to Questions," pp. 174–80 in his *Promises, Promises: Essays on Literature and Psychoanalysis*. New York: Basic Books.
Philpott, Daniel (2001), *Revolutions in Sovereignty*. Princeton: Princeton University Press.
Pichardo, Nelson (1997), "New Social Movements: A Critical Review," pp. 411–30 in *Annual Review of Sociology*, 23.
Pickstock, Catherine (1997), *After Writing: The Liturgical Consummation of Philosophy*. Oxford: Blackwell.
Pieper, Josef (1999), *In Tune With the World: A Theory of Festivity*. South Bend: St. Augustine's Press.
Pinches, Charles (1987), "On Form and Content in Christian Ethics," pp. 4–14 in *Sophia*, 26.1 (March).
Placher, William (1989), *Unapologetic Theology: A Christian Voice in a Pluralist Conversation*. Louisville: Westminster/John KnoxPress.
  (1996), *The Domestication of Transcendence: How Modern Thinking About God Went Wrong*. Louisville: Westminster/John Knox Press.
Plantinga, Alvin (1992) "Augustinian Christian Philosophy," pp. 291–320 in *The Monist*, 75.
  (1993), *Warrant and Proper Function*. New York: Oxford University Press.
Pocock, J. G. A. (1975), *The Machiavellian Moment*. Princeton: Princeton University Press.

Polkinghorne, John (2002), *The God of Hope and the End of the World*. New Haven: Yale University Press.

Polletta, Francesca (2002), *Freedom is an Endless Meeting: Democracy in American Social Movements*. Chicago: University of Chicago Press.

Pollmann, Karla (1996), *Doctrina Christiana: Untersuchungen zu den Anfängen der christlichen Hermeneutik unter besonderer Berüchtsichtigung von Augustinus, De Doctrina Christiana*. Freiburg Schweiz: Universitätsverlag.

(1999) "Molding the Present: Apocalyptic as Hermeneutics in *City of God* 21–22," pp. 165–81 in Fitzgerald *et al.*

Polsgrove, Carol (2001), *Divided Minds: Intellectuals and the Civil Rights Movement*. New York: Norton.

Polsky, Andrew J. (1991), *The Rise of the Therapeutic State*. Princeton: Princeton University Press.

Porter, Jean (1990), *The Recovery of Virtue: The Relevance of Aquinas for Christian Ethics*. Louisville: Westminster/John Knox Press.

(1999), *Natural and Divine Law: Reclaiming the Tradition for Christian Ethics*. Grand Rapids: William B. Eerdmans.

Portes, Alejandro (1998), "Social Capital: Its Origins and Applications in Modern Sociology," pp. 1–24 in *Annual Review of Sociology* 24.

Posner, Richard (2001), *Public Intellectuals: A Study in Decline*. Cambridge, MA: Harvard University Press.

Post, Stephen G. (2003), *Human Nature and the Freedom of Public Religious Expression*. Notre Dame: University of Notre Dame Press.

Postman, Neil (1985), *Amusing Ourselves to Death: Public Discourse in the Age of Show Business*. New York: Penguin Books.

Putnam, Robert D. (2000), *Bowling Alone: The Collapse and Revival of American Community*. New York: Simon & Schuster.

ed. (2002), *Democracies in Flux: The Evolution of Social Capital in Contemporary Society*. New York: Oxford University Press.

Rahner, Hugo (1972), *Man at Play*, trans. Brian Battershaw and Edward Quinn. New York: Herder & Herder.

Rahner, Karl (1966), "The Hermeneutics of Eschatological Assertions," pp. 323–46 in *Theological Investigations* IV. New York: Crossroad.

Ramsey, Paul (1950), *Basic Christian Ethics*. New York: Charles Scribner's Sons.

(1961), *War and the Christian Conscience: How Shall Modern War be Conducted Justly?* Durham, NC: Duke University Press.

(1967), *Who Speaks for the Church?* Nashville: Abingdon.

(1988), *Speak Up for Just War or Pacifism*. with an Epilogue by Stanley Hauerwas. State College: Pennsylvania State University Press.

Raposa, Michael L. (1999), *Boredom and the Religious Imagination*. Charlottesville: University Press of Virginia.

Rauch, Jonathan (2003), "Let it Be." *Atlantic Monthly*, 291.4 (May).

Rausch, Thomas P., SJ (2004), *Evangelizing America*. Mahwah: Paulist Press.

Rawls, John (1993), *Political Liberalism*. New York: Columbia University Press.

(1999), *The Law of Peoples*. Cambridge, MA: Harvard University Press.

Raz, Joseph (1988), *The Morality of Freedom*. New York: Oxford University Press.

Rescher, Nicholas (1993), *Pluralism: Against the Demand for Consensus*. Oxford: Clarendon Press.

Ricoeur, Paul (1965), "The Socius and the Neighbor," pp. 98–109 in his *History and Truth*, trans. by Charles A. Kelbley. Evanston: Northwestern University Press.

(1984), *Time and Narrative* I, trans. Kathleen McLaughlin and David Pellauer. Chicago: University of Chicago Press.

Rist, John M. (1994), *Augustine: Ancient Thought Baptized*. Cambridge: Cambridge University Press.

Roberts, Tyler T. (1998), *Contesting Spirit: Nietzsche, Affirmation, Religion*. Princeton: Princeton University Press.

Rohr, John (1967), "Religious Toleration in St. Augustine," pp. 51–70 in *Journal of Church and State*, 9.

Roof, Wade Clark (1999), *Spiritual Marketplace: Baby Boomers and the Remaking of American Religion*. Princeton: Princeton University Press.

Rorty, Richard (1998), *Achieving our Country: Leftist Thought in Twentieth-Century America*. Cambridge, MA: Harvard University Press.

Rose, Gillian (1996), *Mourning Becomes the Law: Philosophy and Representation*. New York: Cambridge University Press.

Rosen, Stanley (1987), *Hermeneutics as Politics*. New York: Oxford University Press.

Rosenblum, Nancy, ed. (1998), *Membership and Morals: The Personal Uses of Pluralism in America*. Princeton: Princeton University Press.

ed. (2000), *Obligations of Citizenship and Demands of Faith*. Princeton: Princeton University Press.

Rosenzweig, Franz (1985), *The Star of Redemption*, trans William W. Hallo. Notre Dame: University of Notre Dame Press.

Ross, Andrew (1989), *No Respect: Intellectuals and Popular Culture*. New York: Routledge.

Rotberg, Robert I. (2001), *Patterns of Social Capital: Stability and Change in Historical Perspective*. New York: Cambridge University Press.

Rudenfeld, Jed (2001), *Freedom and Time: A Theory of Constitutional Self-Government*. New Haven: Yale University Press.

Rupp, George (2001), "Religion, Modern Secular Culture, and Ecology," pp. 23–30 in *Daedalus* 130.4 (Fall)

Sachedina, Abdulaziz (2001), *The Islamic Roots of Democratic Pluralism*. New York: Oxford University Press.

Sahlins, Marshall (1993), "Goodbye to *Tristes Tropes*: Ethnography in the Context of Modern World History," pp. 1–25 in *Journal of Modern History*, 65.1 (March).

Saletan, William (2003), *Bearing Right: How Conservatives Won the Abortion Wars*. Berkeley: University of California Press.

Salzman, Michele Renée (2002), *Making of a Christian Aristocracy*. Cambridge, MA: Harvard University Press.

Sandel, Michael (1982), *Liberalism and the Limits of Justice*. New York: Cambridge University Press.

(1996), *Democracy's Discontent: America in Search of a Public Philosophy*. Cambridge, MA: Belknap Press of Harvard University Press.

Sandler, Ross, and David Schoenbrod (2003), *Democracy by Decree: What Happens When Courts Run Government*. New Haven: Yale University Press.

Santner, Eric (2001), *The Psychotheology of Everyday Life: Reflections on Freud and Rosenzweig*. Chicago: University of Chicago Press.

Santurri, Edmund N. (1987), *Perplexity in the Moral Life: Philosophical and Theological Considerations*. Charlottesville: University Press of Virginia.

Scarry, Elaine (1999), *On Beauty and Being Just*. Princeton: Princeton University Press.

Scharpf, Fritz W. (2000), "Interdependence and Democratic Legitimation," pp. 101–20 in *Disaffected Democracies: What's Troubling the Trilateral Countries*, ed. Susan J. Pharr and Robert D. Putnam. Princeton: Princeton University Press.

Schell, Jonathan (1986), "Reflections: A Better Today," pp. 47–67 in *The New Yorker*, 61.50 (February 3).

Schindler, A. (1990), "Augustine and the History of the Roman Empire," pp. 326–36 in *Studia Patristica*, 18.4.

Schlabach, Gerald (1994), "Augustine's Hermeneutic of Humility: An Alternative to Moral Imperialism and Moral Relativism," pp. 299–330 in *Journal of Religious Ethics*, 22.2 (Fall).

Schmemann, Alexander (1973), *For the Life of the World: Sacraments and Orthodoxy*. Crestwood: St. Vladimir's Seminary Press.

Schnaubelt, Joseph C., O. S. A., and Van Fleteren, Frederick E. (1990), *Collectanea Augustiniana: Augustine, Second Founder of the Faith*. New York: Peter Lang.

Schoppa, Leonard J. (2001), "Japan the Reluctant Reformer," pp. 76–90 in *Foreign Affairs*, 80.5 (September/October).

Schreiner, Susan (1995), *The Theater of His Glory: Nature and the Natural Order in the Thought of John Calvin*. Grand Rapids: Baker.

Schreiter, Robert (1997), *The New Catholicity: Theology Between the Global and the Local*. Maryknoll: Orbis.

Schuld, Joyce (2000), "Augustine, Foucault, and the Politics of Imperfection," pp. 1–22 in *Journal of Religion*, 80.1 (January).

Schwartz, Barry (2004), *The Paradox of Choice: Why More is Less*. New York: Harper Collins.

Schwartz, Regina (1997), *The Curse of Cain: The Violent Legacy of Monotheism*. Chicago: University of Chicago Press.

Schweiker, William (1990), *Mimetic Reflections: A Study in Hermeneutics, Theology and Ethics*. New York: Fordham University Press.

Scitovsky, Tibor (1992), *The Joyless Economy: The Psychology of Human Satisfaction*. Rev. edn. New York: Oxford University Press.

Sedgwick, Timothy (1999), *The Christian Moral Life: Practices of Piety*. Grand Rapids: William B. Eerdmans.

Seligman, Adam (1992), *The Idea of Civil Society*. New York: Free Press.
    (1995), "Animadversions upon Civil Society," pp. 200–23 in *Civil Society*, ed. John A. Hall. Cambridge: Polity Press.
    (2000), *Modernity's Wager: Authority, the Self and Transcendence*. Princeton: Princeton University Press.

Sells, Michael A. (1996), *The Bridge Betrayed: Religion and Genocide in Bosnia*. Berkeley: University of California Press.

Sennett, Richard (1998), *The Corrosion of Character: The Personal Consequences of Work in the New Capitalism*. New York: Norton.

Shanks, Andrew (1995), *Civil Society, Civil Religion*. Oxford: Blackwell.

Shannon, Christopher (1996), *Conspicuous Criticism: Tradition, the Individual, and Culture in American Social Thought, from Veblen to Mills*. Baltimore: Johns Hopkins University Press.

Shapiro, Ian (2003), *The State of Democratic Theory*. Princeton: Princeton University Press.

(1999), *Democratic Justice*. New Haven: Yale University Press.

(1990), *Political Criticism*. Berkeley: University of California Press.

Shelby, Tommie (2005), *We Who Are Dark: The Philosophical Foundations of Black Solidarity*. Cambridge: Belknap Press of Harvard University Press.

Shiffrin, Steven H. (1999), *Dissent, Injustice, and the Meanings of America*. Princeton: Princeton University Press.

Shklar, Judith (1984), *Ordinary Vices*. Cambridge, MA: Belknap Press of Harvard University Press.

Siebers, Tobin (1988), *The Ethics of Criticism*. Ithaca: Cornell University Press.

(1993), *Cold War Criticism and the Politics of Skepticism*. New York: Oxford University Press.

Skerrett, Kathleen (2003), " Desire and Anathema: Mimetic Rivalry in Defense of Plenitude," pp. 793–809 in *Journal of the American Academy of Religion*, 71.4 (December).

Skinner, Quentin (1978), *The Foundations of Modern Political Thought, I: The Renaissance*. New York: Cambridge University Press.

Skocpol, Theda (2004), "Voice and Inequality: The Transformation of American Civic Democracy," pp. 3–20 in *Perspectives on Politics*, 2:1 (March).

Sloterdijk, Peter (1987), *Critique of Cynical Reason*, trans. Michael Eldred. Minneapolis: University of Minnesota Press.

Smith, Christian (1998), *American Evangelicalism: Embattled and Thriving*. Chicago: University of Chicago Press.

(2000), *Christian America? What Evangelicals Really Want*. Chicago: University of Chicago Press.

(2003a), *Moral, Believing Animals: Human Personhood and Culture*. New York: Oxford University Press.

(2003b), ed. *The Secular Revolution: Power, Interests, and Conflict in the Secularization of American Public Life*. Berkeley: University of California Press.

Smith, Christian with Melinda Lundquist Denton (2005), *Soul Searching: The Religious and Spiritual Lives of American Teenagers*. New York: Oxford University Press.

Smith, Rogers M. (1997), *Civic Ideals: Conflicting Visions of Citizenship in US History*. New Haven: Yale University Press.

Smith, Steven D. (1995), *Foreordained Failure: The Quest for a Constitutional Principle of Religious Freedom*. New York: Oxford University Press.

Sontag, Susan (1966), *Against Interpretation*. New York: Farrar, Strauss, & Giroux.

Soskice, Janet Martin. (1992), "Love and Attention," pp. 59–72 in *Philosophy, Religion and the Spiritual Life*, ed. Michael McGhee. Cambridge: Cambridge University Press.

Sperber, Dan (1985), *On Anthropological Knowledge*. Cambridge: Cambridge University Press.

Steiner, George (1989), *Real Presences*. Chicago: University of Chicago Press.

(2001), *Grammars of Creation*. New Haven: Yale University Press.

Steiner, Wendy (1995), *The Scandal of Pleasure: Art in an Age of Fundamentalism*. Chicago: University of Chicago Press.

Steinfels, Margaret O'Brien (2004), *American Catholics and Civic Engagement: A Distinctive Voice*. Lanham: Rowman & Littlefield.

Stephen, Julie (1998), *Anti-Disciplinary Protest: Sixties Radicalism and Postmodernism*. New York: Cambridge University Press.

Stern, Fritz (1961), *The Politics of Cultural Despair: A Study in the Rise of the Germanic Ideology*. Berkeley: University of California Press.

Stiltner, Brian (1999), *Religion and the Common Good*. Lanham: Rowman & Littlefield.

Stout, Harry (1989), "The Historical Legacy of H. Richard Niebuhr," pp. 83–99 in *The Legacy of H. Richard Niebuhr*, ed. Ronald F. Thiemann. Minneapolis: Fortress Press.

Stout, Jeffrey (1981), *The Flight From Authority: Religion, Morality and the Quest for Autonomy*. South Bend: University of Notre Dame Press.

(2004), *Democracy and Tradition*. Princeton: Princeton University Press.

Stout, Rowland (1996), *Things That Happen Because They Should: A Teleological Approach to Action*. New York: Oxford University Press.

Strange, Susan (1996), *The Retreat of the State: The Diffusion of Power in the World Economy*. Cambridge: Cambridge University Press.

Stuckey, Tom (2003), *Into the Far Country: A Theology of Mission for an Age of Violence*. Werrington: Epworth Press.

Studer, Basil (1990), "Augustine and the Pauline Theme of Hope," pp. 201–21 in *Paul and the Legacies of Paul*, ed. William S. Babcock. Dallas: Southern Methodist University Press.

Sunstein, Cass (1996), *Legal Reasoning and Political Conflict*. Oxford: Oxford University Press.

Surin, Kenneth (1989), "*Contemptus Mundi* and the Disenchantment of the World: Bonhoeffer's 'Discipline of the Secret' and Adorno's 'Strategy of Hibernation'," pp. 180–200 in his *The Turnings of Darkness and Light: Essays in Philosophical and Systematic Theology*. Cambridge: Cambridge University Press.

Svendsen, Lars (2005), *A Philosophy of Boredom*. London: Reaktion Books.

Tanner, Kathryn (1987), "Theology and the Plain Sense," pp. 59–78 in *Scriptural Authority and Narrative Interpretation*, ed. Garrett Green. Philadelphia: Fortress Press.

(1988), *God and Creation in Christian Theology: Tyranny or Empowerment?* New York: Basil Blackwell.

(1992), *The Politics of God*. Minneapolis: Fortress Press.

(1993) "Respect for Other Religions: A Christian Antidote to Colonialist Discourse," pp. 1–18 in *Modern Theology*, 9.1 (June).

(1997), *Theories of Culture: A New Agenda for Theology*. Minneapolis: Fortress Press.

Taussig, Michael (1992), *The Nervous System*. New York: Routledge.

Taylor, Charles (1989), *Sources of the Self: The Making of Modern Identity*. Cambridge, MA: Harvard University Press.
  (1992), *Multiculturalism and the Politics of Recognition*. Princeton: Princeton University Press.
  (2004), *Modern Social Imaginaries*. Durham, NC: Duke University Press.
TeSelle, Eugene (1970), *Augustine the Theologian*. New York: Herder & Herder.
  (1998), *Living in Two Cities: Augustinian Trajectories in Political Thought*. Scranton: University of Scranton Press.
Theusen, Peter (2002), "The Logic of Mainline Churches: Historical Background Since the Reformation," pp. 27–53 in Wuthnow and Evans.
Thiemann, Ronald (1996), *Religion in Public Life: A Dilemma for Democracy*. Washington: Georgetown University Press.
Thompson, Augustine (2005), *Cities of God: The Religion of the Italian Communes, 1125–1325*. University Park: Pennsylvania State University Press.
Tilly, Charles (1975), "Reflections on the History of European State-Making," pp. 3–83 in *The Formation of National States in Western Europe*, ed. Charles Tilly. Princeton: Princeton University Press.
  (1989), *Coercion, Capital, and the European States AD 990–1990*. Cambridge, MA: Blackwell.
  (1993), *European Revolutions, 1492–1992*. New York: Blackwell.
Tinder, Glenn (2000), "Faith, Doubt, and Public Dialogue," pp. 223–41 in Douglass and Mitchell 2000.
Tocqueville, Alexis de (2004), *Democracy in America*, trans. Arthur Goldhammer. New York: Library of America.
Tomasi, John (2001), *Liberalism Beyond Justice: Citizens, Society and the Boundaries of Political Theory*. Princeton: Princeton University Press.
Toulmin, Stephen (1990) *Cosmopolis: The Hidden Agenda of Modernity*. Chicago: University of Chicago Press.
Tracy, David (1991), *Dialogue with the Other*. Grand Rapids: William B. Eerdmans.
Tropman, John E. (2002), *The Catholic Ethic and the Spirit of Community*. Washington: Georgetown University Press.
Turner, Denys (1995a), *The Darkness of God: Negativity and Christian Mysticism*. Cambridge: Cambridge University Press.
  (1995b), *Eros and Allegory: Medieval Exegesis of the Song of Songs*. Kalamazoo: Cistercian Publications.
Turow, Joseph (1997), *Breaking Up America: Advertisers and the New Media World*. Chicago: University of Chicago Press.
Unger, Roberto Mangabeira (1977), *Law in Modern Society*. New York: Free Press.
Uslander, Eric (2002), *The Moral Foundations of Trust*. New York: Cambridge University Press.
van Creveld, Martin (1999), *The Rise and Decline of the State*. Cambridge University Press.
Van Fleteren, Frederick, and Joseph C. Schnaubelt, eds. (2001), *Augustine: Biblical Exegete*. New York: Peter Lang.
van Fraassen, Bas (2002), *The Empirical Stance*. New Haven: Yale University Press.
van Inwagen, Peter (1983), *An Essay on Free Will*. New York: Oxford University Press.

(1989), "When is the Will Free?," pp. 399–422 in *Philosophical Perspectives,* III : *Philosophy of Mind and Action Theory,* ed. J. E. Tomberlin. Atascadero: Ridgeview Press.

Vanderspoel, John (1990), "The Background to Augustine's Denial of Religious Plurality," pp. 179–93 in *Grace, Politics, and Desire: Essays on Augustine,* ed. H. A. Meynell. Calgary: University of Calgary Press.

Vanstone, W. H. (1978), *The Risk of Love.* New York: Oxford University Press.

(1983), *The Stature of Waiting.* San Francisco: HarperSanFrancisco.

Verba, Sydney, Kay Lehman Schlozman, and Henry E. Brady (1995), *Voice and Equality: Civic Voluntarism in American Politics.* Cambridge, MA: Harvard University Press.

Veyne, Paul (1990), *Bread and Circuses,* abridged and introduced by Oswyn Murray, trans. Brian Pearce. London: Penguin.

Villa, Dana (2003), *Socratic Citizenship.* Princeton: Princeton University Press.

Viroli, Maurizio (1992), *From Politics to Reason of State: The Acquisition and Transformation of the Language of Politics 1250-1600.* Cambridge: Cambridge University Press.

Volf, Miroslav (1996), *Exclusion and Embrace: A Theological Exploration of Identity, Otherness, and Reconciliation.* Nashville: Abingdon.

(2000), "The Final Reconciliation: Reflections on a Social Dimension of the Eschatological Transition," pp. 91–113 in *Modern Theology,* 16.1 (January).

Volf, Miroslav, and Dorothy C. Bass (2002), *Practicing Theology: Beliefs and Practices in Christian Life.* Grand Rapids: William B. Eerdmans.

von Heyking, John (2001), *Augustine on Politics as Longing in the World.* Columbia: University of Missouri Press.

Waldron, Jeremy (1987) "Theoretical Foundations of Liberalism," pp. 127–34 in *Philosophical Quarterly,* 37.

Walzer, Michael (1970), *The Revolution of the Saints: A Study in the Origins of Radical Politics.* New York: Atheneum.

(1985), *Exodus and Revolution.* New York: Basic Books.

(1987), *Interpretation and Social Criticism.* Cambridge, MA: Harvard University Press.

(1997), *On Toleration.* New Haven: Yale University Press.

(1998), "The Idea of Civil Society: A Path to Social Reconstruction," pp. 123–43 in *Community Works: The Revival of Civil Society in America,* ed. E. J. Dionne Jr. Washington: Brookings Institution Press.

Ward, Graham (2000), *Cities of God.* London: Routledge.

Warner, Michael (2003), "Styles of Intellectual Publics," pp. 106–25 in *Just Being Difficult? Academic Writing in the Public Arena,* ed. Jonathan Culler and Kevin Lamb. Stanford: Stanford University Press.

Warner, R. Steven (1994), "The Place of the Congregation in the American Religious Configuration," pp. 54–99 in *American Congregations,* II: *New Perspectives in the Study of Congregations,* ed. James P. Wind and James W. Lewis. Chicago: University of Chicago Press.

Warren, Mark E., ed. (1999), *Democracy and Trust.* New York: Cambridge University Press.

(2001), *Democracy and Association.* Princeton: Princeton University Press.

Watson, Gary, ed. (1982), *Free Will.* New York: Oxford University Press.

Weber, Eugen (1976), *Peasants Into Frenchmen: The Modernization of Rural France*. Stanford: Stanford University Press.

Weber, Max (2004), "Politics as a Vocation," pp. 32–94 in *The Vocation Lectures*, ed. David Owen and Tray B. Strong, trans. Rodney Livingstone. Indianapolis: Hacket.

Webster, John (1998), *Theological Theology*. Oxford: Oxford University Press.

Weenar, Leif (1995), "*Political Liberalism*: An Internal Critique," pp. 32–62 in *Ethics*, 106.1 (October).

Weithman, Paul J. (1992), "Augustine and Aquinas on Original Sin and the Function of Political Authority," pp. 353–76 in *Journal of the History of Philosophy*, 30.3.

  (2002), *Religion and the Obligations of Citizenship*. New York: Cambridge University Press.

Werpehowski, William (1986), "Ad Hoc Apologetics," pp. 282–301 in *Journal of Religion*, 66.3 (July).

  (2002), *American Protestant Ethics and the Legacy of H. Richard Niebuhr*. Washington: Georgetown University Press.

West, Cornel (1982), *Prophesy Deliverance! An Afro-American Revolutionary Christianity*. Philadelphia: Westminster Press.

  (1988), *Prophetic Fragments*. Grand Rapids: William B. Eerdmans.

Wetzel, James (1992), *Augustine and the Limits of Virtue*. New York: Cambridge University Press.

White, Lynn (1967) "The Historical Roots of Our Ecologic Crisis," pp. 1203–7 in *Science*, 155 (10 March).

White, Michael J. (1994), "Pluralism and Secularism in the Political Order: St. Augustine and Theoretical Liberalism," pp. 137–54 in *The University of Dayton Review* (Summer).

White, Stephen K. (2000), *Sustaining Affirmation: The Strengths of Weak Ontology in Political Theory*. Princeton: Princeton University Press.

Wilhelm, Anthony G. (2000), *Democracy in the Digital Age*. New York: Routledge.

Wilkinson, James D. (1981), *The Intellectual Resistance in Europe*. Cambridge, MA: Harvard University Press.

Williams, Bernard (1985), *Ethics and the Limits of Philosophy*. Cambridge, MA: Harvard University Press.

  (1993), *Shame and Necessity*. Berkeley: University of California Press.

  (1995), "Moral Incapacity," pp. 46–55 in his *Making Sense of Humanity: And Other Philosophical Papers, 1982–1993*. New York: Cambridge University Press.

Williams, Michael (1997), *Groundless Belief: An Essay on the Possibility of Epistemology*. Oxford: Blackwell.

Williams, Rowan (1987), "Politics and the Soul: A Reading of *The City of God*," pp. 55–72 in *Milltown Studies*, 19/20.

  (1989a), *Christianity and the Ideal of Detachment*, 1988 Frank Lake Memorial Lecture. Oxford: Clinical Theology Association.

  (1989b), "Language, Reality and Desire in Augustine's *De Doctrina*," pp. 138–50 in *Journal of Literature and Theology*, 3.2 (July).

  (1991), "The Literal Sense of Scripture," pp. 121–34 in *Modern Theology*, 7.2 (January).

(1994), "'Good For Nothing'? Augustine on Creation," pp. 9–24 in *Augustinian Studies*, 25.

(1999), *On Christian Theology*. Oxford: Blackwell.

(2000), *Lost Icons: Reflections on Cultural Bereavement*. Edinburgh: T. & T. Clark.

Wimbush, Vincent L., and Richard Valantasis, eds. (1995), *Asceticism*. New York: Oxford University Press.

Winter, Bruce W. (1994), *Seek the Welfare of the City: Christians as Benefactors and Citizens*. Grand Rapids: William B. Eerdmans.

Witten, Marsha G. (1993), *All is Forgiven: The Secular Message of American Protestantism*. Princeton: Princeton University Press.

Wolf, Susan (1986), "Asymmetrical Freedom," pp. 225–40 in *Moral Responsibility*, ed. John Martin Fischer. Ithaca: Cornell University Press.

(1987), "Sanity and the Metaphysics of Responsibility," pp. 46–62 in *Responsibility, Character, and the Emotions*, ed. Ferdinand Schoeman. New York: Cambridge University Press.

(1990), *Freedom Within Reason*. New York: Oxford University Press.

Wolfe, Alan (1996), *Marginalized in the Middle*. Chicago: University of Chicago Press.

(1998), *One Nation, After All*. New York: Viking.

(2001), *Moral Freedom: The Impossible Idea that Defines the Way We Live Now*. New York: W. W. Norton.

Wolin, Sheldon (1960), *Politics and Vision: Continuity and Innovation in Western Political Thought*. Boston: Little, Brown & Company.

Wolterstorff, Nicholas (1984), *Reason Within the Bounds of Religion*, 2nd edn. Grand Rapids: William B. Eerdmans.

(1996), *John Locke and the Ethics of Belief*. New York: Cambridge University Press.

(1997), "The Role of Religion in Decision and Discussion of Political Issues," pp. 67–120 in *Religion in the Public Square: The Place of Religious Convictions in Political Debate*, ed. Robert Audi and Nicholas Wolterstorff. Lanham: Rowman & Littlefield.

Wood, Neal (1986), "*Populares* and *Circumcelliones*: The Vocabulary of "Fallen Man" in Cicero and St. Augustine," pp. 33–51 in *History of Political Thought*, 7.

Wood, Richard L. (2002), *Faith in Action: Religion, Race, and Democratic Organizing in America*. Chicago: University of Chicago Press.

Wright, Paul (2005), "Machiavelli's *City of God*: Civic Humanism and Augustinian Terror," pp. 297–336 in Doody *et al.*

Wuthnow, Robert (1988), *The Restructuring of American Religion: Society and Faith Since World War II*. Princeton: Princeton University Press.

(1994), *God and Mammon in America*. New York: Free Press.

(1997), *The Crisis in the Churches: Spiritual Malaise, Fiscal Woe*. New York: Oxford University Press.

(1998a), *After Heaven: Spirituality in America Since the 1950s*. Berkeley: University of California Press.

(1998b), *Loose Connections: Joining Together in America's Fragmented Communities*. Cambridge, MA: Harvard University Press.

(1999a), *Growing Up Religious*. Boston: Beacon Press.

(1999b), "The Role of Trust in Civic Renewal," pp. 209–30 in *Civil Society, Democracy and Civic Renewal*, ed. Robert K. Fullinwider. Lanham: Rowman & Littlefield.

(2002), "Beyond Quiet Influence," pp. 381–403 in Wuthnow and Evans.

(2003), *All In Sync: How Music and Art Are Revitalizing American Religion*. Berkeley: University of California Press.

(2005), *America and the Challenges of Religious Diversity*. Princeton: Princeton University Press.

Wuthnow, Robert and John Evans, eds. (2002), *The Quiet Hand of God: Faith-Based Activism and the Public Role of Mainline Protestantism*. Berkeley: University of California Press.

Wyschogrod, Michael (1983), *The Body of Faith: Judaism as Corporeal Election*. New York: Seabury Press.

Yack, Bernard (1986), *The Longing for Total Revolution: Philosophic Sources of Social Discontent from Rousseau to Marx and Nietzsche*. Princeton: Princeton University Press.

(1997), *The Fetishism of Modernities: Epochal Self-Consciousness in Contemporary Social and Political Thought*. Notre Dame: University of Notre Dame Press.

Yearley, Lee (1992), *Mencius and Aquinas: Theories of Virtue and Conceptions of Courage*. Albany: SUNY Press.

Yoder, John Howard (1972), *The Politics of Jesus: Vicit Agnus Noster*. Grand Rapids: William B. Eerdmans.

Young, Frances (1997), *Biblical Exegesis and the Formation of Christian Culture*. Cambridge: Cambridge University Press.

Zagzebski, Linda (1996), *Virtues of the Mind: An Inquiry into the Nature of Virtue and the Ethical Foundations of Knowledge*. New York: Cambridge University Press.

Žižek, Slavoj (2000), *The Fragile Absolute: Or, Why is the Christian Legacy Worth Fighting For?* New York: Verso.

Zolo, Danilo (1992), *Democracy and Complexity: A Realist Approach*, trans. David McKie. University Park: Pennsylvania State University Press.

Index

(1) Thesis : Jerusalem and Washington

Theology of public vs. public theology

(4) Bowling alone

(5) Religious right + left

(8) Therapeutic + christianity

(9) Taylor : Ethics of inarticulacy (!!!)

(11) Asceticism

(12) Consumerism/patience

(14) our ultimate hope

(16) In this world or metaphysical mars ; resident aliens

(17) World is eva, not place

(19) Augustine tradition

(20) Augustine's eschatology ?

(21) Augustine's politics

(22) God's love source of all being (!!!)

Nature

(23) Not pro-democracy bro (!!!)

(24) Escapism

(25) christianity = public religion

(33) God near, but absent + God's material action in Christ

(35) Beckett

(36-7) Love + otherworldly

(38) Concern about apocalypticism

(40) God's expectations ; "we live on borrowed time."

(42) Lets think about apocalypse

(43) Faith (!!!)

(44-45) Faith cont, + modernism and Augustine

(46-47) Augustine : autonomy + faith ←important

(48-49) Augustine vs Plato ; Augustine : this-worldly

(50) (???) subjective + objective

(52) Epistemology w/ Augustine

(55) Augustine : (!!!)

(60) Augustine : Where do we get beliefs?

(66) Augustine : Free will

(67) Augustine : Voluntary sin

(77) Augustine : We are truly free in God

(77) "Using the world."

(82) "Love and do what you will!"

(87) Confession (!!!)

(97) Signs

(98) Mathews : "How to read scripture."

(100) God loves material

(101-2) What is ethics

(103) Worldly action is liturgy

(106) Confession + eschatology

(107) Christian community (!!!)

(108) Religion relationship w/ secular

(111) Secular : LCD + tolerance

(112) Consequence of secular

(116) Secularism should be dismissed

(118) Cont, world religions ; exclusivist, pluralist, inclusivist

(119) How Taylor, Macintyre approach these things

(122-23) Conversion (!!!)

(128) Sin + other

(129) Final destination in Christ (!!!)

(134) Hope

(136) Trinity

(138) Inter-faith

(148) Cynicism / political indifference

(149) State (!!!)

(151) Citizens suck right now

(154-56) Problems w/ liberalism

(161) Theology is politics for Christians (!!!)

(162) Hauerwas; What is politics Matthews? ; relation to civic

(165) Churches must be engaged

(166) Humility in politics / christianity

(171) Eisenhower

(177) Republican state

(181) Critique of O'Donovan

(184-85) (!!!) O'Donovan

(190) Augustine! Christ as teacher; authority; worship (!!!)

(197) Faith + Hope

(200-01) State (!!!)

(204) We are faithful citizens (!!!)

(206) Identity

(208-09) Faithful citizens again (!!!)

(213) wrestle w/ God
(223-24) Cavanaugh (!!!)
(238) Cynicism (!!!)
(239) Hope
(254) State critique
(278) Who can? (!!!)
(244) Public life (!!!)

29803326R00236

Made in the USA
San Bernardino, CA
30 January 2016